ENGAGING WITH CONTEMPORARY CULTURE

C000002254

I commend Martyn Percy's new book to Anglican and Catholic laity, pastors, theologians, and bishops. All, with his sprightly prose drawing them in, will find themselves joining his search for authentic paths for Christian faith. All will also find something to disagree with. Percy's well-researched work is not a polite chat about how we can all get along better. His practical theology examines lived faith and ordinary life, where Christianity and culture meet.

Thomas Hughson, SJ, Marquette University, Milwaukee, USA

Martyn Percy has provided an insightful and fresh approach to the dialogue between theology, church and world. He achieves this through a series of penetrating theological sketches touching the everyday life of churches and western culture. The accent is on engagement, the theology is practical and grounded. The result is an intellectually robust, accessible and provocative public theology. He shows himself to be a theologian at the cutting edge of contemporary Christian Theology. A joy to read and plenty of food for further engagement.

Stephen Pickard, School of Theology, Charles Sturt University, Australia

Theology and the churches are often considered to be at the margins of contemporary culture, frequently struggling for identity and attention. In this important new book Martyn Percy argues that a rich form of practical theological engagement is needed if the churches are to comprehend their situation in the modern world, thereby enabling them to engage more confidently with society. Drawing on a range of perspectives in the religion–culture debate, and from case studies in the USA and Europe, the book explores the myriad of ways in which culture is now shaping contemporary Christianity, and how vital an appreciation of this dynamic is for the self-understanding of churches and theology.

This book explores the crucial and continuing contribution that theology can make to public life, in an era that is often perceived to be dominated by consumerism and secularity. It will especially appeal to scholars of contemporary religion, practical theologians, and all those who are engaged in ministerial formation.

Explorations in Practical, Pastoral and Empirical Theology

Series Editors: Leslie J. Francis, University of Wales, Bangor, UK and Jeff Astley, University of Durham and Director of the North of England Institute for Christian Education, UK

Theological reflection on the church's practice is now recognized as a significant element in theological studies in the academy and seminary. Ashgate's new series in practical, pastoral and empirical theology seeks to foster this resurgence of interest and encourage new developments in practical and applied aspects of theology worldwide. This timely series draws together a wide range of disciplinary approaches and empirical studies to embrace contemporary developments including: the expansion of research in empirical theology, psychological theology, ministry studies, public theology, Christian education and faith development; key issues of contemporary society such as health, ethics and the environment; and more traditional areas of concern such as pastoral care and counselling.

Other titles published in this series:

A Reader on Preaching
Making Connections
Edited by David Day, Jeff Astley and Leslie J. Francis

Congregational Studies in the UK
Christianity in a Post-Christian Context
Edited by Mathew Guest, Karin Tusting and Linda Woodhead

Women's Faith Development
Patterns and Processes
Nicola Slee

Divine Revelation and Human Learning
A Christian Theory of Knowledge
David Heywood

Engaging with Contemporary Culture

Christianity, Theology and the Concrete Church

MARTYN PERCY

Routledge
Taylor & Francis Group

LONDON AND NEW YORK

First published 2005 by Ashgate Publishing

Published 2016 by Routledge
2 Park Square, Milton Park, Abingdon, Oxon OX14 4RN
605 Third Avenue, New York, NY 10017

First issued in paperback 2021

Routledge is an imprint of the Taylor & Francis Group, an informa business

Publisher's Note
The publisher has gone to great lengths to ensure the quality of this reprint but points out that some imperfections in the original copies may be apparent.

British Library Cataloguing in Publication Data
Percy, Martyn
Engaging with contemporary culture : Christianity, theology and the concrete
   church. – (Explorations in practical, pastoral and empirical theology)
   1. Christianity and culture 2. Theology, Practical 3. Secularization (Theology)
   I. Title
   261

Library of Congress Cataloging-in-Publication Data
Percy, Martyn.
   Engaging with contemporary culture : Christianity, theology, and the concrete
church / Martyn Percy.—1st ed.
      p. cm.—(Explorations in practical, pastoral, and empirical theology)
   Includes bibliographical references and index.
   ISBN 0-7546-3259-8 (alk. paper) 1. Christianity and culture. 2. Theology,
Doctrinal. I. Title. II. Series.

   BR115.C8P37 2005
   261—dc22

                                                                    2004013983

ISBN 13: 978-1-03-209993-4 (pbk)
ISBN 13: 978-0-7546-3259-7 (hbk)

Typeset by Tradespools, Frome, Somerset

For Stewart, Nick and Tim

Contents

Acknowledgements

I am grateful to a number of individuals and institutions in the writing of this book. To Hartford Seminary for graciously giving me the time and space to continue my research during the summer of 2002, and for the ongoing privilege of serving there as an Adjunct Professor for their estimable theology and ministry programmes. To the American Academy of Religion for providing me with a grant to undertake more fieldwork in Toronto in November of 2002. And, once again, to the Trustees of the Lincoln Theological Institute for their support and encouragement.

I would also like to acknowledge the following publications, and thank them for permission to redevelop material that has been previously published: *Reviews in Religions and Theology/Conversations* (Blackwell) in Chapter 1; *Creative Christian Leadership* (edited by John Nelson), SCM-Canterbury Press, 2004 in Chapter 4. Earlier versions of the essays contained in Part III (Chapters 7, 8 and 9) of the book have been published in the *Journal of Contemporary Religion*, the *Journal of Anglican Studies* and *Ecclesiology* respectively.

I would also like to thank the following societies and institutions for the opportunity to develop materials that were originally delivered as lectures: the World Council of Churches (parts of Chapters 1 and 4); the American Association of the Sociology of Religion (for papers given in Atlanta in 2003 and San Francisco in 2004 – Chapters 3 and 9 respectively); the contextual theology seminar at the University of Manchester (Chapter 2); and the American Academy of Religion (Chapter 7).

Lastly, I once again thank my family for their forbearance during the writing of this book. Their love and support is, as always, beyond price.

Martyn Percy

Introduction

Christianity, Theology and Contemporary Culture

One of the most pressing challenges faced by theology and the churches is how to engage with contemporary culture. For many, engagement, it seems, is a contested and risky affair. Some theological and ecclesiological traditions feel so threatened by the prospect of being overwhelmed or consumed by the task of engagement that they retreat before they have advanced; standing apart from key issues and debates in culture is seen to be the only way of protecting the integrity and identity of the Christian tradition. Others prefer a different strategy – namely one of deep engagement – but, in so doing, can find themselves so transformed that they become alienated from their roots. In either form of engagement, a degree of cultural bewilderment seems inevitable. A Venetian proverb sums up the dilemma: 'The artist swims in the sea, but the critic stands on the shore.'

It is my contention that theology and the churches do not have the luxury of such a choice. To engage with contemporary culture, theology and ecclesiology needs to be both critical and artistic. It needs to be at home in the sea and on the shore. It needs to be able to immerse itself in the turbulence of the waves of the sea, and yet stand apart, retaining a critical distance from the vantage-point of the shore. I further hold that the discipline of practical theology offers the possibility of such reflexivity, and this book is therefore an attempt to sketch some possibilities for the discipline in its engagement with contemporary culture. Such engagements require theology to be open to the insights of cultural studies and alert to the ways in which contemporary culture is shaping religion.

Whilst the term 'cultural studies' is often used very broadly, insofar as it pertains to all aspects of the study of culture, it can also be used more precisely to refer to a particular range of issues and disciplines. Classically, the disciplines of cultural studies have tended to include ethnography, literary criticism and socio-biology; in turn, these disciplines have touched feminism, Marxism, semiotics, aesthetics; and in turn, the field has then extended to include areas of inquiry such as consumption, production, race, class, gender and even religion.

One problem with defining cultural studies lies with the different meanings of 'culture', which vary across contexts. That said, the concept, at least when used academically, is proximate to the notion of culture used in social or cultural anthropology. Instead of being absorbed by 'high' theories of culture, or indeed with sociological meta-theories that are concerned with society, it concentrates on the world in which humanity both lives and creates. In this respect, the study of culture recognizes that human beings exceed that natural world which is their context. Thus, 'agriculture' and 'horticulture' recognize that humanity does something to its environment; it builds and creates, and it also uses a language to describe itself and its activity. This opens up the possibility of studying communication, power relations, values, aesthetics and meaning. Culture is, put simply, the study of what is overlaid, built or imposed on the natural environment. It is therefore concerned with 'artificiality' and the meanings that are given to such 'things' (see Highmore, 2002; Strinati, 1995; Williams, 1986, amongst others).

A project that sets out to engage theologically with culture is therefore immediately faced with some dynamics that it needs to recognize from the outset. First, theology does not precede culture; theology is itself a discrete kind of culture – a system of language, meaning and power relations that attempts to theorize about the knowledge and place of God in the world. Second, churches and other religious institutions are themselves 'cultures', so a discipline such as ecclesiology, can learn much from cultural studies. Third, there is a need to bring theology into some kind of engagement with culture and cultural studies. Moreover, this cannot simply be about 'high' theories of theology engaging with 'high' forms of cultural studies. Granted, such dialogues and synergies will have their uses, but the simpler (and arguably more urgent) task of engaging with everyday life should not be overlooked (cf. Astley, 2002).

Several factors have prompted the writing of this book. At the outset, I wanted to continue developing the agenda begun in *Salt of the Earth; Religious Resilience in a Secular Age* (2001), which had argued for a range of theological and ecclesiological engagements with contemporary culture. In this volume, however, readers will be aware that the use of anthropology (especially Geertz; see also Davies, 2002), congregational studies (especially Hopewell), ethnography (Highmore, 2002; Bender, 2003), and practical theology (Browning, 1991; Farley, 2003) is much more focused. There is also a more concerted attempt to engage with everyday life, especially ecclesial life (see Part III). In this respect, the volume as a whole has a much more explicit ecclesiological focus.

I have also been fortunate to find that *Salt of the Earth* has prompted others to write on Christianity and contemporary culture, and am especially grateful for Ian Markham's critique and modification of my work in his *A Theology of Engagement* (2003). Furthermore, there is now evidence for a burgeoning volume of theological reflection that addresses contemporary culture. Recent work by Kathryn Tanner (*Theories of Culture: A New Agenda for Theology*, 1997) and Delwin Brown, Sheila Davaney and Kathryn Tanner (*Converging on Culture*, 2001), along with a host of others, are now establishing this field as both normative and critical for theologians. There are also fresh and innovative approaches to theology (for example, Jeff Astley's fine *Ordinary Theology*, 2002), and new initiatives evident in the field of ecclesiology, pioneered by scholars such as Nicholas Healy (*Church, World and Christian Life: Practical–Prophetic Ecclesiology*, 2000) and Lewis Mudge (*Rethinking the Beloved Community: Ecclesiology, Hermeneutics and Social Theory*, 2001). This volume simply seeks to continue and extend the engagements and dialogues that others have begun, and enlarge the possibilities for studying theology, Christianity and contemporary culture.

One of the reasons for pursuing the academic agenda (theology, ecclesiology, Christianity and contemporary culture), and why it is so crucial, is that it continues to be, to a large extent, countercultural. Since the early 1960s both the academy and the popular public imagination have been in the grip of secularization theories, namely the simple assertion that as society progressively becomes more modern so it will lose its religious heritage and interests. But in the last ten years, a significant amount of revisionism has been taking place. Most scholars have realized that modernization merely heightens the role of religion on the public stage. That said, no one can survey contemporary cultural life, at least in Western Europe, and conclude that religion is as strong as it once was. But neither is it evaporating in the way that sociologists of religion once predicted. In truth, the socio-cultural changes are more complex than any single or simple theory of secularization can normally enunciate. But what, then, are the factors that have prompted cultural and religious change? Several brief points need to be made here.

First, the rise of religious pluralism has had a marked impact on religion over the past three centuries. However, this pluralism plays out differently across the continents. In Britain, the passing of the 1689 Toleration Act seriously undermined the grounds for enforcing uniform religious practice on the population. 'Dissenting traditions' steadily gained in number and influence, and this weakened the grip of 'state' religion (cf. McCleod and Ustorf, 2003).

Second, the impact of religious pluralism in America had a quite different effect. The absence of officially sanctioned religion for the populace led to a flourishing culture of religious competition that still thrives today. Religion is part of the overall commodification of American life, and choices, as in so many spheres of ordinary life, closely identify individuals and communities (see P. Ward, 2002 and Cronin, 2000). At least 50 per cent of the population go to church, and many more than this identify with a denomination or place of worship.

Third, Western Europe witnessed a gradual, but persistent, loosening of ties between church and state. This led to the gradual decrease in the power of the churches in prominent spheres of public life. In turn, this led to a decline in religious practice, which was only occasionally halted by popular revivals and other movements. (However, Europe is the exception, globally, not the rule. For the rest of the world, religious revival and growth is comparatively normal, even with the growth of modernization and consumerism.)

Fourth, there has been a general agenda of social 'liberalizing' throughout the past century. Laws on abortion, obscenity, marriage, divorce and homosexuality have all correlated with a set of cultural, political and social trends that has seen religion pushed from the public sphere to that of the private. Increasingly, performing religious tasks, duties and rituals is seen as something 'private' that is undertaken in leisure time. Fewer and fewer Roman Catholics attend confession on a regular basis; holy days of obligation, unless they fall on Sundays, are unlikely to be keenly observed.

Fifth, the decline of associations in general has had a deleterious impact upon religious institutions. Although scholars such as Grace Davie have suggested that religion has fared better than, say, trade unions, it remains the case that modern Western society (including America) is entering a 'post-associational' state (Putnam, 2000). Individuals in society are increasingly disconnected from one another, as 'soft' social structures such as the Masons, Odd Fellows and the Women's Institute have rapidly disintegrated. What has replaced these social ties is consumerism and the 'negative social capital' of television and other forms of media, which have become the new electronic public sphere.

Sixth, there is an increasing fluidity about how religious, moral and political beliefs are held within modernity (Bauman, 2000). Consumerism infects not only practice and adherence, but also alters the landscape of belief. Few Christians in the West, even those committed to various forms of conservative belief, will subscribe to literal interpretations of biblical stories or to historic understandings of doctrines, such as hell. In what Bauman calls our 'liquid modernity', more fluid forms of association and belief have sprung up, which, whilst still allowing for the possibility of meta-narratives, nonetheless relate to them differently in the twenty-first century.

Seventh, and finally, the rise of spirituality, in its various 'alternative', 'vernacular', 'folk' and other forms, continues to question the dominance of secularization theories on the landscape of the academy and the public imagination. France, a country where secularity is apparently deep and pervasive, can still boast 40 000 fortune-tellers. Most British newspapers (not just the tabloids) will have a daily or weekly horoscope, fronted by a renowned astrologer. Spirituality is a more fluid (modern?) and pervasive expression of the religious sentiments that continue to shape everyday life in a myriad ways. Theological engagements with culture, then, need to take a serious account of the grounded reality of religion in its typical contexts and situations, and not simply engage with religion conceptually, or as a 'high' and overdefined culture.

So, this book sets out to address the Christianity and culture 'problem', as well as the interrogating of appropriate theological sources and methods for ecclesiology, by exploring and testing a variety of approaches in three separate sections. Part I examines the engagement of theology, religious studies, missiology and ecclesiology with contemporary culture. Part II explores the nature of practical theology and examines the nature of theological education as it relates to churches, Christianity and culture. It also attempts to outline a different vision for theology from that of Radical Orthodoxy, which is briefly critiqued in Chapter 3. Part III, using ethnographies, the work of James Hopewell and Clifford Geertz, takes a more ecclesial turn, and explores (successively) church congregations, movements and denominations as forms of culture. (To the best of my knowledge, this is the first time Hopewellian analytical frameworks have been used to extend our knowledge of ecclesiology beyond congregations, and explore movements within the church and also examine the life and character of a denomination.)

The conclusion argues that, although Christianity is bound to paradox (that is, seemingly contradictory positions or statements) in its theological engagement with culture, this is in itself a sacramental paradigm, rooted in the revelation of God – who is revealed through the ordinary and in agents whose 'nature' (whether ordinary or transformed) are contestable. The paradoxical nature of forms of theological engagement with culture are therefore best resolved in faithfully conceived reflexive theology and ecclesiology, dialogue and further theological reflection. Methodologically, the argument turns towards arguing for a richer form of practical theology that takes 'ordinary Christianity' more seriously and, in so doing, restores some sense of public theology as a critical and yet affirming discourse that is engaged with contemporary culture.

Readers may naturally wonder why this range of issues and particular essays are addressed, and not others. I am more than aware that the Christianity and culture debate is one of the larger and more perplexing fields for theology to engage in. For myself, I have naturally had to write as a male Caucasian Western writer, who sees the subject he addresses from within inside his own ecclesiological and theological traditions. Therefore, I can only point to, following Ricoeur, the 'authorial intention' of the work and recognize that these essays will set off different trains of thought for the reader, which cannot be known (let alone controlled). Ultimately, one can only hope to provide a series of insights, confessionally shaped illuminations and methodological slants that can help guide the reader through the myriad questions and subjects. To be comprehensive is not possible. However, each chapter is an essay in its own right and is an attempt to get at the meanings of ecclesiology and the Christianity and culture debate from various vantage-points (cf. Mudge, 2001, p. 12). Some of the work will require readers to dig more deeply; other parts of the book will simply provide a critically reflective resonance.

That said, some may still want to question why the emphasis is on the here and now; on the social situation of the churches; on what they actually *do* or might think about doing. Leaving aside my concern to address ecclesial concreteness (rather than hypothetical theological correlative theories of what the church could or should be like), there are at least three reasons that justify the ecclesial focus for tackling the theology–Christianity–culture debate.

First, I am clear that churches are cultures themselves, and therefore both form and are formed in relation to their contexts. This has an impact on public theology, ecclesial shape and wider social life. Second, much contemporary Christian faith and practice now bypasses traditional or formal ecclesiology. The situation is, to quote Mudge, one of 'post-denominational Christianity' (2001, p. 3), where many existing denominations find themselves increasingly disabled and new experimental countercultural and pro-cultural Christian communities are on the rise (ibid., p. 64). Third, new cultural shapes for expressing and embodying Christianity make the Christianity and culture debate a key area of engagement both for theology and for churches.

To give one example that encapsulates what I have expressed in the three previous points, I can point to a local Anglican–Baptist ecumenical church partnership, with an Evangelical and Charismatic identity which nestles in one of the more prosperous suburbs of my native Sheffield. The church of St Thomas Crookes has an interesting history with experimentation. It was here that the postmodern 'Nine O'clock Service' (NOS) was born out of the 'Nine O'clock Community', a fusion of Matthew Fox's creation spirituality, various types of theology, hi-tech worship and other elements fused together to create a regular 'planetary mass' for the worshippers. However, the experiment ended in acrimony, and the church literally imploded, when the leader of the church, the Revd Chris Brain, was found to have been engaged in a level of sexual impropriety.

Nonetheless, this same church has continued its tradition of cutting-edge experimentation. It has risen, phoenix-like, from the warm ashes of the scandal that threatened to consume it. Under its new leader, the Revd Mike Breen, it has recently begun its own religious order, with the vicar becoming the Superior. The Order of Mission is Protestant, Charismatic and Evangelical, but has developed a system of tertiary association, as well as encouraging full members of the Order who are committed to a daily cycle of prayer and living in community. The church has bought and developed a new complex – Philadelphia – to enable the evangelization of inner cities throughout northern England. Members of the new Order describe the Philadelphia complex as a 'monastery in an urban setting, for the express purpose of mission'. Meanwhile, the new Superior – embodying the synthesis of globalization and commitment to the local (that is, 'glocal') – now divides his time between a new project in Phoenix, Arizona, and helping to establish new cells of the Order across the largely un-Christianized landscape of England's northern cities and urban connurbations.

The Philadelphia project and the Order of Mission mark a new development in ecclesiological patterning. The Order constitutes a new self-conscious fusion of Charismatic, Evangelical, Catholic and postmodern spiritualities. The order, organization and worship that characterizes the meetings seems to be perfectly in tune with the needs and desires of Christians drawn from the – it has to be said – mostly articulate and professional middle class of a postindustrial city at the turn of the third millennium. But it is exactly this kind of mutation that is taking place in religious life within contemporary culture that makes the task of hospitable and interdisciplinary methods in ecclesiology more urgent than ever, both for the academy and for the church as a whole. It will no longer suffice to speak of churches, in their embodiment of Christ, being 'for' or 'against' culture. The cultural map of the third millennium needs a more complex system of signs and symbols to represent the grounded reality of Christianity.

With these observations in mind, it is worth attempting to say something, finally, about the situation of the churches (and theology) within the context of the twenty-first century. The renewal of interest in religion in the postmodern situation is not without its price and irony. In contemporary postmodern culture, fluidity has replaced the concrete, and certainties have given way to subjectivity and ambiguity. As Lyotard reminds us, ' . . . postmodernism is "incredulity at metanarratives" ' (1984, viii). And as Huston Smith suggests, postmodernism is 'ambiguity elevated to apotheosis' (1990, p. 661). Post-modernism is, of course, not a systematic philosophical system; it is more of a mood and a socio-cultural force (cf. Rengger, 1995). In that sense, the challenge of postmodernism to religion lies in the very nature of the culture in which it now finds itself embedded. This is a culture that accepts its own fragmentation and its lack of obvious moral or cultural coherence.

In such a context, religion undoubtedly lives – but no longer as a meta-narrative. It is, rather, one of the many ideologies and activities that competes for time and interest in an increasingly ephemeral public sphere. Under such conditions, churches and theology have at least three tasks: first, to be able to 'higgle' – the old English (agricultural) word that describes the process of continuing to affect things by degrees; second, to be able to 'thole' – an old Irish word that describes the process of survival under adverse conditions (for example, 'tholing' through bad times at work, or perhaps through a difficult relationship); and third, to be engaged in renewal. Now, renewal can be read in two senses here. It can mean a process of recovery and restoration, but it can also mean replacement. Here I want to suggest that both senses are implied for the churches and theology. The Christian tradition must face the present and the future, but it cannot neglect its past. Correspondingly, for churches and theologians alike, the possibilities and potential for practical theology are especially rich, since the discipline is committed to conversation (with other, non-theological disciplines and with the grounded reality of ordinary situations), as well as bearing faithful spiritual and hermeneutical witness to the Christian tradition. In the essays and sketches that follow, practical theological reasoning has been deployed, in a variety of arenas, in order to test and clarify the forms of theological and ecclesial engagement with contemporary culture that exist at the beginning of the third millennium.

Practical Theology: The Background

The most typical kinds of theological engagement with contemporary culture are confessionally rooted and 'applied'. In other words, they are concerned to defend an existing tradition, and set about doing so by applying biblical particularities or theological priorities to perceived problems that require their attention. Roman Catholic, Evangelical and liberal traditions are all capable of engagement at this level, and an abundance of theological literature exists that either affirms or critiques culture from such standpoints. That said, a much more rarely encountered strategy is one whereby the theological or ecclesial tradition recognizes itself to be part of a discrete culture and then sets itself the task of undertaking several types of dialogue with other cultures. This encounter-based approach is far riskier, since it virtually anticipates change on the side of the inquirer. To *truly* listen will mean being open to the possibility of change (cf. Markham, 2003, p. 48ff). Moreover, I hold that it is precisely this kind of challenge that should, and could, help shape the discipline and practice of ecclesiology.

Having said that, some aspects of theological engagements with culture are less about reception and more to do with change and conversion. Just as there is a balance to be struck in religious resilience between resistance and adaptation, or assimilation and confrontation (Percy, 2001; Markham, 2003), so in engagement there is an equilibrium to be sought between passivity and activity, and receiving and responding. I mention this, since it can sometimes be assumed that any methodology which is crafted for the purposes of inquiry and engagement must somehow be 'neutral'; and where neutrality cannot be located, some kind of confessional bias can be assumed. This is unfortunate, since most scholars in the social sciences would readily admit that there is an inherent partiality in any methodology. Sociology assumes that religion is social; anthropology assumes that it is cultural; and theology assumes that it is 'real', and irreducible. I accept these shortcomings in theories that might guide any method of inquiry. However, it is important to state from the outset that here, in this book, the methodologies are already acknowledged as being in some sense prejudicial. As Bauman notes:

> There is no choice between 'engaged' and 'neutral' ways of doing sociology. A non-committal sociology is an impossibility. Seeking a morally neutral stance among the many brands of sociology practised today...would be a vain effort.... (Bauman, 2000, p. 216)

As readers will discover, the subtext of many of the chapters in this book is that 'ecclesiology itself is a kind of social theory' (Mudge, 2001, p. 12). Contrary to Radical Orthodoxy, the use of, and dialogue with, the social sciences herein is intended to make a richer kind of theology that *engages with this world*. I do not hold, as Milbank does, that social sciences (including political theory) simply consume or nullify theology whenever any kind of fusion takes place. Ecclesiology, based on (or understood as) social theory can read and interpret the stories of the people of God, who are themselves reading the story of God through their tradition, even as they are 'performed' by it. Some understanding of concrete social and ecclesial existence is therefore vital if the churches are to truly engage with the cultures which are their contexts. Correspondingly, I hold (along with Healy and Mudge) that ecclesiology must make full use of non-theological methods and insights, which will help the church to think of itself as an organization, as well as a 'text' that is read and expressed. Thus, the underlying thread of the argument in this book is for a sociologically informed theology (which is, per se, an ecclesiology), and for a cultural–linguistic understanding of Christianity (following Lindbeck) that pays attention to the grounded reality of the church and the cultures that congregations inhabit.

It is for this reason that practical theology is the preferred methodological mode of inquiry that is adopted in the explorations that follow. To be sure, there are many types of practical theology, and it is not my purpose here to rehearse the various schools of thought that ultimately comprises a rich methodological field of inquiry. Fundamentally, practical theology is rooted in a determined form of research that often begins by learning to *listen deeply* and *well* – giving a subject or issue some serious and respectful non-directive attention in the first instance, whilst not foreclosing on the possibility of critiques and the development of a critical practical theology. The listening is undertaken in order to: provide some systematic ordering of complex and contrary materials; to reach some intelligible discernment about their shape and scope; to offer some critical reflection on relevant issues, ideas and theories; and, finally, to discover fresh theological insight. Some of the basic tools for the above would comprise ethnography, fieldwork, interviews, textual analysis and the like.

Of course, no research takes place in a vacuum. In the arts, humanities and social sciences it is very often situated between: theories and practices; ideal situations and ideas; real situations and thoughts; blueprints for the world and concrete reality; modernity and postmodernity. We might also say that research in religion is often caught between the general and the particular; between the local and the macro. Nonetheless, research is normally about making more sense of situations than those people who are in them can normally manage; it is about genuine and free inquiry. Thus, research can be defined as re-searching – retelling or renarrating and reconstructing – either the theories that failed to deliver a sound analysis, or the 'facts' themselves. Re-searching, retelling and reconstructing are critical, related yet distinct stages within the overall penumbra of research. Their sequencing within a study – either linear, which can either be a matter of progression, or a spiral of interaction – requires the researcher to separate out and yet connect description (a range of perspectives), interpretation (a range of options) and analysis (a range of critical perspectives), leading finally to the redescription of the original issue or topic under investigation.

Since practical theology is a listening and reflective discipline, it does not seek to be dogmatic in its engagements:

> Practical theology is a critical and constructive reflection within a living community about human experience and interaction, involving a correlation of the Christian story and other perspectives, leading to an interpretation of meaning and value, and resulting in everyday guidelines and skills for the formation of persons and communities. (Poling and Miller, 1985, p. 62)

There are, of course, several other ways of describing the discipline and its focus. For Woodward and Pattison practical theology is 'a place where religious belief, tradition and practice meets contemporary experiences, questions and actions and conducts dialogue that is mutually enriching, intellectually critical and practically transforming' (2000, p. 5). For Elaine Graham it is transforming practice – the articulation and excavation of sources and norms of Christian practice, a form of *phronesis* (practical wisdom) that helps churches to practise what they preach and preach what they practise. For Duncan Forrester, it is 'the theological discipline which is primarily concerned with the interaction of belief and behaviour' (Forrester, 2000, p. 10). And for Don Browning, practical theology is utterly fundamental:

> ...all theological thinking...is essentially practical. The social and intellectual context in which theology is brought into conversation with the vision implicit in pastoral practice itself, and with the normative interpretations of the faith handed down in the traditions of the church. Theology thus arises from practice, moves into theory, and is then put into practice again.... (Browning, 1991; cf. Woodward and Pattison, 2000, p. 6)

Practical Theology as Methodology

According to Van der Ven (1998), there are four functions in the work of scholarship. The first is 'discovery research'; the second is 'integrative theoretical research'; the third is 'applied research'; and the fourth is 'the scholarship of teaching'. The distinction is useful, since it closely corresponds to the matrix of functions within which practical theology both situates and describes itself. As a methodology, it is critical, empathetic and reflective, but also geared towards transformation and learning. It treats discovery, integration, theory, application and teaching – and their relationship – with utmost seriousness. Thus, in any consideration of theological research and education, there is a necessary interest in not only attending to all four of the functions that Van der Ven identifies, but also investigating the extent to which they interrelate. This is a vital task for the field of theological and religious studies.

A piece of research is, ultimately, a review, reconsideration and a return – perhaps leading to a revolution; this is comparable to the transformative agenda of practical theology at work. It is this type of approach that allows us to study apparently simple things, such as a funeral tea (cf. Clark, 1982) or to ask a basic question, such as: 'Where is the theology of this group located?' Is it in their creeds and articles of faith? Or is it in their habits, customs, rituals and stories? And if the latter, how do we best discover and study them? And once we have discovered them, how do we read and interpret them? And, finally, what are the implications of such studies for the academy, with its methodologies and present understandings? (To help me address such issues, I have leant heavily on the interpretative framework of James Hopewell (1987), and some of the possibilities for his work being applied are sketched in Part Three. Readers who are familiar with my work will also note that this has involved a more anthropological turn in my writing, which has flavoured several of the chapters.)

So to repeat, the key to successful researching in religion lies in establishing that the knowledge we have is inadequate and insufficient, or even 'wrong', despite appearances to the contrary (for example, what we think we know about a church). It lies in identifying new knowledge, or how knowledge reinterpreted, might change the way in which we look at a specific topic or field (for example, history or religion). It then rests on using an established methodology to help answer a set of research questions (which may not have been asked before) and then establishing a *critical* relationship with that methodology. Finally, it leads us into a situation where we can begin to say something entirely new about the apparently familiar.

In a comparable vein, Ziebertz argues that 'practical' theology is not the opposite of 'theoretical'. Practical theology is not like systematic theological disciplines, since it focuses on 'the practice of religion ... real-life human acting within religious practice rather than logic ...'. However, practical theology does not merely seek to describe what it sees, but also to try to come to some understanding of it. In so doing, it habitually turns to the full range of social sciences to gain a deeper understanding of the social situations that it is engaging with (Ziebertz in Roebben and Warren, 2001, pp. 105ff). In this respect there is something essentially hospitable about practical theology. It does not stand on its own dignity; it seeks partnerships and conversations at every stage. It is a fluid methodology fully in tune with Bauman's 'liquid modernity'.

All this, it seems to me, takes the would-be practical theologian well beyond the compass of merely 'reflecting' on ecclesial and cultural situations from a theological perspective, let alone trying to be 'applied'. Practical theology, at its richest, is a form of thinking that allows a range of methods to come together, to be 'tested' by the issues they are addressing, and for some degree of critical fusion to emerge. It is for this reason that I prefer the term 'refracted' to 'reflected' or 'applied' when considering how practical theology might engage with contemporary culture. The idea that the truth and purposes of God are 'refracted' – spread like a band of colour, as it were – is particularly compelling for the issue at hand. A refractive strategy is also, analogically, a good 'fit' for the fusions and strands that make up any one 'culture'. Strictly speaking, of course, 'culture' is a contested nest of issues and categories, and it could be argued that a process of refraction is required for the purposes of separation and illumination.

So to speak of theological refraction within culture is to suggest that there is a fit between the explanatory and analytical process and its subject. Refraction – as a strategy – allows disciplines and issues to pass through one another, and through so doing 'reform themselves in such a way as to manifest their capacity to mediate the primary vitality of life and understanding – that is, to manifest their capacity to integrate that through which they have passed into *their* truth (cf. Hardy, 1996, pp. 1, 203, 323–26). Put more simply, refraction is a proper dispersal of light into its constituent bands of colour, as it passes through a glass prism. In a consideration of theology, church and contemporary culture – which is rightly concerned with sociology, theology, anthropology, cultural studies and more besides – it is vital that the whole 'issue' passes through each of these 'prisms' and that each of these then sees how its own truth is effected by the refractive process.

In theological refraction (or any other discipline), for example, theology can fulfil itself through another discipline and, in so doing, enhance its own capacity to reflect, focus and enhance its primary task. To take this a stage further, refraction is in place for the clear sight of the perceptor. Only when things are 'correctly' perceived – the whole picture taken in, as it were, and processed – can the objects of refraction be addressed, affirmed or changed. Refraction is a process which divides 'strands' and then reconfigures them into an image or an interpretation. Because culture and religion are complicated 'things' to see, and often 'blurred', it is essential that the refraction is as dense and accurate as possible.

Refraction does not just mean 'interdisciplinary'. The dispersal of light – or the sifting of elements and compounds when the term is deployed in chemistry – is about a purification and intensification of original sources. When one light is refracted, the subsequent bands of light can be dazzling. But the actual refraction is not the goal. The actual goal is to discover fuller ways of reflecting and focusing life in this or that band of colour, and not only gaining understanding *in* it, but also *from* it. Refraction, then, is the transformation of light as it passes from one medium to another; as this is done, different images are formed and experienced, and light itself is seen in a different light.

To see the issue of religion and culture as something that requires refraction is to rescue it from 'simply' being *reflected* upon. Too much reflection takes place without proper refraction, and, although much of this may be worthy, intuitive and skilful, there can be no substitute for separating out the constituent issues and disciplines, allowing them to interpermeate (pass through one another) and, in so doing, find their own proper density. Refraction also pre-empts questions of reform or revolution. It is not that refraction is against these two futures; rather, it is more likely that any reform or transformation will be *clearer* and more specific, and then carefully directed to those areas that demand that.

Practical Theology: Further Reflections

David Hazle further argues that two distinct paradigms of theology coexist. The first sees theology as a discipline in which practical theology is one of many subdisciplines. The second conceives of theology as essentially practical, so that all kinds of theology are ultimately interrelated within the sphere of the church as the community of practice. For the most part, the first paradigm has dominated Western theological thinking, and, from such a perspective, practical theology has been merely the 'finishing school' for ministers, equipping them for the task ahead. However, the second paradigm has enjoyed increasing pre-eminence. In particular, practical theology has mounted a challenge to the nature of theology itself, has challenged traditional methodologies for theological reflection and has developed interdisciplinary approaches, especially in conversation with the social sciences. This development has enabled practical theology to evolve into a primary form of theory which challenges both the nature and the boundaries of the discipline.

Hazle builds on the work of Farley, who divides the field of theology in a slightly different way – into four. For Farley, there is, first, theology as a 'habitus' – a way of life that includes prayer, worship and discipleship. Second, there is theology as a 'science' – the grasping and disclosure of the self-revelation of God. Third, there is theology as 'sciences' – a cluster of relatively independent studies that constitute a 'faculty' in which various subdisciplines interrelate. Fourth, there is theology as a systematic or dogmatic constitution, but this is usually one that is to be found operating at some distance from ordinary life and contemporary culture. Hazle, agreeing with Farley, laments the loss of the first kind from the academy. The clericalization and professionalization of theology have removed it from the realm of the ecclesial and the situation of worship, and have driven a (false) wedge between 'pure' and 'applied'.

But what has bequeathed this new life to 'practical theology', given the prevailing separatism that modernism and secularization has visited upon the study of theology? The answer must lie somewhere in the realm of the rediscovery of the contextual, and in the development of 'theories of action' in relation to theology. Typically, such initiatives have emerged from the edge of ecclesial, social and theological thinking. Black, lesbian, gay, feminist and other kinds of theology have been concerned with 'doing' theology; they have understood that the divisions between 'pure' and 'applied' have invariably excluded minority groups and interests. The Caribbean theologian Kortright Davis expresses the moment of epiphany within the discipline simply enough:

> Western theologians are [now] attempting to educate themselves about the new theological surges emanating from the Third World. They have finally realized that there is no universal theology; that theological norms arise out of the context in which one is called to live out one's faith; that theology is therefore not culture free; that the foundations on which theological structures are built are actually not transferable from one context to another. Thus, although the Gospel remains the same from place to place, the means by which the Gospel is understood and articulated will differ considerably through circumstances no less valid and no less authentic.... (Davis, 1990, p. 70)

Quite so. Put another way, we might say that the lesson from Pentecost is that theology (or Christianity) is always spoken in tongues, so that each can understand in their own language. There is no Christianity that lacks a local accent; there is no one, singular 'pure' version. Theology and faith are always contextual, but that does not mean a capitulation to relativism. Indeed, almost any study of Christian 'culture' could illustrate this, but, to illustrate my point, here is an extract from an early-mid-twentieth-century English hymnal, written for children in Sunday School:

> Do you see this Penny?
> It is brought by me
> For the little children
> Far across the sea.
> Hurry, Penny, quickly
> Though you are so small;
> Help to tell the Heathen
> Jesus loves them all....

As Davis says, the Gospel is the same (as God is), but the means of expression will always be variable over space, time and culture.

Hazle concludes his reflection on the nature of practical theology by noting that the discipline is inherently praxis-centred. Because of this, the branches of theology relate both to each other and other disciplines as they encounter fresh situations and new contexts. Theology is, then, a living process of thought and action, which is not simply for the specialist. Theology is the description for the reflective or refractive activity and praxis of the Christian community. And, because it is concerned with living for the kingdom of God, it always has a broader vision than its own self-concerns (Hazle, 2003, p. 366; cf. Forrester, 2000).

To conclude, we can say that practical theology is more concerned with *phronesis* (that is, practical wisdom) immersed in concrete situations than with *theoria* (that is, abstract theoretical reasoning). However, practical theology is heavily theory-laden and, arguably, of more strategic use than other theological disciplines. Critical practical theology and strategic practical theology are therefore engaged in a dynamic spiralling, which engages practice with theory and theory with practice; it refines the purposes of thinking and the deep wisdom of reflection in given contexts (Browning, 1996, pp. 6–10). Or, as I have already suggested, we might refer to this process, analogically, as refraction. Farley, summarizing our thinking, identifies seven theses that describe the scope and trajectory of practical theology as it is being used in this book of essays (Farley, 2003, pp. 42–43):

1   Because practical theology is a dimension of theological reflection and understanding and therefore is all-pervasive in the faith community, it is not restricted to a field of clergy education.
2   Practical theology is that dimension of theology in which reflection is directed to a living situation in which the believer or corporate entity is involved.
3   When response to, and interpretation of, a situation is self-consciously responsible, it can be assisted by a hermeneutic of existing in a situation. The focus of traditional and contemporary hermeneutics by texts and traditions has suppressed and marginalized the interpretation of situations. In practical theological hermeneutics the object of interpretation is the situation itself.
4   The tasks of a hermeneutic of situations are to uncover the distinctive contents of the situation, probe its repressed past, explore its relation to other situations with which it is intertwined and confront the situation's challenge through consideration of corruption and redemption.
5   The clerical activities of the traditional version of practical theology are, as situations, valid and important candidates for practical theological interpretation as are the situations of the believer and churchly communities. A practical theology of these activities and environments will correct their traditional pedagogical isolation through a special hermeneutic of these situations.
6   Practical theology, like other dimensions of theology, can and should be taught both in the church at large and in schools for educating the clergy.
7   Practical theology, as a dimension of theology and as an educational undertaking, can have a rigorous character and should be supported when appropriate by the resources, tools and disciplines of scholarship.

Broadly, we shall be working with Farley's definition of practical theology throughout this volume. Equally, however, we shall not be following Farley's delineation of the field (or that of any practical theologian) slavishly. These essays are intended to be exploratory in nature and are a deliberate exercise in 'trying on' different kinds of theoretical and practical reasoning in relation to the life of the church, the nature of theology and the relation between

Christianity and contemporary culture. They are sketches. The expectation is that the reader will use the book to reflect on their own cultural and ecclesial situations; that they will deepen their understanding of theory and practice; and that they will enlarge their vision for the possibilities of theology within the nexus of today's complex cultural milieu.

PART I
THEOLOGY, CHURCH AND CONTEMPORARY CULTURE

Chapter 1

Church, Authority and the Culture of Credibility

Modern ecclesiology is essentially concerned with describing and analysing the shape of the contemporary church in relation to modern life and its understandings of God. Put another way, it is the internalized social expression of its doctrinal mind; ecclesiology mirrors theology. The missiology of the church, in contrast, can be more detached from the immediate self-understanding of the church. Whilst it will undoubtedly disclose something of the inner heart and mind of any ecclesial body, it can also at once be more pragmatic and experimental: testing the Spirit at work in the world, as it were. In this chapter, the exploration of Christianity within contemporary culture proceeds in two ways. First, a comparative analysis of writers addressing ecclesiological issues in North American Roman Catholicism is offered, in order to gain some preliminary understanding of how the church is developing in response to crises of authority, reception and public perception. Second, there is a broader, ecumenical focus on the teaching authority of the church, and its relation to notions of credibility and identity. Here the discussion expands to include Anglicanism and some recent ecumenical initiatives, although the shape of the argument has implicature for other historic denominations.

Roman Catholicism in North America: Four Writers in Dialogue

Radical blueprints for reforming the Roman Catholic Church are hardly new. Hans Kung, Karen Armitage, Hans Winjgaards, to mention but a few, have all, in their different ways, advocated radical changes in theological and ecclesiological self-understanding. Whether or not one agrees with their agenda is, for our immediate purposes, inconsequential. Rather, it is important to grasp that each such writer argues with a degree of passion, cogency and tenacity for the reform of the church. They have sought to set out a new schema for the church in which its missiological shape and ecclesiological dimensions would better 'fit' with modern times. No self-respecting writer in the realm of 'public theology', it would seem, can leave the issues alone.

Paul Lakeland's recent *The Liberation of the Laity* (2003) carefully charts the situation of the laity before Vatican II, the achievement of Yves Congar, the teaching of the Council on the laity and the new emergent situation since Vatican II. But Lakeland's book contains a second part, which is arguably far more significant. Here he argues for a 'lay spirituality of secularity', the liberation of the laity (from overt clerical domination), the shaping of mission for the postmodern world, and changes in the way the church is governed. These proposals include greater accountability and transparency, women and married people occupying roles of leadership, as well as the eventual elimination of both ecclesiastical careerism and the College of Cardinals. But such contributions to contemporary Roman Catholic ecclesiology (from both within and without) are hardly unusual at the commencement of the twenty-first century. There is widespread debate, which reflects a range of reformist agenda and discontent, as well as a predictably concerted attempt to try to maintain the current shape of the church, despite much criticism. In order to explore this ecclesiological territory in more depth, a comparative strategy will now be deployed.

Four recent books that attempt to engage Roman Catholic thinking with the everyday challenges of contemporary life are Francis Buckley's *The Church in Dialogue: Culture and Traditions* (2000), Anthony Gittins' *Ministry at the Margins: Strategy and Spirituality for Mission* (2002), John Fuellenbach's *Church: Community for the Kingdom* (2002) and Nicholas Healy's *Church, World and Christian Life: Practical–Prophetic Ecclesiology* (2000). The authors are all North American and might, therefore, have the immediacy of their context in mind as they write. No one can dispute that such an agenda is a timely one. Roman Catholics are a diverse body of believers in the third millennium. Furthermore, the relationship between 'official' and 'operant' in American Catholic religion is under increasing academic scrutiny:

> Most observers agree that there is a great deal of diversity among American Catholics.... While there was a certain amount of diversity in the 1940s and 1950s...the beliefs and practices of American Catholics have become increasingly varied since then. Studies done during the 1950s and 1960s indicated that there was more uniformity among Catholics than among mainstream Protestant groups.... More recent research, however, suggests that American Catholics' beliefs and practices are now more diverse than they were prior to the Second Vatican Council.... (Williams and Davidson, 1996, p. 102)

But there are now additional problems to note, besides the diversification of Catholic beliefs. The Roman Catholic Church in the USA has been rocked over the past few years by a series of unfolding scandals that have undermined its authority and power. The *Boston Globe* has led the way, challenging Cardinal Bernard Law and his fellow prelates over their handling of priests who have subsequently been convicted for paedophile offences. August papers such as the *New York Times* have also joined in the fray and have exposed chronic gaps between rhetoric and reality in the life of the church.

In general, it is a widely shared perception amongst the American public that most of the bishops in the Roman Catholic Church have performed very poorly in the midst of this crisis. The bishops have been reticent about being taken to task by secular law, clearly preferring to keep priestly paedophilia as an 'internal matter'. They have resented the growing clamour of voices amongst the laity for greater openness and accountability. The newly formed

'Voice of the Faithful' movement has been quickly suppressed and labelled as seditious and divisive, despite a clear programme that pursues justice and truth. And in terms of delivering any reform in the future, the bishops already seem to have promised far more than they are ever likely to deliver. Commitments to involve the laity more and to compensate victims have already turned sour. In the media overall, the bishops have shown themselves to be flat-footed and lacking dexterity, tenacity and appeal. A number of commentators have noted that, instead of looking like fathers in God, the bishops more likely resemble a disparate collection of minor mafia uncles. Trusting no-one, and having failed their own, they nonetheless expect to rule to the end, remaining above secular law at all times, sorting out their own problems in their own way.

So four books concerned with Roman Catholicism and contemporary culture ought to be timely, refreshing and helpful. Whilst these books could not have hoped to address the ecclesial cancer that was first revealed in the archdiocese of Boston (and is now known to be very widespread), one would nevertheless anticipate that Roman Catholic theological engagements with contemporary life would be able to make some important connections. For example, at a time when attendance at mass is declining and religious observance is moving from the obligatory to *à la carte*, what is the connection between the *authentic* life of the church and its claimed *authority*? How do you catechize new generations of Roman Catholics when the (so-called) 'lapsed' have distanced themselves from many of the arcane customs and beliefs of the church? It is a fact that the majority of Roman Catholics in the USA are in favour of married priests, would not mind ordained women in their parishes and don't believe that Methodists or Muslims are necessarily bound for hell. But the official teaching of the Roman Catholic Church is not quite in step with the vernacular religion of the faithful. Increasingly, 'official' and 'operant' religion finds themselves at odds with one another. For most of the time, this is a quiet, unspoken revolution.

In England, for example, the Roman Catholic birthrate has been falling for years. But good Catholic women do not take contraceptive pills for birth control – only to regulate their periods. The ends justify the means. In the USA it is hardly very different. Even parish priests turn two blind eyes: one to the official teaching of the church, the other to what really goes on amongst their congregations. Williams and Davidson (1996), in their study of American Catholicism, offer a generational explanation for the seismic shifts of the last 50 years. The pre-Vatican II generation (born in the 1930s and 1940s) viewed the church as an important mediating force in their relationship with God. When asked why they were Catholic, many participants in the Williams and Davidson study replied that it was because 'it was the one true church'. The Vatican II generation (born in the 1950s and 1960s), however, were more circumspect about the nature of the church and its absolutist claims. Interviewees were more inclined to see their priest as representing 'official' religion which, in turn, was only one religious source that fed and nurtured their private and individual spirituality. In this sense, the Vatican II generation is pivotal, since the post-Vatican II generation (born in the 1970s and 1980s) has tended to be even more liberal and open. For this generation, mass attendance is not a priority; being a good person is more important than being a good Catholic; faith is individualistic and private – 'what really counts is what is in your heart'. Williams and Davidson conclude their study with these words:

> One thing is certain: the hands of time cannot be turned back. Societal changes, as well as changes occurring within the church, leave no doubt that tomorrow's Catholics will be very different from previous generations. The children of post-Vatican II Catholics will receive their religious education from those who never read the *Baltimore Catechism*, and are likely to know little about the changes brought about by Vatican II. The conceptions of faith post-Vatican II Catholics are apt to pass on to the next generation will look decidedly individualistic in nature.... (Williams and Davidson, 1996, p. 37)

So what kind of hope do Healy, Gittins, Fuellenbach and Buckley offer for the future of their church? How are their approaches to faith and contemporary culture-enabling, enlightening and empowering? Each author has their own approach to the debate, and offers a distinctive take on how Roman Catholicism is attempting to come to terms with the multiple and diverse pressures of modernity. These contributions will be briefly described in a moment. But the main focus of our interest here will be to dwell not so much on what the authors say as on what they don't say. In other words, this conversation should perhaps begin where the books finish. Correspondingly, I want to draw out the possible implications of each author's approach to the subject and invite them to say a little more about what needs to be done.

Francis Buckley's *The Church in Dialogue* (2000) is a warm and thought-provoking work that aspires to 'engage in fruitful conversation with various cultures, academic disciplines and religious traditions'. The scope of the chapters covers a very broad range of topics that will be of particular interest to Catholics: Mary and catechesis, ecumenism, liturgy and enculturation, and so forth. Buckley writes with freshness and poise, and his rhetorical style assumes an easy familiarity with readers. At times, the book almost reads as though one were in a distance-learning process of spiritual formation, being mentored and coached through various stages and negotiations.

Methodologically, the book is apparently influenced by educational studies (although no specific theorists are cited), and Buckley pays considerable attention to narrativity in his treatment of themes. Thus, the chapter on Marian catechesis actively promotes a theology that listens to the inductive reasoning of worshippers (ibid., p. 46), whilst at the same time advocating a deductive approach to the teaching of Marian dogma. The open, listening approach to the insights of the laity for the professional theologian also emerge with some force later (Chapter 6), where Buckley argues for an educational strategy that learns from 'popular religiosity and sacramentality'. Yet despite these encouraging signs, I have substantial reservations about Buckley's agenda. It looks to be charitable, open, committed to encounter and dialogue, and yet the text is riddled with unchallenged hierarchical assumptions.

For example, Buckley states that: 'Christianity is an adult religion, since adults best understand and respond to revelation . . . adults teach children in the family and schools' (ibid., p. 8). What children may be able to teach adults about God, worship, the church, truth, and more besides, does not seem to occur to him. Similarly, in the chapter entitled 'Building Christian Community', Buckley has no difficulty stating that:

> . . . sects tend to oppose sacramentalism and institutional structures as unwarranted compromise with the world . . . [such as] Pentecostals, Adventists and Quakers. . . . In the small sect one feels welcomed, needed, understood, loved, and helped, with a strong sense of belonging. But many drift from sect to sect, searching for the perfect community. (Ibid., p. 140)

Buckley seems to be wholly blind to his paternalism and patronizing tone, as though there was no 'real' problem with the present order he seeks to gently reform but fully support. So what emerges from Buckley's text, finally, is a vision for a church that is more open, accommodating, politer and friendlier to all those that it does not understand or know (in other words, there are *some* good things to say about sects and their members). But the underlying assumption is that all 'aliens', including the Hispanic community, on which Buckley writes movingly, will make little difference to the authority, praxis or shape of the church. The church will continue to be guided by an elite group of males who need to adapt to a new climate of pluralism, but who nonetheless must continue to dominate the church. So, the 'popular religiosity' of the Hispanics is affirmed but, in the same breath, dammed. It has something to say to the church, but this same group are, at the same time, targeted for catechizing, clearly indicating that Buckley sees their 'popular' theology as something less than 'proper'.

For Buckley, enculturation is something that the church accepts, but ultimately expects to be able to overcome. In enculturation, the church may adapt its teachings to fit a context, but there is little sense in which the culture can help to reform the church, calling it to repentance. Perhaps this is why Bernard Law can be seen on television, sitting in court, scowling at the black female judge who is compelling him to answer questions about the practice of his church. I have no doubt that Law thinks he only need answer to a higher authority, and not to an ordinary court of law, and certainly not to a woman. And that is the problem with Buckley's book. Ultimately, I do not think that *The Church in Dialogue* is serious about *true* dialogue. By dialogue, Buckley only means learning just enough about local culture to translate the Gospel into local dialects, so you can then teach the natives the one true language of the church. There is no real commitment to *listen* to the world – especially if it means that the world might change the church.

Theologically, I find that this is highly problematic. If the Holy Spirit cannot speak to the church *from* the world, calling it to new adventures, opportunities and, yes, repentance, then the extensive revelation of God is something less than what Vatican II thought (ibid., p. 5). Now, I am conscious that this is a somewhat harsh reading of a book that tries very hard to be charitable, open and reformist. Indeed, Buckley makes many concessions that some Roman

Catholics would choke on (for example, on intercommunion). But the extraordinary interiority of the rhetoric that peppers so much of the text makes me want to suggest that, to even begin to achieve a fraction of what Buckley might hope for, the Roman Catholic Church might like to begin in a different place and consider itself as a more fallible part of God's universal church, and learn to be a listening body that is as receptive as it is communicative, and as open as it is bounded.

Comparable problems are not located in Anthony Gittins' *Ministry at the Margins* (2002). Here we encounter a sophisticated yet practical theological treatise on 'how mission should be undertaken in practice' (2002, p. ix). Indeed, it is one of the few books about Christian ministry that I think one could commend ecumenically. Gittins states that his book is:

> ... offered to boundary crossers of all kinds ... intended for anyone committed to outreach and inclusion ... [it] is a book about ministry ... a minister is the opposite of a master; not very visible and not self-important, but nevertheless necessary ... margins are minimally important in themselves, yet they mark where inside meets outside ... mission often takes place at the margins .... (Ibid., p. xi)

Each chapter is an excellent exposition on its theme, and Gittins writes with an intellectual depth coupled with passion and elegance that serves to strengthen the force of his argument. For example, his chapter on 'Gift-Exchange and the Gospel' uses the work of Mauss to disclose the reciprocal nature of mission. For Gittins, mission involves a prior commitment to learn and to change (ibid., p. 119). True mission across cultures involves mutuality: the desire to give must be matched by the obligation to receive. For Gittins, there can be no sense in which cross-cultural missiological dialogue can hide the kinds of hierarchies that are consistently implied in Buckley's text:

> We may have talked to people, but actually talked down to them. We may have listened to people, but perhaps selectively. Sometimes we craved relationships, but only as givers. Sometimes we set ourselves to learn from others, but only as teachers ... our listening, our relationships and our teaching have been impregnated with power, righteousness, certainty, and the control of initiatives ... Gift-exchange may provide structure for our ministry and teach us the place of trust and risk-taking, vulnerability and indebtedness, and mutuality in mission .... (Gittins, 2002, p. 119)

Gittins carries forward his theology of mission by carefully sketching a missiology based on the concept of hospitality. His exploration of the value of 'strangers' examines the Christian imperative to receive the alien, to welcome the foreigner, as we too, as Christians, were once aliens. Gittins, quite apart from having a fine socio-anthropological grasp of the stranger–host relationship, is able to take his thinking into finely tuned practical theological insights. Thus, he offers perspectives on the host – that is, rights, duties, obligations and ambivalence (ibid., p. 126) – and on the stranger – that is, as receiver, resource, alien and guest (ibid., p. 131) – before bringing this analysis together in an assimilation of the insights. These include a discussion of how the church can become a more incorporative community, sharing histories, pooling resources, generating solidarity, enriching lives and mediating in the midst of hostilities.

The final chapter from Gittins is an apt crescendo for the book: 'the missionary as stranger'. Here the author offers a rewarding account of his own missiological experiences, but coupled to rich theological reflection. What is so attractive about Gittins' work is his ability to see the familiar in a strange, new and more illuminating light. Thus, Jesus on the road to Emmaus becomes a missiological paradigm – a stranger who needs to be received, in order for the Gospel to be proclaimed. But there is also the need to set this insight, as Gittins does, alongside Jesus' own teaching in relation to welcoming the stranger. The church cannot simply cast itself in the role of 'revealed' visitor, expecting the world to receive it. There are many occasions when the church must be the host to the Christ-like visitor and be transformed by the Christophany that is manifest in the face of the hungry, the stranger, the beggar and the prisoner.

John Fuellenbach's *Church: Community for the Kingdom* (2002) is a relatively traditional if well put together treatise on the church. Fuellenbach is well aware that the Roman Catholic Church has woken up to the advent of late modernity and found itself in a different world. Noting that there are several 'megatrends' that affect the church today (2002, pp. 100ff), he writes that:

> People's needs for God are no longer met in the present structures of ministry. A whole range of new ministries is required. There are 400,000 [Catholic] priests. Of these, 68 per cent care for the 40 per cent of the Catholics who live in Europe and the United States and 32 per cent minister on behalf of the remaining 60 per cent. There are not enough to take care of the sacramental needs, never mind mentioning other pastoral necessities. The church has to develop different ministries and new styles of ministry.... (Fuellenbach, 2002, p. 102)

Fuellenbach is wise enough to know that this crisis – and others within the Roman Catholic Church – will not be set straight by achieving a new level of 'objective' talk about the church (ibid., p. xiii). He understands that the sources of theology themselves are multiple: the Bible, tradition and the magisterium; the ongoing life of the worshipping community; the life situation of the committed community; and, finally, the presence of the Holy Spirit. This allows Fuellenbach to constantly talk about the church as only part of the celebration of the kingdom of God, which is, from my point of view, an intriguing and fruitful repositioning of ecclesiology.

On balance, Fuellenbach's missiology is both richer and denser than that of Gittins or Buckley. There are times when his proposals for mission and ministry, and his description of the local church, sound close to the kinds of theology one more generally finds in Congregational Studies and Practical Theology. I mean this as a compliment. Fuellenbach has managed something that few Roman Catholic writers achieve: a compelling thesis that would engage and enlighten many Protestants who are searching for a similar vocabulary to redefine their missiological purpose. There are only a few instances where I would want to quibble with his insights. For example, his description of enculturation as 'a process by which the gospel enters into a culture' (ibid., p. 101) suggests that there is a notion of a 'pure' and *a*cultural gospel lurking somewhere in his thinking, even though the statement is qualified by his admission that the Gospel 'takes from culture all that is already gospelled, and is enriched by it'. Fuellenbach is well aware that cultures can challenge 'the Gospel' and expose those aspects of it that are merely Western.

Fuellenbach concludes his study by calling the church to two tasks. First, the church should recognize that it is no longer in an era of linear change. Second, it should establish a renewal of faith in God and a new understanding of 'God's saving plan for all God's kingdom' (ibid., p. 221). This leads to the identification of two major issues that the church will have to face if it wants to remain faithful to the kingdom: enculturation and solidarity with the poor, both of which are 'within the process of globalization'. The way forward for the Roman Catholic Church will not merely be to anticipate, predict or respond to the future. In an engaged church, it will make the future through a radical recommitment to 'Jesus' own life principles and to his message of the kingdom' (ibid., p. 222).

Finally in this section, we come to Nicholas Healy's prescient work, *Church, World and Christian Life* (2000), which argues that the authority of the church (including what the church teaches about itself), has to pay more attention to the authentic, the concrete, the ordinary and the lived or actual experience or discipleship of its people, and not just try to live its life out of 'blueprints' based on ideology or notions of revelation. To do this, Healy describes contemporary ecclesiology as an antinomy: namely the tendency on the one hand for theologians to describe the church in 'ideal terms', whilst on the other failing to address the church and its problems or possibilities of everyday life – what Healy dubs 'concrete ecclesiology'. Healy argues that the gap between the idealist and the concrete traits tends to inhibit the church in its discipleship and witness, and, furthermore, stifles the production of a coherent prophetic ecclesiology that might arise out of contextual theologies that pay greater attention to ethnography, sociology and other cognate disciplines. Healy sets about his thesis by exposing the weaknesses of what he terms 'blueprint ecclesiologies'. He writes:

> If we generalize from the wide range of ecclesiological styles of the last century or so, it is possible to detect five key methodological elements. One is the attempt to encapsulate in a single word or phrase the most essential characteristic of the church; another is to construe the church as having a bipartite structure. These two elements are often combined, third, into a systematic and theoretical form of normative ecclesiology. A fourth element is a tendency to reflect upon the church in abstraction from its concrete identity. And one consequence of this is, fifth, a tendency to present idealized accounts of the church . . . . (Healy, 2000, p. 26)

The discussion proceeds from here and shows how, for example, an ecclesiologist such as Dulles, in identifying 'models' of the church such as 'herald' and 'sacrament' (five models in all), allows the models to be used in both explanatory and exploratory ways. Although this approach is initially illuminating, it follows a trend that is common to many modern theologians who reflect on the church, namely the identification of an authoritative 'supermodel' as the pre-eminent way of conceiving of the church, and then determining its authority. Thus, for Barth it may be 'the Body of Christ' that is deemed to be denotative; for Rahner it may be 'sacrament'; for Tillard it may be 'communion'.

To this analysis, Healy brings the following insights. First, all 'models' are in some sense deficient – something Dulles also acknowledges. Second, the New Testament offers what he calls 'an irreducible plurality of ways of talking about the church'. Third, the doctrine of the Trinity itself requires us to 'keep shifting our perspective[s]', and to acknowledge that no one perspective is ever 'adequate', but, rather, each needs the 'corrective pressure' of another in order to do justice to the rich and multifaceted faith we know as 'Christianity' (ibid., p. 34). As with the Trinity, so it is with the church; we are bound to a relation of intradependent competing convictions in which no one insight or model has supremacy. This leads Healy to conclude that theologians who deduce a 'complete and normative systematic description of the church from the definitive model of the church's essence' have missed the point. That is not to say that all 'models' are pointless; it is, rather, to say that the models need to be used 'contextually' in ways that aid the exploration of the many facets of the Christian church. That said, Healy still wishes to warn against what he terms 'blueprint ecclesiologies':

> ...[they] display to some degree a tendency to concentrate their efforts upon setting forth more or less complete descriptions of what the church should ideally become...the images and concepts used to model the church are almost always terms of perfection.... (Healy, 2000, p. 36)

The danger of this is that theologians can give the impression that it is 'necessary to get our thinking about the church right first, after which we can go on to put our theory into practice'. As Healy points out, blueprint ecclesiologies therefore assume that there can be agreement on the starting point for a theology of the church – and, of course, there is no such agreement, not even in the New Testament. Blueprint ecclesiologies are problematic for other reasons, too. In using models of perfection, they fail to distinguish between the church militant and the church triumphant, and between the pilgrim church and the heavenly church. Blueprint ecclesiologies tend to foster a disjunction between normative theories and accounts of ecclesial practice, and between ideal and concrete ecclesiology, thereby 'undervaluing the theological significance of the *genuine* struggles of the church's membership to live as disciples within the less-than-perfect church within societies' (ibid., p. 38).

Healy suggests that the deficiencies identified above are best corrected by a proper contextual theology. This is not to separate the church from its context but, rather, to recognize that the concrete church performs its tasks in the world, a place of ever-shifting contexts that inevitably has an impact on shaping its performance (ibid., p. 39). Here Healy pleads for greater attention to the cultural history of the church and for ethnography and sociology to help guide the practice of the church, in order to develop a 'practical-prophetic ecclesiology' that makes use of non-theological disciplines, but without turning away from ecclesiology's primary functions, namely 'to aid the church in its task of truthful witness within a particular ecclesiological context'. Or, as I have been hinting, it is important to move away from epic accounts of the church or blueprint ecclesiologies that 'describe the church in terms of its final perfection rather than its concrete and sinful existence', and from 'normative' accounts or models rather than 'presenting careful and critical descriptions of its activity within the confusions and complexities of a particular theological context' (ibid., p. 54)

What are the implications of this for the Roman Catholic Church in its attempts to engage in contemporary (Western) culture? Healy's work appeals for a more open encounter with 'grassroots' insights that will make the church more 'real' and authentic as a teaching community. Instead of ideologies and truths being imposed on the laity from lofty heights, Healy proposes an *engagement* with the complex reality of the world that can countermoderate traditions. In other words, praxis may have an impact on the idealized blueprint. The suggestion that emerges in the book – more implicit throughout than it is ever explicit – is that teaching must be authentic if it is to be authoritative. Since much of the teaching that the church aspires to deliver is (apparently) authoritative, yet at the same time is lacking in authenticity (that is, not grounded in genuine encounters and the like), the authority can appear to be coercive and imposing rather than engaging and liberating.

So where do these four authors take us in our reflection on the present state of the Roman Catholic Church in America? Of the four, Healy seems to have articulated the most promising theological paradigm that might enable the church to transform itself. Gittins' missiology is enchanting and practical. Buckley's work, although promising in places, is less secure in its theological outlook. Fuellenbach's well-articulated but relatively traditional ecclesiology is certainly able, but seems to be reticent when faced with sharper contextual questions. Doing more for the poor and embracing enculturation is easier said than done, and I remain unclear as to how Fuellenbach's recipe, if fully practised by local congregations, will impact the wider structures and hierarchy of the church.

Of course, it is for the authors to say a little more about how they think their theology might enable the Roman Catholic Church to regain its credibility and re-engage with both believers and public alike. I am conscious that I have approached the American agenda as an English Anglican, so certain allowances will have to be made for what may have been misconstrued. I readily acknowledge that there may be perspectives and insights that I have missed, and some that I have misunderstood. Of course, that is one of the purposes of conversation: clarification. But at the risk of repeating myself, the agenda for the American Roman Catholic looks increasingly complex and awkward, and it will take much tenacity, wisdom and humility to negotiate the hurdles ahead. In particular, three issues come to mind, and I pose these as questions.

First, how can a church have authority when it is perceived to have lost its authenticity and integrity? It is all very well continuing to insist (in a hermetically sealed theological vocabulary) that the church is still *the* authority, but such assertions sound hollow and lack credibility when weighed against public disgust at the handling of paedophile priests and other scandals. Put another way, suppose we ask this question: what if the world does not want *this* church? Suppose the world only wants the church imagined by Fuellenbach – one where solidarity with the poor and enculturation are its distinguishing features?

Second, if the church is to learn from culture, where and at what point does it judge culture, and by what criteria? This question is more complex than it sounds, since many post-Vatican II Catholics now think that 'being good' is more important than 'being a good Catholic' (Williams and Davidson, 1996). If Catholicism is now a mere resource within the wider common pool of civil values and virtues, its claim to be universal and complete begins to look suspect – an archaic way of speaking about the church that nobody really believes to be true. What can be done about this is beyond the scope of the books we have discussed but, I suspect, not beyond the imaginations of the authors. Each, in their different way, is in favour of listening to the laity, learning from congregations and having theology reshaped through such conversations: but how far will they really go?

Third, what can our four authors suggest for the renewal of the church, especially when there is an emergent generation where believing through spirituality seems to matter more than belonging to a congregation? Does the church need to radically rethink itself or, perhaps, attempt a more substantial and imaginative type of re-evangelization? As Bernard Law continues to struggle to talk to, and listen to, the world around him, one can only hope that fresh voices and more attentive ears will emerge. At least these four authors, with their missiology, pastoral and practical theology, and in their different ways, offer much promise and hope for a church that often looks as though it lives its life through its past and struggles to cope with the present. Given these remarks, we now need to consider the nature and purpose of teaching in more depth.

Teaching Authority

Not so long ago, I was invited to an august ecumenical gathering in Europe, and invited to lecture on the following subject: 'How can we teach with authority?' The premise of the question appeared to be that what the church mainly lacked in its engagement with contemporary society was *authority*, and that, without this, the church cannot be heard, is not given its due respect and can be ignored. Of course a body – of belief or believers – that is not held in high regard by the public at large and is ignored by the masses has a dubious claim on being an authority. It can preside over and proscribe for its followers but, to outsiders, the grammar of assent simply looks like a quaint curiosity or, perhaps worse, something between a hobby with too many rules and a totalitarian regime.

So, 'how can we teach with authority'? It is a simple enough, six-word question. And yet to answer it requires some genuine honesty about the premises that fund such an inquiry. We might begin by asking, 'Who is asking the question?' Who is the 'we' of this question? (The question is explored in some depth in Visser't Hooft's *Teachers and the Teaching Authorities* (2000), where a helpful distinction is drawn between the *Magistri* and the *Magisterium*.) Is this a concern of bishops, theologians, pastors, priests and educators? And, if so, is there any evidence that the laity cry out with the same voice? (I doubt it.)

I suspect that the 'we' of the question reflected the angst of many religious *professionals*, who perceive that *their* authority has been eroded by a pottage of cultural and intellectual trends, including modernity, secularization, consumerism, postmodernity, and who knows, perhaps even ecumenism. The reality of these forces allows religious consumers to compare, contrast, choose and, yes, contest their *given* sources of authority. Or one could name any other inimical force that apparently rivals Christianity's *uni*versal claims. There is, for many believers, not one universal authority, but rather a *cosmos* of competing convictions, in which universal claims look increasingly pre-Copernican in outlook. But this observation is only to point towards the fact that, behind the question, we are probably dealing with a neuralgic response to a perceived crisis. The underlying assumption seems to be that that there was once a time when, for the church at least, teaching authoritatively was (relatively speaking) plain sailing. Correspondingly, the hope and aspiration of many is to try to reclaim this pre-eminence in social and cultural positioning, and of course within the interior landscape of ecclesial communities themselves, such that the church can *command* attention by virtue of the charism of its authority.

Now, it is not my purpose here to have a debate about the nature of secularization and its relationship to the teaching office and authority of the church. That would be a separate project in its own right. Suffice to say, the situation of late modernity or postmodernity is more complex and ambivalent than it is stark. In many European countries, religion has a significant public role, and the utterances of church leaders can have, under certain circumstances, significant moral and social impact. It is not the case that secularity (whatever that is – and it is far from clear, and often poorly defined) is squeezing the life out of the role and influence of faith communities in the public spheres. In Europe, religion mutates in modernity; it doesn't disappear as some scholars have argued. People believe, but without necessarily belonging. Faith or spirituality is there, but it is more colloquial in character than those who might aspire to the mythic utopia of Christendom (Davie, 1994, 2000; Percy, 2001). I argue, following Keith Thomas, that faithful indifference to religious authority is commonplace throughout English history and not a modern malaise.

Similarly, in the USA, where the contours of public and civic religion are rather contrary, 'private' or differentiated faith continues to enjoy substantive public adherence (Casanova, 1994). Here again, however, I am bound to say that scholars, having explored contemporary North American religion, can point to considerable spiritual pluralism in the foundation of the USA. 'One

Nation Under God' was an inclusive Deist slogan in the first instance, and not a radical reinvention of Christendom for a new postcolonial nation. Of the 54 people who signed the Declaration of Independence in 1776, only three were *not* practising Freemasons – which is not to say that they were not *also* Christian. As Robert Fuller argues in his recent book (Fuller, 2001), Americans have always been fond of religious and spiritual pluralism and syncretism. So perhaps North America is not so different from Europe? And in the developing world, as if it needed to be said, religions and faith remain utterly fundamental. Indeed, following Grace Davie, I cannot help wondering if the question 'How can we teach with authority?' is a peculiarly European question (Davie, 2000, 2002).

But, given that this is the question before us, how might we proceed? As an Anglican priest, and as a practical theologian with a strong interest in contemporary ecclesiology, the religion–culture debate and ministerial formation, I find the acuity of the question to be more than testing. But I want to set about addressing it in a somewhat atypical way. To my mind, such questions are not that well served by quoting familiar dusty answers, drawn from the shelves of past ecumenical debates. Nor do I draw much inspiration from 'agreed statements' or from mono-denominational responses that simply restate the grounds for their authority and their reasons for teaching what they do.[1] To be sure, such statements and documents have their merit, but they seem to lack imagination and public engagement; they seem to assert rather than argue; they seem to be more anodyne than authoritative. But, by and large, their purpose is one of clarity within the context of interiority, and this means that they don't engage with the *public* character of the question.

In order to address the issue, I want to explore the relationship between *authority* and *authenticity*. The reason for this is simple enough. The etymology of both words lies in the prior word 'author', meaning 'the person who originates or gives existence to anything', 'the inventor, constructor and founder', and so on. Or, put more theologically, the Creator. Generally speaking, definitions of authority flow from this: 'power or right to enforce obedience', 'moral or legal supremacy', 'the right to command', 'give an ultimate decision' and so forth. 'Authentic', in turn, proceeds from authority. The authentic is 'entitled to respect', is 'authoritative' and 'entitled to belief'. But to be authentic can also involve being 'reliable, trustworthy, first-hand, original, real, actual, genuine'; it is identified more colloquially – in other words, not with ideology but with reality.

The tension between the authentic and authority is, in my view, one of the most important (but relatively unexplored) keys to understanding the apparent crisis in contemporary ecclesial identity. Put simply, people's perception of the authentic can question the authority they are placed under, just as much as an authority can interrogate the prevailing establishment. This leads to a debate

---

[1] A recent example of this was the meeting of the 38 Anglican Primates, who at the end of their deliberations issued a statement affirming that they believed in 'a living God; an incarnate God; a triune God; a faithful God; a saving and serving God'.

about the *Author* of a particular aspect of authority – does the dogma under question come from the Creator or the created (*Opus Dei* or *Opus Hominum*)? Equally, is the authentic *given* by the Author (that is, part of the created order) or called into a new existence by the Authority that is above it? (I am well aware that this antinomy is fundamentally false, since inspiration and revelation all comes *through* the agency of created order. Nevertheless, the division between the authentic and authority will serve our purposes well here, in establishing the contours for the debate.)

Authenticity and Authority

Let me start this section by giving two examples – one ancient, and one modern – where authority is linked to the authentic and has a direct bearing on the contours of contemporary ecclesiology. We'll take the ancient example first: in what sense is St Paul an Apostle? Paul claims to have been 'the last' to see Jesus, and partly bases his apostolic claim on being a witness to the resurrected Christ, which appears to have been a criterion for being numbered amongst the elite who quickly came to be known as 'the Apostles'. Yet the writer of the Book of Acts insists that what Paul saw on the road to Damascus was not Jesus himself, but a *vision* of Jesus or a hearing of his voice. It was not an encounter with the risen Jesus in the way the Apostles or the stragglers on the road to Emmaus had known. But Paul, to keep his mission alive, needs the *authority* of an Apostle to carry the Gospel to the gentiles, so he stretches the definition of what an Apostle is by shrewdly rewriting history. But what is the truth of the matter? Paul was still a zealous Jew when Jesus ascended, and he only turned to persecuting the church after it was formed, which was at Pentecost. So he could not have met the risen Christ, and probably never met the earthly Jesus either; the fact that he never quotes Jesus directly in his letters rather confirms this. And yet he wishes to affirm, that he, 'untimely born' was the last witness to the resurrection and that he has 'seen Jesus our Lord' (1 Cor. 15:8 and 1 Cor. 9:1). The Acts of the Apostles manages to subtly undermine the claim, yet without leaving Paul's apostolic claim twisting in the wind. In the Book of Acts, Paul is not converted until one-third of the way through the treatise of Acts (9:1ff) – we have had eight chapters of early church history, without an earthly Christ, before Paul even appears on the scene.

Here is a second, more modern example, and one to which I have alluded already. The current difficulties of the Roman Catholic Church in the USA are now well documented, and they do not need rehearsing here. There is perhaps nothing new about cardinals, cover-ups and child molestation, and it is worth pointing out that there is probably no ecclesial community that could hold its head high and say that it might have handled sexual scandals in a better or fairer way. Leaving aside the financial settlements and outstanding legal issues in the USA, there can be no doubt that the more serious issue for the Roman Catholic Church in the long term is the injury done to its *credibility*. In a legal deposition, Cardinal Law (of the archdiocese of Boston) was forced to admit that it was diocesan policy to 'avoid scandal'. (Cardinal Law has since resigned.) Thus, a letter sent to the cardinal in 1982, detailing the molestation of seven boys by one priest, was 'hushed up'; avoiding controversy was thought to be more important than exposing a crime.

The problem is this. The church uses a language about itself which is potentially problematic: phrases such as 'indefectable', 'infallible in teaching and morals', 'unerring', 'authoritative', 'complete' and 'untainted' come to mind. The scandal of the archdiocese of Boston highlights the gap between rhetoric and reality; the chasm between the authoritative and the authentic are exposed. The authority of the church lies in tatters because it has attempted to preserve its authority by hiding or ignoring the authentic – in this case, genuine abuse.

I am more than conscious that this might appear to have spun off from my original concern: authority in contemporary ecclesial theology. However, there is method in such an atypical approach, which will become apparent as the discussion proceeds. The relationship between authority and authenticity remains a fundamental concern of mine, and it, in turn, has a direct impact on establishing a theology that articulates the nature and purpose of authority, and, therefore, of education and formation. In my recent commentary on the final ARCIC document, *The Gift of Authority*, I take issue with the assumption that reaching this kind of top-level theological consensus (that is, agreements between very senior ecclesiastical and theological persons) constitutes a proper way of setting about the business of doing theology (Percy, 2003).

I make several criticisms of the ARCIC document, although I am supportive of its findings. The first criticism is that the report pays no attention to the significant doctrinal and liturgical differences between Roman Catholics and Anglicans. In ignoring these (presumably because they are deemed to be either too contentious or peripheral), the report assumes that an agreed statement makes for an agreement. It doesn't. By ignoring the genuine differences (and social histories), the nature of the report, although clearly authoritative, lacks a dimension that would give it more authenticity.

Second, the absence of local grassroots conversations, dialogues and exchanges constitutes an impoverished kind of theology. If the Report were a more extensive kind of research, it would have listened to the genuine and lived experience of those on the ground, who are practising their faith in Anglican–Roman Catholic ecumenical projects on a day-to-day basis. The authors of the Report would have wrestled with stories: with the difficulty of impaired communion – yet similar liturgies; of invalid orders – yet mutual respect. Of historic and cultural hermeneutics of suspicion – yet much personal warmth and trust. The issue of authority must be addressed in these places and by these people, but their stories do not feature in the ARCIC report.

Third, there is an assumption that cherished cultural particularities (which inevitably have theological significance) can be swept aside by a form of ecumenism that seems to presuppose its own authority. For example, the nature and purpose of the Church of England invests something in the monarch being its supreme governor, which, in turn, partly characterizes the ambivalent and open nature of English religion. At the same time, the pope is a head of state, as well as presiding over an ecclesial system in which the nature and practice of authority 'feels' rather more proscribed to that which might be encountered in Anglicanism. Yet the ARCIC document mentions none of these matters as an impediment to full and visible unity, as though 500 years of political history and cultural conditioning were somehow irrelevant. Again, in not dealing with authentic differences, the report's authority looks thin. If people's genuine grassroots concerns have not been taken into account, exactly *how* does the report carry weight?

Part of the problem, to my mind, lies in an impoverished notion of what constitutes learning, teaching and formation in ecclesial communities. Paulo Freire understands this better than most, and in his seminal *Pedagogy of the Oppressed* (1972) he sets out the problem:

> A careful analysis of the teacher–student relationship at any level…reveals [a] relationship between a narrating Subject (the teacher) and patient, listening objects (the students)…. The teacher talks about reality as if it were motionless, static, compartmentalized and predictable. Or else he expounds on a topic completely alien to the existential experience of the students. His task is to 'fill' the students with the contents of his narration…. (Freire, 1972, p. 45)

Granted, this is a characterization of teaching and is designed to undermine the (usually unacknowledged) authority of the teacher and the power of knowledge. Nonetheless, Freire's critique is sharp and penetrating. He sees that this approach to education turns students into 'containers – into receptacles to be filled by the teachers'. Education becomes an act of depositing; instead of communicating, the teacher issues communiqués. Students 'bank' knowledge, and in so doing, claims Freire, '[file] themselves away through [a] lack of creativity'. In the 'banking system' of education, knowledge is a gift bestowed by those who consider themselves knowledgeable upon those who are considered to be ignorant. Freire sees this as a form of oppression, negation and stifling of genuine inquiry.

Freire's anti-thesis is a libertarian approach to education, which 'drives towards reconciliation'. Rather than the 'banking system' with its endemic paternalism, he proposes a philosophy of education that is collaborative and 'problem-posing', namely the undertaking of a process in which power relations are suspended and then explored, placing the whole focus of inquiry and its objects (that is, students and teachers alike) within a reticulate intradependent educational context. Freire then argues that 'authentic liberation' (part of the purpose and goal of education – 'the truth shall set you free') is a process of humanization, which cannot be imposed, since it is not a deposit to be made *in* people but is, rather, part of the praxis of liberation. Thus, liberating education 'consists in acts of cognition, not transferrals of information' (ibid., p. 53).

The implications of Freire's work for the question of authority now begin to emerge. Teachers and students become jointly responsible for a process in which they grow and are liberated: 'In this process, arguments based on "authority" are no longer valid; in order to function, authority must be on the side of freedom' (ibid.). This leads Freire to conclude that 'banking education' has a tendency to '[mythicize] reality, to conceal certain facts which explain the way men exist in the world... [it] resists dialogue'. On the other hand, liberating and problem-posing education stimulates creativity, reflection and critical thinking. It affirms praxis, and is characterized by 'revolutionary futurity' (ibid., p. 57).

Freire's concerns correspond more or less directly with those that I briefly sketched in my discussion of the ARCIC report, *The Gift of Authority* (see Percy, 2003). The failure of the authors to consult widely means that certain issues and realities are overlooked. I must also add a further concern. In what sense can 'authority' be truly a 'gift'? Only, it seems to me, if it is asked for, wholly offered (that is, not imposed) or appreciated for what it gives of itself. But to be a true gift, in any conventional sense, it no longer becomes the property of the donor, since it becomes part of the economy of exchange – it can be received with thanks, or rejected as unsuitable. Authority, as a 'gift', implies a covenant relationship, in which obedience cannot be commanded as of right. Of course, *The Gift of Authority* belongs to that economy of education that believes in 'banking' select portions of knowledge (and ignoring others), and the ARCIC report is, arguably, its final deposit, and a way of ordering that knowledge hierarchically. The 'gift' is not given; it is insistently imposed. Moreover, the 'gift' never becomes the property of the receiver, or something to share, since it is clear that the true owners remain the authors and definers of the range and capacity of authority.

To sum up, *The Gift of Authority*, though laudable in so many ways, *lacks* ultimate authority because of its insufficiency in grounded authenticity, and is therefore part of the problem (not the solution) to the crisis of authority in ecclesiology and ecumenism. If such reports don't deal in 'real' issues and don't consult with 'real' Christians and their churches, it will not gain the authentification of the masses of the laity that it *needs*, which will ultimately deprive it of any authority – the very thing it presupposes it has. It is simply theological double-speak to say that a document still has authority even when no-one pays attention to it, or believes in it.

For many, Freire's philosophy of education will appear to be far too risky for the status of ecclesial authority. If faith is turned from monologue to dialogue, from the credal to liberating praxis, and from the concrete to the fluid, will it be meaningful to talk of authority at all any more? Indeed, isn't this precisely the problem for churches and theological educators today? There are disagreements not only about the identity, nature and purpose of fundaments, but also about how they should be read, interpreted and applied. Again, to partly address this question, it is necessary to draw on insights from the philosophy of education. I make three brief points.

First, it must be remembered that there are various types of knowledge that constitute the Christian communities of which we are part, and which form the basis of ecclesial authority or the personal fundaments that construct the Christian lives of individuals. There is considerable plurality amongst the churches. For example, those that are liturgically or doctrinally formed (that is, through tradition), may struggle to relate to those churches where certain experiences (for example, speaking in tongues) validate membership and give grounds for authority. For some, the authority of orders will be pre-eminent. For others, the validation of authority rests on charismata, experiences of the numinous and the ability to reify the life of the Holy Spirit within the midst of the congregation. Within this matrix, the weight of authority given to scripture, tradition, reason and culture will vary enormously. In other words, Christian 'knowledge' (and therefore authority) is a deeply contested concept.

Second, knowledge, and therefore the authority that proceeds from it, is not an inert corpus of material lying 'out there' in some ethereal world (Barnett, 1990, p. 43) but is, rather, part of the dynamic discourses that constitute communities. That is not to say, of course, that knowledge is *only* a social construction of reality (to parody Berger and Luckmann, 1971). It is, rather, to own the fact that knowledge requires *commitment* in order to assume an authority, and this must be an ongoing dynamic process which is open to constant renewal. Furthermore, knowledge has different competencies that are related to its purposes. Practical knowledge has a different authority to that of academic knowledge (Barnett, 1994, p. 160). A knowledge that ceases to have value or meaning for a community inevitably loses some of its authority. Knowledge and authority must therefore be continually rediscovered in the ordinary processes of dynamic sociality; it can never assume a right to privilege without the sacrifice of engagement and debate. (Here we speak of nothing less than 'the word made flesh': God's communication and truth is propositional and relational; eternal, yet dynamic; established and given, yet open and eschatological.)

Third, and following the previous two points, we might ask how authority functions in the church as a *learning* community. To what extent are ecclesial communities equipped with the resources to become communities of critical reflection, or exploration, and of distinctiveness? This question goes to the heart of the knowledge–authority axis and makes further demands on the assumptions about the kinds of knowledge that underpin authority. We might say that in a modernist mindset, the contours of authority are well articulated, and the purposes of knowledge attainment clear and precise. But in a more postmodern climate, there is an almost in-built sense of indecision, indeterminacy and openness (Doll, 1989, p. 250). The ends that may be perceived turn out to be only beginnings: rule books become guidebooks; the pillar of flame a beacon to guide rather than a light to follow; and the shaping of ecclesial communities becomes a process of development rather than a comparatively static correspondence to a finite body of knowledge.

Having made these points, it is important to acknowledge that considerable ecclesial and theological difficulties would be involved in inculcating them wholesale into the life of the church. At worst, an uncritical adoption of the philosophy outlined above could lead to a vapid relativity in terms of definition and distinctiveness. Churches do (and must) stand on some kind of authority that is supported by its corpus of knowledge. However, this brief excursion into contemporary educational philosophy highlights a major problem in consider- ing authority within ecclesial communities. The problem, simply put, is one of reception rather than content. If churches are unwilling to embrace new (more collaborative and less doctrinaire) philosophies of learning and teaching, then the authority of the church is no longer *received* in the same way. Being more imposing (even if this is for the sake of a predetermined unity) is no substitute for the liberation of enabling – even if that does lead to distinctiveness and difference.

Authority and Discipleship

To return to the crisis in ecclesial authority, one could begin almost anywhere, but I hope you will forgive me if I confine my comments to the Church of England and the Anglican Communion, to which I belong as a priest and theologian. Like many churches these days, we seem to have no need of external critiques, as we seem to grow our very own prophets of doom. Norman (2002), for instance, argues that the Church of England has lost its authority because of its uncritical inculcation of humanism, pluralism, secularity and materialism. His views on knowledge are the antithesis of mine. Writing of the encroaching secularization within the church, he asserts that:

> The crucial switch was from confessional instruction to liberal education . . . educated opinion of the time used the word 'indoctrination' pejoratively; indoctrination, however, is what every ideology needs to practise in order to secure its survival . . . the result for the propagation of Christianity has been catastrophic. (Norman, 2002, p. 15)

Norman's attack on authority within his own Communion is therefore short on surprise. He blames the 'imprecision' of definition and 'the modern individualising of religious choice' for the crisis (is this really new?). Yet, despite identifying the 'absence of a coherent source of authority' as the modern malaise for the Church of England, Norman argues that the repository of authority is 'the People of God': '[Christ] established a means of communicating his truth . . . and committed the message not to a philosophical system, or even to written texts, but to an organic agency, a living body of people . . . ' (ibid., p. 93). So, although, to be fair, Norman acknowledges that authority and truth have always been contested within the church (even the pages of the New Testament reflect this, as we have already noted), what is to be done about this?

Norman's guarded uncertainty about what to do in the absence of clarity raises a familiar spectre in the church. If no-one can be absolutely sure about what texts and traditions guide us in our teaching and deliberations, then certainty will prove elusive. And yet this is precisely the point. We walk by faith, not by sight. The need for certainty is, as Robert Towler pointed out some decades ago, a pathology rather than a pathway (Towler, 1984). And yet it is the differences and disagreements between and within churches that raise the prospect of division, which, in turn, appears to further undermine authority. But need this be so?

In David Brown's two recent treatises (1999 and 2000), he argues that it is the very pluralism of scripture itself that can help address the contested field of authority. In *Tradition and Imagination* (1998) he is concerned to maintain a strong emphasis on revelation, but at the same time combine it with an account of tradition, which is the main medium of revelation. In other words, he sees the medium and the message as inseparable, thus allowing him to identify places where developing tradition may correct misunderstandings of truth, and where truth may continue to reform tradition. Behind this process, Brown sees the hand of God 'continuing to involve himself intimately with humanity' and a role for the community of faith in helping believers discern where the process of revelation has now reached. In *Discipleship and Imagination* the argument is taken a stage further:

> ...in the Bible and beyond more often than not truth has emerged through lively *disagreement*, and not simply by formal acceptance of an existing deposit or simple deductions from it. The ability to envisage alternative scenarios has thus always been integral to the healthy development of the tradition. Unilinear theories of development must therefore be abandoned, and the search for consensus *within* conflict be taken with much more seriousness, whether we are thinking of later church history or even the Bible itself. (Brown, 2000, p. 291, emphasis added)

Brown's point resonates with the earlier excursions into educational philosophy. But where does this leave the authority of the church? The question has been put badly and deliberately. In the (so-called) Great Commission (Matt. 28: 18–20), Jesus states that 'all authority in heaven and on earth has been given to *me*...therefore go, and make disciples of all nations'. Where is the authority of the church here? It is ultimately with Christ, which is not to say that that the church has no authority. It is, rather, to remind the church that it does not possess the truth; it is, instead, possessed by the Truth, which is not the same.

This change of emphasis places the church at the feet of Christ and reminds the disciples that they continue to be a learning, disciplined and discovering community of believers who are gathered faithfully around the Word and sacrament, and continue to be fed, nourished and transformed by the living triune God who creates, redeems and sustains. The teaching authority of the church can therefore only rest upon how the church itself allows itself to continue to be taught; how it listens, and models its conversation and education, must be as important as what it says and does in the name of the authority that it has been given.

It is sometimes tempting, when surveying the global Anglican Communion, to imagine that the church will be split asunder by its inability to agree on the ordination of women, the place of homosexuals in holy orders, or indeed any other matter that is held to be inimical to its coherence. The arguments can be bitter, with authority claimed by all who are deeply engaged in such disputes. Yet, at the same time, there is also ample evidence to suggest that conversation and negotiation leads to fresh perspectives on what it means to be a church.

In a recent article on same-sex relations and the debate in East African Anglicanism, Kevin Ward shows how 'the attempt to make definitive pronouncements on sexual ethics and human relationships cannot foreclose on the continuing struggle to establish and foster appropriate human relationships and the institutions which sustain them' (K. Ward, 2002, p. 111). Ward's work shows that, for the church to establish a definitive authority on same-sex relationships, it will have to *engage* with the authentic and complex sexualities it is attempting to rule on. Perhaps inevitably, it will not be able to indoctrinate, for the world is too complex and multifarious. But to educate, and to teach with authority, it will need to be a participant within conversations and encounters that it might not either be able to initiate or control, listening to the Spirit within, whilst also understanding that the same Holy Spirit may choose to speak to the church from the outside, and from the unexpected places.

At this point, it would be right to recognize that many will still be fearful for the fate of faith and order if the question of unity is decoupled from that of authority. But this is where the burden of this chapter starts to emerge. I am advocating more open and faithful disagreement (celebrating the diversity of discipleship) as a part of ecumenical dialogue and truth-seeking, which in turn is to be seen as a truer pathway to the churches owning a more authentic teaching authority. But how can I be sure that such a programme will be faithful to tradition? To answer this, I turn to an area of research that was my first love: Christian fundamentalism. As I argued almost ten years ago, the structure of fundamentalistic thinking is, far from being simple and clear, highly complex, differentiated, accommodating and fluid (Percy, 1996a). Exegesis, eisegesis, interpretation and exposition abound. The Bible can function almost totemically in some communities, whilst in others it provides illumination, inspiration and canonicity, but is rarely read or regarded as wholly inerrant.

There is, in short, no *precise* agreement on the nature of the Bible and what it determines of itself for fundamentalists. Some have 'high' views of inspiration, but have abandoned inerrancy. Others qualify inerrancy, insisting that the doctrine only applies to original autographs, excludes grammatical errors or misspellings and is exempted from lack of precision in certain matters, or apparent contradictions. This leads scholars to identify at least five different versions of the doctrine of inerrancy: *propositional* (absolute); *pietistic* (that is, a kind of spiritual biblicism); *nuanced* (some portions of scripture weigh more than others); *critical* (identifies non-essential errors); and *functional* (limited inerrancy or particular infallibility).

I have deliberately taken the discussion slightly 'off-piste' here to show that, even in fundamentalistic communities, there is considerable divergence on what constitutes an inerrant Bible. And bearing in mind that, for such communities, authority flows *from* the inerrancy of scripture (which is to say that ecclesial and ministerial authority is regarded as being *under* the Word), the patterns of authority and teaching in such communities will vary widely. Where there are similarities between them, they may be morphological rather than doctrinal (style, not substance). Of course, a review of the authority of the Bible in different denominations would reveal a similarly significant range of diversity. Some treat the sacred text as a 'rule book' (instructions to be followed, carefully), others as a guidebook (a few rules, many recommendations, warnings, suggestions and so on), and most interchange between the two. (But is it not the case that the parabolic tradition of Jesus gives the church precisely this permission to act so fluidly?) We may have agreement on *what* the fundaments of tradition are, but not on how to understand them, what weight to place on different aspects of faith and order, nor how to *be* Christian in the contemporary world. (But even this is far from secure. The Salvation Army neither baptizes nor celebrates the Eucharist, but in what sense, though, can they *not* be regarded as Christian? For many in the world, they are a pre-eminent sign of the presence of God and the ministry of Christ, incarnate in some of the most demanding places.) Ecclesial communities are unavoidably hermeneutical rather than (vapidly) receptive. They are *within* the (ultimate) parable of Jesus Christ – experiencing God's story of incarnation, redemption and resurrection as it continues to unfold within them and around them, the Word made flesh (McFague, 1975).

Thus, the authority of the churches – at least in public life – is constituted in the calibre, character and depth of its discipleship. If this sounds too slippery, we would do well to remember that the New Testament offers remarkably little by way of definition as to what a Christian actually is. Christians are known by what they do (activity and vocation), some words that they say (confess), and by what they have (the Spirit of God). But the New Testament does not give the churches a credal definition of what, precisely, a Christian must (or must not) believe in order to count themselves amongst the saints. To be sure, creeds are important, if not vital, for maintaining unity and identifying authority, both internally and externally. But the authority of the church depends primarily on an authentic discipleship that manifests the love of God for the human race and for the whole of the created order. 'We' are known by our fruits, not our seeds.

The stress on discipleship as the fundamental basis for teaching authority takes us back to the start of this chapter and the insistence on the need for parity between authenticity and authority. An emphasis on discipleship also indicates why, on certain occasions, the church fails to be *received* as an authority by the world, since it lacks authenticity and characterful discipleship. Put more strongly, I would argue that the teaching authority of the church rests not on dogma, but on discipleship. And this is surely why, in the (so-called) Great Commission of Matthew 28, there is an explicit link between authority, teaching and the making of disciples. It is a reminder of some words that are usually attributed to St Francis: 'Go and make disciples of all nations. And if absolutely necessary, use words.'

Chapter 2

Christianity and Consumerism

Preamble: Going to Church in Atlanta

The means and modes by which religion can reflect culture, and culture religion, are myriad and multifarious. It is never easy to say at what point culture has appropriated religion and at what point religion has consumed culture, and then begun to sacralize it. In this chapter the exploration is once again centred on the churches and Christianity, but with specific attention being paid to the contribution that religious studies can make to the analysis of the religion–culture debate. Of course, to consider a field as large as this would require more space and time than can be given in a volume such as this. Correspondingly, the foci of the chapter, for the purposes of contextualizing the discussion in the concrete life of the church and contemporary, will rest in a consideration of the impact of consumerism and choice on the shaping of religious identity and behaviour.

By way of preliminary reflection, let us consider two examples of contemporary church life, both drawn from a single day of churchgoing in Atlanta, Georgia. A visit to the Lutheran Church of the Redeemer suggests that it might be a fairly ordinary experience. The church was founded in 1903 and was the first English-speaking Lutheran congregation in the city. The building is of stone and, in its architectural aesthetics, exhibits influences from late nineteenth-century Protestantism. More modern extensions have been added to provide offices, a library and education facilities.

Arriving early for the 9.45a.m. Jazz Service, one is confronted by a gathering that reflects both the theological priorities of the church together with its adopted jazz culture. The main lobby that one first enters from the street feels spacious and airy and is carpeted much like a conference centre. In the middle of this lobby a long series of tables are laid out for a breakfast buffet, with other tables positioned in the corners and at the sides of the room serving coffee, lemonade and other refreshments. The table is a place of gathering: people arriving for the service meet with those who are leaving from the end of the 8a.m. Eucharist. In one corner, a saxophonist, pianist and percussionist lead the gathering in casual hymn singing, set to a jazz beat. Children watch, some dance lazily in the warmth, others sit in comfy chairs and just watch, whilst many adults join in the mellow preamble to the main worship service. The service has no obvious formal beginning, but the music and the beat draw attendees into the emerging spirit of the worship.

This is 'jazz religion' – orchestrated but free, ordered yet casual, easy-listening and entertaining, yet somehow worship. As the gathering thickens, the choir, acolytes and clergy join in the throng, mingling with the worshippers.

There is no formal procession to lead people into the church itself, but somehow the music reaches a level of intensity that begins to move the congregation from the lobby into the main sanctuary, where they take their places in pews and chairs. The lobby is the 'gathering place' – where worshippers meet and greet, and begin to turn to the sanctuary space.

In the service itself, formality (which included a baptism that week) is mixed with more free-flowing jazz praise. The hymns, all of which are traditional, have been set to an upbeat jazz tempo. The congregation participates in the act of worship by singing, but also by responding to the requests for prayer. A time is set aside for worshippers to write down their prayer requests, and, while this is being done, a soft and haunting jazz melody plays. The clergy then move amidst the congregation, collecting the pieces of paper in baskets. They then take them to the sanctuary steps and read a précis of these requests, which is itself shaped within the overall intercessory pattern. This moment is, arguably, the height of the service: the clergy gather the needs of the congregation and then place them before God, but in such a way that the whole congregation can share in the needs expressed. The service concludes with more jazz hymns and improvised music.

The service seems to be intensely personal, and yet also corporate. The gathering and the offering of the prayer requests at the high point of the liturgy, which is at once both casual and ordered, creates a sense of immediacy within the congregation, which the jazz worship appears to complement. The jazz shapes the sacredness of the liturgy, but the liturgy also consecrates the moods, motifs and concerns of the individuals that make up the congregation. Religion and culture are set together in a paradoxical, dynamic and rich fusion. (For further discussion of pragmatism, jazz, spirituality and religion, see Dean, 2002).

A quite different experience can be encountered within the gay subculture of the same city. The New Covenant Church of Atlanta is a gay and lesbian 'mega-church' that proudly proclaims that 'the Spirit of God is being poured out upon all people (Acts 2:17)'. The church has a core membership of several hundred, and attendance figures can easily run to a couple of thousand for certain high days and holy days. But if this seems like an example of niche ecclesial marketing, it is nothing in comparison with the work of the Gospel Girls and the (self-styled) Revd Morticia de Ville, two 'drag queen' acts that lead singing and services in the Atlanta gay bar scene. Journeying out to Burkhart's Pub, one is confronted by a normal American bar, packed out on a Sunday evening. But what marks out the venue for special attention is the entertainment, which is simultaneously secular and sacred. The singers, who clearly dress to impress, use a repertoire of jazzed-up hymns, spirituals and popular music that clearly evoke a form of vernacular spirituality, to which the audience responds.

Similarly, at the nearby Buddies Bar, the Gospel Girls are engaged in both entertainment and ministry. It is not easy to say where one begins and the other ends. The evening closes with the Gospel Girls moving amongst the audience, exchanging the peace in an extended moment of fraternal piety: the whole experience almost defies definition (c.f. Althaus-Reid, 2003).

Both these events are more obviously a cultural representation of religion, but in the very act of representation, religion is given its own (new) life within a fresh and surprising context. Just as with carol singing and other kinds of corporate sharing in 'vernacular' or 'folk' religious songs, the two 'drag gospel bars' of Atlanta show that religious materials and artefacts (that is, hymns, sentiments and so forth) are part of the cultural furniture and not simply confined to what religious institutions express, celebrate and formally reify. The division between religion and culture cannot easily be sustained and can be shown to be premature, or perhaps even false (Hall, Neitz and Battani, 2003, pp. 43–44). Religion and culture are not to be divided. As Niebuhr perceptively notes, the attempts of churches to free Christianity from culture are always doomed to failure:

> Christ claims no man as a purely natural being, but always as one who has become human in culture; who is not only in culture, but into whom culture has penetrated. Man not only speaks but thinks with the aid of the language of culture. Not only has the objective world about him been modified by human achievement; but the forms and attitudes of his mind which allow him to make sense of the objective world have been given him by culture.... (Niebuhr, 1951, p. 69)

Religious Studies, Culture and Contemporary Christianity

Although Emile Durkheim asserted that the cardinal distinction between the sacred and profane lies at the heart of all religions ('things set apart...and forbidden'), the focus of culture within the field of religious studies clearly questions such sharp definitions and distinctions. The turn of religious studies towards cultural studies is by no means new, but the recent attention given by scholars to religion and popular culture has had a profound impact on the shaping of other debates. For example, the volume of material devoted to popular culture and religion has seriously questioned the adequacy of secularization theories, as well as their proponents. If religion can indeed be found almost everywhere and anywhere (for example, theology and film, religion in *The Simpsons*, spirituality and consumerism – see Pinsky, 2001), then any understanding of apparent religious decline in the Western hemisphere must be revised and redescribed. New explorations and evaluations of religion and contemporary culture are needed to make sense of the changes that are now taking place, such as the processes whereby religion is increasingly subject to privatization, individuation, differentiation and dissipation but, in all probability, not to secularization.

The agenda sketched here is continually raised (though not resolved) in a burgeoning range of studies that concern themselves with religion and popular culture. For example, Elaine Graham's *Representations of the Post/Human: Monsters, Aliens and Others in Popular Culture* (2002), for all its anticipated advancement in the field of practical theology, is rather overwhelmed by the fields of cultural and religious studies that it engages with. Exactly where does theology end and cultural studies begin? In this study, and many others like it, it is not clear. It remains a fascinating but ultimately inconclusive scholarly adventure. There is plenty of attention to anthropology, cultural studies, gender studies and the like, but it is not clear whether this is a work of theology per se or, rather, a contribution to theological studies with a focus on ethics. The study, for all its sagacity and penetration, takes us to the edge of potentially rich theological engagement, but it does not enter the Promised Land.

Similarly, Mazur's and McCarthy's (2001) study of religion in popular American culture offers an impressive meta-mapping covering an almost limitless sphere of inquiry but, inevitably, can do little more than generalize about particularities and particularize on generalities. However, their approach is promising, insofar as it focuses on the concentrated context of North American religion in popular culture. The book covers a vast field: subjects range from barbeques (food and faith), holidays, commercialism, sport, TV and the like. The main methodological and interpretative approach is set within a Geertzian frame of reference:

> ...his functionalist – rather than essentialist – framework permits [the authors] to explore what religion does for its adherents rather than what religion is...religion and culture are not really things in and of themselves; they are systems of meaning that humans give to things, to the stuff of everyday life.... (Mazur and McCarthy, 2001, p. 5)

Following Geertz, religion and culture are conceived of as 'webs of significance' (ibid.) that connect human thought and behaviour. But, in turn, such connections cannot always be so easily discerned. Mazur and McCarthy warn:

> ...[these] things cannot be calibrated, measured, replicated or easily diagrammed. They are real enough – or rather, their perception is clothed with 'an aura of factuality' – and they are based on things out there (somewhere), but their significance lies in the meanings given to those things by the people who use them in whatever fashion. Using this view here, we are relieved of the burden of finding religious things, and can look more widely for the religious meanings attached, explicitly or not, to such activities as eating, dancing, and calling in to a radio talk show... (Ibid.)

The question arises: is this theology simply capitulating to cultural studies and evacuating its essentialist preoccupations for a vapid functionalism? Or is it setting out on a journey of discovery and engagement that will enlarge its own self-understanding? In the best traditions, it is (hopefully) the latter, and one of the reasons why the matrix of practical theology is such a compelling methodology within this field is precisely because it is committed to risk, engagement and interdisciplinarity: it seeks sagacity within the contemporary cultural milieu. The search for meaning is a legitimate concern for theology, and as individuals, groups and societies clearly look for and find religious meaning outside the proscribed 'formal' religious dogmas and institutions, theology has an obligation to move beyond its more familiar frontiers and in to the hinterland of cultural studies.

Such a move will necessarily relocate theology within a larger definition of religion, which in itself will require theologians to pay attention to those scholars who are less interested in defending theological priorities and are instead more deeply engaged in the rich task of describing and understanding the religious world and its many meanings and subtleties. Here, we turn to Clifford Geertz:

> The notion that religion tunes human actions according to an envisaged cosmic order and projects images of cosmic order onto the plane of human experience is hardly novel. But it is hardly investigated either, so that we have very little idea of how, in empirical terms, this particular miracle is accomplished. We know that it is done, annually, weekly, daily, for some people almost hourly; and we have an enormous ethnographic literature to demonstrate it. But the theoretical framework which would enable us to provide an analytical account of it ... does not exist. (Geertz, 1973, p. 90)

Thus, for Geertz, religion is:

> (1) a system of symbols which acts to (2) establish powerful, pervasive, and long-lasting moods and motivations in men by (3) formulating conceptions of a general order of existence and (4) clothing these conceptions with such an aura of factuality that (5) the moods and motivations seem uniquely realistic.... (Ibid.)

Geertz fully appreciates that enormous weight rests on 'symbol' in this definition. Moreover, 'symbol', like 'culture', is being used to cover a huge compass of activity. Nevertheless, the definition works at many levels, precisely because religion is also encountered in a myriad ways. As Geertz notes, for one person, a dark cloud is a sign that bad weather is on the way. For another, it is an omen of ill-fortune. For yet another, it is an answer to a prayer: God is sending rain. For another person still, the cloud is a sign from a deity that points to something beyond mere meteorology.

Geertz also sees that just as temporal symbols (such as clouds) may be ascribed meaning, so other, more material, objects 'store' meaning for individuals and groups (ibid., p. 127). Thus, a cross, rosary or a crescent will each provide an instant trigger that cascades meaning to their bearers, relating ontology and cosmology, aesthetics and ethics. Similarly, stories contribute to ideology as a cultural system (ibid., p. 193). Meaning is found not just in plain 'dogma', but also in the myths, stories and folklore that inhabit and shape religious identity:

> The culture of a people is an ensemble of texts, themselves ensembles, which the anthropologist strains to read over the shoulders to whom they properly belong.... But to regard such forms as 'saying something of something', and saying it to somebody, is at least to open the possibility of an analysis which attends to their substance rather than to reductive formulas professing to account for them.... As in the more familiar exercises of close reading, one can start anywhere in a culture's

repertoire of forms and end up anywhere else. One can stay ... within a single, more or less bounded form, and circle steadily within it. One can move between forms in search of broader unities or informing contrasts. One can even compare forms from different cultures to define their character in reciprocal relief. But at whatever level one operates, and however intricately, the guiding principle is the same: societies, like lives, contain their own interpretations. One only has to learn how to gain access to them ... (Geertz, 1973, pp. 452–453)

At this point, the synergy between religious and cultural studies is especially rich. However, it is important to state, for the purposes of this study, that the attention given to religion through the social sciences or cultural studies does not necessarily anticipate a reductionist reading. Although it may be true that a significant number of scholars engaged in these disciplines would assume that their interpretative methodologies were almost inherently secular, it need not be so. Religious studies can, in other words, be sufficiently self-composed to be 'related' rather than 'relative'. A comparative, social or neutral standpoint (which, as Milbank (1991) reminds us, are a form of secular violence or tyranny attempting to 'police the sublime') need not be an end in itself. Correspondingly, the kind of (French Enlightenment reductionism) sentiments expressed in Pascal Boyer's *Religion Explained* need not be representative of religious studies:

Rituals do *not* create social effects but only the *illusion* that they do .... Thoughts about the social effect and thoughts about the ritual sequence are combined since they are about the same event. So rituals are naturally *thought* to produce social effects .... (Boyer, 2002, p. 292, emphasis added)

In contrast to Boyer, I hold that it is presumptuous to assume that religious rituals merely create the impression of being affective and effective. To my mind, this is a genre of socio-cultural studies that has strayed a little too easily into territory that it need not concern itself with. Questions of meaning are not the same as those of ultimacy and ontology. Boyer's explanation for religion, although compelling, is interpretative rather than complete. Given these preliminary remarks, we now turn to the specific question of religion, choice and consumerism. The discussion is then extended by a consideration of Christmas and some of the recent scholarly work that has focused on its religious, cultural and theological significance.

Choice, Consumerism and Christianity

In this section, we begin with another vignette that is in keeping with the Geertzian approach that flavours much of this thesis. But, this time, the story is more personal. I begin with a confession: timekeeping is not my strong point. So, as I drove purposefully down the road one wet, April evening a few years ago, I was already slightly late (as usual) to pick up my son from Cubs. But, I mused, there was no need to panic, since the ever-enthusiastic Cub leader normally overran the meetings by at least 10–15 minutes. Sure enough, I arrived at the entrance to the church hall to discover a group of parents waiting somewhat tardily for their offspring to come out. However, as I joined the small throng preparing to show solidarity in patience, I realized that I had walked into a rather terse and tense discussion. Each parent was clutching a letter from Akela, which reminded parents and Cubs that Sunday was St George's Day, and that Cubs were expected to attend church parade (indeed, the letter stated that it was 'compulsory'). Smart kit and clean shoes were also specified.

The parents stood around, discussing the word 'compulsory'. One looked bewildered and cast around for empathy as he explained that his son played soccer on Sunday, so attendance was doubtful. Another mused that the family were all due to be away for the weekend, and that changing plans for a church parade was neither possible nor desirable. Another looked less than pleased that a 'voluntary' organization such as the Cubs which, she added, her son attended by choice, should now be using words like 'compulsory'. There was no question of obligation; attendance and belonging was a matter of preference. (Presumably the oaths which her son had taken were simply part of a traditional and quaint ceremony that had little actual meaning.)

At the beginning of the twenty-first century, a small vignette such as this is not untypical in Western Europe. Since the Second World War era, the culture of obligation has rapidly given way to one of consumerism. Duty, and the desire to participate in aspects of civic society where steadfast obligatory support was once cherished, has been rapidly eroded by choice, individualism and reflexivity (see Putnam, 2000). Granted, this is not the place to debate such a cultural turn. But its undoubted appearance on the landscape of late modernity has posed some interesting questions for voluntary organizations, chief of which might be religious establishments. Increasingly, churches find themselves with worshippers who attend less out of duty and more out of choice. There is, arguably, nothing wrong with that. But under these new cultural conditions, churches have discovered that they need to be much more savvy about how they shape and market themselves in the public sphere. There is no escaping the reality: the churches are in competition – for people's time, energy, attention, money and commitment.

But it is that last word, 'commitment', that has become such a slippery term in recent times. Few regular or frequent churchgoers now attend church twice on a Sunday, as was once normal practice. For most, once is enough. Many who do attend on a regular basis are now attending less frequently. Even allowing for holidays and other absences (say, through illness), even the most dedicated churchgoer may only be present in church for 70 per cent of the Sundays in any given year. Many clergy now remark on the decline in attendance at Days of Obligation (that is, major saints days or feast days, such as the Ascension). The committed, it seems, are also the busy. The response to this from the more liturgical churches has been to subtly and quietly adapt their practice, whilst preserving the core tradition. For example, the celebration of Epiphany may now take place on the Sunday nearest to 6 January and not on the day itself. A number of Roman Catholic churches now offer Sunday mass on Saturday evenings, so that Sunday can be left as a family day, or for whatever other commitments or consumerist choices that might now fall on the once-hallowed day of rest. In a survey of American Christians undertaken in 1955, only 4 per cent defected from the faith of their childhood. Thirty years later, a comparable survey revealed that one-third had left their spiritual and religious roots in search of something new (Foster and Hertzog, 1994, p. 23). The culture of choice is transforming churches into market-led spiritual suppliers, especially as worshippers expect their faith and religious values to be a matter of selection rather than obligation. (On this, see P. Ward, 2002, pp. 69ff). As we saw in Chapter 1, the age of the *à la carte* Catholic has already come.

It is not my purpose here to venture into a debate about the precise nature of secularization. Whatever that process is supposed to describe, it seems to me that it can never do justice to the intrinsically inchoate nature of religious belief that characterized the Western European landscape and its peoples long before the Enlightenment, let alone the Industrial Revolution of the nineteenth century and the cultural revolutions of the twentieth century. The trouble with standard secularization theories is that they depend on exaggerating the extent and depth of Christendom. They assume a previous world of monochrome religious allegiance, which is now (of course) in tatters. But in truth, the religious world was much more plural and contested before the twentieth century ever dawned. So what, exactly, has changed? Despite my reticence to accede too much ground to proponents of secularization theses, I readily acknowledge that the twentieth century has been the most seminal and challenging period for the churches in all their history. Leaving aside their own struggles with pluralism, postcolonialism, modernity, postmodernity and wave after wave of cultural change and challenge, the biggest issue the churches have had to confront is, ironically, a simple one: choice. Increased mobility, globalization and consumerism have infected and affected the churches, just as they have touched every other aspect of social life. Duty is dead: the customer is king. It is no surprise, therefore, to discover churches adopting a consumerist mentality and competing with one another for souls, members, or entering the marketplace itself and trying to convert tired consumers into revitalized Christians.

One such initiative is the Alpha courses, begun by Nicky Gumbel from Holy Trinity Brompton, in London. The Alpha courses have attracted millions of followers worldwide and have arguably achieved the distinction of becoming the first internationally recognized global 'brand' of Christianity. In an important and timely study of Alpha courses, Stephen Hunt (2003) uses the well-established sociological framework of the spiritual marketplace (drawing on Ritzer, Lyon and others), in order to illustrate something of the impact of commodification on contemporary religion. Significantly, he demonstrates that the increasingly consumerist cultural turn adopted by the churches that advocate Alpha does not necessarily lead to an increase in the level of religiosity. Or, perhaps put more acerbically, the number of customers for the courses does not necessarily translate into a new army of dedicated converts.

Correspondingly, Alpha is more like a creature of its culture, and far less countercultural than many of its champions imagine. Its features chime almost too perfectly with postmodern consumer culture: a stress on relationships; a definite nod to the therapeutic; dogma presented with a distinctly 'light' touch; a course to try, but not necessarily a long-term commitment. This is not a criticism, I should add: it is merely an observation. Alpha is arguably the first example of 'mass branding' for Christianity, replete with its own logo, publications, clothing, cookbooks and other non-essential, but-desirable, merchandise such as baseball caps, fleeces, t-shirts, pens and the like. (On popular religious materialism, see McDannell, 1995.) Just as Sidney Carter once lamented those churches that had made their version of Jesus or salvation 'copyright', we now have a version of Christianity that is 'patent pending': the Alpha brand enjoys legal protection, in order to distinguish itself from any pale imitator.

Besides the 'marketplace' framework that Hunt deploys in his analysis, his book is also to be welcomed for its firm grounding in ethnography. As a discipline, ethnography comes in all shapes and sizes: some is mainly quantitative, whilst other kinds can be mostly qualitative; some depend on formal questionnaires and clearly proscribed methods, whereas other kinds are more like 'participant observation' and accept the partiality of the observer/ interpreter as a given. Hunt's journey through planet Alpha (he is both a pilgrim seeking answers and a stranger entering a world he does not belong to), enables the reader to glimpse, perhaps for the first time, how a form of religion, far from challenging consumerism, has itself been consumed by it. Again, this is not a criticism so much as a commonsensical observation. Recent work by Giggie and Winston (2002) shows that modern cities (replete with their pervasive commercial cultures) and religious traditions interact in dynamic, complicated and unexpected ways, producing expressions of faith that aspire to rise above the conventional cacophony of everyday city life. Alpha is just such a product: a faith *of* the market and a faith *for* the market. As David Lyon perceptively notes:

> ...consumerism has become central to the social and cultural life of the technologically advanced societies in the later twentieth century. Meaning is sought as a 'redemptive gospel' in consumption. And cultural identities are formed through processes of selective consumption. (Lyon, 2000, p. 74)

Put more strongly, we might say the regard of humanity for Western modernity is an expression of a piety in which capitalism has itself become a global religion, at least in practice, if not always belief (Goodchild, 2002). So, is Alpha doing no more than successfully marketing a specious brand of Christianity within the wider consumerist cultural milieu, wherein the 'commodification of religion' is taking place? Laurence Moore's seminal study *Selling God* provides a partial answer. Moore argues that secularization theories should give way to an understanding of religion in the modern world, whereby it has become one of a number of 'cultured' and 'leisured' activities that individuals now purchase or subscribe to. Once, religion might have taken a somewhat 'standoffish' attitude to consumerism, and would have only entered the marketplace to censor and condemn it. But now, argues Moore,

> ...the work of religious leaders and moralists in the market-place of culture [is] immediately entangled in a related but distinguishable enterprise. Rather than remaining aloof, they entered their own inventive contributions into the market. Initially these were restricted to the market of reading material, but their cultural production diversified. Religious leaders...[started to compete] with the appeal of popular entertainments. By degrees religion took on the shape of a commodity.... (Moore, 1994, p. 6)

Hunt's important study is devoted to showing just how far that process of commodification has been reified in Alpha, and how religion can both consume and be consumed by the processes of free-market capitalism. But we can also add a further insight here. Alpha is also a creature of culture. Its structure is a 'fit' for contemporary culture, where the therapeutic and relational have superseded the hegemony of rules and regulations in the formation of churches and Christian life. As one trinity of sociologists note:

> ...the modern project destroyed religious culture based in interdiction (rules) and replaced it with therapeutic culture based in relations.... (Hall, Neitz and Battani, 2003, p. 25)

Quite so. But what does it really mean to talk about 'consumer religion'? Hall, Neitz and Battani's study of culture is riddled with references to the power of consumerism; they describe a society in which religion has to a large extent, been marginalized – pushed into the sphere of the private (ibid., pp. 130ff., 250ff). So, if the Geertzian definition of religion advanced earlier was both reasonable and fair, some description of consumerism is also necessary here. The idea that capitalism has produced a consumer society is primarily a postwar perception. Typically, the 'consumer society' nomenclature identifies a series of trends that have moved in parallel: the shift from heavy industry to new technology; service providers and entertainments as the new 'industry'; increased consumption as a focus of social activity; the gradual triumph of lifestyles and choice over discipline and obligation; and the shift from associational societies to post-associational societies (see Putnam, 2000).[1]

Of course, these remarks are mere characterizations, but they are not without foundation. Veblen's (1953) account of 'conspicuous consumption' charts the rise (in modern societies) of a new bourgeois and leisured class that is identified less by class and occupation and more by its association with lifestyles that express choice and status. In a different vein, Horkheimer and Adorno (1972), in their discussion of the culture industry, suggest that late

---

[1] 'Post-associational' refers here to First World industrialized and urbanized communities where 'soft' forms of social ordering – such as intracommunal participation through voluntary organizations, shared leisure, charitable or other pursuits – has been steadily eroded by the rise of individualism and consumerism. The impact of this can be measured through the decline in affiliation to, amongst others, local or national political organizations (for example, scouting), the Freemasons or Women's Institutes. The shift in social patterning is profound – from implicit cohesion to one of explicit adhesion.

modern and postmodern life is a distinct mode of production. Commodities are then, perhaps strangely, those materials that society produces to combat alienation. The advantage of this view is that it rescues the 'culture–consumer' debate from the crude and unsophisticated charge that consumers are merely passive pawns within a clever capitalist conspiracy. Instead, consumers are colluding with the forces of material and social production by 'purchasing' pleasure, meaning and fulfilment in what is an otherwise alienating and highly constrained mode of social existence.

The fusion of religious and cultural studies can be enriched further if one considers the central place of shopping in contemporary life (see Miller, 1995, 1998). As an activity, shopping is not only necessary but also, for many, a pleasure. The phrase 'retail therapy' has entered the vocabulary of vernacular life. In theorizing from the perspective of cultural studies, shopping is 'quasi-utopian'; it points towards a future in which there is time and leisure to enjoy the commodities that have been acquired. Their acquisition symbolizes a future with less stress and more time. The shopping mall (cathedrals of consumerism) provide a social focus that encompasses eating, entertainment and gratification, centred on an understanding of humanity that elevates the autonomy and individuality of the consumer. Consumption, then, is a major mode of social expression, and it is perhaps inevitable that it would find its way into religion. But in what ways can such influences be charted?

McDannell's (1995) work shows that Christianity's absorption with consumerist culture is longstanding, but has accelerated in the capitalist optimism of the postwar years. In her richly descriptive and analytical book she examines how the production of religion has shifted from the textual (that is, books, tracts and so on) to encompass the ephemeral (for example, baseball caps, fridge magnets and the like). Inevitably, specious Christian critiques of religious and secular consumerism – themselves, ironically, a product of consumerist culture – are never far behind. Tom Beaudoin's *Consuming Faith* (2003) argues for a spirituality that 'integrates who we are with what we buy'. Interestingly, the premise of this thesis is that what individuals buy, eat and wear says much about their deepest values. Correspondingly, this thesis calls for a deeper practical wisdom in engaging with consumerist culture (but otherwise sees no way out of it, and accepts it as a given).

A different perspective can be gleaned from Graham Ward's intriguing treatment of religion and consumption (Ward, 2003). Here, Ward argues that religion is inherently driven by consumption because it is so tied up in desire. In his illuminating discussion of Herman Melville's *Moby Dick*, he shows how some of that desire is misconceived and, equally, how it is also shaped by events and destiny, and ultimately refined. However, he also warns that:

> ...the momentous growth in consumer culture that began in the nineteenth century paralleled the new Smithsonian economics of free trade and the avaricious drive for conquest, are reflected back in the fears, fascinations and figurations of 'religion', the turns to cosmotheism, the Romantic metaphysics of the absolute spirit, the deity who dominates, and the aesthetics of the sublime. A series of related works cross and recross these various discourses: 'consume', 'consummate', 'consumer' (we might

even add the medical term 'consumption'). This Promethian will, commanding and indomitable, is driven and haunted by a lack as infinite as it is unappeasable. The obsession is death-bound and mad with an absence it can only surrender itself to . . . .
(G. Ward, 2003, p. 113)

This characteristically acerbic (but richly and densely expressed) critique is at variance with more empathetic critiques that can be harvested from that of other scholars whose work might be best expressed as a fusion of theology and cultural studies. For example, Pete Ward's exemplary *Liquid Church* (2002) suggests that shopping characterizes most of contemporary life. Drawing on the work of Bauman, Baudrillard, Bourdieu and James Twitchell, Ward notes that:

> Our competency as a shopper is challenged not so much by the choice of products, events, and experiences but by what they represent: the hopes and dreams, the aspirations and pleasures. To shop is to seek for something beyond ourselves. To reduce this to materialism is to miss the point, or more importantly it is to miss an opportunity. For this 'reaching beyond ourselves' indicates a spiritual inclination in many of the everyday activities of shopping. Rather than condemn the shopper as materialist . . . [the] church [should] take shopping seriously as a spiritual exercise . . . .
> (P. Ward, 2002, p. 59)

The turn towards ecclesiology and missiology takes us back to one of the more central concerns of this book, namely understanding and interpreting contemporary culture and its relation to religion. Ward continues his excursion into the world of the 'spiritual shopper' by reminding his readers that what consumer culture craves is not objects, but their meaning. Thus, conspicuous consumption is not rampant materialism, but is rather a means of exchange and the enjoyment of meanings. Citing the work of Twitchell again, Ward suggests that advertising culture can therefore be understood as being like religion:

> . . . [they are] part of a meaning-making process. Religion and advertising attempt to bridge a gap between ourselves and things, and they do this by offering a systematic order . . . . (Ibid., p. 60)

Consumption is therefore more about meaning than acquisition; consumerism is more about identity than materialism. Strictly speaking, then, the threat posed by consumerism to Christianity is not the material versus the spiritual. It is, rather, a competition between systems of meaning and identification. In this regard, we can suggest that advertising has a teleological and utopian dimension to it: it suggests a new order that is to come. In effect, it offers a promise of salvation within a culture that is already saturated with meanings and materialism. Advertising – pointing towards, bearing witness to and proclaiming – is a fundamentally evangelistic art-science. That which is raised up on the hoardings, reflected on our screens or placed in our hands through mailings or literature is offering ultimacy and dependency. In effect, it is a (seductive?) way out of multiple meanings and materialism through *this* offer or *that* product. Advertising adds meaning and interpretation to the objects of desire. Advertising, as an industry and art form, recognizes that desire, not need, drives our choices and shapes our consumption. It understands that the culture of obligation and assumption has ceded the moral high ground to that of consumption. Correspondingly, authority, institutions and ideologies have to be desired and liked; they can no longer be imposed (but, for an alternative view, see hooks, 1994).

If evidence were needed that the age of the 'Worshopper' had arrived, one needs to look no further than the mega-churches of North America. These are churches that are catering for several thousand members and employing large numbers of staff in substantial sites. I have visited several over recent years, and their most striking feature remains their capacity to engage with the scope of human desires. A drive to South Barrington near Chicago will surely draw you to Willow Creek Community Church, one of the largest and most prominent mega-churches. The church – in reality a giant conference and meeting centre, with a bookshop, several restaurants, lecture theatres and a large sanctuary – can accommodate about 5000 people at any one time. As a result, the church runs four identical services over the weekend: two on Saturday evening and two on Sunday morning (see Hoover, 2000).

The church as a whole is mostly devoid of explicit religious symbolism, and the services are a fusion of uplifting folksy Christian messages, moral (but not too prescriptive) advice and some singing. The services are 'performative' set pieces that adopt a 'magazine-type' format – carefully choreographed, sensitively hosted and thought-provoking. They are stirring and compelling, but without being demanding or intrusive. However, it is the resources centre that is arguably the most striking feature of the church. The sheer range of self-help, support and encounter groups is overwhelming. There are several types of social group: bowling, soccer and other leisure pursuits for all ages. The therapeutic provision is comprehensive and engaging. There are groups for 'Moms and Daughters Hurting', 'Fathers and Sons Bonding', individuals coping with their own sexuality, or individuals who suspect that they might have problems with the sexuality of their partner. There are support groups offering counselling, help through bereavement, loss, eating disorders (obesity and anorexia) and more besides. On my visit there I counted more than 40 different kinds of self-help, therapeutic and support groups, as well as several dozen groups devoted to sport and leisure activity. The total number of people involved ran into several thousands.

The composition of Willow Creek's membership mostly reflects its context. The congregation is mainly white, affluent, college-educated and working in the city, with a large percentage aged between 30 and 50. The sermons carry an evangelistic timbre coupled to a politically (slightly) left-of-centre appropriation of ethics. In some ways, the ethos of Willow Creek could be reasonably characterized as the 'First Church of Christ the Democrat'. However, a fuller and deeper ethnography of Willow Creek would, I suspect, identify the gathering as a distinctive brand of consumer church: worship, lunch, family activities, leisure events and self-help groups fuse together in a seamless consumerist experience. The division between secular and sacred is utterly obliterated.

Christmas, Christianity and Culture

The absence of clear or obvious divisions between the secular and the sacred is undoubtedly puzzling for many within the Christian tradition. This, added to the ascendancy of consumerism, presents a perplexing problem for the churches at a time when they are seeking to recover their identity within an age besieged by assumptions relating to the triumph of secularization. Arguably, this is especially concentrated in the meaning and purpose of Christmas. For many within the Christian tradition, the consumerist appropriation of the festival produces an almost neuralgic response. However, such concerns are hardly particular to modernity. As Jennifer Rycenga notes:

> ...shunned by the Puritan authorities of early New England because of its connections to pagan seasonal celebrations and to sexual and alcohol excesses, the colonial Christmas was celebrated mainly by the working class as an occasion for public revelry and carnival. The eighteenth century often became riotous...the transformation of Christmas into a domestic holiday coincided with the growth of consumer culture in nineteenth century America.... (Rycenga, 2000, p. 142)

Similarly, Nissenbaum (1996) argues that Christmas was transformed in relatively recent times. True enough, the New English Puritans of Massachusetts banned the festival. They had their reasons, and argued that it simply encouraged drunkenness and riot, with poor 'wassailers' allowed to extort food and drink from the well-to-do. Nissenbaum notes how seventeenth- and early eighteenth-century diarists described the festival:

> 'highly dishonourable to the name of Christ...[The people] are consumed in...playing at cards, in revellings, in excess of wine, and mad mirth...' (Revd Increase Mather, Boston, 1687)

> 'The Feast of Christ's Nativity is spent in revelling, dicing, carding, masking and in all licentious liberty...by mad mirth, by long eating, by hard drinking, by lewd gaming...' (Revd Cotton Mather, 1712)

> '...the festival is a scandal to religion, and an encouraging of wickedness...a pretence for drunkenness, and rioting, and wantonness...it is the occasion of much uncleanness and debauchery... (Revd Henry Bourne, Newcastle, England, 1725)

According to Nissenbaum, Revd Bourne noted that Christmas carols, though sung enthusiastically, were often 'done in the midst of rioting and chambering [a common term for fornication] and wantonness...' (Nissenbaum, 1996, p. 7). Yet, by the nineteenth century, the festival had been transformed into one of domesticity and consumerism. Nissenbaum shows how this social transformation depended, to some extent, on drawing upon earlier spiritual traditions, such as St Nicholas, Baboushka and other popular folk tales. The practice of giving gifts (especially to children) also marked a new economic and social confidence, which also coincided with significant cultural and political changes in attitudes to children. The elevation of Christmas to its present celebratory epoch also draws upon older cultural traditions: the observance of the winter solstice, a brief period of leisure and plenty in an otherwise demanding agricultural year, and so forth. Indeed, the current 'tradition' is replete with ironic overlays. The origin of the legend of St Nicholas (*c*. 300 AD), a patron saint of children, can be traced to modern-day Turkey, a predominantly Muslim country. The story was subject to many variations over several centuries. The image of Santa Claus was transformed in 1844 by Clement Cark Moore's saccharine poem ''Twas the Night Before Christmas', causing many artists to portray Santa as an elf-like figure in a green cape. But the red cape and white beard is primarily the work of another artist, Haddon Sundblom, who dressed Santa in red as a part of the commercialization of Christmas that was propagated by Coca-Cola. The result was the white-bearded, red-caped, black-booted jolly old man we now associate with the festivities (Witzel and Witzel, 2002, pp. 1001–117). But Santa's journey has been a long one: a Christian saint from a country that later became Muslim, to becoming the icon synonymous with Christmas, who owes part of his identity to a global commercial corporation.

Santa's evolution shows that it is almost impossible to draw precise lines between consumerism, culture and religion. The churches' initial collusion in eliding Christ's birth with a range of more secular or non-Christian celebratory themes has meant that their hold over Christmas has been rather tenuous. For some, it is a time of piety; but for many, it is a carnival. Christmas is, ironically, a difficult holiday to Christianize (Nissenbaum, 1996, p. 8; Marling, 2000, pp. 321–55).

However, Rycenga, amongst others, argues that even the modern consumerist-saturated Christmas represents some form of deep, nascent 'residual Christianity'. The season has the potential for the 'consecration of dense symbols' in a cluttered calendar: the giving of gifts, the family, the vulnerability of a newborn child and so forth. Thus, according to Rycenga, and using the work of Grimes, even something as 'simple' as Christmas shopping is at least a secondary act of religious ritual, for it is:

> ... performed, embodied, enacted, gestural (not merely thought or said), formalised ... not ordinary, unadorned) ... repetitive ... collective, institutionalised ... patterned ... standardised ... ordered ... traditional ... stylised ... deeply felt ... sentiment laden, meaningful ... symbolic, referential ... perfected, idealised ... ludic ... religious ... conscious, deliberate .... (Grimes, 1990, p. 14)

In such a reading, the shopping mall can be interpreted as a 'cathedral of consumerism': laden with altars, icons and votive opportunities, it speaks of gift, desire and fulfilment. Of course, such comparisons only take the analysis so far. But to its credit, it is the provenance of religious studies to locate and interpret the religious that is beyond the immediate or obvious bounds of faith traditions. And, in a consumerist society, there can be little doubt that the synergy between consumer culture and religion is complex and interactive. According to David Docherty, the key to reading the relationship between religion and consumerism lies:

> ... not in the opposition between the symbols of natural and transcendent faiths, but in the analysis of the way the former appropriates the latter only to discover that it has swallowed something alien, something that at some stage will burst out and consume the social order that initially consumed it .... (Docherty, 2000, pp. 82–108)

Thus, Christmas is a place where culture and religion collide and compete for meaning. And beneath that synergy of consumerism and spirituality lies a battle for the control of Christmas. However, it cannot be obvious where, precisely, the battle-lines are to be drawn, for what some may regard as plain consumerism, will, for others, be gestures that richly and ritually symbolize gift, love and a gesture towards the transcendent. Susan Roll's fascinating (1995) exploration of the origin of Christmas goes further than most theological treatises by suggesting that the key to the debate lies in developing a theory of time. Roll's central thesis is that the great feasts of Christianity are not, by nature, historical commemorations of actual episodes in history linked to specific and verifiable dates. The feasts are, rather, linked to the explanation of religious ideas (Roll, 1995, p. 23).

Epiphany can be taken as one example of this. The actual date of the coming of the Magi is, relatively speaking, of secondary importance in the Christian tradition. Indeed, some Christians may regard the story of the 'three wise men' as a myth. But this is unlikely to impact on the celebration of Epiphany (literally, 'manifestation'). The feast, because it takes account of the flight of the holy family into Egypt and Herod's massacre of the innocents, is habitually interpreted as being concerned with journeying, exile, violence, refugees, coming and going, visions, dreams, recognition and disguise, and 'true' wisdom. The story is laden with meanings that have embellished the tradition down the centuries. It can be taken to symbolize a range of representative powers recognizing the lordship of the Christ child: gentile, occult, Eastern, non-Christian – all have scope within the brevity of the Gospel account. Other Christian traditions emphasize the aspect of pilgrimage and searching; of surprise and gift; of the vulnerability of the Christ child. But in all these forms of ritual and theological remembrance, the actual time or history of the event is secondary: it is the meaning of the events that are primary.

This leads Roll to suggest that, for several centuries, commercial time has been 'normative'. The time of the church and the time of the merchant (or farmer) are no longer the same. This change can be traced back to before the Industrial Revolution, Reformation or Renaissance. In truth, argues Roll, it is the church that has always adapted to culture and the seasons, by investing them with particular meaning. There are three reasons for this. First, humanity does not look for meaning in time; it creates meaning in time. Second, human activity searches for meaning and sustenance beyond basic needs and seeks to enrich life. Third, money and consumerism form the basic mode of exchange and interconnectedness (Roll, 1995, p. 38).

Building on this observation, Roll argues that there are two types of time in Christian tradition and culture (ibid., p. 236ff). *Anticipative* time refers to a rhythm of time in which the build-up leads to a peak, followed by rapid decline. *Extensive* time, on the other hand, refers to a pattern in which the high point occurs at the start of the time-segment and is developed during this period. The distinction is useful in several ways. For example, we can immediately see that 'secular' Christmas time is mainly anticipative in character: it can begin when the shops first start selling and advertising wares (say, September), and ends on 1 January. On the other hand, more formal Christian Christmas time is primarily extensive in character; its time of preparation begins in Advent and the season officially concludes at Epiphany.

But the two become blurred, of course. Advent, although anticipative in one sense, is almost wholly lost on the secular world (except through Advent calendars). Churches also make significant concessions to (extensive) secular and consumerist time. Only the strictest churches will avoid carol services during Advent; many will hold Christingle services, nativity plays and other liturgical events, whereby the Christmas message intrudes into Advent. However, these observations merely strengthen Roll's thesis, since they show that in Christianity, at least in its multifarious vernacular forms, actual time (and what it signifies) is less important than the meanings that are attached to festivals.

To earth this discussion more practically, I need only consider the array of events that typically takes place in my local parish church during December. The most popular service is Christingle, which is developed from a Moravian tradition. The children are all given oranges (symbolizing the world), with a candle stuck in the middle (symbolizing the light of Christ). The oranges are made into orb-like objects by red ribbon that is wrapped around the middle (symbolizing the blood of Christ), and four sticks that hold sweets or dried fruit (symbolizing the gifts of God in creation). The high point of the service is when the lights of the church are dimmed, the candles all lit and carols are sung. This service always takes place on the Sunday evening before Christmas Day, and for many families and individuals it is their 'Christmas' service.

In contrast to this emergent and popular tradition, the celebration of Epiphany is markedly low-key. In a number of churches the festival will be celebrated on the Sunday closest to 6 January and not necessarily on the day itself. Correspondingly, in my own home, we have a ritual of inscribing C + M + B, and the date of the new year on our front door, and then processing around the house with the Wise Men from the nativity set. This is a deliberate countercultural shared activity that says something else about the nature of the season and time. However, it is a moot point as to which visitors to our house would understand the alphabetical formula that is chalked up in our porch each year.[2]

---

[2] C + M + B = Casper, Melchior and Balthasar – traditional names for the Three Wise Men.

Given the drift of the discussion so far, it might be tempting to imagine that consumerism, coupled to notions of secular anticipative time, is eclipsing religious notions of time and their meaning. Is there, indeed, a distinct loss of sacred time against normative commercial time? Superficially, it would seem so. Where there is no link with consumerism, sacred time often suffers a loss of extensive meaning. One need only think of feasts such as Ascensiontide, or Whit Monday, and see that their celebration and marking within the public sphere has deteriorated significantly in the last 25 years. Once public holidays cease to be linked to religious events, the sacred loses something of its pre-eminence. On the other hand, Christmas and Easter flourish, arguably, because of the continuing consumerist links with the festivals, and the fact that the religious events are still marked with public holidays. However, lest this sound complacent, a number of Northern European countries are ambivalent about Good Friday being a public holiday. Increasingly, this means that many who celebrate Easter may have fairly inchoate views about Holy Week. Easter Monday as a holiday, on the other hand, flourishes because of its consumerist ties, which is ironic, since Easter Monday has no significant Christian meaning.

However, there is a double irony at work here. The very fact that consumerism continues to draw upon and inhabit religious ideas and events for its own ends also means that religion continues to quietly peddle its countercultural message. As Roll points out, the sentimentalizing of the nativity story at the height of consumerist indulgence creates alternative spaces for different meanings. The lighting of candles, the deliberate elevation of memory, the effort of kinship: each nuance of the Christmas story can act against the consumerist culture that has brought it into the public domain (Roll, 1995, p. 239). Ironically, it is the commercialization and enculturation of Christmas that saves it. It acts to: give alternative meanings to consumerism; give added meaning to consumerism; and take people from the material and functional to the transcendent and mysterious (ibid., pp. 243–73).

Put another way, it is possible to see festivals such as Christmas as secular/sacred and public/private 'felt' Days of Obligation, in which many more will participate than those who actively identify with a formal religious group. Conceptually, this is an aspect of 'believing without belonging' (Grace Davie) or of the social 'structure of feeling' (Raymond Williams) that revolves round a season (ibid., p. 240). Thus, we might return to our Geertzian perspective and restate that it is useful to regard religion as a culture (Warren, 1997, p. 23). It is a signifying system, which demands allegiance. Thus, religion and culture conflict and conflate in equal measure. Religion structures feeling and mystery, orders life, and is itself ordered by life. But it is precisely because religion is a culture (based on the resources of hope and vision) that it can critique contemporary culture (ibid., p. 190). And it is at its richest when it does this in ways that chime with contemporary culture and resonate with the totality of human life and experience. The duty of theology, then, is to be both temperate and engaging, for it can never easily divide religion and culture:

> ... perhaps one way to express the task, or *a* task, of theology, is that of structuring mystery. One might go a little farther and call it even imposing structure on mystery,

but this involves crossing a boundary into an arena where humans have little power, and what we have merely tends to encourage *hubris* .... (Roll, 1995, p. 9)

Christianity in a Secular Society

This chapter has not attempted to deal systematically with theories of secularization. This has been a deliberate choice, in order that fresh vistas of insight can be opened up on the 'Christianity and contemporary culture' debate. However, in this concluding section, it is perhaps appropriate to say something about perspectives on secularization that I have adopted and which, to some extent, condition the remainder of this monograph.

Secularization is, of course, a highly contested concept. In general, the word is used to describe the relatively recent decline of religion in the Western world. However, even with this very basic understanding, there are some immediate problems. First, religious affiliation in the USA – in theory a liberal, modern state – remains vibrant. Second, Europe seems to be the exception, rather than the rule, when it comes to a general decline in religious interests. Third, it is far from clear that religious interests necessarily decline in direct proportion to the rise of industrialization, modernity, globalization and the like. At the height of the Industrial Revolution in Victorian Britain, church attendance stood at record levels. In post-Second World War Britain new denominations and new religious movements have flourished.

Several objections can be raised against the secularization thesis. First, apparent religious decline (in terms of formal attendance at a place of worship or belonging to a religious organization) must be measured against member-ship of other voluntary organizations or associations. Granted, fewer people belong, formally, to a Christian denomination when compared to the interwar or Victorian periods. But almost all forms of association have declined steeply since those days (cf. Putnam, 2000). There are fewer Scouts and Guides, trade union membership has waned, and there are now fewer members of the Conservative Party than there are Methodists. Recreationally, there are fewer people in our cinemas and football grounds than 70 years ago.

Second, there is reason to doubt the idea that fewer and fewer people are turning to official or mainstream religion. For example, the Victorian period saw a revival of religion and religious attendance that lasted for about 40 years. Yet the trend at the beginning of the eighteenth and nineteenth centuries was the very opposite of this: church attendance was, on the whole, derisory. The evidence for church attendance during medieval times is contestable; some scholars assert that religious observance was strong and others argue that it was, at best, patchy.

Third, statistical surveys continually support the thesis that Europe is the place where the vast majority of the population continues to affirm their belief in God, but then proceeds to do little about it. As a result, church attendance figures tend to remain stubbornly low. Yet this is not a modern malaise, but is rather a typical feature of Western societies down the ages. Granted, there have been periods of revival when church attendance has peaked. But the basic and innate disposition is one of believing without belonging – of relating to the church and valuing its presence and beliefs, yet without necessarily sharing them.

Correspondingly, scholars are divided on how to interpret contemporary society and its apparent secularity. Sociologists such as Peter Berger have effectively repented their predictions of the 1960s, and now argue that Western society, with all its capitalism and consumerism, remains religious. Historians can now show that increased church attendance may be a response to social unease and dislocation. The Industrial Revolution and the resettlement of postwar Britain both saw a rise in church attendance that may be viewed as a reaction to social upheaval.

Other scholars, such as Callum Brown, have argued that secularization is neither a product of the Industrial Revolution nor of Enlightenment thinking, but is in fact a rather more recent phenomenon. In *The Death of Christian Britain* (2000), Brown argues that the cultural revolution of the 1960s has broken the cycle of intergenerational renewal that was so essential to Christianity's survival. Arguably, the rise of popular culture has done more than any other thing to marginalize Christianity (and religious observance in general) and provide people with other arenas for absorption and entertainment.

Similarly, Robert Putnam's *Bowling Alone* (2000) shows that the rise of popular culture in the USA has had a deleterious effect on many different types of association and voluntary society. Putnam's thesis demonstrates that 'negative social capital' has built up to such an extent that religious affiliation may ultimately be affected. In a country where churchgoing is a normal activity – as many as 50 per cent of the population attend on a regular basis – Putnam's thesis may point to some interesting future trends.

That said, Danielle Hervieu-Leger's (2000) work suggests that religious memory still persists in societies that are apparently acquiring religious amnesia. Although the cycle of intergenerational renewal may be distorted by the invasiveness of popular culture, her work suggests that religion only mutates under such conditions. It may be pushed from the public sphere to the private realm, but it still appears to be able to shape society at critical points. Far from turning their backs on religion, modern societies seem to be perpetually absorbed by it – something argued more than a quarter of a century ago by David Martin (1978).

But lest this sound too complacent (on behalf of the churches), it is important to remember that there is *something* in secularization. There can be no denying that people's perception of social ordering now seldom depends on theological, religious or meta-moral constructions of reality. Society has shifted in its orientation – from a reliance on (or at least a reference towards) theological metanarratives to one that is altogether more pragmatic and contigent, where ambiguity has been raised to a level of apotheosis.

Added to this, we can also note the rising number of 'new' spiritualities, the range and volume of which have increased exponentially in the postwar era. Again, choice (rather than upbringing, location and so on) is now a major factor in determining the spiritual allegiances that individuals may develop.

Moreover, it is not easy to discern where the boundaries now lie between leisure, exercise and spirituality. As the consumerist individual asserts their autonomy and right to choose, clear divisions between religion and spirituality, sacred and secular, and church and society are more difficult to define. Thus, consumerism and choice simultaneously threatens, but also nourishes, religion and spirituality. Spiritual self-help books and other products, various kinds of yoga and meditative therapies, plus an ample range of courses and vacations, all suggest that religious affections and allegiances are being transformed, rather than being eroded, in contemporary society. 'Secular' society seems to be powerless in the face of a curiously stubborn (and growing) social appetite for inchoate religion and nascent spirituality, in all its various forms. So whilst it is true that many in Western Europe are turning from being religious assumers to religious consumers, and are moving from a culture of religious assumption to religious consumption, in which choice and competition in the spiritual marketplace thrive, there may be less cause for alarm than has been assumed.

Ultimately, religion and culture should never be divided up as subjects or objects. Their relationship is fundamental to religion and has been conceived by some as inherent to the nature of society. Cultures include hereditary values that lead to individual, social and collective views on behaviour, beliefs and attitudes. It is generally a mistake to try to define religion outside such social patterning. Religion and spirituality provide a variety of templates for the ordering of individual and collective courses of action, and for culture more generally. Often, religion gives expression to the most cherished or critical moments of social life. Moreover, most major religions have social vision: they wish to see some degree of congruence between social organization and the faith that they espouse.

Typically, the presence of religion within society is characterized by both sacred and social cultivation. Even in faiths which claim a high doctrine of revelation, the expression of the spirituality will be social and disseminated. However, the complex connectedness between religion and society can most easily be seen in national, local or state religions. For example, occasions such as Remembrance Sunday, Mothering Sunday, Harvest Festival and the celebrations of Christmas and Easter within the Western Christian tradition can be highly flavoured with cultural artefacts that have not originated from within the heart of the religious tradition. Medieval mystery plays, equally, can be nascent spiritual vehicles for pursuing a particular social agenda that is relevant to its cultural context. The popularity of carol singing at Christmas is an example of commonplace spiritual and cultural material being widely used outside the control of mainstream religion.

As etymologists of the word 'religion' have noted, the portmanteau word comes from two older Latin words meaning 'to persistently bind together'. Religion, by its very nature, is socially experienced and expressed, and is concerned with having an impact on social realms that are beyond the sacred. Correspondingly, divisions between 'religion' and 'society', although common-place, are invariably false. This is because religion exists not only in its own right, but is also public and finds that its materials, sacred truths, stories, images and ideas are part of the wider cultural furniture. As I have hinted already, even an apparently innocent phrase such as 'Happy Christmas' bears testimony to this. Religion is so thoroughly a part of society that it cannot be separated out entirely from its context as though there is somehow a pure essence that could be studied. Equally, and to repeat, society takes such a hand in creating and ordering religion, that society itself cannot be properly understood without some reflection upon religious ideals and practices.

In conclusion, three particular issues that focus the study of religion and culture are worthy of further attention. First, globalization appears to lead to an increase in spiritual pluralism. Under such conditions, societies that have been ordered through one particular religion now find themselves having to adjust and accommodate a range of faiths within the public sphere. This can create some ambiguities and occasionally lead to tensions between competing convictions. At this point, society can appear to be less coherent and may struggle to reconcile some of its religiously-funded but implicit values with other more explicit faith claims.

Second, there seems to be little evidence that religion is becoming less of a feature within contemporary culture. For example, the interest in spirituality – religious and sacred sentiment outside the immediate control of formal religion – has been burgeoning for many years in the Western world. It would seem that, in the midst of consumerism and secularization, people are turning more than ever to texts and techniques that inspire and enchant. This appears to result in the continual (if somewhat diffuse) infusion of inchoate spirituality at every level of society, suggesting that society, no matter how atomized and incoherent, persists in its quest for sacral meaning amidst the everyday reality of mundane modernity.

Third, vernacular Christian spirituality appears to thrive in the gaps between the ideal and the real, and between formal and operant religion. At its most visible, a faith offers a means for expressing and ordering public grief, celebration and memorialization, at local, national and international levels. It is precisely at the breaking points of human existence that religion lends the strength and vision to society to reconfigure itself and imagine new beginnings. Religion, in other words, still has the marked capacity to enable society to exceed itself and, in so doing, improve upon the present and build for the future. Religion is that which 'binds' things together; spirituality is its expression. Individuals, ideas, communities and nations, set alongside their pain, grief, hopes, healing and celebration, are brought together in ways that continue to sustain and nourish societies, enabling them to see beyond the immediate and transitory and catch a glimpse of the timeless and the ultimate. Societies, it would appear, have always needed this. Religion not only provides it; it also gives meaning to the very cultures that continue to seek the something that is more than human.

Chapter 3

Theology and Cultural Challenge

Introduction

During the last 50 years, and since Niebuhr's ground-breaking *Christ and Culture* (1951), a significant number of theologians have attempted theological engagements with 'culture'. Broadly speaking, there have been two major modes of engagement in relation to contemporary culture, which have to some extent bifurcated. The first tradition broadly conceives of the engagement as a form of interlocking combative encounter with contemporary culture. The second broadly sees it as a form of intrarelated binding, covenant or commitment. Both lead to the formation of their own distinctive cultures (for example, characteristic missiological and ecclesiological outlooks), which increasingly do not know how to talk to one other. Although the adoption of both strategies delivers a certain degree of poise and reflexivity, their inability to relate to one another leads to an impoverished form of public theology. In effect, both traditions could be said to be somewhat culturally dyslexic (the etymology of the word lies in a conflation, from the Greek *lexis*, 'to speak', and the Latin, *legere*, 'to read'). Thus, and of culture, it could be said that modern theologians and the churches tend neither to speak properly nor read well.

Niebuhr suggests that there are five theological responses to the complexity of a Christian faith immersed in culture. The first type stresses the opposition between Christ and culture; this is the Christ *against* culture. The second type is diametrically opposed to the first: 'there is a fundamental *agreement* between Christ and culture'. This is the Christ who is *of* or *for* culture. These two basic types represent the two primary faces of engagement that can be identified in the life of the church, and the remaining three types all flow from these two primary typologies. However, there are also four distinct types of religion–culture relationships that can be identified: religion is part of culture; culture is part of religion; culture may be 'religious'; and religion and culture can undertake a variety of serious academic dialogues. It is the last of these that we are mainly concerned with in this book, although that will enable a 'reading' of the other three types.

Given the issues already sketched and critiqued in the preceding chapters, the incompleteness of both faces of engagement may already be apparent. Rather as Troeltsch thought, the bearers of the Christian tradition long to give something to the world, but invariably do not know how (or what, perhaps?). On the one hand, Christians can provide symbolic legitimation for the prevailing society and culture, thereby generating the 'church type' of interaction that theologians such as Barth were so critical of. On the other hand, there can be protest against the prevailing powers and an attempt to set up a counter-society, thereby generating the 'sect type' response that Tillich was so critical of.

Arguably, the resolution of this is far from easy. It may partly depend on appreciating the axis of paradox that is inherent in engagement, and seeing it as a necessary device for poise, theological commitment and discernment. However, no sooner is this contemplated than another paradox begins to emerge: God meets us 'outside' conventional forms of revelation, but then also comes to us in culture and engages with us through the ordinary, even as we attempt to delineate the tradition and experience through our own paradoxes such as the Radical Orthodox.

It could be argued that a theology of culture needs to be a *collation* of the two faces of engagement if theology is to re-inhabit public space. In so doing, it can be both a 'thick description' of reality as much as it can become a critique or affirmation of the same. As we have already hinted, such an argument may be pursued by paying some attention to specific and commonplace religious motifs and practices that have become part of the 'cultural furniture' of society, including sacramental practice, such as baptism, or the celebration of Christmas. The actualities of these beliefs and practices – Christian traditions that have deep roots within culture – *require* theologians and the churches to rethink their *pastoral* nature as part of a new theological understanding – what Nicholas Healy might call 'practical–prophetic ecclesiology' rather than 'ideologies of the church'.

So to return to Troeltsch, baptism, for example, is not administered adequately by either the 'church type' or 'sect type' orientation, since the controlling ideology normally restricts the mode and tenor of cultural engagement. Yet if the ministry of the church is to reflect God's self-gift in Jesus Christ, then there will be an element of praxis in the pastoral which will actually *shape* the gift that is defined and delimited by the ideological. Baptism (or in more vernacular lingua, 'christening') will be at once an ambiguous sacrament of welcome at the very *borders* of the church even as it proceeds from its *centre* and speaks of a specific intensity of faith. Thus, rightly conceived, the sacrament invites a church–world 'negotiation' (between 'culture' and 'religion', or 'orthodoxy' and 'vernacular religion') as a sign of God's grace and inclusivity, but without penalizing the borders of its necessary exclusivity. As one cultural commentator notes: 'religion is not effective because it is otherworldly, but because it incarnates this otherworldliness in a practical form of life...a link between absolute values and daily life' (Eagleton, 2000, p. 38).

Thus, a theology of culture that understands a social–sacramental approach to the religion–culture divide might invite us to get beyond an imagination that traces a transition from a secular reality (that is, bread, water, and so on) to a sacred state (that is, of transformed materials), and to no longer belong to the categories we thought we imagined. Rather, we would belong to a transformed community that has a wisdom that is above the inherently false secular–sacred divide. Ironically, it is in the pastoral that the paradoxes of the two faces of engagement can begin to be resolved, for they are 'lived out' in other forms of creative tension. The church can relearn the art of becoming a 'genuine community of argument', marked by mutual respect, diverse discipleship, common engagement and respectful critique.

Such a view might lead us to explore the identity of culture as a hybrid or relational affair, and a theology that closely corresponds to that reality, yet without actually mirroring it. In other words, there is the space for the paradox to affirm and critique what is created. There can be a sense of the gap between the sign and referent, even though a social sacramental theology may 'saturate' such a space. Because Christian identity itself is both contested and relational, it hinges both on cultural engagement and being open to direction from the free grace of God. This might allow us to relate the 'core' values of religious belief to society/culture in a more reflexive manner, which in turn creates new possibilities for theology as a public discourse. Drawing inspiration from writers such as David Tracy, *conversation* can be commended as a major mode of theological engagement. Equally, *collage* can be considered as an analogical and methodological description for how theology is to be constructed in relation to culture. In so doing, theology is able to attend to whole areas of human experience and understanding that are normally neglected by faith communities. But such a move requires a risk – namely of theology ceasing to operate as an autonomous discipline ('private grammar of faith') – and to take its place as a distinctive mode of discourse that seeks to operate within wider social and academic contexts.

Ultimately, theology should not be considered as a mode of reflection that can be placed at the margins of culture; it should claim its full citizenship as a member of that culture. The particularity of theology should not be allowed to collapse into, or be confused with, privateness. Particularity and publicness are not opposed. A theology of engagement that makes a virtue out of paradox (as an axis that brings poise and reflexivity) can seek to be *empathetically participative* within culture and can make a distinct contribution to public life.

In view of these preliminary remarks, we now turn to consider and critique three different types of theological engagement with contemporary culture, each represented by a key figure. The divisions (or rather characterizations) follow the work of Peter Berger and his *The Heretical Imperative* (1980), which attempts to systematize the responses of theologians in three distinct modes. The first is the deductive possibility. Here the Word of God (or the tradition) is the starting point, and there can be no other way of knowing God. The gain of this theological outlook is certainty and mastery in the mist of cultural confusion. John Milbank and 'Radical Orthodoxy' have been chosen to represent this outlook. The second mode is the reductive possibility, where it is deemed that the tradition has to be rationalized in order to be credible for the modern age. In reductionism, the core of the tradition (ethics?) has to be rescued from the thick veneers and overlays of myth that have obscured the tradition over time. 'Faith' has to be freed from 'religion', and reflexivity is a byword for this approach. The Belgian theologian Lieven Boeve has been selected to represent this tradition. The third approach, according to Berger, is the inductive possibility. Here there is a movement from tradition to experience or, more accurately, the recovery of experience as a means of reconstituting the tradition in the modern world. The inductive possibility traces the religious experiences that began the tradition. In that sense, it is profoundly sociological, but at the same time not reductive. David Martin has been chosen to represent this approach. In considering all three, our focus remains firmly ecclesiological. In other words, we are concerned with these authors' theology in terms of its capacity to shape the church in the task of engaging with the complexity of contemporary culture. In pursuing this line, we are drawing on the agenda outlined earlier, and in particular the challenge laid down by the work of Nicholas Healy, namely to identify models of the church that take a serious account of the actuality of ecclesial life rather than 'blueprints'.

The Deductive Possibility: John Milbank and Radical Orthodoxy

As Gavin Hyman suggests, one of the great ironies about the end of foundationalism is that it has heralded the return of religion. As institutions and ideologies collapse and decay at the beginning of the twenty-first century, religion (that which was dormant and repressed) has reappeared. There are undoubtedly many reasons for this: making sense of life in the midst of chaos; providing consolation in the midst of alienation; offering hope in the midst of doubt. Hyman suggests that there have been two principal theological responses to the resurgence of religion. The first, ironically, has been to reassert anti-foundationalism. Typically, such theological strategies are represented by figures such as Don Cupitt and Mark C. Taylor. Although their theological projects are quite distinctive, they nonetheless 'write within the post-Nietzschean space of the death of God and the postmodern space of the end of metanarratives' (Hyman, 2001, p. 2). The second tradition is arguably broader and represents an attempt to recuperate theology, even though it will now be informed by postmodern thought. The principal 'school' that champions this move is Radical Orthodoxy, identified through writers such as John Milbank, Graham Ward, Gerard Loughlin and Catherine Pickstock. Radical Orthodoxy, as a movement – and simply expressed – is an attempt to recover premodern modes of theological thought, fusing them with postmodern thinking, in order to counter the 'apotheosis of modernity'. This gives rise to various labels for the theological school and its stratagem: 'postmodern Augustinianism', 'conservative postmodern theology', 'post-modern orthodoxy' and, finally, 'Radical Orthodoxy' (see Milbank, Ward and Pickstock, 1999).

It is important to understand that the Taylor–Cupitt and 'Radical Orthodox' strategem, although quite different, are linked by the fact that they are both responses to modernity. The former sees modernity as inevitable and, to some extent, desirable. The latter regards it as a form of violence and oppression that has resulted in 'secular tyranny' (Hyman, 2001, p. 52). However, the rich irony of this assertion is that it is itself a form of violence. In refuting, dismissing and attacking modernity, Milbank's insistence becomes a kind of compelling form of intolerance that reasserts Christian 'mastery' over all other narratives and cultures.

It is not my purpose here to engage systematically with the entire range and depth of Milbank's work. My primary concern here is to offer an evaluative sketch that will explore the adequacy of Radical Orthodox theology as a form of engagement with contemporary culture. This immediately brings us to one of the most critical points of interest in relation to Radical Orthodoxy: the role and scope of the 'human sciences'. For a significant number of theologians (for example, Farley, Lindbeck and Martin), the use of the human or social sciences has been an important and staple complement to their theological work: 'the sociological imagination as classically deployed undercuts religious and theological pretensions' (R. Roberts, 2002, p. 191). Milbank, in contrast, sees such alliances as problematic and deadly. He asserts that such partnerships are doomed either because theology becomes an adjunct of secular reason or because theology then alienates itself by confining itself 'to intimations of a sublimity beyond representation' (Milbank, 1990, p. 1). In response, a number of theologians claim that the social sciences have been misnarrated in order to be outnarrated. As Roberts notes:

> Sociology as a discipline should not be construed *reductively* and *exclusively* in terms of the perverse metanarrative of secular reason. Sociology and the social sciences may also be classically understood as the *critical representation* and *clarification* of patterns of social organisation necessary to the sustenance of humane societies, rather than (as Milbank would have it) the partner in the promotion of an allegedly necessary and totalitarian violence of order. The tasks of theology and sociology are mutual at least inasmuch as they address the human condition in exploratory and interpretative terms, and do not subsume (in however virtuosic a fashion) *everything* under the dance of death and totalitarian logic of Western secular reason. Moreover, sociology and theology which embody concerns for the other cannot afford to neglect or express contempt for ethnography, that is the effective representation of and interpretation of what is actually happening in human lives. Both theology and the social sciences should be concerned in their distinctive ways with life and with how things are – and might be. (R. Roberts, 2002, p. 206)

Put another way, a theology that is uninformed by the social sciences may turn out to be very clever and erudite in some sense, but it may also be ultimately 'unreal'. But there are other concerns with Radical Orthodoxy as a suitable theological means of engaging with culture. First, Radical Orthodoxy is a peculiar alliance of the premodern and the postmodern. That said, it would not be fair to describe it as 'anti-modern': it isn't. But the movement is concerned, generally, with the scale of influence that modernist and Enlightenment thinking has had on theology. It regards that influence with suspicion. In this respect, Radical Orthodoxy wants to reinstate theology as a primary narrative for social, political, cultural and philosophical discourse. It critiques and demonizes social sciences as 'modernist meta-narratives' that are, in reality, the illegitimate kith of theology (although they are apparently unaware of their parentage). Radical Orthodoxy holds that there can be no neutral 'social' readings of the world or traditions that do not depend on a prior ontology of knowledge.

Second, Radical Orthodoxy, as a term, is a curious oxymoron. Postmodern and paradoxical, it shifts a little too easily between conservative and liberal positions, dogmatism and praxis. One is tempted to ask: what is the difference between Radical Orthodoxy and conservative heterodoxy? It is an ecclesial programme, often guilty of a degree of idealism and imperialism. It pays little attention to other faiths and the grounded reality of pluralism, or indeed of complex local congregations. It treats the church as a given construct – the City of God. In contrast, I take the view that there is no version of Christianity that is without a local accent. No-one can speak, or ever has spoken, of 'pure' Christianity or 'pure' theology. The dialect is always particular: Rome, Geneva, Canterbury, Atlanta – Christianity speaks in tongues that are tinged and tilthed in local contexts. In my own recent writing I point out how Radical Orthodoxy resembles the missiology of Leslie Newbigin – with its insistence on the reality and primacy of Christendom – but with Radical Orthodoxy having overdosed on metaphysics. Correspondingly, some critics describe Milbank's programme as a kind of postmodern quasi-fundamentalism.

Third, and a point that may seem odd to some, although relevant to the discussions on modern ecclesiology that follow, I note that most of the leading lights in Radical Orthodoxy are English Anglicans (with 'catholic' tastes), and I want to suggest that this has a particular bearing on the shape and identity of Radical Orthodoxy. If I am right – that Radical Orthodoxy is a marriage of the premodern and the postmodern – then what we have is an alliance (or versions) of Patristic, Scholastic and Renaissance thinking fused together with continental philosophy, with its face set squarely against modernity. But is the target not also liberal Protestantism? I think it must be. (Milbank, for example, ridicules 'the poverty of Niebuhrism' – see Lovin, 1995). But more particularly, Radical Orthodoxy could be read as a movement that tries to *renarrate* the church. I find this interesting, because Anglicanism's peculiar genius is *not* to have solved the problem of its own identity – although that looks increasingly ragged as a virtue, at present. Anglicanism is episcopal, yet synodical; Catholic, yet Protestant – the *via media*. It is no surprise, therefore, to discover that most of the leading lights in Radical Orthodoxy are of the Anglo-Catholic tradition. Indeed, there is something rather Tractarian about Radical Orthodoxy. Perhaps this is unsurprising, given that the spiritual crucible of the key figures of Radical Orthodoxy is Anglo-Catholicism, with its emphasis on aesthetics, romanticism and idealism. So the Protestants were right. If episcopacy was not extirpated, it would come to dominate the church. Ultimately, Radical Orthodoxy wants to impose a basic kind of 'solvedness' on the church and society. In Radical Orthodoxy we witness a kind of assertive intellectual episcopacy that believes it is ordained and consecrated to control. Its programme is simple: to reorder the world and church by outnarrating its existing meta-narratives. Hence, the premodern and postmodern unite to refute the modern – a classically Tractarian move, but with a postmodern twist.

Fourth, it is worth contrasting Milbank's work to Ward's. Milbank's is striking, strident and original. Ward's work, however, is original in a quite different sense: as interpretative montages and pastiches. Ward's work ranges perceptively, imaginatively and often deeply over vast fields of intellectual inquiry. In a matter of a few pages, one can find oneself rubbing shoulders with poets, philosophers, political thinkers, theologians and novelists, with the subject matter fusing together doctrine, sexuality, psychology and sociality. It is, strangely though, a form of theology that is a product of its culture and time. Access to material makes fast, penetrating and absorbing critiques or theses possible. But there is a strange sense in Ward's work in which one feels one is watching a master-artist of bricolage or montage at work. It is postmodern reconstructionism: artful, inventive and subversive. For example, what makes Ward's (1995) treatment of Barth and Derrida an intriguing theological project is not that he has read either one correctly; most of his critics seem to agree that he hasn't. It is the fact that he has put them together at all that makes a statement, which is as once performative, dramatic and affective, even as it is ultimately unpersuasive. But such work should not be confused with other kinds of art.

So we might say that Ward's work turns out to be something akin to an elaborate Luboc montage. Or then again, perhaps a better comparison is to a (great) contemporary fashion design. It captures the spirit of the age (late 1990s and early twenty-first century), and yet pushes those boundaries of taste in a voguish and intriguing manner. The cut and styling of the theology is sharp, attracting the eye. The paradox of the theological composition is daring yet familiar – urban chic meets Oxbridge tweed? This is avant-garde theology, to be sure. But for all its novelty, it is strangely unoriginal. For Ward is primarily a designer and shaper of materials; but he does not spin his own yarn, nor weave his own cloth. Ward's theological substance is constituted in a style of fusions. Here, postmodern theology has come of age.

These points assume a greater relevance when they are set within the field of modern ecclesiology, Christianity and contemporary culture. Modern ecclesiology, as conceived by Nicholas Healy, Edward Farley and others, is concerned with the shape of the church in relation to modern life. Modern ecclesiology does not reject 'idealist' claims for the church – such that it is 'the body of Christ' – and so forth. It takes such theological claims with utmost seriousness. But it also understands the church to be a social gathering, and one that is therefore open to the kinds of interpretations and clarifications that are normally gleaned from the social sciences. Modern ecclesiology is therefore always more than a simple restatement of theological principles; it takes account of context, and understands the church to be both ascription and description, projection and revelation. It is as much about excavating the 'archaeology of the house of faith' as it is about any ontology. Radical Orthodoxy, in contrast, although advocating a kind of recovery of the past, is nonetheless an exercise in inventive imagination. It gives birth to thought, but not to action. It reconceives the church of the intellect, but not the church of the ordinary world.

Towards the end of *The Word Made Strange* (1997), Milbank offers an analogy of faith, comparing it to a giant gothic cathedral. It can never be seen as a whole, yet it is; it is always complete, yet never; it is enclosed, yet boundless. Milbank's analogy is, I think, an ironic moment of self-defeat for Radical Orthodoxy, since the analogy expresses that, no matter how much a cathedral is a given, a sacred space and more than the sum of its parts, it is also the work of human hands.

That is why I am drawn to Nicholas Healy's *Church, World and Christian Life* (2000), where he calls upon theologians to take more notice of the 'concrete church' and of social sciences such as ethnography. He argues that too much ecclesiology is shaped by 'blueprint' or 'ideal' descriptions of the church – what the church could or should be like, but not what it is actually like. Put another way, modern ecclesiology ought to take more account of its actual shape and context than it normally does. In such an equation, theology need have nothing to fear from social sciences when it comes to understanding and interpreting the church. Modern ecclesiology will always be apples and oranges – the proverbial fruit salad. It will explicate and interpret claims to be the body of Christ against the observations and interpretations of sociologists and those others from the social sciences. It will come to see that, no matter how churches imagine themselves theologically, they can also be understood sociologically and without that being a necessarily reductive exercise. This is a vital task in theological engagements with culture, which will include recognizing the cultural determinants within any given theology. Ultimately, the debate is not whether sociology can contribute to modern ecclesiology – it clearly can. The question is in what ways, and by how much? Verily, there are many rooms in my father's house.

The Reductive Possibility: Lieven Boeve and Reflexive Theology

Beyond the Cupitt–Taylor theological tradition, which might be understood as a capitulation to modernity, and the tradition of Radical Orthodoxy (a refutation of the same) there is a vibrant range of theological approaches to modernity that constitute a 'third way'. Writers such as Tanner, Farley and Browning make a serious attempt to engage the tradition in ways that are deep yet reflexive. Indeed, their arguments usually depend, to some extent, on understanding Christian tradition as being inherently and dynamically 'open'. Their views will be touched on later. But, from a European perspective, let us first examine Boeve's theological approach to the crisis facing Belgian churches in the twenty-first century. Boeve's diagnosis is as follows:

> ... the church is so out of touch with modern culture and society that the church is obstructed in its efforts to initiate. Only when the church is able to bring its doctrine, ethics, spirituality and organisational structures up to date will faith become a credible option once again ... the diagnosis leads one to the unavoidable conclusion that an ever-increasing gulf exists between contemporary culture and the Christian faith. The days of 'traditional', cultural Christianity are numbered .... (Boeve, 2003, p. 6).

Boeve's thesis rests on a number of assumptions. He accepts that the Catholic Church (at least in his own context of Flanders) once determined the shape and scope of human sociality. However, that same church is now struggling; the transmission of faith is flagging, and this has had a deleterious effect upon the cultural domain, which has become rapidly de-Christianized. Traditional Christianity is, in effect, worn out. Boeve argues that the church needs to accept that it is ill-equipped to face the challenges and questions posed by contemporary culture. It then needs to recontextualize its presentation and meaning and, in so doing, create a new and more respectful dialogue between Christianity and contemporary culture. Granted, the foundations for the thesis are contestable. But Boeve's response, interestingly, is not to reassert the tradition. It is, rather, to find modes and patterns of engagement that will 'rescue' the church from a kind of self-imposed private exile. This assertion is based on his sophisticated understanding of secularization, which is primarily problematized as a range of cultural moments that have pushed religion from being a public discourse and praxis into the realm of the private:

> ... secularisation emerged as the direct consequence of functional differentiation ... diverse sub-systems emancipated themselves from the all-embracing religious horizon ... [religion] lost its prominent role [the] all-encompassing source and point of reference for human values and convictions ... religion was forced to take on the form of a sub-system, developing, among other things, its own logic, institutions and role patterns. Religion came to focus exclusively on the promotion of the religious function in society, side by side with, yet distinct from, the other institutions. In doing so, religion was forced to withdraw from public life, its relevance reduced to the organisation of the private arena and intimate relationships, side by side with the fulfilment of a comfort/consolation function.... A second consequence was the generalisation of values. Where the local community once derived its convictions with respect to truth and value entirely from its own traditions, this was now only viable (and to a lesser and lesser degree) in the private arena .... (Boeve, 2003, p. 39)

These observations resonate strongly with our earlier remarks on consumerism, religion and culture. The collapse of ideologies and meta-narratives is mirrored in the demise of institutions and forms of public and civic association. The ties that bind society are increasingly undetermined, at least by any obvious moral force. Sociality is thus rendered more fragile, and depends on collections of individuals to make up the gap that is created in a post-associational culture. Boeve, noting this cultural turn, writes:

> The root causes of individualisation are to be found in the centuries old process of modernisation ... [1] increased education; [2] increased economic capital which guarantees material independence; [3] urbanisation; [4] mobility; [5] massively expanded leisure possibilities; [6] persistent rationalisation of life .... (Boeve, 2003, p. 53)

For Boeve, postmodernity can actually be defined as 'reflexive modernity'. Correspondingly, he readily accedes that the overall narrative in which Christianity is now situated is one of 'marketisation' – this is the only master narrative. In such a context, Christians operate reflexively within the reflexive society. However, there is a danger in this:

...there is evidence of the religious consumer exercising his or her right to self-determination. The result is an a la carte religious identity. Religious communities often fall in line with this process and become 'service providers'.... (Boeve, 2003, p. 55)

But Boeve argues that even in the market-driven world, stories continue to be told and faith survives. He calls on the churches to engage in open, rather than closed, narratives of tradition. What does he mean here? The open narrative is framed, but inviting. But it is not overly dominating; it is not a 'meta' in the 'over' sense, but in the 'with' sense. Jesus, rather like the parables he tells, invites us into a realm of questions and multiple interpretative possibilities. Jesus is, in some sense, 'the open narrative of God'; the incarnation is an aspect of the reflexivity of the life of the Trinity.

To speak of reflexive theology is, then, to speak of a semi-fluid but substantial mode of being. Theology is always more than just thinking about God. It is art, dance, liturgy, protest and practical. It is an *activity*. As Paul Van Buren reminds us, it is the movement of people 'struck by the biblical story, in which they undertake to revise continually the ways in which they say how things are with their present circumstances, in the light of how they read that story' (Van Buren, 1969, p. 53). Where and when the story strikes, there is power, response and religious community: the body of God, the church. Indeed, following Pierre Bourdieu, it is possible to see sociology as fieldwork in theology (Bourdieu, 1990, p. 28). Because God does not come to us 'neat', but through agents and ambiguity, it is necessary to examine how power is diluted and distorted – and perhaps even expose how we are deceived. It is not only theology that can speak about the power of God. Sociology may test the agents of power, as much as political science may examine their moral use and abuse: the 'monarche' of God is generally transferred to states, individuals and ecclesial structures. It is in these places that we find the power of God translated. In view of these remarks, three points for further reflection seem an appropriate point with which to conclude this section.

First, orientation in the culture of late modernity remains a serious issue for many who are religious and wish to defend some conceptualization of God, whether it be absolute or qualified. In part, a better orientation may be achieved if modernity and postmodernity are better understood. A clue to how this might be achieved comes, ironically, from a sociologist. Anthony Giddens prefers the term 'post-traditional' to postmodern, and suggests that society is now engaging in 'social reflexivity' (Giddens, 1991, pp. 21–43). According to Giddens, people have to filter rapidly growing amounts of information for themselves, such that they are increasingly reflexive about how they are influenced by ideas and, in turn, how their actions influence society. Social reflexivity is an individual and communal process of reflection and action that allows foundationalism or meta-narratives to have a bearing on the world without necessarily dominating. In other words, ideology participates in the world without becoming totalitarian. In Giddens' view, therefore, moral fundamentalism is a much greater danger to society than (controlled?) moral relativism.

Reflexivity is an important concept here. It is no accident that post-liberals and 'post-evangelicals' are at the forefront of constructing meaningful dialogue between traditions that were once alienated from each other (Phillips and Okholm, 1996). But there are dangers to be heeded as well. Theology and ecclesiology might be swayed by culture rather than discerning it and exercising discrimination (Williams, 1989, p. 103). It is not clear what would test 'reflexivity': the very concept itself risks engulfment (Flanagan, 1996, p. 26). Reductionism, relativism and failure most likely lie ahead if the reflexivity does not correspond to some form of revelation. As von Balthasar notes, there must be a sociality that relates to what is limitless, beautiful, radiant, revealed and transcendent: reflexivity without this is just choice and self-evaluation (von Balthasar, 1982, p. 28). The Christian traditions of immanentism and interventionism could combine to counterbalance reflexivity and, in some ways, re-inhabit the gap created by the discourses of modernity.

And yet, second, and linked to the first point, it does not follow that reflexivity with foundations leads to their compromise and eventual erosion. The suggestion being made by Giddens is that a post-foundational culture presents new opportunities for relating to fundaments. In an even more positive vein, Kieran Flanagan has suggested that power 'may reach a perfection in a theological context' that sociology and 'culture' cannot match, and that theology can enable (sociological) reflexivity and, in effect, call it to account (Flanagan, 1996, p. 207).

Third, and linked to the second point, what Middleton and Walsh call 'anti-totalizing' meta-narratives become highly desirable commodities as vehicles for the power of God in this new post-foundational[1] situation (Middleton and Walsh, 1995, p. 107). The question, already put, is how can any meta-narrative be anti-totalitarian? 'Meta', when used in conjunction with narrative, means 'above': dominant, or reigning over. But in other usage, it can mean 'with', 'by' or 'beyond', as in the case of metaphysics. Perhaps the task for narratives about the dominion of God in a postmodern world is not to be 'over' the world, but in reflexive theology to be both with it and beyond it. In other words, stories of power and domination become rewritten as stories about love and relationship. Furthermore, 'with' implies a journey, where truth is encountered in the future through teleology or eschatology. Christianity is transformed from a propositional religion into a pilgrimage, in which God goes with us, yet is beyond us. This, it seems to me, is the heart of Boeve's theology – it is deeply reflexive reductionism that seeks to engage faith with contemporary culture.

---

[1] 'Post-foundational' refers to societies that have moved beyond accepted meta-narratives and embraced a more postmodern ethos.

The Inductive Possibility: David Martin and Socio-theology

The selection of David Martin's work to represent the Bergerian inductive theological strategy may seem puzzling to some, especially as Martin is primarily known as a sociologist of religion. However, David Martin's scholarship also extends into several types of theology. He is comfortable working within doctrinal, ecclesiological and homiletic fields; he is also equally at home operating within pastoral and practical theology. Arguably, his work is too diverse and complex to be easily categorized (although this could also be said of Boeve and Milbank). To be sure, it is not immediately obvious how Martin's theology might be identified as inductive. However, a few preliminary observations can set the scene. First, Martin's sociological foci dispose him to concentrate on the social constructions of reality that have a direct bearing on the shaping of (religious) experience. Second, his interests in ecclesial cultures (perhaps especially Pentecostalism) suggest that he is more alive than most to the possibilities of experience being recovered in order to reanimate tradition. Third, Martin is also well aware of the socio-theological dynamics of in-duction, whereby the cyclical movement between tradition and experience is constantly reborn in ecclesial contexts that are themselves immersed in contexts that demand a memory and resonance of the past in order to shape the present and the future. Such trajectories of thinking can be traced in *A Sociology of English Religion* (1967), a profound reflection on practices, attitudes, beliefs and opinion, to explanations and structures of belief, to the more homiletic tone of *Christian Language and Its Mutations* (2002), which examines the aesthetics, fundamentals and dynamics of belief in relation to modernity. Throughout, Martin is consistent in taking 'ordinary' Christian experience seriously, and in reflecting upon it sociologically, theologically and inductively.

So, whether it is doctrine, liturgy, Pentecostalism, Methodism or Anglican-ism, Martin's work has often brought new insights to those communities, as much as his writing has illuminated other scholars. Undoubtedly there are personal reasons why this may be so. David Martin is a scholar who is critically engaged with his subjects, but also deeply aware of their own reality and integrity. But in order to consider Martin's inductive theological approach, let us first examine his distinctive approach to the sociology of religion:

> ... at the simplest level he can organise surveys based on sound principles of selection and questionnaire construction to elicit given ranges of fact ... the next level could be that of interpreting and collating survey results ... quite clearly, this level of interest includes an assessment of all these various kinds of data in historical perspective. There remains the level of what may be called institutional analysis: the relation between the social structures of the Church and the structures of society at large at the national and local level. The task here includes a long-term and intimate knowledge of 'geological' shifts in this structure.... (Martin, 1967, p. 107)

Lest this presumes too much omni-competence on the part of any sociologist, Martin is at pains to stress the limits of their discipline. He states that, whilst on the one hand, 'without such research, comment is useless', the only possible comments after research are in fact 'cautionary': a sociologist can only 'indicate the range of possible interpretations... before any [one] interpretation can become persuasive'. Thus, '[he] is a man with a set of tools, a training, a group of relevant queries... some accumulated insights which probably bear on the problem in hand... [he] is not a conjuror...'. Then, critically, he adds that a sociologist must have, built into their intellectual armoury, 'a scepticism about conventional "images" and how the world "works", or explanations of current social phenomena' (ibid.).

Here, Martin's description of sociology contains more than a hint of rigour. He is arguing for a form of inquiry that goes beyond appearances and generally held assumptions, which in turn propels us into the original reasons and motivations for actions, structures, beliefs and organizations. In particular, Martin is critical of the extent to which the culture of well-meaning but amateurish guesswork guides so much of the church's thinking. Martin points out that the Church of England collects 'just enough statistics to know that it has a variable temperature, but supports no investigation to find out why' (ibid., p. 108). His work often criticizes the churches for their absence of a real research culture and calls upon them to reconsider their 'empirical condition' (in other words, to reflect inductively on their experience) as well as the methods of investigation and interpretation that can service their actuality.

The epicentre of Martin's agenda for the churches, arising out of his inductive stratagem is simple enough to narrate. His theology is not 'pure' in that he does not begin with metaphysical or philosophical questions. Generally speaking, Martin's theological reflection, begins with the lived experience of individuals or groups or with the professed creeds in relation to their contexts. It is, in other words, engaged. In that sense, it is proper to describe Martin's theology as classically 'practical', meaning that he is prepared to see how culture, contexts and experience shape the range and trajectory of theological discourse, on the basis that it has always done so. This, however, does not lead to reductionism. It is precisely because experience is taken so seriously in relation to tradition that Martin can be identified as a practical theologian in the inductive tradition. (Practical theology in the deductive tradition is normally called 'applied' theology, and in the reductive tradition it is termed 'contextual'.)

To press these distinctions further, the difference between proper practical theology and systematic theology can often be as stark as that between an artist and an engineer. At the risk of extending the mechanistic metaphor further, Martin is well aware that the church largely prefers to commission and collect ornaments, but it seldom builds machines. And when it attempts the latter, the design is normally a good decade or so out of date. This is a tendentious remark, granted; but it should be obvious to many sociologists that churches do not normally know how to organize or investigate themselves, are poor at gathering accurate data about their own ecclesial life, and even poorer at interpreting it. In short, they are aesthetically gifted, yet often structurally frayed and dated. Martin's practical sociology (or perhaps his understated ecclesiology) takes this dynamic seriously. He is aware that beauty (even when it is simply constituted in order, creeds or liturgy) is what shapes experience, and it is this that gives birth to tradition.

David Martin's sociology and practical theology is, correspondingly, sharp and coherent when he comes to address the English parish church. In a now famous essay, he notes that 'sociology cannot answer evaluative questions about the social role of the church; it can however clarify thinking by elucidating unacknowledged presuppositions which may be shaping current thinking' (Martin, 1988, p. 43). It is with such inductive socio-theological thinking that he can rein in some of Leslie Newbigin's theological reflection on the nature of the church, describing it as 'eloquent' but 'tenuous'.[2] Martin, as a theologian and sociologist considering the apparent increase in 'associational' patterns (that is, a more congregational–denominational approach to mission) for the church, prefers to begin with social reality rather than Newbigin's dubious biblical eisegesis. To do this, Martin narrates a picture of the situation in England as being somewhere between Northern Europe and Northern America. He is characteristically generous to the American 'associational' model, pointing out (rightly) that some churches that have 'only been put up within ten years [are] riddled with community functions...doing an extraordinary business in putting out tentacles into the wider community' (ibid., p. 46). In Scandinavia, the 'competition is *very* limited', but the service the church offers to the community is 'utterly ecumenical', by which he means socially and theologically comprehensive. This picture describes the broad sociological context. But why has the parish church declined?

Martin is not sure that it has, exactly, and as with his work on confirmation, he presses the church to look a little harder at the material it is offering and a little longer at the audience that it supposes it has lost. That said, he makes some remarks that are sociologically cautious and are in turn designed to caution the church. For example, he points out, following Hugh McLeod, that between 1880 and 1930, various social and economic factors caused the rich and powerful to lose interest in the church. Labour movements, expanding public services and consumerism all played their part: England became progressively more areligious (but note, *not* anti-religious).

Martin then sets about discussing and critiquing various strategies that attempt to address the decline in the status of the parish church. North America and Europe are discussed, but neither offers a viable model for the Church of England. 'Modernising' or reforming is put up and then pulled down; Martin does not think that 'producing a new book of liturgy...is somehow going to transform the overall situation' (ibid., p. 49). So far, he is proved right. The sudden introduction of the *Alternative Service Book* for the Church of England was certainly no panacea, but Anglicans cannot know (because they have not researched) whether modern rites have arrested decline or, in fact, caused it.

Martin's assertion that ecumenism is 'associated with weakness' is equally worthy of attention. So far as Martin is concerned, denominational collaboration is unlikely to 'make much difference'. Besides, there is no

---

[2] Newbigin's ecclesiology could be justly characterized as Evangelical, adopting a hostile and negative stance on Christianity's relationship with post-Enlightenment culture.

sociological evidence that competition between denominations impedes the overall mission of the church, even if it is theologically and ecclesiologically undesirable. Martin also rejects the 'less means more' argument: that if only the churches could lose financially draining church buildings, clergy and so on, there would be resources to do more. He cites some examples of Finnish churches, which are fantastically equipped and resourced but otherwise comparatively empty; only 4 per cent of the population attend church on average, dropping to 0.5 per cent in the inner cities. The other strategies discussed are handled in a more polemical way. Martin rejects liberalizing trends in theology, ranging from left-wing proclamations to process theology. Finally, he also dismisses the recovery of communitarian models of the church as a viable strategy, believing that it does not really cut into the problem.

The conclusion of Martin's essay is as an eloquent apologia for the parish church as one will ever read from a sociologist: a homily, if you will. Writing out of a deep sociological consciousness that is richly informed through practical theology, he notes that, despite so many social trends moving against the parish church, it nevertheless retains strengths and virtues. He points out that:

> ...many of the networks of charity, of voluntary work and of the arts, especially music, link up with the social network of the parish...then there is latent 'folk' religion which....does have some kind of focus in the parish church, notably through rites of passage...the parish church [also] offers some kind of meaning which is embodied architecturally...it [is] often the only non-utilitarian building in certain areas. It is *there*...[suggesting that] people are still in some ways located, whatever social or geographical mobility does to them...[enabling] them to retain a sense of place, a sense of origin, a sense of continuity...[this] goes back several hundred years. (Martin, 1988, p. 51)

One might accuse Martin of preaching at this point, but that would be unfair. But in terms of the theology and sociology on its own ground, Martin is again ahead of his time here, quite consciously writing a language of enchantment, imagination and nostalgia into the discipline. It is this sort of work that makes Martin's sociology and practical theology so engaging and persuasive. It is a practical theology and sociology rooted in the contextual situation of the churches, helping them to meet triumph and tragedy in social trends and statistics, to deconstruct the academic and cultural trends that impact belief, and to inculcate the wisdom of discernment.

In Martin's inductive thinking, the sociology of religion emerges as an attempt at categorization – 'establishing normative epochs' for meaning (D'Costa, 1996). It concerns itself with describing phenomena in commonsensical ways, creating categories of meaning and knowledge in order to give a 'social' account of what it sees. Thus, 'religion' tends to be treated like a 'thing' – an 'object' of scientific analysis – and deconstructed accordingly. Correspondingly, religion is broken down into its (alleged) constituent parts (for example, sacred–profane and so on) or referred to in functional terms (such as 'social legitimization', 'projection' and so on). Like many modernist human sciences however, it often fails to see *itself* as a construction of reality – social or otherwise. As Catherine Bell points out, 'that we construct "religion" and "science" is not the main problem: that we forget we have constructed them in our own image – that is a problem' (Bell, 1996, p. 188).

In saying this, Bell is suggesting that a 'pure' description of phenomena is not possible. Any good inductive theological strategist would know this. But scholars in both the human sciences and theology are engaged in an interpretative task and describe what they see according to the prescribed rules of their grammar of assent. Sociology of religion has often tended to assume a humanist-oriented perspective which has sometimes imagined itself to be 'neutral'. Thus, sociologists describe what they see, whilst theologians and religious people are said to 'ascribe' meaning to the same phenomena. On the other hand, those who have had religious experiences feel that what they experience is 'real', and the sociological account is therefore deemed to be at best complementary and at worst unrepresentative. Invariably, both approaches forget that 'religion' is a complex word with no agreed or specific definition. It is the task of the inductive theological strategist to understand the present, seek the wisdom of the past and, in so doing, change the future.

Reflexive Religion and Contemporary Culture

To return to contemporary culture, we are now in a position to reinstate the normality of religious practice as primary material with which theology should be rightly concerned. The danger of being preoccupied solely with a theological stratagem for engaging with contemporary culture is the possibility of assuming that the primary locus of religious activity is organized (in churches) and easily observed. But, in reality, any post-associational (Western) society has hundreds of different outlets and expressions of spirituality and vernacular religion. For example, Flory and Miller's recent work draws attention to the practice of tattooing within Evangelical youth subcultures. Despite the clear biblical prohibitions on marking the body (Lev. 19: 28), the authors have uncovered new attitudes to baptism that are countercultural and yet pro-foundly Christian (Flory and Miller, 2000, p. 15). Granted, the connection between baptism and tattooing may not strike one as being immediately obvious, but Flory and Miller are able to show that, just as baptism is an invisible mark (of the cross, and usually on the forehead) so tattooing can, in certain types of youth counterculture, be a deliberately visible and indelible mark that signifies the promises and fruits of baptism: repentance, rebirth, and belonging. In this way, the tattoo performs the same task as the sign of the cross with water and oil; it is the outward sign of an inward grace. Similarly, Grimes has recently drawn attention to the vernacular spiritual responses to the Estonia ferry disaster of 1994, in which several hundred lives were lost (Grimes, 2003). Once again, the shaping of religious experience in response to traumatic events is discovered to be a delicate fusion of 'official' and 'operant' religion, in which the culture of grief and loss is reified into a newly constituted spiritual expression.

These two examples, though apparently slight, lead us to a provisional observation – namely that any assessment of adequate theological engagements with contemporary culture must rest on three specific tests. First is the extent to which such a theology is *reflexive* within modernity. Second is the ability of that theology to cope with *events* that are basically outside its control or obvious purview. Third is the degree to which such a theology is prepared to *engage* in empathetic dialogue with culture, listen and take account of the views of others. Each of these characteristics assumes that theology (and ecclesiology) can no longer afford to sit on its dignity. Nor can the discipline of theology judge the world or other disciplines from a position of privilege. In other words, theology should be capable of risking itself in all kinds of social, intellectual and cultural intercourse, since it depends, to a large extent, on a quality of engagement for its value as a public discipline.

To test this further, we now turn to one of the most seminal and defining global events in the twenty-first century, namely the events of 11 September 2001. Almost everyone will have their own personal recollections of this day – where they were, how they heard the news, what they did and how they reacted in the aftermath. I arrived home that day for my youngest son's fifth birthday party. I had been at a conference all day and was quite unaware of the news. When I walked into the house, at around 5.15p.m., I was prepared for the usual bunfight. But instead of the frantic celebratory atmosphere, the mood was sombre, anxious and uncertain. Nobody quite knew what was happening – only that a lot of people had died that morning, and that you had to keep watching repeats of sparse news footage to drink in the magnitude of the events.

Earlier in the day, a colleague in Connecticut, about two hours' drive from New York, had just started a seminar on Jewish–Christian–Muslim relations, hosted by Hartford Theological Seminary, a renowned research institute. By 9a.m. the seminar had stopped, and the leaders of different faiths had gathered around a TV to watch the breaking news. By noon, they had moved to the chapel to offer collective prayer, united in their disbelief and shock, and yet bound together by faith. The outcome of that day is a remarkable book called, unsurprisingly, *11 September: Religious Perspectives on the Causes and Consequences* (Markham and Abu-Rabi', 2002), in which theologians reflect on the events and their significance.

Theologians are often not the best people to reflect on events; their eyes are more usually fixed on the timeless and on those select issues that might affect the future of faith. But 11 September is one of those pivotal moments in time that prods theologians and asks them what they are doing to facilitate dialogue and understanding across the faiths, especially when one of the underlying causes of 11 September centres on contested sacred space many thousands of miles distant.

Ian Markham, one of the authors and editors of the book, identifies four major responses to (or discourses surrounding) the 11 September attacks. The first is the mainstream American interpretation that sees the assault on the World Trade Center and the Pentagon as an attack on freedom, democracy and the American way of life. The second response understands the attacks to be an indirect assault on Israel by Arab terrorists. A third response by some Americans is to see the other side of this claim and adopt a more empathetic attitude to the plight of the Palestinians, and therefore question American foreign policy in the Middle East. Fourth, a significant number of Americans adopt a 'mainstream' Christian fundamentalist stance and understand the attacks of 11 September to be, in part, the judgement of God upon an increasingly secular and liberal America. God, in other words, has allowed this to happen in order to punish America for its national sins and immorality. Such views were faithfully recorded in a discussion between Pat Robertson and Jerry Falwell, with Falwell claiming in a live television broadcast that '[to] all of them who have tried to secularize America, I point the finger in their face and say, "You helped this happen".'

As Markham points out, there is little dialogue taking place between these groups and distinct discourses, and interreligious conversations that might foster better understanding are still relatively rare occurrences. But, if there is to be any real hope, institutions and faiths must begin to take responsibility for promoting such dialogue. This is all well and good, but I wonder whether there is room for a fifth mode of discourse at the table – that of the ordinary Americans and their responses to 11 September?

When I was next in New York myself, I caught a taxi from the public library down to the General Theological Seminary. I chatted with the driver as we dodged the traffic and asked what she had been doing on the day. She recalled her bafflement at the plumes of smoke coming from downtown Manhattan and how, when the roads had become gridlocked, a man selling newspapers ran out to her cab and told her to turn on the radio. When she realized what was happening, she set off for the Twin Towers and began ferrying people, but soon the roads became blocked completely. 'It was then', she said, 'that people started drifting past me in slow files, like a kind of well-ordered biblical exodus.'

Take a trip round Manhattan now, and the fencing surrounding the World Trade Center Church is festooned with photographs, messages, flowers and candles. Up near Bleeker Street, a shop selling ceramics has appropriated a whole street corner and covered the fencing with individual glazed tiles that carry messages of grief, hope and peace. Brightly decorated, the tiles have turned a major road into a shrine. In fact, almost everywhere you turn in downtown Manhattan, you can see a flag, a candle, a picture or a message. The vernacular religion of New Yorkers – which the British became familiar with at Hillsborough and after the death of the Princess of Wales – is everywhere to be seen. At the heart of this most secular city, religion seems to be leaking out on to the streets. But what are we to make of this?

In a recent collection of essays, Peter Grimes suggests that there are three approaches to ritual that demand theological attention. The first conceives of ritual as unchanging and being almost independent of human agency. In such a view, ritual is 'highly symbolic acting', covering the annual and transitional points of life. Exponents of this outlook include Victor Turner and Mary Douglas. A second view regards ritual as focusing on the 'changeless', with 'high rituality' now becoming immersed in everyday life, especially for those on the margins of society. A third view places an emphasis on performance and process that then defines actors. In other words, the ritual is assessed through its capacity to help shape the social construction of reality when that reality is itself shattered or challenged. Thus, in terms of event-driven theological reflection, a reflexive form of theological engagement that takes a serious account of people's experience has more to commend it, especially in terms of its capacity to discern how and why operant religion or vernacular spirituality operates in response to traumatic events.

Grimes, noting how society responds to events such as the Estonia ferry disaster, suggests that ethnographies that explore religion and society reveal several things. First, the church continues to provide rites and other mourning tools that provide shape and meaning for society. Second, in public memory the church buildings continue to serve as sacred places. Third, priests and ministers continue to function as symbolic representatives and ritual actors in social situations. Fifth, for many individuals, lighting a candle is a symbolic action. Sixth, church bells have resonant symbolic functions in times of grief and solace. Seventh, the significance of prayers and orchestrated silence has a public value far beyond the meaning that can be intended (Grimes, 2003, p. 191). Whilst this does not amount to an especially sharp theory of religion in public life, the commonsensical nature of the observations should not be underestimated. The treatment of ritual reminds theologians that religion is public and is part of the cultural furniture; it is a resource for more than just the faithful. Correspondingly, a theology of engagement needs to be continually committed to dialogue, overhearing that is, patient and attentive listening to the conversations of the world in which the churches and theology are habitually not included, and to an encounter and event-based mode of praxis.

That said, and to return to the events of 11 September, it would not be unfair to suggest that, for most New Yorkers, the dominant mode of discourse in the wake of 9/11 continues to be one of incomprehension. On one of my earlier trips past Ground Zero in 2002, a woman who had lived in New York for 20 years turned to me and said: 'I can't believe they did that. All those people in that building. Why? I can't believe it.' Some years on, I suspect she still speaks for most Americans. And it is not difficult to see why. The sudden and violent removal of the Twin Towers has left a permanent visual scar on the New York skyline and on the collective memory of its inhabitants. They grieve not just for their people, but for their city and its wounds. They are still a people numb with shock; they cannot believe what they no longer see.

The reactions of theologians to 11 September are as diverse as they are interesting. Consider, for example, this response to the events from a Radical Orthodox perspective:

> I had been attending a conference on paradise that day when I heard the news.... The shadow of the twin towers of the World Trade Center stretch across this whole work, yet I have remained silent about the events in the United States on 11 September 2001. That demands an explanation, on moral grounds. I am not certain I can ever provide such an explanation...I could not weave...11 September into my

narrative as if I understood the part it played in the unfolding logic of 'true religion'.... (G. Ward, 2003, p. 154).

Events, in other words, seem to confound the Radical Orthodox perspective. And this particular event comfortably neutralizes the 'outnarrating' agenda that lies at the heart of the theological movement. In contrast, however, Markham and Abu-Rabi''s contribution to understanding the events is located in dialogue, listening and engagement. Starting with 'events' as 'pivotal moments' that can change theology, Markham recognizes that moments outside the separate world of theology can have a profound impact on its course and weight as a discipline and field. He sees dialogue (not just talking) as an essential component in constructing a new theology that can cope with the cataclysmic events of 9/11 (Markham and Abu-Rabi', 2002, p. 206). But what makes the book all the more theologically rich is the variety of perspectives that are brought into dialogue with one another and also with the events of 11 September. Jack Ammerman's essay explores the theological priority of moving from data collection to documentation, and ensuring that ethnography is at the centre of any future theological reflection on the events. Nancy Ammerman examines the vitality of religion and social capital exhibited in the wake of the tragedy. Perspectives from Ibrahim Abu-Rabi' and Ingrid Mattson critique the role of the violent Islamic praxis.

Is there any hope of these discourses about 11 September leading to something more? As I have already hinted, I suspect the answer lies with the ordinary American people. But it also lies in being prepared to engage with others on a basis of mutuality and exchange. Furthermore, and as Ian Markham points out, such engagements may be costly and may themselves turn into transformative encounters rather than static exchanges. In 'overhearing' the world of another, one is naturally invited to reconsider the foundations of one's own beliefs. To truly engage will be to change and to discover something of the richness and diversity in the traditions of others, as well as the depths and reflexivity of one's own (Markham, 2003, pp. 8–15). Equally, a practical theology of engagement needs to consider that there are moments when assimilation is appropriate; when resistance is essential; and when dialogue, encounter and deliberately conceived 'overhearing' are vital, if a larger understanding is to be arrived at (ibid., pp. 48–56).

If I may offer a simple illustration of this at a practical ecclesial level, I recall a visit I made in 2002 to a small city in the Mid-West to audit a college for a British university. I go every year, and our hosts, always most gracious in their hospitality, duly escorted us to their favourite restaurant. Now, it turned out that most of the staff at the restaurant were Muslim (or at least Middle Eastern), and on 13 September 2001, several large black sedans had rolled up to the premises and taken the staff away for questioning. Their families had no idea where they were taken to, and no idea when they would be back. The usual courtesy telephone call to one's attorney seems to have been set aside. The shroud of 'national security' in the wake of the attacks seemed to snuff out any talk of civil liberty. (Just recently, Congress has passed a bill allowing the government to 'monitor' all cellphone calls.) But with no staff, the business could not run and was in danger of closing. A local church leader, hearing of the restaurant's plight, arranged for local Christian volunteers to help run the restaurant until the Muslims were released. This duly happened after several weeks, but the church, meanwhile, had kept the restaurant viable.

I offer this story because the Muslims and the Christians in this small city had had little to do with each other up until this point. It was a prime example of events causing what Markham calls 'overhearing' in engagement; this is the praxis of deeper listening. My guess is that had this taken place in Britain, most Christians would have written to their MP and protested, but the business would have closed due to lack of staff meanwhile. In other words, the contours of 'civic religion' run differently and deeply in America, and they appear to be shared across faiths: respect for your neighbour, and a belief in their future and yours, together. Granted, it is not much of a discourse, but it is a sign of hope when people of different faiths can come together over a shared and common interest, even if it is only lunch at an American diner.

Theological Engagement

The burden of this chapter has been to explore the potential and limits of three types of theological engagement with contemporary culture. Granted, Milbank, Boeve and Martin could each be said to exceed the category into which they have been placed. All three are, in fact, richer and more sophisticated than Berger's categorizations allow. However, as a guide to the task of engagement, Berger's work serves its purpose. We can see that Boeve's reflexivity is well motivated and does not necessarily lead to an ecclesial or theological impoverishment. Milbank's reassertion of tradition – a fusion of the premodern with the postmodern – is no less engaging, even if many will struggle to articulate what kind of church this theological agenda actually envisages. (Radical Orthodoxy is, strangely, somewhat impotent when it comes to looking at ecclesial vision and the fruit that might issue from such a daring ensemble of theological perspectives.) David Martin's strategic thinking, more sociologically informed than the work of Nicholas Healy, takes the grounded experience of the church seriously as a major component within the structuring of theology and the life of the church. It begins with engagement and consistently leads to a rich form of *phronesis*.

However, ecclesiologically and in terms of theological engagements with culture, I suspect that a fusion of reflexivity (or limited reductionism) and inductive approaches will be the principal mode of orientation for theology and the churches for the future. As I have already hinted, Martin's inductive strategy can work for the church, perhaps producing materials that complement or form practical or pastoral theology, or various boundaries for ecclesiology. This is because sociology tries to offer empiricism married to imagination – forming, exploring and critiquing social reality no less than religious tradition and theology. How strange, then, that Radical Orthodox has worked so hard to distance theology from the social sciences in order to preserve the 'purity' of theology. Milbank's book, *Theology and Social Theory*

(1990) still remains one of the key rallying posts for the Radical Orthodoxy camp. It is, in many ways, a brilliant and sharp book yet, as I have argued before, it is also a 'hermeneutic of suspicion about hermeneutics of suspicion': strangely anti-liberal and anti-modern; oddly pro-Christendom. Whilst there is undoubtedly plenty to admire from Radical Orthodoxy, its trajectory is troubling in places. Subsequent offerings from the Radical Orthodoxy camp have attacked the 'discipline' of religious studies or emphasized that all social sciences are 'descended' from theology, either as legitimate heirs or as distant bastard children. Such critiques possibly have their merits, but they lack generosity.

For example, what father or mother tells each of their children, throughout their lives, that all their achievements are really those of their parents? Or that without them, they would not exist, so, please, always acknowledge your debt and know your place? Radical Orthodoxy does not argue so much for the restoration of theology as 'queen of the sciences' as it does for the church and theology being the father of us all. Even if this is entirely true – which I doubt – what about some considered praise for other 'disciplines' that can now teach theology, inform it, civilize it, dialogue with it or even outnarrate it? Is theology so small and shy, or old and grumpy, as to be unable to acknowledge the breadth and depth of other constructions of reality, even if it still wishes to be considered as revealed? David Martin's work offers a sociology and inductive theology in the service of the church, but in a spirit of gentility and humility. It does not threaten but, as we have seen, it does challenge. Theology must take account of such voices if it wishes to be in any way public and 'practical'.

In contrast, it would hardly be unfair to characterize much of Radical Orthodoxy as profoundly docetic: a kind of disembodied rhetoric that, for all its eloquence and brilliance, lacks any real earthiness. In its dismissive attitude towards other strains of theology and the social sciences, it also sets itself apart from, and above, other potential conversational partners. It is a character-istically tough and abrasive form of theological discourse, despite its playfulness. This, I suppose, makes it a kind of pushy theological bullying accompanied by an element of self-justification. Furthermore, because it almost never starts from where people are, it fails to produce any kind of ecclesial vision or realism into which individuals and communities might wander. So where does all this lead us? Mudge, in his vision for sociology and theology fused together to form a critical ecclesiology, suggests that the problem with Radical Orthodoxy is that:

> ...[it] risks a kind of institutional docetism. I fear as well that Milbankian communities are going to be unable to communicate with Christian communities of other persuasions, but only with other Milbankian communities, a prospect which looks very like the birth of some new communion. [But] I want churches to share many of the common preoccupations of a world that human science is helping to make one. We may all find affinities between ecclesiological social science and social theories of other kinds, owing, it may be, to common origins or common aims. But whether or not this happens, we want ecclesiological social theory to hold other viewpoints in respect; to be in conversation with them. They can help keep us honest. (Mudge, 2001, pp. 6–7)

So Radical Orthodoxy is indeed a curious phenomenon in theology when one considers that there are many forms of ecclesial correlation for each of Berger's three types of theology. The deductive, reductive and inductive, in turn, have many forms of ecclesiological manifestation that express their theological priorities. But to press the question again, where would the church of Radical Orthodoxy be, and what would it look like? The mere fact that we don't know the answer to this question suggests more than just aloofness; it also points to a reticence, possibly a lack of commitment, and arguably to a deficiency in engagement. One can imagine several kinds of church that embody a deductive theological stratagem: Evangelical, conservative or even Catholic. Likewise, reductive churches that embody radical or contextual traditions are common-place, especially within the liberal Christian tradition. Ecclesiologies that embody an inductive theological stratagem are more difficult to identify, but they probably find expression in Pentecostalism, Quakerism and in other spheres where spiritual experience is a valued theological priority.

But it is simply not easy to imagine, let alone locate, the church of Radical Orthodoxy. For all the talk of 'outnarrating' modernity, Radical Orthodoxy is a curiously unengaged theological movement. Like its Tractarian ancestors, it lives in the world of aesthetics, imagination and play; it splices together the premodern and the postmodern, and opposes the modern; and it is usually above conversation and beyond comprehension. Such an end point is no place from which to begin a strategy of theological and ecclesial engagement with culture. More listening, humility and openness will be needed if the churches are to recover their poise in the public sphere as agents of social transformation and socio-spiritual renewal. It is to this exercise we now turn in Part II of this book where we attempt to sketch a vision for theology and education that genuinely engages with cultural complexity.

PART II
ORDINARY THEOLOGY

Chapter 4

Acuity, Clarity and Practical Wisdom

Introduction

A theologian, on being approached by an earnest young student, was asked: 'What is your methodological starting point?' The theologian replied simply; 'A theologian is always beginning in the middle of things' (R. Williams, 2000, p. viii.). The wit, clarity and acuity of the reply says something important about the nature of theology and about what it is engaging with. In this chapter we now turn to considering the nature of theological formation by exploring it in relation to contemporary culture through the discipline of practical theology and paying particular attention to the shape of theological education. The study, like the discipline of practical theology itself, is critically reflective, refractive, meditative, praxis-based, searching and inquiring. It seeks to challenge and transform existing understandings of theology, theological education and contemporary culture in ways that are empathetic and constructive.

We might begin by noting that, oddly, the history of specialized theological education, at least in England, is curiously brief. When the bishop of Gloucester tested his clergy in 1551, of 311 priests only 171 could recall all ten of the commandments from the Old Testament. In 1530 William Tyndale complained that few priests could recite the Lord's Prayer or translate it into English (Percy, 2001, p. 87). But perhaps this is not so surprising, since there were no seminaries or theological colleges in which to train priests. Indeed, technically, there were no degrees in theology or divinity to be studied at Oxford or Cambridge, since what we now call 'classics' and 'philosophy' were the only subjects read. Theological colleges emerged in the nineteenth century and were a response to the increasing secularization of the universities, contemporary culture and part of the general movement within many professions to separate out specialist institutions for training within general education. As medical and law schools emerged, theological colleges were born too, shaping the identity of a 'profession' that had, hitherto, seldom relied on specialist knowledge for the practice of theology – what we now call 'professional ministry'.

This chapter is not, however, about the origin and development of theological colleges. Undoubtedly, it would be interesting to subject religious seminaries to a thorough Foucauldian analysis, but that is beyond the scope of our enquiry. However, beginning with a brief discussion of formal (professional) theological training is no accident. Many of the assumptions about the character of theology are formed, in seminaries, not by the theology itself, but by the underlying (and normally undisclosed) culture of education. Sometimes this culture is practised unwittingly by the staff, perhaps under the guise of supporting a particular dogmatic or ecclesial position that reflects the values of the college. At other times, the college may deliberately set out to unsettle the beliefs of students, challenging them and questioning them, acting as an agent of disturbance or as a catalyst for change. Much of this can be observed almost casually in most seminaries, and yet, oddly, it is seldom reflected upon.

In this chapter I want to draw away from the conventional antinomies that characterize most debates about the nature of theology and contemporary culture, theological formation and education. Typically, these antinomies pitch liberal against conservative, traditional against progressive, dogmatic against radical, and more besides. To be sure, this kind of dialectic has its place in educational philosophy; for example, in tension, students may discover a middle path. But such assumptions can presume too much; that this method (which can be, at times, aggressive), automatically leads to the student reaching their own position of accommodation. This may happen, of course, but equally it may not. Some students may become dissatisfied with the polarity and conclude that the antinomy renders the subject itself to be highly suspect.

The genesis of this argument lies in a simple, commonplace idea within the philosophy of education: there can be no teaching without learning. Or, put another way, excellent teachers must first become learners. However, beneath the surface of this apparently obvious observation lies a penumbra of questions about the relationship between teachers and learners, amidst the art and craft of education. In the field of theological studies, and in the education and formation of the church more generally, those who hold the office of 'teacher' are seldom perceived or identified as learners. Education is, in other words, a process in which the teacher disseminates knowledge to learners. The learners seldom obtain the opportunity to instruct their teachers or to enter into any kind of serious theological dialogue. But this is, as we noted in Chapter 1, not surprising in a culture where the church can sometimes speak of itself in terms of perfection, indefectability and God-given authority, justified by a range of terms such as '*ex cathedra*', 'infallible' and 'revealed'. In an educational economy of this kind, knowledge is immutable; learning can only mean 'banking' knowledge, and adapting or applying it to specific situations. Indeed, the etymology of the term 'seminary' (that is, a place of formation and training for religious professionals, leaders and teachers) is closely linked to the more static term 'dissemination' – the 'spreading around' of seeds or knowledge.

Whilst I readily acknowledge that this is a characterization of sorts, it is hardly unfair. Many who teach in the church – leaders, educators and pastors – are trained and formed in an environment that assumes that the task of education is to implant (correct) knowledge in those contexts where they minister. The training process does not assume that a congregation or context will be able to teach the teacher. The training process does not teach people how to continue learning. Any consideration of what constitutes teaching and learning within a discipline is invariably timely. In this section, our exploration is concerned with the meaning of theological education (especially focusing on ministerial formation – the relationship between theological colleges or seminaries and the churches that the ministers serve in) and how its definition and scope can both be broadened and deepened.

Correspondingly, the style of this chapter (continuing the strategy of pursuing a meditative critical–reflective or refractive approach) is intended to resonate with, and reach, a theological public who may already have concerns about theological training and formation. Throughout the United Kingdom, churches have had to face a series of challenges that have raised questions about their nature and purpose. Financial difficulties, secularization, critical engagement with traditionalism, lack of resources, disenchantment, consumerism and other forces have all played their part in creating a climate of uncertainty for churches. Educationally, one might say that many churches and denominations are now finding that they still possess (and cherish) the answers to questions that no-one is asking any more. It is my contention that addressing the crisis in teaching and learning (and their relationship) within the church is an important and necessary agenda. The guiding assumptions that have shaped ministerial training and formation are in serious need of urgent reform. To paraphrase Paulo Freire, the time for oscillating between naive and ironic (or shrewd) readings of the church is past, for both will maintain the status quo. Only a revolution will do.

But a revolution will depend on having some understanding of what theological education could or should be. Clearly, this type of theological education could only be a small contribution to a debate – a debate, incidentally, that is hotly contested within the churches. But the contribution is intended as a meditative–critical reflection on the possibilities for theological education, and although primarily focused on the concerns of Anglicans, the insights nonetheless may have wider implications. In advocating a strategy and philosophy of education-for-change, I offer a thesis that is intended to counter and question the prevailing assumptions about theological education in church and seminary culture, namely the expectation that theological education is there to inform, support and consolidate tradition – but not to change it.

In contrast, I hold that theology that fails to be critically reflective and transformative is not only a failure to inculcate advances in educational philosophy and practice, but an actual betrayal of the Christian tradition itself and a failure of nerve in the field of theology. In relation to this, it is important to understand that there is still, in many universities, an implicit and residual relationship between the structure and shaping of degree courses and the kind of theology that is also pursued in theological colleges. A number of older university departments in Britain can still (comfortably) accommodate trainee ministers within their degree programme (as part of their training), suggesting that 'Divinity' lives on in the academy. Newer university departments that tend to concentrate on 'religious studies' tend to have little, if any, connection with theological colleges. So there is a kind of double impoverishment at work here. Even where theological colleges and their ordinands are strongly linked to university departments of theology and religious studies, it tends to be the older, more established departments that offer 'Divinity' degrees.

The type of research offered fits in with Van der Ven's first, second and third types (1998: cf. the Introduction): discovery, theoretical–integrative research and applied research. But, critically, it has an impact on the fourth dimension of scholarship: teaching. It is this matrix that is assessed through the methodology of practical theology. Furthermore, and mindful that my concern and subject is primarily the Anglican Church, I nonetheless want to suggest that my own use of the word 'research' in this essay means 're-search', which is only to say that I take a new and original look at a very old subject. The relationship between teaching and learning, and their actual definition, in theology and in the churches, forms the crucible of concern that governs the reflections in this chapter. It is my contention that seminary education simply misunderstands the nature of education, culture and the church itself – a primary arena of shared learning that is a 'community of practice'.

The implications, however, for epistemology, practice, transformation and development, should be far-reaching. A piece of re-search is, ultimately, a re-view, re-consideration and a re-turn – perhaps leading to a revolution; this is comparable to the transformative agenda of practical theology at work. I am conscious that to reflect on theological education is, ultimately, to offer a critique of the definition and scope of the actual discipline of theology. In other words, a critical–meditative chapter of this kind, focused on the meaning of theology and educational practice in relation to contemporary culture, is an inherently and unavoidable political critique of the term 'theology' – what it means, who does it and where it is to be found. But that last sentence is something for the reader to make a judgement upon sometime later.

To shape this sketch a little more, I want to briefly return to the recent writing of Edward Norman, an Anglican priest and scholar, former Reith lecturer and noted conservative and scourge of liberalism. In his *Secularisation* (2002), Norman attacks the church for its uncritical and wholesale embracing of modernism. His study of secularization is, by the publisher's own admission, '*not* a systematic attempt to describe and identify every feature of the fading religious landscape'. It is more of a *Tract for the Times* than a methodical appraisal of religion in the crucible of contemporary life. Norman's book will confirm the mindset of all those who are 'saddened by the decline of institutional religion in Britain', but it offers little by way of comfort to those who might want to extricate the church from the milieu of modernity.

Norman writes with clarity and candour. At times the argument is sweeping and irresistible, and yet it is always presented in the most economic prose. Norman has no time for the 'is the glass half-full or half-empty?' debate when it comes to the Church of England. For Norman, the Church of England is not so much a sacred vessel as a kitchen colander – so full of holes that it can hold nothing. Moreover, the Church of England has brought about its own downfall by its wholesale accommodation of vapid liberalism, which has inevitably had a deleterious effect on its identity, authority, teaching, truth, leadership and ministry.

Thus, Norman can confidently assert that the problem behind falling church attendances is 'the absence of a systematic teaching office' which is 'at the root of all their difficulties' (note 'theirs', not 'ours'). He continues:

...when an organism cannot identify its enemies it gets taken over by them...the body needs immunology...it has long been a feature of modern Anglicanism [that] it cannot, as an institution, resist the adoption of alien ideas and attitudes, of false doctrine, when it does not have an immune system. (Norman, 2002, p. 121)

And so Norman goes on to attack 'modern' spiritual relativism, 'decades of reductionism and scepticism' and the like. It seems that only Catholics, who adhere to an indefectible teaching office, and Evangelicals, who are 'loyal to scripture', are capable of resisting Norman's imagined invasion of cancerous liberalism and secularism.

Some will doubtless applaud this less than subtle attack on the church and feel that it rings true and hits home (hard). But a thesis of this kind is very shaky for all kinds of reasons. Here are just a few. First, it assumes that the (alleged) present crisis is a new one and a particular creature of liberalism or modernity. But, if this is so, how are we to account for miniscule church attendances in centuries that pre-dated the Enlightenment? Second, Norman misconstrues the heart of liberalism, which is to engage faith with modernity; it is a way of holding and valuing Christianity and rarely an evacuation of its content. Far from being vapid, liberalism attempts to be creatively faithful to Christ in a changing world. Third, Norman's polemic, for all its poise, represents an odd kind of *alliance* with secularization. Like a number of Catholic and Evangelical commentators, he seems to need to believe in secularization more than ever in order to reclaim the church for his own agenda. As I have remarked before, after newspaper editors, the only people who really *truly* believe in secularization are scholar-priests like Norman, who then seek to make educational, doctrinal and ecclesial capital out of opposing it (Percy, 2001). Put more sharply, the attack on secularism is really only another way of opposing liberalism, which is then turned into a crusade for the imposition of conservativism, which is held up as the guarantor of truth, teaching and authority.

In contrast to this agenda, I want to suggest that an important key to a practical and effective theology that engages with contemporary culture lies in hospitality rather than exclusivity. Or, put another way, we might say that the only way to develop a critical conversation with contemporary culture is through discerning accommodation. Henri Nouwen has suggested that (theological and spiritual) hospitality consists of:

...the creation of a free space where the stranger can enter and become a friend instead of an enemy. Hospitality is not to change people, but to offer them space where change can take place. It is not to bring men and women over to our side, but to offer freedom not disturbed by dividing lines. It is not to lead our neighbour into a corner where there are no alternatives left, but to open up a wide spectrum of options for choice and commitment. (Nouwen, 1975, p. 51)

This leads us to an early but critical point in our argument about the nature of engaging theology within contemporary culture. Can it be a discipline that listens? Can it be a place that receives the stories and experiences of strangers? Can it practise genuine hospitality? The turn towards stories and narratives at this point is no accident. The ability to listen to, and receive, the stories of others is one of the primary ways in which the practice of reception and hospitality can be identified, since it indicates the degree of openness within the host. As Daniel Taylor suggests:

> ... story gives us a kind of knowledge that abstract reasoning cannot. One of the advantages of *story knowledge* is its concreteness and specificity. Stories give us individualised people in specific times and places doing actual things. Rationality tends to sidestep the messy particulars to deal directly with the generalised concepts behind the particulars. In doing so, it often strip-mines reality, washing away tons of seemingly useless details to get to the small golden nuggets of truth .... (Taylor, 1996, p. 30)

Of course, one of Paulo Freire's aims was to help people achieve 'deep literacy' – to become aware of the far from innocent forces that can shape lives and institutions. Freire argued that deep literacy comes through dialogue. It is in conversation and reflection that we become aware of how we are *determined* by our cultural inheritance. Moving beyond that can be achieved if we are willing to critically question what we think we know (Morisy, 1997, p. 66).

'Story knowledge' will be seen by many to be a weak substitute for the concreteness and certainty of doctrine and creedal formulae. And yet the power of stories for conveying theological material should not be underestimated. Jesus, after all, spoke in parables. Moreover, there is substantial evidence to suggest that churches are (in a memorable phrase coined by James Hopewell) 'storied dwellings'. Churches are cultures that are shaped by world-views and particular kinds of theological stories that continue to have an impact on, and resonance amongst, individuals and communities. As a result of this, a real focus on the kinds of stories that congregations both store and tell can reveal much about the church's theological priorities and its praxis.

Having made these points, it is important to acknowledge that some, at least, would have considerable ecclesial and theological concerns in inculcating such insights into the life of the church. If all churches do is receive the stories of strangers, what else are they there for? I suspect that, at worst, some would fear that an uncritical adoption of the philosophy outlined above could lead to a vapid relativity in terms of definition and distinctiveness. Churches do (and must) stand on some kind of authority that is supported by its corpus of knowledge. However, this brief excursion into one aspect of contemporary educational philosophy highlights a major problem in considering authority within ecclesial communities. The problem, simply put, is one of reception rather than content. If churches are unwilling to embrace new (more collaborative and less doctrinaire) philosophies of learning and teaching, then the authority of the church within contemporary culture itself is no longer likely to be *received* in the same way. Being more imposing (even if this is for the sake of a predetermined unity) is no substitute for the liberation of reception and enabling – even if that does lead to distinctiveness and difference.

So, is there some middle ground between Norman and Freire? Is there a philosophy of education that treats tradition and imagination with equal seriousness? Is there a way of conceiving of theological education that respects tradition and truth whilst also acknowledging the value of doubt, criticism and openness? Part of the answer to these questions may lie in an apparently unlikely place, since the educational philosophy that I want to propose in this essay is liberal in character. Let me say at once that I do not use the term 'liberal' as an opposite to 'conservative'. Rather, I use it in the most constructive sense. I see liberalism as an 'open frame of reference', a way of regarding truth and valuing wisdom, rather than an evacuation of the content of faith or some kind of demystification. Indeed, the phrase 'frame of reference' works analogically.

As someone who was raised 'low church' in my childhood and gradually evangelicalized throughout my teens and twenties, I became very aware, even if uncritically at first, as to how many of the truths we held were controlled by prior frames of reference. For example, it is obvious that the Bible does not speak of itself at all, let alone as an infallible text. And yet 2 Timothy 3:16 would be regularly used to frame all debates about biblical reliability: 'all scripture is inspired by God . . .' was a frequently intoned mantra. But no-one ever bothered to say where the Apocrypha fitted into this, let alone mention the synoptic problem. Similarly, for debates on sexuality, where the Bible is confusing and reticent, key texts conditioned not only how we looked at the rest of the Bible, but also how we viewed the world. We were framed, and in turn we framed everything we saw.

Looking at life through a frame has its advantages; the picture remains in focus and frozen. The view never changes; only your view on the view alters. But for the curious, there are too many unanswered questions. Who made the frame? What lives and moves outside the frame? What aspects of the picture are obscured by the frame? It is at these junctures that an enquiring liberal mind and an accompanying spirituality start to take root. For myself, I soon realized that the frames of reference I was working with were too particular; to parody J.B. Phillips, 'your frame is too small'. The realization that the portrait of faith I had been staring at for most of my life actually *surrounded* me, totally (but openly, not suffocatingly) changed not only my theology, but also my spirituality. Moreover, I began to appreciate the ways in which I myself was in the picture. The frames suddenly became almost redundant; they now remain useful for capturing detail and focusing on issues, but their limits (as well as their relativity and selectivity) are recognized for what they are.

Expressed more conventionally, an authentic liberal philosophy of theological education works with boundaries, not barriers. In liberal theological education the borders of faith are open, because it is recognized that God is both outside and inside those borders. This then assumes that the only acceptable frame of reference is an open frame, which allows the viewer to look beyond the immediate and catch a glimpse of the ultimate. The missiological dimension of this is explored in writings such as Vincent Donovan's *Christianity Rediscovered* (1982) and J.V. Taylor's *The Go-Between God* (1972). Open frames of reference let God in, who is, *de facto*, not the property of the church. Or, to paraphrase Sydney Carter, 'Jesus is *not* the copyright of the church'.

Practical Theology, Ecclesiology and Formation

As I noted in the Introduction, the methodological approach to the question of theology's identity and of theological formation is drawn from the arena of practical theology. If practical theology begins anywhere at all, it is in the recognition that the nature of theology is both practical and public as it seeks to make some sense of the relationships between belief and practice, faith and the world, and church and society. As I noted at the beginning of this chapter, it is in the nature of practical theology to 'begin in the middle'. Practical theology is a listening and reflective discipline; it does not seek to be dogmatic in its engagements. For Killen and de Beer, the discipline is about a level of critical–reflective engagement with tradition:

> ... exploring individual and corporate experience in conversation with the wisdom of a religious heritage. The conversation is a genuine dialogue that seeks to hear from our own beliefs, actions, and perspectives, as well as those of the tradition. It respects the integrity of both. Theological reflection therefore may confirm, challenge, clarify, and expand how we understand our own experience and how we understand the religious tradition. The outcome is new truth and meaning for living.... (Killen and de Beer, 1994, p. viii)

This suggests that, in terms of education, aspects of practical theology closely correspond to certain types of educational philosophy. One thinks immediately of Brookfield's 'critically reflective teacher' (1995), or Van der Ven's distinction (following Levi-Strauss), between the engineer and bricoleur. The engineer systematically thinks, conceives and executes. The bricoleur, in contrast, builds something out of the disparate elements through doing, experiencing and reflecting (Van der Ven, 1998, p. 40). Clearly, theological education is more bricolage than engineering. Kathryn Tanner in describing the tasks of 'mainstream theology', almost accidentally articulates a type of practical theology (and the nature of theological education) that is fundamental to the identity of the discipline:

> The basic operation that theologians perform have a twofold character. First, theologians show an artisanlike inventiveness in the way they work on a variety of materials that do not dictate of themselves what theologians should do with them. Second, theologians exhibit a tactical cleverness with respect to other interpretations and organisations of such materials that are already on the ground.... The materials theologians work on are incredibly diverse ... theologians use a kind of tact requiring numerous ad hoc and situation-specific adjustments. In contrast to what the values of clarity, consistency and systematicity might suggest of themselves, even academic theologians do not simply follow logical deductions where they lead or the dictates of abstract principles when arriving at their conclusions. They do not construct their theological positions by applying generalities to particular cases, or emend them by

trying to reproduce the same clear meanings in the terms of a new day, so as to convey them across putatively accidental differences in circumstances and vocabulary. Instead, they operate by tying things together – the Latin meaning of *religare*, after all, is to bind.... (Tanner, 1997, p. 87ff)

Tanner's description of theological method is one of skilled and discerning praxis. Tanner displays a characteristic ease in describing the discipline of theology, locating its functioning in active formation. So practical theology becomes a critical and creative *art* – something that is created and shaped within each context and is appropriate to its environment. Within contemporary culture, it is aware that it is both culturally formed, as well as being an agent within culture for the express purposes of ongoing social formation. But this notion of practical theology being a discipline (like religion itself) that binds is also worth paying attention to. One might reasonably ask, 'Bind what, exactly?'. Certainly practical theologians are used to bringing together different materials and holding them in tension.[1] But perhaps what makes practical theology so appealing as a discipline within contemporary culture is its ability to pull together different strands of thinking and material into a new kind of relationship and purpose.

So what are the hallmarks of practical theology? In what ways does a practical theological approach constitute a method or discipline? Woodward and Pattison suggest 14 characteristics:

1   Practical theology is *transformational activity*...

2   ...not just concerned with the propositional...[it] finds *artistic and imaginative* ways of thinking and expressing pastoral theological insights...

3   *confessional and honest*...truthful about the world and religious experience...

4   *unsystematic*...it continuously has to re-engage with the fragmented realities and changes of the contemporary world and the issues it presents....

5   *truthful and committed*...[it tries] to discern the reality of situations...committed to helping people and situations change...

6   *contextual and situationally related*...explore and contribute to immediate contexts, situations and practices...

7   *socio-politically aware and committed*...[learns] from praxis-based liberationist theologies that apply the tools of suspicion to theology as well as to the social and political order...

8   *experiential*...takes contemporary people's experiences seriously as data for theological reflection, analysis and thought...

9   *reflectively based*...lived contemporary experience is an important starting point for engaging...

---

[1] If I might be use a mechanistic analogy at this point, there is something 'Gripple-like' about practical theology. A gripple is a device (varying in size) that brings broken or loose wires together. A gripple can be used to mend wire fences, but also to suspend lights or other objects using wires. Its function is (a) binding; (b) holding materials in tension; (c) supporting weights that are far greater than itself.

10 *interrogative*...[not] monolithic and instructional [but] more interested in asking good questions than...trying to confine [people] within the restraints of [tradition]...

11 *interdisciplinary*...uses...methods and insights...that are not overtly theological...

12 *analytical and constructive*...help[s] people to construct ideas about how they might change...

13 *dialectical and disciplined*...critical conversation...practical theologies hold in creative tension a number of polarities such as theory and practice, reality and ideal, what is and what ought to be, etc...

14 *skillful and demanding*...there is much to learn about how to work with different methods, types of material, situations, etc.... (Woodward and Pattison, 2000, pp. 15–16, adapted)

These methodological observations are the substantial criteria that explain how and why theology is being explored and evaluated, and also to what ends. Practical theology, in other words, is the vehicle for a critical–meditative reflection on the place and meaning of theology within the 'real' church, with special attention being paid to praxis and transformation. Two American writers distil Pattison and Woodward's categorizations into just eight hallmarks. For these authors, practical theology is:

[1] a distinct genre of theological discourse; [2] formally analogous to secular ideology; [3] grounded in a dialectic of theory and praxis; [4] works from a critical construction of the essence of a religious tradition; [5] creates distinct theological models of self and history; [6] with the help of other genres of public discourse it leads to social policy formation, decision and action; [7] establishes a mode of socialisation; [8] that is truth dependent. (McCann and Strain, 1985, p. 209; cf. Kinast, 2000)

I have already hinted that the notion of theological education as liberation (following the work of Freire) has been influential on my thinking. Education as the practice of freedom and theological education as transformative pedagogy have reshaped my views on what it means to be free and open, critically constructive, experiential, visionary, culturally reflexive, life-forming, constructive and interactive. This has partly come about through reconceiving theological education as 'conversation' – balancing the 'hermeneutics of retrieval' (as Ricoeur might say) with the 'hermeneutics of hospitality' – as Nouwen might affirm (see Astley *et al.*, 1996, p. 159) – or, put more colloquially, balancing the obligation to teach and speak with the need to listen and learn. Theologically, and following scholars such as Lindbeck (1984) and Schreiter (1985), we might say that it is useful to distinguish between *traditio* (that is, what is taught) and *tradita* (that is, how things are taught). Exactly how the church conveys its message may say more about its theology than it really knows; the mode of education may reveal what educationalists are often wont to call 'the hidden curriculum'. Some of these matters will be returned to later on, where questions of praxis can be more properly addressed, and where we return once more to the discipline of practical theology. But, for now, we turn to a deeper consideration of the work of James Fowler and James Hopewell, and its implications for 'concrete ecclesiology'.

Describing Faith: Some Perspectives

For almost any student of theological or Christian education, the standard point of departure for the voyage is James Fowler's seminal study, *Stages of Faith*. Fowler's work was written in 1981, and the book has effectively established itself as a 'classic' text for explicating the journey of faith – through the motif of stages. Fowler's work is arguably the major portal gateway into the burgeoning world of theological education, providing a reliable and incisive model of progressive understanding that appeals to educationalists and theologians alike. Fowler's work, by his own admission, is heavily influenced by the approaches of Kohlberg and Piaget and seeks to build bridges between theologians and scholars of human behaviour. Indeed, we might say that what Kohlberg and Piaget did for moral and cognitive development respectively, Fowler achieves for faith development; the subtitle of the book does not overreach itself when it states that the volume is concerned with 'the psychology of human development and the quest for meaning'. Fowler postulates that there are six stages of faith, and these need briefly describing before a foundation of critical reflection can be laid for the remainder of the chapter. It will become apparent that, whilst Fowler provides a useful starting point for reflecting on theological education, there are certain gaps in the approach, as well as particular assumptions that need to be challenged.

Fowler's first stage is the 'Intuitive-Protective': 'the fantasy-filled, imitative phase in which the child can be powerfully and permanently influenced by examples, moods, actions and stories of the visible faith . . . most typical of the child of three to seven' (Fowler, 1981, p. 133). Fowler regards this stage as being the one where the imagination is at its most explosive and productive and where logical thought does not inhibit either the visualization or actualization of belief. On the positive side, Fowler sees this faith stage as part of the birth of the imagination. More negatively, the mind of the child can be 'possessed' by the very images it produces. The key to moving on to another stage lies with the child, and is concerned with sifting fantasy from reality, and to 'know how things are'. (It is this stage, or rather the failure of a young girl to evolve from it, that is wonderfully captured in the semi-autobiographical novel of Jeanette Winterson, *Oranges Are Not The Only Fruit*, 1991.)

The second stage is the 'Mythic-Literal': 'the person begins to take on for [themselves] the stories, beliefs and observances that symbolize belonging to [their] community . . . beliefs are appropriated with literal interpretations . . . symbols are taken as one-dimensional and literal in meaning' (Fowler, 1981, p. 149). The key features of this stage are the rise of narrative and the emergence of story, drama and myth as primary vehicles of faith which, in turn, give meaning and coherence to experience. However, the stories must be 'balanced' (or fair and reciprocal, according to Fowler), such that paradox and tragedy are, by and large, excluded from this stage. Thus, a typical reciprocal story from a school assembly is this. In hell, people have plenty of food to eat, but the knives, forks and spoons that are used are too long to get the food from plate to mouth, so everyone starves, yet all the while being surrounded by food. Heaven is identical, but different in one respect only: people have learned, with the same implements, to feed each other. The story bears a resemblance to the ancient classical legend of Tantalus, from which the English language derives the word 'tantalize', although the school assembly story 'balance' is less brutal in its resolution than its classical counterpart.

The third stage, 'Synthetic-Conventional', understandably makes some of the inroads that the second stage cannot achieve. Fowler rightly assumes that, by a certain age, the child has a social network beyond the immediate family, with many new spheres demanding attention. Correspondingly, faith 'must provide a more coherent orientation in the midst of that more complex and diverse range of involvements'. It must 'synthesize values and orientation ... [and] provide a basis for identity and outlook' (ibid., p. 172). According to Fowler, the third stage still lacks a perspective where one can stand outside beliefs and reflect upon them systematically. Fowler suggests that this may not happen until a child begins to leave home, which suggests he has teenagers in mind. However, 'teenage' denotes a stereotypical mindset here, rather than an age band. The third stage has scope for rebellion and rejection but is, at the same time, looking for deeper patterns of integrity and may still be quite idealistic in orientation.

The fourth stage is described by Fowler as 'Individuative-Reflective faith' (ibid., p. 182) and is characterized by a number of key movements: from individuality to group commitment; from subjectivity to critical reflection on one's own strongly held beliefs; from self-fulfilment or self-actualization to social service; from absolutism to relativity. In this fourth stage a form of adulthood emerges that becomes self-aware of its own frames of reference and world-views, and their relative contingency. It is possible that a certain amount of deconstruction or demythologizing may take place. Correspondingly, the stage, as a stage of faith, may actually implode at this apparent point of maturity: confidence in conscious processes of thought and their ability to 'master' faith may lead to its rejection altogether. Thus, the rite of confirmation, normally offered in the Church of England at about the age of 14 as a rite of passage into adulthood, can be justly described by the sociologist David Martin as 'the Church's Leaving Certificate'.

The fifth stage, 'Conjunctive Faith', involves the development of those elements that were suppressed or overlooked in stage four. Citing Ricoeur, Fowler notes how this stage can constitute a 'second naivete', in which older symbolic power from earlier stages are now re-united with conceptualization at an adult level. In other words, there may be 'a new reclaiming and reworking of one's past ... [and] an opening to the voices of one's "deeper self" ... ' (ibid., p. 198). Fowler regards this stage as being 'unusual before mid-life', partly because the sustainability of this stage depends on the development of the ironic: 'a capacity to see and be in one's or one's group's most powerful meanings, while simultaneously recognizing that they are relative, partial and inevitably distorting apprehensions of divine reality'. In other words, this stage can subject faith to radical doubt, but without tearing apart the very fabric of belief or losing any affinity with it. There is a paradox inherent in this stage, as one would expect. Whilst this is Fowler's ultimate stage of maturity, a retreat into original religious habits and beliefs becomes possible. Adults can regress in faith, but usually know what they are doing – at least at some conscious level – and have the ability to return to the ironic and relative at any time.

The sixth stage, Universalizing, is closely related to the fifth stage but is, in Fowler's view, 'exceedingly rare': 'the persons best described by it have generated faith compositions in which their felt sense of an ultimate environment is inclusive of all being...they become incarnators and actualizers of the spirit of an inclusive and fulfilled human community' (ibid., p. 201). To illustrate the stage, Fowler chooses representatives such as Gandhi, Martin Luther King Jr, Dietrich Bonhoeffer and Dag Hammarskjöld, individuals who, in Fowler's view, cherish particularities, but only as 'vessels of the universal'. The vision narrated here is one of mystic–social connectedness, in which divine principles transform both individual lives and socio-political situations through an appeal to human futurity and transcendence.

In describing these stages, it should be immediately recognized that Fowler himself acknowledges that journeying from one to another is not a simple matter of linear progression. The formation of faith is complex: cyclical and oscillating; the movement is more typically a dynamic spiral of transformation than a matter of simple advancement. But having said that, there are some particular problems with the motif of stages, suggesting that, whilst Fowler is a useful gateway through which to forge into the territory of theological education, his work does not provide a map or vessel which offers comprehensive navigational support. Three brief points need making here.

First, Fowler's work focuses on individuals. Whilst this undoubtedly has its strengths, I suspect that it underplays the extent to which the faith communities can form faith, and, in turn, the 'stages theory' tends to ignore the significant *demands* that religious bodies can make upon believers. Put another way, there may be a nascent schizophrenia between private beliefs and public faith, with the individual selecting or screening aspects of their apparent formation. A good example of this might be assenting to a literal belief in hell, whilst at the same time expecting to be reunited with all one's 'unsaved' loved ones.

Second, although Fowler tries to distinguish between types of knowledge, he doesn't go far enough. In fact, most of the 'knowledge' that Fowler describes seems to be fairly settled and concrete; it is only the perception of it that alters the individual. A similar charge can be levelled at Freire (1973), who in critiquing the 'banking theory of knowledge' (with its deposits), treats knowledge as a mainly static, unchanging body of information. In fact, many kinds of knowledge have a life of their own (Christian tradition even talks of 'the *lively* deposit of faith'), which can continually transform the receptor. In other words, although Fowler is primarily interested in how people process knowledge, he seems to be unaware of the power of knowledge to process people. This is not mere semantics; it is an important distinction – some types of knowledge convert their receptors altogether, and do not merely move them on a stage.

Third, in failing to attend to different types of formative knowledge, Fowler manages to ignore what behavioural psychologists call 'qualia': subjective but shared experiences and knowledge of the world, such as the smell of coffee, the taste of mango or the look of love – or, come to that, the smell of incense, the taste of bread and wine at the altar rail, or the kiss of peace[2] (see also Barnett, 1990 – 'knowledge captured in action, in performance, in practice and in sheer experience'). Granted, there may be certain types of physiological, biochemical or neurological tests that can be applied which deconstruct these 'tastes', but we are not concerned with proving their existence. My point is that many aesthetic dimensions to life are forms of knowledge that are not easily described or taught (for example, the taste of coffee). And, in my view, this is particularly true in religion, where habits, apparently informal practices, visual images, sounds, symbols and what might seem to be fairly ordinary human interaction can play a significant part in faith development and theological education (Graham, 1996).

We will return to this final point in a moment, but before leaving Fowler for the time being, we should remember that the primary burden of his work is to offer a childhood-to-adult theory of theological education. In so doing, he unavoidably commits himself to the proposition that 'adulthood' equates with 'maturity', and that stages one to four are all prone to 'break[ing] down' at some point – usually because of the individual's inability to move on to stage five. This theory is developed for a more corporate climate (that is, communities) in *Becoming Adult, Becoming Christian* (1984), where greater attention is paid to the inner landscape of adult Christian life. The agenda is also taken up with some force in the writings of John Hull (1985), amongst others. That said, Fowler still sees movement between stages as being most likely to be precipitated by crises, and his rhetoric in *Stages of Faith*, at several points, seems to imply that each stage, until stage five is reached, is ultimately unsustainable and naturally immature (or at lest deficient in maturity).

In other words, and to summarize, the framework he offers us for understanding faith development is already interpretative and laden with value-judgements. What I want to suggest in its place in the rest of this chapter, and to moderate and complement Fowler's work, is the idea that a 'world-view' also predetermines the character of theological education and formation, and that this may be a more helpful lens through which to view theological education. But before doing so, it is necessary to develop my earlier remarks on qualia.

What is Theological Knowledge?

In theory, 'theology' is derived from two Greek words: *theos* (god) and *logos* (word or reason) – knowledge of God.[3] In practice, however, theology covers a

---

[2] For an amusing discussion of qualia, see David Lodge's novel *Thinks* (2002).

[3] See Grigg (1990, p. 1): 'it is broadly construed as any kind of talk or reasoning about the divine . . . .'

broader range of concerns. Whilst it may primarily be concerned with metaphysics, philosophy, systematic and dogmatic theology and the primary texts that bear witness to what is deemed to be revealed, the discipline is not only 'of' God but also 'about' God. Theological knowledge deals with those traditions, texts and penumbra that mediate revelation, and is therefore rightly concerned with human history and social development. Like many disciplines within the humanities, it has a contested hierarchy of subjects and disciplines. In church history, for example, those who work in the field of Patristics are more likely to be concerned with doctrine than, say, those who work on more recent developments. Similarly, a subject like pastoral theology is invariably something of a Cinderella compared to dogmatic or systematic theology.

But where theology is more unusual amongst the humanities, and perhaps unique, is that the discipline is purveyed, practised and performed in churches and communities by millions of 'non-specialists' – at least in academic terms. In other words, there are numerous non-professional and non-academic contexts in which theology is practised 'unofficially'. Without at all wishing to be patronizing, an average church congregation is just such a context. Whilst it is likely that the minister will have professional theological training, and perhaps a degree in theology, the chances are that the vast majority of the congregation will not be conversant with academic theology. Nonetheless, theological views will be apparent at every turn; the congregation will most likely know what it is committed to, and what it is not. Furthermore, there may be a high quality of articulated faith, which suggests that faith or theology has been 'learned' in ways that are not commonly thought of as teaching. The most obvious example of this is, I suppose, liturgy, where the regular and rhythmic recitation of creeds and formulae seem to 'school' individuals and communities into their belief system and common Christian practice. Worship is a form of learning and therefore a form of teaching. No less significant is the built environment for worship. A plain whitewashed walled 'preaching box' carries an important theological message and is no less a theological treatise – a sermon in stone, if you will – than an ornate Gothic cathedral or a rambling country church (see Visser, 2001).

Two less obvious examples may also focus attention on the practice of theology. Consider, for example, the phenomenon of the funeral tea – a virtually indispensable part of a mourning ritual. After the service has taken place, the event seems to have no obvious theological value. However, if one were to read the tea as part of the response to loss, it takes on a different hue. The event can signify respect, solidarity, humanization, the need for conversation and reminiscence, and suggests reliability in the face of uncertainty. It can also be a highly ritualized event in its own right, reflecting social order and reordering in response to loss and trauma (Clark, 1982, p. 110; Nieman, 2002). In other words, the event – apparently devoid of theological meaning – can be read as an extension of the theological sentiments that are expressed in the liturgy: 'blessed are they that mourn, for they shall be comforted'. But the importance of funeral teas is never explored or taught at theological colleges; their value is something that most congregations learn and perpetuate in the midst of loss; their occurrence needs no academic or professional prompt. At the same time, the manner of the hospitality clearly reveals something about the theological priorities of ecclesial communities.

A second example concerns dress codes. In a North American church, one of the ten elders elected by the congregation refuses to wear a suit and tie as the others do. He is also late for meetings and sometimes does not turn up at all. The nine elders petition their pastor to have the errant elder removed, claiming that the casual mode of dress signifies disrespect (to God), and is mirrored in 'sloppy attendance habits'. The pastor makes enquiries of the dissenter and discovers that he has his reasons for dressing down; he wants the church to be more relaxed and less stuffy; he thinks formal attire inhibits worship and suggests a more mellow, relaxed God, to which, of course, he is committed. So he does not miss meetings to be rude or to make an obvious point; he simply doesn't think it matters that much, *theologically*. And that, of course, is itself theologically significant.

These two examples show something of the almost casual way in which theological knowledge is held by non-specialists, and practised and purveyed by congregations. But if these examples are part of the economy of theological knowledge, it raises a question as to what actually constitutes theology. Three brief observations about the purposes of theology can be made in this respect. Following Nieman (2002), I hold that theology is, first, a matter of *identity*: an innate and self-conscious language in which the church says something about what it intends to be. To be sure, assertions about God are vital here, but no less vital are the invitations to stay behind afterwards for coffee and refreshments, or someone offering to visit in the week. Second, theology constitutes a *world-view*; it presumes and promotes a cosmology which can enable or constrain behaviour. Thus for some, raffles and lotteries are a good (and fun) way to raise money for the church; for others, it is gambling and therefore a vice. Third, theology is *critical*; it offers, discerns and transforms as it sifts material, enabling individuals and communities to regulate their roles in relation to their fundaments (Nieman, 2003, pp. 200–201).

I am conscious that this is an unusual way of describing theology, but my purpose here is a simple one, namely to challenge what is meant by and counts as theology. I want to say at the outset that I do not think that every single practice within a faith community constitutes theology. However, I do want to suggest that many apparently 'ordinary' customs and routines arise out of deeply embedded theological commitments that deserve more serious attention when considering the process of theological education within faith communities. If we are to explore the meaning of theological education, the implicit needs as much attention as the explicit; the practice as much as the theory; the vernacular faith as much as the credal beliefs that are espoused. In view of this, I concur with James Nieman, and offer this (modified) definition:

> Theology is about fundamental assertions that sustain individuals and communities, rejuvenate beliefs, support institutions, and reify power. (Nieman, 2002, pp. 202–203)

Let me briefly unpack this. Fundamental assertions are claims made by the adherents as well as those claims made upon them. Sustenance follows immediately from this, since the ultimacy of fundamental assertions must provide nourishment and be sufficiently buoyant and reflexive to carry individuals and congregations through bad times as well as the good. Rejuvenation of beliefs does not necessarily mean revision, but is instead meant to imply something about the renewing character of theology. Equally, support of institutions, involves a qualification: it is not necessarily an affirmation of the status quo in any static sense, but, rather, connotes the sense in which theology legitimizes and transforms practice. Finally, the reification of power is the production of effects or materials from ideas and results in faith communities being able to see and experience the fruit of their reflection and labour.

Stated like this, theology is found almost everywhere (that is, it is located and widespread within all ecclesial communities), and is no longer confined to the academy, seminary or solo professional working in an apparently non-theological context. It also affirms Wade Clark Roof's assertion that:

> Theological doctrines are always filtered through people's social and cultural experiences. What emerges in a given situation is 'operant religion' will differ considerably from the 'formal religion' of the historic creeds, and more concern with the former is essential to understanding how belief systems function in people's daily lives. (Roof, 1985, pp. 178–79)

In short, I am promoting a theology of the qualia as a serious focus of inquiry for identifying what theology is, especially in regard to teaching and learning. Furthermore, the theology of congregations – normally implicit – will shape how gatherings are construed and practised, and will normally be able to indicate what significance can be attached to apparently unstructured practices (Graham, 1996). This means that, in studying theology (working with a broader definition), many types of knowledge can be included within the theological penumbra that would normally be excluded. Demography, geography, local history, architecture, custom, order and organization, and a study of activities, can all reveal the sorts of theological knowledge that are present within local churches.

Of course, this approach to the subject of theology opens it out considerably, but my purpose in doing this is twofold. First, if types of theological knowledge are more broadly conceived, then deeper questions about the nature and purpose of theological education can be asked. Conversely, and, second, in challenging the traditional limits that are normally set around theology, as a discipline, we may be able to interrogate the hidden curriculum that has hitherto guided many academies, seminaries and colleges. To take this argument further, I want to suggest that world-views (rather than stages of faith) present a more viable way of examining theology and theological education. In the next section, therefore, we briefly examine the work of James Hopewell (as a contrast to Fowler), before moving on to some brief closing comments in this chapter.

World-views

James Hopewell's distinctive approach to congregational studies has potentially rich implications for the study of theological education. James Hopewell
died in 1984, but his posthumously published *Congregation* (1987) became a
seminal study in contextual and practical theology. To summarize briefly,
Hopewell maintained that the theology of a congregation, its values, virtues
(and therefore, most probably, its discrete learning and teaching practices)
were not carried in formal dogma, but were rather bound up in shared stories
and complementary world-views. (This is explored and applied in more detail
in Part III of this book.) Hopewell based his theory on sensitive ethnography,
coupled to a rich understanding of the power of narrative for framing group
and individual ecclesial identity. Using the work of Northrop Frye (*The
Anatomy of Criticism*, 1957), Hopewell developed a simple 'world-view test'
which was able to position congregations and individuals in terms of their
theological outlook. The grid proposed by Hopewell consisted of four 'points'
or genres.

First, the Canonic genre is likened to Frye's notion of tragedy. Individuals or
communities that are primarily Canonic tend to rely on an authoritative
interpretation of the world 'often considered [to be] God's revealed word or
will, by which one identifies one's essential life' (Hopewell, 1987, p. 69). The
Canonic genre, when tested, is most evident in conservative religious groups
and outlooks. (Interestingly, where I have used the world-view test and
adapted it for interreligious groups, Evangelicals and Muslims score heavily in
this genre.) Second, the Gnostic genre relies on a more intuited process of a
world that develops from 'dissipation towards unity'. Hopewell regards this
genre as similar to Frye's conceptualization of comedy. (The Gnostic genre is
most commonly encountered in strength in Quaker and Buddhist individuals.)
Third, Hopewell suggests that the Charismatic genre requires 'reliance upon
evidence of a transcendent spirit personally encountered, where supernatural
irregularities are regularly witnessed'. This is linked to Frye's explicit notion of
'romance'. (Pentecostals, Revivalists and Charismatically-oriented Christians
do seem to fit this third category.) Fourth, Hopewell suggests that the Empiric
genre has a tendency to rely on evidence and is fond of realism. In turn, this is
linked to Frye's notion of irony. (Most 'liberal-minded' religious adherents are
heavily Empiric – and are also fond of irony, paradox and so on.)

The implications of Hopewell's programme for investigating the meaning of
theological education may not at first be immediately obvious. However, three
brief points need to be made in order to establish the superiority of the 'world-
view' approach over that of Fowler. First, Hopewell links his genres to a grid,
which allows individuals and congregations to be heavily oriented towards one
genre, whilst also being affected by their sympathies to other points on the grid.
In the world-view test, it is rare for individuals or communities to emerge with
results that exclude one or more of the genres entirely. Thus, someone who is
heavily Empiric may also be partly Gnostic and slightly Charismatic, but may
score only one or two points for being Canonic. Equally, very few come out
with four equally balanced scores. The suggestion of the world-view test is that

people's attitude to faith is preconditioned by their world-view. This may, of course, be theological in origin, but the point is that this continues to shape attitudes to learning and teaching. Put another way, Hopewell offers a lens through which it is possible to identify how people process information and what knowledge they value – as well as what is set aside.

Second, Hopewell also shows how differing types of knowledge and information material can help form religious adherence. Instead of a linear progression through stages (*à la* Fowler), Hopewell offers a pattern of reticulation in which competing convictions and tensions (the four different genres) can be used to *negotiate* the world with a more reflexive faith. Furthermore, as if to underline this theory, Hopewell compares potential church attendance to the commercial activity of house-hunting, noting how individuals and communities reflect different values (Hopewell, 1987, p. 19ff). The implications for teaching and learning are rich. Hopewell points out how some house-hunters focus on the *contextual* nature of the dwelling: 'viewed in this way, a dwelling is a texture whose weaving reveals the strands that originate in the larger context of the neighbourhood'. Alternatively, some focus on *mechanisms*, 'and how well the house does its job'. Typical features of 'mechanistic' approaches to church life and education focus on aims, outcomes, programme effectiveness and demonstrable success. Hopewell likens mechanistic approaches to church life to engineering. This approach is in stark contrast to those who value churches as *organisms*, where the interior and exterior of the house are primarily assessed on their aesthetics and the ability of the building to 'fit' with the natural biography of the house-hunters. Hopewell equates this approach to church life as architectural. The *symbolic* approach explores how the building conveys and reifies meanings, and what it communicates to its wider context. Symbolic concerns typically focus not on effectiveness, but on reception and meaning within a wider community. In each of these approaches (rather like the genres of the world-view), knowledge, learning and teaching is handled and valued in different ways by individuals and communities. Apparently trivial knowledge (for example, 'How does our church *look*?') takes on a whole new significance.

Third, in concentrating on narratives and world-views rather than stages, Hopewell avoids the trap that Fowler baits for himself by implying a linear progression from one stage to the next. Even allowing for a cyclical understanding of Fowler (in which there can be oscillation and regression as well as progression), I find Hopewell's approach to be altogether richer because of its stress on *narrative* as a primary place of learning and development (Hopewell, 1987, p. 46ff). If Hopewell is right to assert that congregations' and individuals' self-perceptions are primarily narrative in form,[4] its communication is mainly by story and that it participates in wider society thorough social narrative structures, then we can begin to see a rather different approach to theological education emerging. This would be one in which judgements are

---

[4] See also Hauerwas, 1996, p. 97ff, in which Hauerwas argues that everything the church is and does is 'religious education'.

not made on what is believed or what is taught (formally or dogmatically), but rather on what story or plot is being followed, with proper and due attention paid both to the qualia (the apparently insignificant or trivial) and the world-views that seem to play a major part in performing the type of theological education that may occur in any given situation.

The turn towards narrativity is one of the more striking features of Hopewell's work, and it resonates with our earlier observations about stories and their importance. How and what congregations *recollect* identifies their *plot* and its course or cycle. Without recollection, congregations drift; with it, they narrate their lives together in communion with God, in the midst of triumph and tragedy, opportunity and adversity, and more besides. As Charles Winquist puts it:

> Storytelling can be allied to homecoming because homecoming is more than the collection of actuality. It is more than a bare statement of facticity. Homecoming is a recollection of experience. Our remembrance is an interpretation. We tell a story about the actuality of experience to lift it into the context of meaning that speaks out of the reality of possibility as well as actuality. The *prima material* of meaning encompasses the possibilities from which the particularity of historical fact is made determinant. The re-collection of experience attends the fullness of reality. As strange as it may seem, re-collection allows us to think ahead to the original ground of experience and become conscious of the finality of meaning that coincides with the origination of the actual. (Winquist, 1978, p. 108)

So, in telling the story of the congregation, we unravel its plot:

> ...church culture is not reduced to a series of propositions that a credal checklist adequately probes. The congregation takes part in the nuance and narrative of full human discourse. It persists as a recognizable storied dwelling within the whole horizon of human interpretation. (Hopewell, 1987, p. 201)

If this last point sounds a little too far-fetched, we may do well to remember that Paulo Freire's own educational philosophy actually starts to chime quite well with Hopewell's insights.[5] Freire believes that individuals and communities reach points of understanding and gain self-consciousness by recognizing themselves sequentially in time: 'they develop their power to perceive critically the way they exist in the world with which and in which they find themselves [when] they come to see the world not as a static reality, but as reality in process, in transformation' (Freire, 1972, p. 70). Hopewell suggests that, here, Freire has perceived that, to achieve liberation, people need first to discover their own historicity: they need to discover themselves in the historical plot, not in abstract mechanistic concepts (Hopewell, 1987, p. 198). But, if anything, Freire goes further, arguing that individuals and congregations need to embrace 'conscientisation' (that is, education for critical consciousness) where

---

[5] See also Tony Harland's (1997) work on stories about small-group teaching, which uses a problem-based approach to reflect.

traditionalist approaches ('unquestionably allied to the ruling classes') are set aside in favour of an education that is an instrument of transforming action (Astley *et al.*, 1996, p. 167). Or, as Brookfield (1995) suggests, teaching needs to lose its 'innocence' if it is to avoid being blamed for failing to deliver education; only critical reflection can break the spiral for educationalists as they seek to impart knowledge that transforms.

Summary

The primary burden of this chapter has been to establish sufficient grounds for 'faithful doubt' both in the identity of theology and in the enterprise of theological education in relation to any kind of engagement with contemporary culture. The purpose of this approach has been to show that there is no clear agreement on the nature of theology as a discipline, whilst at the same time there is no real clarity about the nature and purpose of education and formation in relation to theology, nor any measure of agreement as to what constitutes teaching and learning in theological communities. The work of James Fowler, although extremely promising in so many respects, has been described with the aim of showing (albeit briefly) its shortcomings. Indeed, other critics of Fowler have pointed to his problematic use of the term 'faith' as though it were a more or less conscious choice in which persons moved from stage to stage of their own free will (Dykstra and Panks, 1986, p. 9).

In contrast, I have tried to show how many different types of (theological) knowledge within ecclesial communities, as well as personal experiences and individual spiritualities, actually constitute part of the learning and teaching process. This is what Astley (2002) calls 'ordinary theology'. Through the more adequate lens of world-views (proposed by Hopewell), we have been able to catch a glimpse of how knowledge and learning is 'pre-framed' by outlooks which are themselves, no doubt, created by dogma, experience and other types of knowledge. By paying attention to Hopewell's richer 'narrative matrix', stories take on a more significant role in formation, but without excluding the more obviously credal or dogmatic formulations that are assumed to be the basis of catechesis. This is important, and something to which we shall return in Part III, for it constitutes a kind of research that is often given scant attention by academics, who all too easily divide research between 'pure' and 'applied'. But strictly speaking, the word 'research' needs to be understood against its Enlightenment definition and etymology (Van der Ven, 1998, p. 66). To 'research' meant to break away from the notion that knowledge was based on a given authority and, regardless of how assertive or commonplace that knowledge was, to reassess its claims in the light of new questions. Research, properly conceived, therefore always has a profound effect on tradition-bound institutions – such as universities, colleges or churches – especially within contemporary culture.

With these thoughts in mind, the argument may now advance a step further and begin to explore theology as a critical and reflective 'habit of wisdom' (Farley, 1988), whereby theological knowledge begins to become part of the economy of practical wisdom, in which mechanistic conceptualizations of teaching and learning are set aside in favour of more holistic approaches to the discipline. This is crucial for the development of models of theological engagement within contemporary culture. In order to pursue this, I will be offering a novel treatment of theological education that owes much to feminist insights, which in turn, as has been suggested, has implications for the self-understanding and self-description of theology. As we have already noted, no consideration of theological education can avoid some inherently political reflection on the actual nature of the core discipline itself. Correspondingly, redescribing the shape of theology (as a culture) will have implications for how the discipline engages with contemporary culture and arrives at a different point of self-understanding.

Chapter 5

Mother Church[1]

Introduction

Once asked to characterize the differences between the present generation of ordinands and those that were ordained in the 1960s and were now near retirement, I made a simple observation. To my mind, those who are presently being trained (through theological education) for ordained ministry seem to be influenced by an educational culture that is centred on being 'answer-based'; correspondingly, they often do not know how to ask questions. In contrast, their predecessors from 40 years ago were drawn from a 'question-based' educational culture, but they were often reticent about answers. I suspect that the difference (and, granted, it is a characterization) can be traced in other professions besides ministerial formation. And yet the observation exposes a profound cultural shift between enabling faithful doubt and belief on the one hand, and depositing information as a means to education on the other. We have already seen how various 'models' of theological education don't quite do justice to the richness of the enterprise: Fowler's stages have been critiqued; Freire's notion of 'banking' and its remedy is also deficient; and Hopewell's world-views, whilst arguably most promising, can only be preliminary.

In this chapter we move from models to metaphors (or more accurately, a single metaphor), and work with insights from feminist theology. In practice, feminist theologians have paid more attention to issues of inequality, power, leadership and hermeneutics than they have to theological education itself. However, there are some notable exceptions that are briefly worth mentioning, which in turn will inform the argument on metaphor.

Rebecca Chopp's *Saving Work – Feminist Practices of Theological Education* (1995) argues that the contours of theological education must be transformed as increasing numbers of women are enrolled into college, seminary and university theological programmes. Chopp maintains that one of the major paradigm shifts for theological education is that women have now moved away from 'merely' being subjects in the discipline to becoming practioners. Moreover, women bring with them a collection of concerns, insights and skills that are normally excluded from male-dominated theological programmes. Chopp, citing authors such as Dykstra and Panks (1986), suggests that *bodiliness* (a refusal to accept the conventional antinomy between the spiritual/intellectual and the emotional/physical) and *habitus* (not only ordered

---

[1] I am especially grateful to the Revd Emma Percy for her writing and thought in this area, which first encouraged me to take the arena seriously.

learning, but also space for the emotional, aesthetic, affectional, spiritual, spatial and empathetic) are amongst the qualities that distinguish feminist approaches to theological education (Chopp, 1995, p. 17). Building on this foundation, she presses for the practice and inculcation of narrativity in theological programmes (again resonating with our use of Hopewell), which in turn can challenge and enhance 'the practice of ekklesia' (ibid., pp. 45ff) on issues such as sin and patriarchy. The book concludes by employing the metaphor of 'quilting' to describe the practice of feminist theological education. This is suggestive, hinting at the collective, collating and colourful ways in which theological insights are brought together, besides drawing attention to the (normally underrated) aesthetic dimensions in creating theology, and the (apparently) more common reticulate habits of women in sharing their lives and work:

> ...[the] quilt is made from hundreds of scraps of material of all different sizes, textures, colours, and shapes. It is beautiful in its diversity...[and] represents the piecing together of our everyday experience in a communal act of love and the acceptance of all people and life experiences. It redefines beauty, and by redefining what beauty is beautiful, feminist theology deconstructs and reorders values, norms, and structures.... (Chopp, 1995, p. 96)

Chopp's approach to theological education is part of a rich vein in feminist theology that challenges the habitual compartmentalization and disembodiment of theology, as though the discipline were not about life itself. For example, Francis Schussler Fiorenza (1988) explores and analyses three 'typical' theological approaches to theological education. The first focuses on the nature of the subject; the second on the church (mission and identity); the third on ministry. Fiorenza argues that each approach has its limitations, and calls for a more integrated and comprehensive approach that can 'clarify both the possibilities and limits of theological reflection on theological education' (Fiorenza, 1988, p. 101).

Similarly, Mary Elizabeth Moore (1991) approaches the subject of theological education with *stories* that are designed to highlight the conventional segregational character of theology. Working within a North American context, she challenges the cherished division between the sacred realm and public space, which habitually confines religion to being a 'private' matter. In place of this dualism (which she identifies as 'destructive' of women's lives and stories), she proposes an alternative world-view in which the 'sacred and the public are held together'.

From a British perspective, Mary Grey (1989) suggests several 'feminist images of redemption' that are centred on mutuality and empowerment, which might then be applied to theological education. Grey discusses reclaiming (or recovering), self-affirmation, self-knowledge and mutual empowerment, which in turn support the underlying thesis in which human wholeness is fundamental to the teaching–learning enterprise. Again, what is distinctive about the feminist approach here is the attention to the embodied and the emotional, and the refusal to allow physical–mental or spiritual–material dualisms to suffocate valid world-views:

> Accepting the truth of relationality as underlying existence and claiming this as power for development, means mutual empowerment in ever-deepening levels of mutuality. But as long as the ... separatist model prevails in society, will mutuality seem merely a soft option, accused of lacking intellectual rigour? ... Redemption in education means all these things: refusal of the victim situation, recovery of self-image, the process of coming to self-knowledge and the discovery of layers of connectedness. But it will be an ongoing story: redemption is also reclaiming, the reclaiming of those despised areas of the self, of memories and forgotten experiences of wholeness. It is also the reclaiming of stories which are yet to be told.... (Grey, 1989, p. 26)

Grey's work propels us once more into the inherently political character of reflecting on the meaning of theological education within the church. Grey is well aware that 'salvation' involves liberation-through-education, delivering women and the church from a range of materials that are explicitly or implicitly oppressive and thereby impair identity:

> [Education] will reclaim images and symbols from sexist and exploitive connotations ... [reclaim] the silences beyond the boundaries of language and culture barriers ... [whilst] being creative in pushing to the telling of new stories ... redemption for education ... focuses on the total well-being and becoming of the human person ... redemption as mutuality challenges even when human brokenness and finitude prevail, and calls for just relation[s] to be established as part of an ongoing process.... (Grey, 1989, p. 27)

The connection between Freire, Hopewell and feminist insight is now emerging more clearly, and it continues to raise one of the original questions that we set out to address earlier, namely 'What is theological knowledge?'. From the writers discussed so far, it should be obvious that theological education is now beginning to be renarrated as a more extensive collection of disciplines and insights, in which life-experience and narrative can be equally and mutually formative and challenging. Culturally, within most ecclesial communities, this is an important threshold to appreciate when education and formation are issues for consideration, since some may see attention to the experiential and the narrative as too threatening and subversive for the credal and dogmatic. The pressure to marginalize the feminine is almost irresistible within some ecclesial communities. At times, it feels as though the very existence of the church depends on maintaining a dualism between thinking and *feeling*, as though what is felt, sensed and expressed would undermine the ordered hierarchies of truths and those that protect them. In what follows, therefore, I propose to reconsider a traditional metaphor within the church for teaching, learning, nourishment and formation: mothering. As we shall see, proper attention to the depth and capacity of the metaphor offers considerable scope for revisiting the nature of theology and the purposeful lives of the communities that are formed out of the discipline.

Mother Church

An immediate foray into the (academic) territory of mothering, feminism and theological education fails to reveal very promising results. Mothering is an issue that lives on the edge of feminist praxis and thinking for obvious political and social reasons; it only becomes an issue when it prevents women from achieving their goals. Similarly, mothering is not a subject on which many theologians in 2000 years of Christian theology have had much to say. Generally, what has been said has been patronizing, paternalistic and prescriptive. Where feminist theology has made a contribution in challenging the tradition, it has more often than not focused on the oppressive 'idealization' of women (for example, virgin-mother, submissive wife, silent women, deacon[ess], martyr-saint and so on) that has continued to serve male power interests. Women achieve recognition through loyalty, self-denial, virtue and purity, not by their wisdom, courage or leadership. Alternatively, if 'idealization' fails, then women (in the Christian tradition) have often been seen as a source of ecclesial threat, impurity, sin, divisiveness and more besides. In short, it is rare to find feminist reconstructions of the Christian tradition (in relation to education, formation and leadership) that work with the fairly ordinary metaphor of 'mothering'.[2]

This is a pity, especially when one considers the breadth of primary biblical material that dwells on mothering as a metaphor for conveying something of the character of God. In Margaret Hebblethwaite's reflective essay 'Motherhood and God' (1984), she draws our attention to the variety of support that exists within the Judaeo-Christian tradition. For example, Psalm 131, verse 2 states:

> I have calmed and quieted my soul, like a weaned child at its mother's breast, like a child that is quieted is my soul ....

This, perhaps strangely, implies that the *weaned* child may return for comfort and nourishment, suggesting that the process of formation does not proceed in an orderly, linear way. The emerging child or adult may move freely between dependence and independence. The relational dimension of the mothering metaphor is also found in other books of the Bible:

> Can a woman forget her suckling child, that she should have no compassion on the [fruit] of her womb? Even these may forget, yet I will not forget you. (Isai. 49: 15)

> Like newborn babes, long for the pure spiritual milk, that by it you may grow up to salvation; for you have tasted the kindness of the Lord ... (1 Peter 1: 23–2: 3)

---

[2] See, for example, Moltmann-Wendel, *The Women Around Jesus* (1982) and Joan Chittister, *Women, Ministry and the Church* (1983), who offer, respectively, a Protestant and Roman Catholic perspective on women in education and leadership. Moltmann-Wendel does discuss Jesus' attitude to mothers, but seems to be unaware of the potential of the metaphor in the wider biblical tradition. Chittister, although a Benedictine nun and Prioress (and therefore presumably *very* aware of titles such as Mother Superior, and all that this may mean), ignores the metaphor altogether.

Here, suckling is not a form of regression, nor indeed is it especially linked to an infantile stage. Rather, the metaphor is being used to make an association between the salvation and formation of persons and the loving constancy of God. Hebblethwaite extends her argument further by drawing on post-biblical Christian tradition. Augustine, for example, speaks of God feeding Christians from her breast: 'what am I but a creature suckled on your milk, the food that perishes?' (Augustine, 1961, p. 71). Both Anselm and Julian, in the more mystical tradition, work with the mothering metaphor, as does Catherine of Siena and Teresa of Avila (Hebblethwaite, 1984, p. 135). However, Hebblethwaite is most concerned to turn these metaphors into some kind of educational currency, and she ultimately argues that 'much [theological education] is *non-verbal*' (my emphasis). Furthermore, where it becomes verbal, it is first and foremost *story*, long before it becomes credal and dogmatic – or perhaps we should say 'detached'. And this simple observation takes us to an important place in developing the metaphor of mothering as a primary way of conceiving of theological education. It serves to remind us that the learning experience within the church is, initially at least, a suckling one. And that, whilst detachment, individuation and maturity may be appropriate at a later stage of development, the intradependency of weaning is not necessarily cast aside; the close relational bonding of spiritual and theological nourishment through suckling may continue.[3]

Yet there are deeper reasons – both sociological and theological – why the metaphor of mothering for theological education and formation deserves further attention. For a start, and to put it rather bluntly, 'mothering' is a very different act to that of 'fathering'. A child can be fathered in seconds, but, even leaving aside the period of gestation, the act of mothering bears a different timeframe, extending 16 years or maybe more than that. There are other differences, too. A child is dependent on a mother in a way that a father may never know; a mother must let go of a child if he or she is to mature, in a way that a father can never quite comprehend.

As we have already noted, there is a strong theological tradition that emphasizes God (and Jesus) as being mother-like, just as the Holy Spirit can also be referred to as 'she'. Yet this aspect of our analogical imagination has been repressed over time by the establishment of God as 'male' and a 'father'. It is the masculine language that is the dominant tradition in Christianity; the feminine language, most especially that of motherhood, has been largely forgotten. Yet for medieval mystics such as Bernard of Clairvaux, feeding off Christ's blood was like suckling God's breast milk; it nourished the soul. Indeed, the mystics often celebrated the maternal nature of God and Jesus as a way of stressing divine tenderness and instinctive love. Sometimes the imagery

---

[3] For a slightly different discussion see Hodgson (1999). Hodgson argues that the true pedagogue (the Greek *pais* (= child) and *aegin* (= leader)) is the 'child leader'. However, in the community of the church this makes us all children, and Hodgson correctly points out that this dynamic was not lost on early church fathers such as Clement and Origen, who understood their instructive role to be one of guide, 'helmsman' and teacher.

would be sentimental, but its purpose was to remind believers that gestation, birth and nurture were, so to speak, aspects of God's feminine or maternal side. As Caroline Walker Bynum points out in her *Jesus as Mother* (1982), St Anselm (1033–1109, and an archbishop of Canterbury) can write quite unapologetically in one of his devotional writings:

> But you Jesus, good Lord, are you not also our mother? Are you not the mother who, like a hen, collects her chickens under her wings? Truly master, you are a mother...for by your gentleness, those who are hurt are comforted; by your perfume, the despairing are reformed. Your warmth resuscitates the dead; your touch justifies sinners...you, above all, Lord God, are mother...'. (Anselm, cited in Bynum, 1982, p. 114)

A concentration on God or Jesus as mother had profound implications for the structuring of ecclesial authority and theological formation in medieval Christendom. Indeed, the irony of focusing on the mothering metaphor is that it can actually help to overturn the patriarchy that has been so inimical within Christian institutions for many hundreds of years. True, the centrality of Mary in Christian teaching has celebrated the various virtues of motherhood, but it has still tended to ascribe a subordinate, even passive, role to women through Mary's example. Yet those who once led monastic communities – including men like Bernard of Clairvaux – were keen to promote their leadership in terms of being 'mothers' of their communities, not just fathers. For Bernard and his contemporaries, the maternal imagery offered a way of ordering relationships within monastic communities. Correspondingly, terms like 'mother', 'nurse', 'breast', 'womb' and 'feed' carried a particular authority for religious leaders that transcended gender, for they were linked to education, formation and the very life of faith. Thus, to a novice whom he fears has departed the monastery for the world, Bernard of Clairvaux writes:

> I nourished you with milk, while yet a child, it was all you could take...but alas, how soon and how early you were weaned. Sadly I weep, not for my lost labour but for the unhappy state of my lost child...torn from my breast, cut from my womb.... (Bernard of Clairvaux cited in Bynum, 1982, p. 116)

But where do these reflections on the mothering metaphor take us? To what extent can the metaphor be a viable way of renarrating the theological task and the nature of theological education? Here, several observations come to mind, which subtly subvert received traditions and understandings and construct a novel form of feminist theological thinking applied to the field of theological education.

First, the metaphor of mothering is a 'cluster metaphor', which draws in several themes and ideas that are central to educational theory. Briefly, the metaphor can celebrate connectedness and also (as we noted earlier), eschew the formal and disembodied boundaries that divide the physical from the emotional. 'Mothering' is one of those metaphors that tie relationships and learning up in bundles, but not necessarily in a suffocating or restraining way.

Relationality is affirmed, but so is the ambiguity and messiness of 'coming to be' and the necessary dependency on another – in a series of acts and within a relationship, rather simply a single 'deposit'. Therefore, some paradoxical parallels begin to emerge in the process of educational formation with which the mothering metaphor 'fits'. Whilst autonomy is desirable for some, the relational remains important. Equally, it is in the act of 'letting go' that mothering is fulfilled; and yet, it is precisely at this point that a further relationship of mutuality (to quote Mary Grey again) becomes possible. There is also something deeply ordinary about mothering, which is perhaps again suggestive of the educational task that faces churches – commonplace, intimate nourishment that leads to maturity and freedom.

Second, the mothering metaphor takes us into rich areas of cultural practice and biological reflection. We might ask, 'How is mothering learned?' And the answer is, of course, seldom through training, but rather through example and instinct. To be sure, effective mothering can benefit from training and reflection, but the primary recognition in this observation is that Christianity is something that is mainly caught and not taught. In other words, and in relation to theological education, there are various kinds of theological knowledge – some of which are known at a deeper level than the creedal and dogmatic.

Third, motherhood profoundly alters theological outlooks in a myriad ways. Whilst cool, reasoned detachment may have its place in formation, the continual activity of parenting can also prioritize *passion* in the relationship. Immediacy can also be reconsidered; the deep instincts and reflexive processes that are 'natural' to mothering and not thought through before being enacted are also suggestive for theological education. Perhaps it is also true to say that pregnancy provides one of the first opportunities to truly reflect on the mystery of creation and the extent to which what is created is free, or obliged to its creator. Furthermore, mothering may be seen as a residual form of resistance to a society dominated by technology under the heel of capitalism (Rothman, 2000), which, again, has implications for educational praxis.

Fourth, the whole process of mothering is itself mysterious and ambiguous, and perforates many of the traditional barriers that pervade theoretical constructions of reality. As Bonnie Miller-McLemore (1994) notes, in the pregnant body the self and other coexist; lactation subverts the artificial boundaries between self and other, inside and outside. Mother love is, ultimately, not a 'power over', but a 'power with' – precisely what the feminist theologians discussed earlier have been saying. As Trudelle (2001) notes, becoming a mother involves becoming an educator and learner all at once; the antinomy between teaching and learning is dissolved.

Fifth, as a mother gives birth, so must she also die. There the creative and generative forces must face their own *telos*. Yet it is in giving that she receives, and it is in the very act of sacrifice that there is gain. At this point the mothering metaphor perhaps reaches its most intense meaning. Mothering is a gift, and a gift that sets free, liberates and enables adult human life to be and to flourish. At the same time, there is an irony here, since good mothering could anticipate (but not expect or demand) the return of the child – not as a child, of course, but rather as someone who has become fully 'other', yet conscious of mutuality and intradependency. In some respects, the mothering metaphor is, at this point, a good 'fit' for a healthy development in the supervisor–postgraduate relationship. In year one, the student learns from the supervisor; in year two, they learn together; in year three, the supervisor learns from the student. In connection with Hopewell's world-views, we might also point out that mothering attends to the contextual, organic, relational and symbolic. Furthermore, 'canonic' mothering is a very different kind of nurturing to that found in the 'ironic' genre, as much as the 'romantic' and 'gnostic' will be oppositional.

The mothering metaphor remains, of course, just that: a metaphor. But it is one that I believe has promise and potential for re-imagining theological education as something that is reciprocal, generative and creative, involving passion, commitment, sacrifice and vocation. At the same time, it is ordinary, pedestrian, demanding, draining and utterly absorbing. I strongly suspect that when educational praxis is experienced as 'bad mothering' that pupils strive to quickly individuate and then to perpetuate independence and isolation in ongoing learning processes. However, when educational praxis is experienced as 'good mothering', rich possibilities of relationality and mutuality occur.

To summarize, education as mothering helps us to see that there are several layers to theological education. Some is learned behaviour; some natural; some reflexive and habitual; some biological; and some ascribed and designated (as in adoption).[4] Education-as-mothering is, in other words, a varied activity in which many participate unwittingly, a few self-consciously, but nearly all significantly. As a metaphor, it points us all towards something more inclusive: better parenting, in which nurture and nature combine to form persons, as the parents themselves are transformed in the activity of self-gift, sacrifice and the shaping of others. Furthermore, the reciprocal nature of the discipline, redescribed here, is suggestive for the patterning of theological engagement with contemporary culture. With these thoughts in mind, we now turn to some further analysis of the metaphor and its capacity for transforming the practice of theological education.

Metaphor and Metamorphosis

One potential problem of the mothering metaphor is its innate capacity to idealize the infantile stage. In ordinary parlance the phrase 'mother knows best' is generally used to terminate further questions and imply a hidden and higher source of knowledge that is not immediately available to all. Similarly, the phrase 'father knows best' can be encountered in particular ecclesial communities – normally those of a male priest – to infer that there are questions and matters that need addressing, which are beyond the competence of the laity and are best left to the professionals. Clearly, in using the metaphor

---

[4] Of course, the whole idea of the mothering metaphor also serves to suggest that there are different ways of knowing. See Belenky *et al.* (1986).

'mother' for the church as a community, no such hierarchy is meant to be implied. However, mention of the mother–child relationship (as a metaphor) does invite further reflection on the process of nurturing and development and, in particular, on the educational process. By way of preliminary comment, several things can be said, linking to the earlier critical description of Fowler's work.

First, and linked to Fowler's proposed early stages of faith development, we can concur with Edward Farley's notion of 'the fragility of knowledge' (Farley, 1988). Because theological knowledge is relational as well as propositional, personal as well as public, and emotive–expressive as well as reasoned, there is a particular task that falls to ecclesial communities in handling questions, doubts, crises and the like. Moreover, the fragility of theological knowledge is something that is normally only understood from the vantage-point of maturity. Under such circumstances, *how* knowledge is held becomes as important as the content of faith itself. This is where the 'mothering church' can anticipate some of the pastoral and practical issues that surround theological education, and help to nurture individuals and communities through different tiers of understanding and alternative hermeneutical insights, leading to new horizons of possibility.

Second, the mothering metaphor leaves a door open to a subject that is rarely, if ever, mentioned in theological education: play. By 'play' I do not mean a leisure activity that is divorced from the serious. On the contrary, playtime and activity are amongst the most formative arenas of human development. It is here that imagination and creativity are ignited. It is in play that a sense of justice and competition can be developed. It is at play that we can also learn to work together. And, of course, play is part of the activity and space that is provided by good parenting as well as by institutions such as schools. But what would it mean to speak of play in relation to theological education? Without wishing to impose a pun, it may give permission for individuals and congregations to toy with texts and traditions in inventive ways that allow for new types of creative flourishing. The idea of play also suggests, helpfully in my view, that not everything in religion should be treated seriously and reverently all the time. A religion (and an education) without laughter is a bleak and impoverished experience. Play and laughter permit new perspectives, and may open up additional possibilities for teaching and learning (Alves, 1972).

Third, there is a relationship between the need for certainty and the fostering of faithful doubt. In Robert Towler's ground-breaking work (1984), a critique of 'conventional religion' is offered that looks at the pathological and neuralgic need for varieties of religion which refuse to mature. Although the work is a product of a particular sociological imagination, its implications for education are immediately apparent. Towler perceives 'a lust for certitude' (Towler, 1984, p. 99) that is inimical for faith development: 'Certitude is the absence of doubt. The need for certitude is the attempt to escape from doubt' (ibid., p. 107).

I could not, of course, claim that the mothering metaphor as a suggestive approach to theological education in contemporary culture immediately overcomes this apparent problem. However, I suspect that a practical understanding and exercise of the metaphor does hint at the type of educational nurture that should be at the heart of all Christian communities. This would be one where various types of certainties, at various stages of development, are set aside or built upon until a relationship of mutuality and maturity is established. Granted, this standpoint presupposes that the nature and substance of theological material can be agreed upon – and very often it is not. What to some is a 'childish' belief is, to another, a non-negotiable fundament. So how can the stalemate be addressed?

I have already noted in my critique of Fowler that change does not necessarily come about through linear progression. Furthermore, in this treatment of the mothering metaphor, I have been careful to point out that the mothering task is a shared ecclesial vocation, and not one that lies solely in the hands of religious professionals. In Bruce Reed's remarkable study of religious change (1978), the author advances a compelling theory of 'oscillation'. For Reed, religious behaviour comprises two elements. The first is a human *process* of alternation between states of dependence and autonomous living, which Reed maintains is natural and universal in the life of the individual and is synchronized in social units such as groups, institutions and societies. The second is a *movement* which provides a rationale, in myth and theology, for the symbolic acts and objects through which the process manifests itself. Reed then goes on to identify patterns of church life which, according to the forms taken by the process, can be restrictive, functional, destructive or enabling.

The value of Reed's insights for the development of theological education are buried deep within his analysis and methodology – but they are there. For example, the oscillation theory resonates with some of my earlier remarks on good mothering. Reed recognizes that the processes of development are less linear and more cyclical-spiral. Regression may accompany transformation; dependence may lead to extradependence and finally flourish into intradependence – but there may still be some space for regression (Reed, 1978, pp. 73 and 170). The burden of Reed's work is to expose the ways in which flight, fright and fight lead to impoverished forms of dependency within ecclesial communities and therefore prevent the furtherance of theological education and increasing maturity. Thus, a retreat to 'sectarianism' or 'ecclesiasticism' (ibid., p. 79) which, on the surface, look very different, are in fact two sides of the same coin. Both represent an inability to cope with the multiple overwhelmings of modernity, and they constitute a theological stance that has terminated further theological questioning and suspended 'ceaseless wondering'.

From a more feminist perspective, Sara Ruddick (1983) proposes a theory of 'maternal thinking' that also has implications for education. Although not writing from a faith, Christian or theological perspective, Ruddick nevertheless offers reflections that complement our earlier observations. She draws attention to processes of nurturing in motherhood and suggests a triangle of virtues that are intradependent yet also mildly conflicting. On the one hand, mothering is committed to the preservation of the child. On the other hand, it is committed to the growth and individuation of the child, which requires sacrificing preservation: children, to come in to maturity, have to be allowed to discover, take risks and experiment. The third point of the triangle is that of acceptability, whereby the adult seeks to socialize the child into the world. But this is done, mindful that skills in questioning and subverting the social order are part of the 'entry requirement' for adult life ('shaping an acceptable child'). Ruddick suggests that the mother/teacher undertakes her task with a combination of humility and hope,[5] and that maternal thinking, applied to education and formation, is more about 'holding' than (the more male) notion of acquiring.

Unsurprisingly, the agenda that emerges from Reed's and Ruddick's work is closely associated with the focused attention we have directed on to the mothering metaphor. We are left with binary paradoxes that are not there to be solved, but are there, rather, to act as guides. Thus, we can say that, whilst mothering anticipates and desires change (in the self and in the child), each stage is cherished for what it is, and a degree of relational regression (within an overall economy of increasing maturity) is permitted, if not desirable. Equally, whilst individuation is to be welcomed, and a mature autonomy encouraged, affiliation and intradependence are also nurtured for their own sake. The metaphor, in other words, is suggestive of a particular type of metamorphosis, in which the mother learns as the child grows, and the mother grows as the child learns. The church, as the 'mothering community' (in terms of theological education) is not only a source of creativity and nourishment; it is also a repository of the reciprocal and intradependent, in which teaching and learning is exchanged mutually.[6]

Another difficulty with Fowler's 'stages' is that the individual must lose his or her mother-theology at each stage in order to progress to the next. One of the attractions of Hopewell's world-views is that there is a type of theological mothering that corresponds to each of the proposed genres. In the case of the Canonic, the nurturing is strict and uncompromising, but for the sake of the child's (eternal) safety. In contrast, the Empiric is mellow and ironic, and perhaps almost too 'hands-off' and liberal. The romantic genre may be characterized as cloying, smothering and directional, with the Gnostic as semi-detached and faintly alternative or even mystic.

However, it is important to grasp that intradependency is not Reed's goal. Certainly, we have moved away from independence – the fifth stage of Fowler's spiritual development – as a goal. Instead, intradependency is the very ground of possibility for teaching and learning: it is a way of being. It is in the

---

[5] Her actual phrase, following Spinoza, is 'resilient cheerfulness' (Ruddick, 1983, p. 218).

[6] See Hodgson (1999). Hodgson draws our attention to the Socratic notion of education as midwifery: 'Socrates' mother had been a midwife, and he said that he learned from her the art of bringing forth ... the art he used was that of questioning, dialectic, by which he was able to draw the idea of the good, the true, the universal out of the experiential particularities of his interlocutors. He was the first to arrive clearly at the great insight that truth is brought forth by thinking, thus that it is discovered within our own subjectivity, and that subject and object are one' (p. 16).

realization that we are interconnected and interrelated at every level – social, emotional, personal and formative – that the intradependency can become a foundation for becoming a learning and teaching community. This is something to strive for. But it is also something that does not cast aside the stages and world-views of others.[7]

These observations are partly made in jest, but they have a deeper purpose, namely to remind us, finally in this chapter, that there are many different styles of mothering and that these styles correspond to a variety of outlooks and values. To be sure, mothering is a substantial activity. But like education itself, the 'how' can be as important as the 'what'. I am reminded of a gentle rule that was once imparted to me at a Romanian monastery, where the discipline seemed to be severe and yet everyone was cheerful. The rule was this: nothing is demanded; everything is suggested. Theological education, like good mothering, probably asks for no more than this. How it is offered will, to an extent, determine what is returned.

The Nature of Theology

In the Introduction and in the previous chapter, I argued that the church needed to be taken seriously as a place in which theological education is present and formative, quite apart from any explicit teaching that might be offered. Architecture, music, ambience, the structuring of social relations, the organization of ecclesial polity and other factors may all make a substantial contribution to theological or Christian education and formation. We have also noted that the *how* of education may be as significant as the actual content. But we can go a little further at this point, and say that the *how* is pregnant with theological significance and cannot easily be separated from content.

For example, in ecclesial communities where there is less stress on mechanistic effectiveness and outcomes, and more emphasis on symbol, the organic and the contextual, it is reasonable to suppose that means often matter more than ends. Indeed, even in the most ardent and devoted congregation where mechanistic priorities remain high, the underlying power of the polity of civility should not be underestimated. It can be far more important to conduct a thoughtful, appreciative, well-ordered, civilized (but ultimately inconclusive) debate than it can be to cut to the quick and reach a decision. Many congregations, and not a few of their ministers, have discovered that the imposition of directive decisions (which may be ultimately *right*) is often unwelcome if those decisions circumvent consultation, the coming together of minds and hearts, debate and mutual learning.

Theologically, and following Lindbeck (1984) and Schreiter (1985), we can reaffirm the useful distinction between *traditio* (that is, *what* is taught) and *tradita* (that is, *how* things are taught). Indeed, it is Lindbeck (1984, pp. 30–45)

---

[7] Strictly speaking, Fowler's sixth stage is the mystical intradependent stage. But in spiritualizing and idealizing it, he makes it a remote and rare possibility, not an essential social foundation.

who alerts us to the *performative* aspects of doctrine (that is, experiential–expressive and cultural–linguistic). A theological emphasis on the incarnation, for example, leads to a particular style of ministry and a particular form of missiology and church polity. Equally, a preferred form of behaviour can help select and shape the preferred theological fundaments. Exactly how the church conveys its message may in fact say more about its theology than it really knows; the mode of education may reveal the 'hidden curriculum' and the underlying theology.

So what of the nature of theology in relation to educational praxis and the church? Following Nieman and Rogers (2003), four observations come to mind. First, theology is *public*. It is the work of groups, congregations and conversations. Creeds or formulae are rarely formed in a vacuum or designed by specific individuals without reference to social questions and contextual pressures that are exterior to the life of a congregation, church or more extensive communion. Second, theology is *practical*. It explicitly sets out to discern the linkages between belief and behaviour, and addresses particular issues that concern the internal life of the ecclesial community. Third, theology is *plural*. Since congregations contain a multiplicity of theologies and world-views, competing and complementary convictions, and more besides, the *expression* of theology arises out of both unity and plurality, and its effectiveness is judged against its performative capacity to speak for more than one voice or viewpoint. Fourth, theology is *particular*. Specific to itself, theology articulates the self-conscious identity of congregations: 'we believe...'. But it is also bilingual, since a church has one language for speaking within, as it were, its own house, and quite another for the public domain, which takes us back to the first point.

Understood like this, the nature of theology can be understood as something that is essentially practical and concerned much more broadly with listening, learning and teaching. Moreover, the manners, codes and customs of ecclesial polity are often in common and ambiguous ownership. The way in which children are schooled into receiving consecrated bread and wine at the Eucharist will invariably be determined by a significant range of largely hidden theological assumptions that are present in any local congregation. In this regard, Schreiter (1985) is wise to draw our attention to the structure of local theologies, in which particular hermeneutics (local readings of sacred texts *and* meanings), certitude (what a congregation thinks is sure or fundamental knowledge) and praxis (practical wisdom) play a part in the ongoing educational formation of ecclesial communities.

The fourfold definition of the *nature* of theology, following Nieman, resonates with our earlier observations concerning the primary *purposes* of theology. First, theology articulates *identity* in which the church says something about what it intends to be. Second, theology constitutes a *world-view*; it presumes and promotes a cosmology that may enable or constrain behaviour. Third, theology is *critical*; it discerns and transforms material, enabling individuals and communities to regulate themselves in relation to their fundaments.

As we have already hinted, it is in the arena of worship that much theological education and Christian formation takes place. So it is perhaps surprising that so little attention has been focused on the grammar of assent, behaviour and symbolization that might occur in worship.[8] There are numerous theological treatises on the meaning and interpretation of worship, and, also within the discipline of theology, a significant amount of work devoted to homiletics and to liturgy (mainly from a historical or pastoral perspective). As Jeff Astley helpfully points out, part of the difficulty may be that worship 'produces' learning, even if it is not itself 'education' (Astley *et al.*, 1996, p. 244). However, this observation has to be balanced against the fact that worship does *not* in fact have an educational purpose: 'Religious people do not worship in order to do or become anything else, to teach or to learn. Worship is an end in itself' (ibid., p. 245).

Nevertheless, it is clear that worship can school, shape, teach and enculturate participants at some of the deepest levels possible. As Anton Vrame's intriguing meditation, *The Educating Icon*, (1999), shows, participation comes before explanation; experience comes before understanding. In this respect, Vrame argues that the early Christians had a distinctive philosophy of education long before they could articulate one. Vrame looks to the work of Elliot Eisner (1979, 1985) in the support of his thesis. For Vrame, catechesis is part of the 'sacrament of education' (Vrame, 1999, pp. 181–201); Christians are informed, formed and transformed in dynamic relationality; the 'hidden' curriculum is the discovery of the sacred in the gaze of the image or icon, as well as the relationship between the viewer and the object.

Similarly, Astley offers several penetrating observations about the character of worship in relation to learning. First, worship not only expresses certain religious attitudes, experiences and affections, it also *evokes* them, and they, in turn, then become part of the active learning memory. Second, learning *about* the worship of another (person, faith, community) also influences the shape of belief and what might ultimately constitute education. Third, individuals and communities learn *from* their experiences of worship. They understand that certain words, images, kinds of music, activities and aesthetics actually produce effects that further shape the contours of belief (Astley *et al.*, 1996, p. 246).

These observations prompt Astley to use a word about worship that we have already employed earlier in relation to doctrine: 'performative'. In other words, certain words, phrases, statements and sentences don't merely *mean* something, they also *do* something – they perform. It is not appropriate, at this point, to become drawn into the wider debate about speech–act theory and the technicalities of locution (a 'simple' statement), illocutionary acts (that is, making a judgement, issuing a demand) and perlocutionary acts (that is, what I

---

[8] My own analysis of charismatic worship as laying a foundation for religious experience and subsequent teaching has become a familiar landmark in the analysis of charismatic ecclesial communities. However, I have yet to see any similar applied to more mainstream/historic denominations. See Percy (1996a).

do by saying something – intimidate, warn, encourage and so on).[9] Suffice to say, worship is an activity that is far more than verbal assertion. It is an utterly transformative pursuit in which the worshipper is taught and can teach, learns and is learned, regresses and progresses.

Astley builds on these insights with the work of the Canadian philosopher Donald Evans (1979), in particular his notion of 'attitude-virtues' which he describes as 'pervasive stances for living, or modes of virtue in the world' (cited in Astley *et al.*, 1996, p. 247). Attitude-virtues, perhaps naturally enough, are in opposition to 'attitude-vices', with the virtues proclaiming 'what ought to be'. They are therefore close to the more performative aspects of doctrine and correlate closely, at least conceptually, with our definition of nature of theology and its purposes. Expressed like this, worship becomes a mode of discourse and behaviour in which learning about the way the world ought to be is regularly remembered and celebrated. Or, as we said earlier in this essay, religion is 'caught' before it is 'taught'; but in the very activity of catching, there is learning.

This brief mediation on worship as an alternative way of conceiving of the nature of theology resonates with some of our earlier observations relating to the nature of theological education. By focusing on worship, we can begin to sense that the totality of activity and experience within any given ecclesial community can constitute the teaching–learning environment. Moreover, in pulling away from narrow and static definitions of doctrine, we have also been able to gain some sense of just how plural Christian formation is – in other words, how the pedagogical activity of the church involves the whole person and not just the mind. It is in this 'totality' that doctrine is learned and taught. As John Bernstein notes:

> ... the early catechists showed in their pastoral activity that the Christian teachings demanded the life of the affections. Their concern for the latter, however, did not represent the commitment to an experiential catechesis as against, say, an instructional one. The disposition of the heart was of such importance not as surrogate for the church's teachings but precisely in virtue of the place those teachings must find in the life of the newly baptised. The fear, remorse, zeal and joy of the paschal season were marks of religious understanding... (Bernstein, 1978, p. 194)

The Nature of the Church

Having considered the nature of theology, we now turn to the nature of the church. Here it will be necessary to build upon the earlier insights about the public, practical, plural and particular nature of theology (all of which produces doctrine which is ultimately performative) and try to identify and establish the types and styles of ecclesial polity that foster the *how* (rather than

---

[9] Astley is in debt, of course, to the work of J.L. Austin. See Austin (1962).

the *what*) of theological education. We might begin by offering a skeletal outline of the different ecclesiological approaches to instruction and education, which are themselves rooted in doctrine and ecclesial assumptions. We have already seen that the world-views offered by Hopewell can be roughly equated to ecclesial types, styles and norms (for Canonic read 'conservative', for Ironic read 'liberal' and so on). But here we are more concerned with ecclesial polity than outlook (that is, structure as an expression of value), in order to reflect more fully on the meaning of theological education within its primary environment. To achieve this I am going to work with conventional vernacular descriptors for churches – 'low', 'middle' and 'high' – briefly discussing each in turn.

In the 'low' paradigm, words and texts are presented as being pre-eminent. The basis of faith and unity will be constituted in agreed statements, and the catechesis will be didactic in character: belonging means agreeing with what has already been said and is likely to be said. Symbols, customs, aesthetics and what we have termed the 'theological qualia' of individuals and communities will, of course, be significant. But their place and interpretation will, to a large extent, be governed by a notion of teaching and learning that has already come to a mind on apparent peripherals – that is, the Oreologians will already have decided on the 'core' and 'central' issues with which theology is to be concerned and therefore, by definition, will have identified those matters that are held to be of marginal interest. An example of education/induction in 'low' ecclesiology is the Alpha course, which consists of 12 short meetings that introduce the uninitiated into the 'basics' of Christianity through didactic methods.

'High' ecclesiology is traditionally associated with an emphasis on sacraments and symbols as primary mediators of the presence of God. This does not mean that words are unimportant but, rather, that, in 'high' ecclesiologies, there is an in-built interpretative and experiential pluralism which can only be managed not by words, but by positioning power and authority in a recognized office (such as a bishop). 'High' ecclesiologies are more likely to see education as a broad form of induction into the Christian life, in which worship may feature significantly. An example of education/induction in 'high' ecclesiology is the Roman Catholic Adult Initiate Curriculum, which lasts about two years and teaches through multifaceted exposure to the presence of the church.

The 'middle' ground, suffice to say, may combine insights from the high and the low in varying proportions. However, it is important to understand that the middle ground is not simply occupied by broad or liberal-minded souls who accept accommodation and pragmatism. For example, Pentecostal groups that combine word and experience may also belong in the middle category, since they seek not only to teach, but also to evoke experiences of the numinous as a means to furthering education. Notably, many who occupy the middle ground use a range of courses that stress such motifs such as journeying, pilgrimage and searching. In so doing, they may offer basics or fundaments as guides, but are unlikely to suggest that such things can all be known at the beginning: much is to be 'discovered'.

Of course, this outline sketch is a mere characterization of ecclesial educational praxis. Its main problem is its presumption that churches possess a settled and uniform nature that renders the adoption of different types of learning and teaching unlikely. In fact, nothing could be further from the truth, and this is what makes reflecting on the nature of the church in relation to educational theory so compelling. For example, consider the ways in which many denominations have attempted to use Alpha courses. Equally, consider the number of churches that have adopted more long-term programmes of induction that concentrate on presence, relationships, spirituality and pilgrimage.

Inevitably, questions of ecclesial praxis return us to the debate on the nature of theology. During the latter half of the twentieth century, theologians squabbled over the 'practical' nature of theology, and the relationship between orthodoxy and orthopraxis. Generally, the latter is deemed (at least by its opponents) to have confused witness or action with theology. By its proponents orthopraxis is held to be a more earthed, genuine and engaging way of *doing* theology (see McCann and Strain, 1985). The distinction is again helpful when it comes to considering the specific forms of educational habits that might embody many ecclesial communities. McCann notes that orthodoxy has been 'shunted aside like a senile but still tyrannical relative, more embarrassing than awe inspiring' (McCann, 1985, p. 39). Quoting the work of Charles Davis (1980, p. 130), who is no fan of orthopraxis himself, McCann continues the critique:

> Religion when maintained as orthodoxy claims a permanent self-identity, remaining unscathed by social and practical changes. It involves some purely theoretical center of reference to serve in an abstract speculative way as a norm of identity. There are indeed conflicting orthodoxies, but the differences are conceived as basically theoretical. Then presupposition of orthodoxy is the contemplative conception of knowledge, according to which knowledge is the result of disinterested viewing of reality by individuals. Orthodoxy is that contemplative conception applied to religious truth. (McCann and Strain, 1985, p. 39)

Once again, this critique draws our attention to the performative aspects of doctrine and ecclesiology and also raises questions about the nature of the church in relation to its wider environment. In fact, it is something of a myth to suggest that there is anything like the kind of purist doctrine that Davis attacks, any more than there is a 'pure' church. All ecclesial communities are, in their own way, socially engaged accommodations of contemporary culture, even if the nature of that response is one of self-conscious withdrawal. In other words, each form, type or style of ecclesiology (and its education) is a form of orthopraxis; there is no body that is working in a vacuum. As Edward Farley notes:

> Theology, that is, ecclesial reflective inquiry, does not itself determine or originate the realities that attend the ecclesial community. Theology does not found these realities but is founded by them. Thus, a theological failure is a failure to bring such realities to expression in the mode of understanding. (Farley, 1982, p. 183)

This is not a particularly startling observation, except perhaps for those who imagined the (or their) church to be an *a*cultural body that was shaped by revelation and tradition, and never by society. This is why Farley argues that the nature of theology is partly concerned with 'the attempt to bring pretheological apprehended realities to formulations intended as true...' (ibid., p. 183). For Farley, the nature of the church therefore has something to do with making the experience of reality more real, concrete, comprehensible and true. In other words, the nature of the church is interpretative and educational; it is a catalyst and agent through which life may be experienced more fully, deeply and clearly – 'a *depth continuity* which undergoes major or minor alterations' (ibid., p. 373).

So what does it mean to belong to the church that has a nature such as the one I have outlined? Is it reasonable to describe the church as a crucible of educational praxis? Several points can be made by way of concluding this middle section. First, we can say that Christian identity, doing theology and belonging are linked, and that these are critical markers for a consideration of theological education and Christian formation. We have already noted that Christianity itself is both a propositional and relational religion. When Jesus writes, he does so only in the sand. The 'word made flesh' is witnessed not by an autobiography, but by other writers and interpreters who construct their own narratives of significance; it is these ambivalent and multifaceted traditions that constitute what is revealed.

Second, hermeneutics – what Lucien Richard (1988) economically describes as 'getting across distances' – is part of the nature of the church; it is an interpretative community. In terms of educational praxis, the church in its teaching, worship, aesthetics and general qualia offers a rich and absorbing framework not only for interpreting life, but also for locating and discerning, for that same world, the transformative possibilities that are associated with the power and presence of God.

Third, the church (like theology) is plural, and yet not divided. The collective and shared memory of salvation, spoken and celebrated on a regular basis in worship and teaching, is also experienced and anticipated in a myriad different ways. It remains possible to speak of the church as an integrated learning community, one of praxis whereby 'people come into their own' and yet have a deepened sense of belonging: in Farley's words, 'a depth continuity'.

Finally, the church is a community of openness; even the most sectarian and communitarian are necessarily incomplete and open to new vistas of interpretation and fresh horizons of possibility. In this sense, the nature of the church is partly concerned with hospitality, which is a core value and attribute of ecclesial nature. Orthopraxis is unavoidable, and, in many respects, highly desirable. As John Cobb puts it:

> ... the more deeply we trust Christ, the more openly receptive we will be to wisdom from any source, and the more responsibly critical we will be both of our own received habits of mind and of the limitations and distortions of others ... (Cobb, 'The Religions' in Hodgson and King, 1982, p. 299)

From these observations, we now move to a deeper consideration of the nature of theological education.

The Nature of Theological Education

Given the different types and styles of ecclesiology, there can be no surprise at the different forms of theological education. Three types were outlined in the previous section, but these were descriptions that were derived from a relatively arbitrary ecclesiological taxonomy. As I noted at the time, this was more of a characterization than an analysis. More substantial attempts to describe the field do exist, such as Jack Seymour's and Donald Miller's *Contemporary Approaches to Christian Education* (1982). In an earlier exploratory journal article (with the same title as the book), Seymour makes the case for there being at least six types of Christian education: religious instruction; socialization/enculturation (in other words, the development of particular lifestyles and ecclesial characters, habits, customs and so on); development; liberation; 'educational system' (Seymour uses this term to refer to Christian schools when church and state are separated); and interpretation. To some extent, we have already touched on each of these, and Seymour's work makes it clear that the approaches are not necessarily mutually exclusive; there can be overlaps, adaptive mixtures for particular contexts and other types of partnership. The burden of Seymour's work is to plead for an approach to theological education in which 'the educating church, the school of Christian living, must be built', such that education is not marginalized as just one aspect of the life of the church. In Seymour's and Miller's view, becoming the learning, teaching and ministering church requires the reinstatement of education as a priority at every level of its being (Seymour and Miller, 1972, p. 10).

However, this is easier said than done. We have already referred to the work of Edward Norman (2002), his attacks on secularization and liberalism within the church, and his advancement of a thesis claiming that the church no longer instructs 'the faithful in the faith'. Although we have disagreed with his dismissal of liberalism and have begun to argue that churches provide cultures of discrete learning that are not immediately obvious or didactic (that is, qualia, and so on), there can be no question that churches devote remarkably little time to reflecting on education. For Edward Farley, the church must redress this balance by conceiving of education as 'ordered learning', whilst also recognizing that the vast majority of churchgoers 'remain largely unexposed to Christian learning' (Farley, 1985, p. 158). Farley advances his argument in a number of ways.

First, he points out that 'teachers' are listed in Paul's *Letters* as one of the earliest historic offices of the church. The tradition of teaching is, in turn, linked to the more ancient Hebrew and Greek notion of *paideia*, meaning to 'nurture' and 'discipline'. Jesus himself adopted the term 'Rabbi', which again points to the centrality of the educational task in early Christian tradition. So far as Farley is concerned, education is 'a social necessity' if a movement is to perpetuate itself. At the same time, however, Farley is aware that education in the church has a deeper purpose; it enables individuals and communities to discern truth from falsehood, deceit from wisdom, and to link faith and reality, which is done *through* theology. But this last point begs a question. If theology is a central, mediating and discerning discipline that is intrinsic to the nature of the church, why is theological education so rarely practised at grassroots levels? As Farley says:

> ... what history has done to the word 'theology' is reduce its meaning to its objective referent (a series of doctrines, beliefs) and then narrow its locus to the specific school and scholarly enterprise which deals with doctrines. Given this objectification and professionalisation of the term, theology becomes the possession of schools and a group of scholar-teachers ... these narrowings are now so stamped on the church ... that the rescue of the word is highly unlikely .... (Farley, 1985, p. 161)

Farley argues that, in the older sense of the word, 'theology' was:

> ... not just the scholar's possession, the teacher's trade, but the wisdom proper to the life of the believer ... faith was practical knowledge having the character of wisdom because it had to do with the believer's ways of existing in the world. (Farley, 1985, p. 162)

This leads to Farley arguing for the fostering and nourishment of 'practical wisdom' as a means of enabling the ordered learning that individuals and communities seek. It is this kind of programme that will assist Christians in interpreting their faithful responses to reality, which will in turn be resourced by interpretations of tradition and heritage, hermeneutics and educational stratagem.

Third, Farley critiques three areas that might prevent the establishment of a more widespread educational culture within the churches. These areas, which have already led to 'educated clergy' and 'uneducated believers', are: the professionalization of theology; the paucity of the homiletic tradition; and the generalizing of the meaning of education. At this point, Farley's critique is close to the borders of those educationalists who write within the tradition of liberation theology. Farley wants to see theology taken out of the 'private' hands of professionals and an ecclesial elite and restored to its proper place as a common language in which all can participate. This approach to the *nature* of education, then, assumes a much wider range of participants and a far more practical (rather than theoretical) discourse that is related to everyday life. It questions apparently given hierarchies and, in so doing, interrogates the very meaning and material of the subject.

If Farley is right, and theology has indeed shifted from being a general (but deep) *habitus* of wisdom to becoming a term that is more commonly associated with a system of doctrines, what else might be said about the nature of education that can help rescue the term 'theology' from the private–professional world of theologians and clergy and restore it to its proper public place within contemporary culture? Part of the answer, I suspect, lies in a recovery of a *spirituality* of education. The term is used quite deliberately, and in using the word 'spirituality' I adopt a term that is ambiguous, 'spongy', imprecise and yet accessible, open, identifiable and substantial. Spirituality, unlike theology, is something that many may possess and articulate; it need not be 'official' or 'approved', but can function, nevertheless, as a sustaining world-view.

Spirituality also implies a more dialogical, open, empathetic and grounded approach to religion and everyday life. Furthermore, if the nature of theological education is to be primarily conceived as a form of spirituality, we can then reconnect the educational agenda with some of the sentiments expressed earlier in the chapter about mothering, individuation, maturity and intradependency. Spirituality is also suggestive for the character and vocation of teachers:

> The purpose of education is to show a person how to define [himself] authentically and spontaneously in relation to [his] world – not to impose a prefabricated definition of the world, still less an arbitrary definition of the individual himself .... (Merton, 1979, p. 3)

Margaret Guenther (1992), in her provocative book on spiritual direction, argues that both the term and the role need demystifying. In much the same way as we have been arguing for theological education, Guenther suggests that real spiritual direction is grounded in daily life, in the ordinary, in the mundane and in the ambiguities of everyday experience. But her reflections go deeper and connect with many of the threads of our previous argument.

For Guenther, spiritual direction is *hospitality*. The teacher or mentor must be able to operate as a listener/learner as well as a speaker (Guenther, 1992, p. 6ff). (We have already stated that theological education must involve a hermeneutic of hospitality.) It is from this place that the spiritual director can become a *teacher*, although Guenther reminds us that teaching is 'a dangerous activity': it stirs hearts and minds and causes us to question prevailing standards and norms. Moreover, good teaching lies not in giving answers so much as in educating people into asking questions (ibid., p. 54). Guenther concludes her tripartite model by identifying the spiritual director as a *midwife*, and expresses similar sentiments to those we touched on in Chapter 2. The midwife brings to birth, enables and assists. The midwife coaches and encourages, and draws out the strengths and new life in others. Ultimately, for Guenther, theological and spiritual teaching is a kind of reciprocal guidance. The teacher leads individuals and communities to thresholds and is present when they are encountered, at the moments of transition and engagement. Teaching, then, is an art form in itself, part of the mystery of education in which persons are drawn to new vistas of openness and expanding horizons of opportunity and reflection.

Described like this, the potential or actual nature of theological education seems a very long way away from what most people will encounter in churches: dogmatic glaciation, static truth and no sense of journey. Furthermore, churches too easily assume that people learn in the same way and therefore adopt a 'one size fits all' approach to their catechesis. Again, this suggests that the churches have an impoverished philosophy of education that guides them in their teaching. For example, Everding *et al.* (1998), building on the work of Fowler, identify four different types of theological learner: affiliating, bargaining, conceptualizing and dialectical. All have resonance with our earlier suggestions for a theology that engages with contemporary culture. But with rare exceptions, such differences of learning perspective amongst the laity (or the clergy, for that matter) are seldom recognized. Perhaps this is why there is a perceptible rise in the number of adults who belong to various 'post-church' movements – post-evangelicals, post-liberals and more besides. People's dissatisfaction is probably not so much with the content of Christian faith as with the underlying educational philosophy that delivers it and often fails to admit to certain types of hermeneutic, particular lines of questioning, and the use of imagination and creativity in rereading the tradition. Alan Jamieson (2002) is right to suggest that the only remedy to this can be conversation between post-church groups ('leavers') and those who remain.

Conclusion

To conclude this chapter, we need only say one thing: that there is a relationship between nature and nurture that ecclesiologists would do well to reflect on further. In the Christianity and culture debate, this is critical and vital for the shaping of theology. Whether it is the nature of theology, the church or of theological education, the actual attention to the nurturing of those who encounter these things is no less a vital task for educators. To understand the church as educational praxis is to begin to appreciate that it is in its very life, care and intellectual nurturing that its truer nature is expressed. Too often, the nature of the churches' teaching is preached as though it were an abstract, and the nurturing added as an afterthought.

In contrast, I am arguing that the nature of the church is deeply connected to educational nurturing, and that, therefore, different types of learning, experience, encounter and questioning should be treated with the utmost seriousness. As Astley notes:

> ... that the church is the fundamental context for Christian education is not in itself controversial, and it might even be argued that the life of the church simply *is* Christian education.... Ecclesiological reflection upon Christian education, however, is always in danger of a kind of abstraction and idealization which must be corrected by attention to the life of the churches, as communities with a range of functions and activities.... (Astley *et al.*, 1996, p. xvi)

It is therefore vital that orthopraxis sits closely with orthodoxy in any consideration of the church as educator or learner. It is not simply the case that 'we are *what* we teach', but also 'we are *how* we teach'.

Chapter 6

Formation, Transformation and Liberation

Introduction

Central to the concern of Part II of this book has been the argument that the life of the church, with all its ambiguity and richness, constitutes a major place for, and resource of, theological education. This argument has been set against the prevailing assumption that theology is only for academic or clerical professionals and is a specialist subject requiring particular types of formation that are open to only but a few. Furthermore, in pressing for a more inclusive and accommodating philosophy of education within the church, the argument has, inevitably, challenged the nature of the discipline itself, calling into question distinctions, boundaries and identities. In this chapter I want to look more specifically at the shape of theological training for clergy, but without losing sight of the wider picture for ecclesial communities. At the same time, we will retain a focus on the church as a primary place for formation, transformation and liberation.

Perhaps unsurprisingly, there are a number of mainstream theologians who are already at the forefront of this debate, although very few of them are 'applied' in their thinking, or are developing a form of practical theology of education that might address some of our deeper concerns. But one senses that this agenda is still quite fresh for the discipline of theology, and that, despite the inevitable political difficulties we have hinted at, there is an inherent spirit of 'reception' within the subject that makes it look beyond its borders for fresh insight and wisdom. Consider, for example, these two recent contributions in the field of theology and religious studies.

First, Ursula King challenges the dominant enlightenment paradigm for studying religion, which assumes that religion could be apprehended and comprehended through 'some form of objective, scientific knowledge' (King, 2002, p. 382). Arguing that such approaches are becoming *passé*, she suggests that the new scholars of religion need to strike a balance between being generalists, comparativists and specialists. Moreover, there is also a need for the scholar to recognize that a certain amount of empathetic immersion into the field of inquiry is no bad thing, since this also constitutes part of the learning process, to which, presumably, universities and individual researchers are committed. Thus she writes:

> Our specialized findings should not remain imprisoned in an ivory tower existence but, rather, need to be integrated into meaningful knowledge related to human praxis and a viable life world ... the viable transformation of religious studies will depend on whether it has sufficient flexibility to respond to different ideas, to a different

context of study, and to the need for a different purpose.... This is a tall order, but I believe passionately that religious studies can fire people's minds and hearts; it can help them to know and understand, to analyse and explain, but also to love, to grow strong and confident and to care and be compassionate. In other words, as an object of human enquiry the study of religions can communicate an empowering intellectual and emotional vision.... (King, 2002, pp. 383–84)

Such a passionate plea for (so-called) 'neutral' religious studies has an almost confessional ring to it, but it clearly strikes a note for a different kind of learning experience and intellectual formation.

Second, and similarly, David Ford argues from a theological perspective that the churches need to take their identity as 'learning communities' more seriously. A learning community is one which 'facilitates the learning of all of its members and consciously transforms itself and its context'. Thus:

...perhaps [the church's] main contribution is to be a good learning community itself, where there is joy in knowledge, understanding, insight and wisdom. Can it be a place where people learn to love God with all their minds and to relate everything – all fields of knowledge and all of life – to who God is and what God does? (Ford cited in Archsbishop's Council, 2001, p. 32)

Here Ford appeals to the vocational dimension of the church, arguing that intellectual hospitality is vital to the discipline of theology and to the life of the church. As we have noted before, the church can be strong on its 'teaching office' (or ministry), but it is less clear about how it is a learning organization, a listening body and a reflexive entity.

Taking such an agenda forward would, of course, require a more collaborative approach to learning. Unfortunately, with rare exceptions, such programmes are rarely found. Commenting on the fragmentation and concentration of theological training programmes in the USA, Poling and Miller note how ordinands (or seminarians) are pulled deeply into isolated and disconnected wells of expertise, such as biblical studies, church history and various types of (competing) theologies. In contrast, they argue for a process of:

...community formation [establishing] critical awareness of the tradition, focused community planning...reinterpreting the interplay of covenant and tradition...the [pastor/priest/minister] relates so as to stimulate the formation community... [standing] between the interpretive and political processes...as midwife to community formation.... (Poling and Miller, 1985, p. 147)

Poling and Miller are conscious that there is a deep problem in theological education and formation. First, its lack of groundedness in the real or authentic life of the church means that ordinands or seminarians quickly unlearn, forget or distrust all that they have been taught at theological college. Second, this leads to a weakening of their ties with their congregations, because what has been offered (and quickly discarded) was essentially abstract and verbal. Third, the former students learn to distrust not only their teachers, but also the idea of teaching; they quickly lapse into 'what works', and, at best, manage a kind of orthopraxy:

> Action and reflection methodologies encourage instant theologising, quick responses to whatever is offered. The disciplines of scholarship are replaced by agility of response. (Poling and Miller, 1985, p. 149)

More likely, however, they will be slightly schizoid in theological orientation: cherished theories seldom match practice. The irony here is that the depth of theological formation has probably not gone deep enough. Interestingly, Poling and Miller suggest that the missing element from many theological programmes is any serious attention to the ways in which a sense of *community* is a major part of the process of formation.[1] Rather, as I have been arguing throughout, it is as and when the community recognizes that the environment and context itself is educative that something deeper can commence. Once students realize that the theological college or seminary itself is merely *part* of the schooling process, they can begin to understand how what they are studying relates to who and where they are, what they are about, and what they are about to become.[2]

Inevitably, we are drawn to saying that most theological education rarely reflects on itself (as a dynamic, process and so on), and is seldom able to evaluate its performance. This is extraordinary when one considers the all-pervasive nature of theological reflection across faith communities, which is by no means restricted to professional clerics or academics. Edward Farley, in one of the more influential essays in the field of theological formation, calls for a 'hermeneutic of situations' in which the taught and skilled interpreter will learn to:

> ... uncover the distinctive contents of the situation, will probe its repressed past, will explore its relation to other situations with which it is intertwined, and will also explore the 'demand' of the situation through consideration of corruption and redemption ... a practical theology of these activities and environments will correct their [that is, the clergy's] traditional pedagogical isolation through a special hermeneutics of these situations.... (Farley, 1987, p. 67)

Again, this approach challenges some of the fundamental assertions relating to the nature of theology. In Farley's thinking, the situations are themselves the crucible for learning and teaching, not something other to which theology is 'applied'. In theological education, therefore, stories, world-views and narratives take on a new significance as the *place* of engagement and interpretation. Or, put more theologically, Christian education becomes an expression of the incarnate dimensions that it ultimately bears witness to.

---

[1] Poling and Miller also criticize theological colleges for being 'in bondage to upper middle-class interest[s]' and male interests: 'the concerns of blacks, Hispanics ... native Americans, Asian and African Christians are seldom represented ... '. (1985, p. 148).

[2] For an alternative vision, see Pobee (1997) and Ferris (1990).

One final point relating to the place of evaluation needs to be made in this brief section. We have already suggested that critical self-reflection, for the church and its theology is a difficult issue. Because the church believes that it teaches 'The Truth', questions of performance and evaluation seem to imply a certain relativity to what is essentially timeless. For many Christian traditions, evaluation simply drags revelation down to the level of the world. But it need not be so. Evaluation is an opportunity to reflect critically on how effective theology might be for its tasks, including the formation of individuals and whole communities for ministry. Evaluation should be seen as a potential partner, not a secularist policing activity that has invaded the realm of the sacred. But a certain parable puts it better:

> In the beginning God created the heavens and the earth . . . and God saw everything He made. 'Behold,' said God, 'it is very good'. And the evening and the morning were the sixth day. And on the seventh day God rested from all his work. His archangel then came unto him asking: 'God, how do you know that what you have created is "very good"? What are your criteria? On what data do you base your judgment? Aren't you a little close to the situation to make a fair and unbiased evaluation?'
>
> God thought about these questions all day, and His rest was greatly disturbed.
>
> On the eighth day God said, 'Oh Lucifer, why don't you just go to hell!?'
>
> Thus was evaluation born in a blaze of glory. (Adapted from Pattison and Woodward, 2000, p. 301)

Transformation

We have already touched on the hesitancy and fear surrounding evaluation in relation to theological education and formation. But we also maintain that evaluation is an essential component in the service of transformation. Of course, evaluation is nothing more and nothing less than judging the worth of an activity, and, as such, *informal* evaluation takes place in ecclesial communities all of the time (Pattison and Woodward, 2000, p. 302). However, the hostility to its formal inculcation is a serious problem for the churches as they seek to transform themselves and adapt to the new environment of the twenty-first century. In truth, the problem is deeper and more widespread than is at first apparent. The churches, in valuing their tradition, are not only slow to change; they are also often guilty of resisting it. Proper admiration of the past quickly becomes a dialectical mode: modernity versus the sacred, change versus tradition, and more besides. Paradoxically, transformation can be seen as a sign of weakness and a lack of depth.

Reflecting upon this dynamic more personally, two stories come to mind. First, in attempting to investigate the changing patterns of healthcare chaplaincy in England, I was able to secure a generous grant from a prestigious research body to enable the appointment of a Research Fellow. In the process of designing the research, I naturally approached the Church of England's Hospital Chaplaincy Council to see if they would contribute to or participate in the research. I was surprised to be turned down flat on the basis that 'we know all there is to know about the field, and we can't really see what you are doing this research for' (see Orchard, 2000). The research went ahead anyway, and, unsurprisingly, the Research Fellow discovered a wide range of practices in hospitals related to the delivery of chaplaincy services. Some NHS Trusts had proper systems of accountability, and worked hard to make (state-funded) chaplaincy religiously inclusive by thoroughly involving non-Christian faiths in the shaping of the service and the profession. On the other hand, the Research Fellow also discovered hospitals where the chaplaincy service was ill-defined, poorly managed, lacking in sensitivity to non-Christian faiths and generally offering a poor service to patients and hospital alike.

One can only guess as to why the Church of England should resist research into its own performance at this level, particularly when hospital chaplaincy is mainly funded by the state. But the educational implications are, arguably, the more serious issue here. Research-led investigations into ministerial perfor-mance (evaluation) could feed directly back into the present state of theological education. One might ask: 'How are Anglican chaplains (who constitute almost 70 per cent of the state funding for hospital chaplaincy) supposed to relate to ministers of other faiths and build religiously-inclusive chaplaincy teams?' It is not as easy as it sounds when one considers that the study of non-Christian faiths (or even, for that matter, other Christian denominations) is not part of the approved curriculum for trainee ministers. Neither does the subject become an issue during continuing ministerial education. In other words, the church is deficient in research-led education to enable processes of transformation. And because of this lack, it resists change, including self-critical reflection that would lead to transformations of its own educational formation.

Second, a similar problem exists when it comes to analysing why clergy leave ordained ministry. Each year, approximately 220 clergy leave full-time ordained ministry in the Church of England.[3] The data is collected, but has never been reflected upon. The educational cost alone of this apparent 'wastage' is surely substantial, and yet researching the phenomenon – which might lead to transformations in selection, training, the management of clergy and so forth – is fiercely resisted at almost every level. Again, one can only guess as to why the Church of England would not wish to look at such an obvious area of research. But the lack of critical self-reflection continues to prevent any kind of transformation.

Now, in advocating evaluation, I am, of course, conscious of its limits, especially in relation to theology and the church. Not everything can be counted: skills are not easily measured; teaching and learning may resist certain types of commodification. Besides, theology is an art, not a science, and its appeal and argument are more usually aesthetic than systematic. This leads me to say that the deeper philosophical purpose of evaluation lies in *valuing*. Teaching people to value something or someone is one of the higher callings in

---

[3] Substantial studies do exist in the USA. The Hartford Center for Religion Research has conducted a number of surveys for different denominations that examine why clergy leave full-time ministry.

the vocation of education, so it therefore follows that the politics of evaluation must be securely located in the economy of valuing, in which worth is affirmed, but flaws can also be identified, discussed and, where possible, corrected (see Pattison and Woodward, 2000, p. 303).

The advantage of considering questions of transformation from the perspective of valuing is that it anticipates critical self-reflection in the service of improvement and broader social flourishing. In her ground-breaking *Transforming Practice* (1996), Elaine Graham uses the Aristotelian concept of *phronesis* to identify the type of 'practical wisdom' that ecclesial communities need to seek in order to adapt and transform themselves. Using the work of Don Browning (1991) as an additional foundation, Graham argues that practical theology as transforming practice can come about when it is reconceived as 'the articulation and excavation of sources and norms of Christian practice' (Pattison and Woodward, 2000, p. 104). By this phrase, Graham means much more than is immediately apparent. She is suggesting that theological education (especially pastoral studies) needs to pull away from alliances with 'soft' therapeutic sciences and clerical concerns and move towards seeing practical theology as something that is 'primarily undertaken with and by intentional communities of faith'. In other words, as I have been arguing throughout, theological education needs to take seriously ecclesial communities as a primary *place* and *focus* of theological education. But how would this become transforming practice? Five points need to be made here.

First, one understanding of practical theology is to enable churches to 'practise what they preach'. To do this, particular attention needs to be paid to the habits, customs and beliefs of churches, in order to identify what it is they value and espouse. Graham argues that this kind of inquiry requires a 'postmodern' methodology of *bricolage* (Lakeland, 1997) – one that pieces together fragments of knowledge, aware that disclosure of identity is often ambiguous and incomplete (Graham in Pattison and Woodward, 2000, p. 106). (Suffice to say, these sentiments complement the feminist perspectives offered in Chapter 4, which meditated on the quilting metaphor.)

Second, Graham argues that the postmodern is less of a successor to modernity and more of a complementary and critical corrective to it. It is through postmodern templates that the hubris of modernity can be questioned; its optimism, literalism, imperialism, objectivism and totalitarianism can be interrogated, and its limits probed. From here, the *alterity* of communities (including churches) can move from the margins into the mainstream as their voices are heard afresh.

Third, a focus on the entirety of Christian practice allows for a new opening up of the boundaries and horizons of Christian education. Once *praxis* and *context* is seen to be 'hermeneutically primary', Christian experience is properly repositioned as the *origin* of theological formulation, and not the application of 'learning' upon experience. Correspondingly, ecclesial communities are once again established as the primary ground of theological education, as a critical discipline that interrogates the norms and values that shape and guide all corporate activity, through which 'the community enacts its identity' (Graham, p. 109).

Fourth, practical wisdom, which emerges out of the first three stages, now breaks through the typical theory – practice or abstract – applied dialects and now sees all writing, speaking, theorizing and activity within churches as performative *practices* that bind communities together, enabling them to share commitments and values. Thus, the *phronesis* of an ecclesial community is both inhabited and enacted. Theological education and spiritual formation is an innate part of the *ordinary* life of the church.

Fifth and finally, Graham's attention to *alterity* (otherness) invites churches to reflect on their diversity and inclusiveness. Distinguishing between disclosure and foreclosure, Graham notes how certain groups, practices, needs, insights and agendas are often overlooked or silenced by the churches. True theological education, therefore, in order to fulfil its transformative vocation, must pay constant attention to 'the other'. This requires not only openness (in terms of boundaries and horizons of possibility), but also a hermeneutic of suspicion that will have the capacity to excavate norms and sources with a critical–reflective mind (Graham, 1996, p. 112).

To earth these observations a little more, let us return to an instance that we referred to earlier in this section: clergy leaving full-time ordained ministry. With Graham's insights to hand, we are now in a better position to understand why the agenda (in terms of research, better pastoral care and a review of selection and training methods) is so easily marginalized within the churches. To explore this area would require the registering of pain, the recognition of failure, the hurts and wounds that institutions inflict on individuals, as well as those that individuals inflict on institutions. It is a messy, complex arena to address, and one that could only begin to be approached through narrative *bricolage* (that is, a sensitivity to people's stories, an acuity for the latent oppression inherent within many practices and organizations and so on) and methodological *bricolage* (that is, ethnography, ecclesiology, pastoral studies and the like). Furthermore, it requires the church to explore its own types of marginal alerity and, in so doing, revisit its praxis in the light of its conventional norms and sources, excavating their meaning and application. So, we might ask, what does Christian tradition have to say to people who, for whatever reason, fail in Christian ministry? What do the codes and rules of the church say, and, more importantly, what do they *convey* to those who have departed or been forced to leave? How is the pain and grief of the laity who lose a minister addressed or recognized? How is the hope of redemption manifested in disciplinary procedures (occasionally trials) and other measures that are sometimes taken against a departing minister? It is in addressing the pain, here, in the body of Christ itself, that transforming practice can begin to emerge and offer the genuine possibility of the renewal of theological education.

Liberation

Our observations take us, quite naturally, back into the field of liberation theology, a term that is loosely used to describe a variety of theologies that makes the specific liberation of a group (marginalized or oppressed by virtue of class, race, gender, sexuality, wealth, ethnicity and so on) its primary purpose and a theological fundament. The roots of liberation theology lie principally in Latin American theology and also in the civil rights struggles within the USA. But at the very base of these roots lies a theory of education that was first developed by Paulo Freire. For Freire, two approaches to education must be rejected. The first is the traditionalist, which defends 'class interests, to which that faith is subordinated'. Here, Freire cites an example of how faith is narrated as something to be 'protected' against the potential ravages of revolution or Marxism. Second, he opposes the alternative modernizing agenda, which is deemed to offer reform so as to only 'preserve the status quo'. Freire rejects both these options in favour of a prophetic perspective on education that envisages education as 'an instrument of transforming action, as political praxis at the service of human liberation' (Freire, 1973, p. 544; Astley *et al.*, 1996, p. 167). For Freire, that will necessarily involve a further, more radical excavation of norms and sources. Thus:

> They [that is, the churches] discover through praxis that their 'innocent' period was not the least impartial . . . [when others] insist on the 'neutrality' of the church . . . they castrate the prophetic dimension . . . . (Freire, 1973, pp. 524–45)

Freire's agenda has been taken forward by a variety of scholars. For example, Thomas Groome (1980) argues (rather as I have) that Christian praxis is the normative form of theological education. This contribution, from a more mainstream (Western) theologian opens up the possibility of theology beginning with the praxis of the poor. But, at the same time, the more radical edge of liberation theology should not be lost in the milieu of praxis-centred theology, for the *desiderata* of liberation theology remains liberation, not development. There is a perpetual rawness to liberation theology that refuses to be consolidated and consoled by accommodationist strategies that do not fully embrace a radical revolutionary revision of structures and contexts.

Again, this type of assertion about the nature and purpose of theological education takes us back to one of our prior questions: the nature of theology itself. What or, perhaps, who is it for? There are several different answers to this question, but our purpose in opening up this brief section on liberation with attacks on neutrality is to show that there is no point on the theological compass that is non-directive. In other words, an inquiry into the nature of theological education is an inherently political process that challenges the shaping and ordering of the discipline itself, long before anything is ever 'taught' by anyone.

That said, liberation theology still stands within a broader tradition of theology – that of the hope of transformation. As Richard Grigg perceptively argues, religion itself can be defined as 'a means toward ultimate transformation' (Grigg, 1990, p. 8; cf. Streng *et al.*, 1973, p. 6). But although one might try and distinguish between theology and religion – theology being the 'intellectual approach to the infinite' – the distinction barely works in practice, since:

... the infinite that theology attempts to understand is just that infinite which can aid us in dealing with fundamental practical dilemmas connected to our finitude... theological reflection tends always to point to religious practice (Grigg, 1990, p. 8)

Grigg extends his theorizing to reflect on the particularity of liberation theology and what is methodologically distinctive about its programme for the field of theological education. Drawing on the work of Robert Long (1978), Grigg identifies six characteristics of liberating hermeneutics.

The first is 'a different starting point'. Instead of beginning with abstract theories, liberation theology commences with the 'experience of being marginalised or excluded'. Second, there is a different interlocutor. Liberation theology does not seek to persuade non-believers with intellectual or philosophical doubts; rather, it works with the people who are oppressed. Third, liberation theology uses different tools. It sets aside metaphysical speculation and opts for the insights of sociologists, political theorists (often Marxist) and historians. Fourth, liberation theology offers a different analysis. Instead of assuming a harmony between peoples and a degree of neutrality in methodology, it presumes that injustice is already in-built. Fifth, there is a different tone to the engagement. Instead of assuming that there will be a definitive Truth or principle to be arrived at, liberation theology maintains that the struggle for justice and truth will be ongoing and be known only in perpetual praxis. Sixth and finally, liberation theology proposes a different kind of theology. Instead of truth 'from above' (that is often then imposed on the world), liberation theology seeks to discover liberating truth in praxis, through a process of critical reflection. It is these six characteristics that, together, will begin the process of transformation that may actually and ultimately enable liberation (Grigg, 1990, pp. 75–76).

Having discussed liberation theology and education, it is important to state that the promulgation of formation, transformation and liberation as essential characteristics of theological education are by no means confined to the field of liberation theology. Postmodern writers have been quick to identify the agenda as one that is consonant with their own hermeneutics of suspicion in relation to modernity. Consider, for example, the African-American literary scholar, bell hooks:

> To educate as the practice of freedom is a way of teaching that anyone can learn. That learning process comes easiest to those of us who teach who also believe that there is an aspect to our vocation that is sacred; who believe that our work is not merely to share information but to share in the intellectual and spiritual growth of our students. To teach in a manner that respects and cares for the souls of our students is essential if we are to provide the necessary conditions where learning can most deeply and intimately begin.... (hooks, 1994, p. 13)

As Hodgson (1999, p. 4) notes, hooks sees that teaching 'touches, evokes, energises the very depths of the human, liberates peoples to realise their potential and transform the world'. He links hooks' work to that of John Dewey (1966) who maintained that teaching and education has a sacral dimension to it precisely because it is the means by which human beings maintain themselves through renewal. But how exactly is education the 'practice of freedom'?

Peter Hodgson (1999, pp. 71–80) argues that the tradition is an ancient one, although more implicit than explicit in early theological writings. Gregory of Nyssa, for example, saw Christian *paedia* as renewal, liberation and transformation through individuals imitating Christ. It is here, claims Hodgson, that we first encounter a language of transformative pedagogy. The theme of freedom and education also emerges in the work of Herder and Hegel, with the latter showing particular concern for families and the state and the education of children. Where poor children were put to work at an early age, lack of education meant lack of freedom and a form of economic slavery. Here, the practice of freedom took priority over the consciousness of freedom: Hegel's work is unavoidably political.

Hodgson develops his thesis by suggesting three separate areas where theological education and liberation combine to make a richer theology. To some extent these areas already echo points I have made earlier, but they merit some further elucidation here, as we seek to establish the meaning of theological education. First, Hodgson agrees with Freire's assertion that liberation is not a deposit made in humans. Rather, it is a praxis: 'the action and reflection of human beings upon their world in order to transform it' (Hodgson, 1999, p. 75). As Freire notes:

> The teacher is no longer merely the-one-who-teaches, but one who is himself taught in dialogue with the students, who in turn while being taught also teach. They become jointly responsible for a process in which all grow.... (Freire, 1972, pp. 66–67)

What Freire is saying here is that the subject matter *gives* itself (especially in theology), and that teachers and students are caught up in the dynamic of this gift, which in turn creates, sustains and then transforms their relationships. To be taught, then, means not to be taught *things*, but to be taught *how* to think, which alone can then enable transformation and liberation.

Second, education as the practice of freedom is about radical democracy and social transformation. However, this transformation may not only be about resisting and challenging established social norms, it may also involve enabling society to live more peaceably with its many differences and diversities. One of the higher vocations of education is to enable 'the celebration of differ-ence...[but] persons must learn how to play the politics of difference' (Hodgson, 1999, p. 77).

Third, education as the practice of freedom is potentially conflict-midden and painful. Education presupposes transformation, and this will necessarily involve clashes with prejudices, habits and 'acceptable' forms of behaviour. In other words, it is only when truth is disputed that truth can emerge. And it is only by entering the debate that a dispute can take place. This takes us back, again, to the character and shape of theology. It is not something settled, signed, sealed and delivered. It is, rather, a way of educating: one that is forming, transforming and liberating. Freedom, then, is not easily attained.

The road to liberation (through the practice/praxis of education) is full of traffic with competing interests and travelling in different directions. The would-be traveller is not guaranteed a safe and smooth passage.

Thus far, this chapter has sought to show how theological education might be reconceived as a process of formation, transformation and liberation, culminating in the idea that it is the practice of freedom. I have offered an overview of how this might work, recognizing that the application of the essentials discussed will take on markedly different characters in various types of ecclesial communities. However, I have also sought to show how education as the praxis of freedom is a corporate, dynamic and collaborative exercise, rather than something that is done to or for individuals. Inevitably, the debate and discussion is political in character, since the excavation of the meaning of theological education takes us back to challenging the nature and purpose of the discipline itself. However, we cannot leave the debate at this point, poised as it were, for an endless number of ongoing political disputes.

Hodgson suggests that the way forward for transformative pedagogy is to recognize that it has a dual responsibility quite apart from its vocation to challenge and liberate. The first is to offer 'connected teaching'. Hodgson reverts to the Socratic midwife analogy that we noted in Chapter 2. Teachers draw out truth from their students and enable the dialogical processes of education. The creation of this 'space' also enables spiritual formation and resists the 'banking' model of education in favour of nurturing, encouragement and trust. 'Connected teaching', in other words, assumes a level of cooperation with the student; it requires grace, communion, reserve, inspiration and inclusion.

Second, learning is seen as cooperative. Hodgson asserts that teaching and learning is at its best when the role of the teacher shifts from 'expert/authority figure to facilitator/coach' – one who 'observes, monitors and answers questions'. Again, recognition of the shared nature of learning is at the heart of a transformative pedagogy, and this, in turn, questions many of the prevailing assumptions about the nature of theological education that are present in most churches. Certainly, the recipe advocated here is one fraught with risk, but it issues a simple invitation. Can churches learn to be learners again? And can its teachers learn to truly teach, rather than simply indoctrinate?

Wisdom

In Part II of this book, I have been arguing that theology and theological education needs to be reconceived as a more holistic endeavour, rather than conceiving of theology as a discipline that is solely within the provenance of academics and professional clerics, one in which the whole church participates in the shaping and transformation of its life. Inevitably, this has raised questions about the nature of theology itself, and, in turn, has led to the inference that much of the present (confessionally-led) theological education for ministers in seminaries and theological colleges is too tied in with clericalism and pseudo-professionalism. Of course, many clergy *are* professional in the conduct of their day-to-day ministry, and this is to be applauded and encouraged. But full-time ministers are not 'professionals' in the ways in which other professions (such as lawyers or doctors) understand the term. Clergy can function professionally, but they do not possess skills and knowledge that easily separate them from the laity. They may have specific functions (ontological, or of representation, for example) that set them apart from their congregations, and these may include the power to absolve, bless, consecrate and the like, but there is not the same gap between professional and non-professional that are encountered in other types of work.

Part of the difficulty in reflecting on theological education is in addressing the question: 'Who is it for?' Clearly, many individuals and congregations would assert that, within reason, it is for everyone. And as we have already argued, the life of the church itself constitutes a kind of theological education in its own right. Beyond this, many would assume that theological education is the 'discipline' of the 'professionals'. But this is doubtful, since the clergy of most denominations can, at best, only be described as 'semi-professional', on account of the fact that pay, structures, patterns of accountability and reviewing procedures are, at best, ad hoc. The vocational nature of the clerical 'task' ensures that clergy are free to practise their 'trade', within reason, how they wish. The demands on their time may be many and varied, but the actual ecclesial or sacramental obligations only constitute a small percentage of their duties.

This observation is in no way meant to deny the clergy of their skills. On the contrary, it is intended to draw attention to the fact that, theologically, the wisdom of God is not 'something' that is in the possession of only a few. Strictly speaking, it is a gift that is part of the whole church and can be exercised and discerned by any number of individuals or groups at various times. Moreover, the wisdom of God is not something that is necessarily 'learned' in any conventional sense, as though at school or college. It is sometimes formed out of spiritual experience; equally, it may also come from the qualia of the church, or from worship. It is no accident that spiritual directors and mystics talk about 'the school of prayer' or 'spiritual lessons'; they are pointing to a different kind of knowledge and to a different aspect to the theological formation of the church that is not concerned with curricula.[4]

Most writers in the field of theological education have an understanding of this dynamic. Hodgson, for example, in describing education as 'paideia', confesses that:

> ...for education to happen in its most fullest and most radical sense the paideutic power of God is required. This is what makes education an intrinsically religious endeavour.... (Hodgson, 1999, p. 87)

---

[4] For example, the classic 'spiritual fruits' that are prayed for at confirmation for each candidate are acquired through disciplined discipleship and the free bestowal of God's graciousness. They are: grace, wisdom, understanding, counsel, spiritual strength, knowledge and true godliness.

Hodgson looks back at the Old Testament and New Testament tradition of Sophia (the wisdom of God) and, using theologians such as John Cobb, David Kelsey and Edward Farley, identifies wisdom as a [new] way of seeing (ibid., p. 89), where reasoning, contemplation, the affections and action are brought together in a new and enhanced harmony. This leads him to reflect on the teaching of wisdom, and quite naturally, as a Christian theologian, he identifies Jesus as 'the incarnation of wisdom':

> What is distinctive about Jesus is not incarnation as such but the uniquely powerful manifestation of divine Wisdom in his teaching, which is at once his praxis of care, healing, and gathering. His teaching assumes a normative, paradigmatic quality in human history. It simply has the power in a profound way to draw people out of their daily preoccupations and petty provincialisms into an encounter with the eternal, with ultimate truth and value, with unbounded love, with a radical, transformative freedom. Jesus does not set this forth in a series of propositions, laws or theoretical statements. Rather, very much like Socrates, he engages in conversation with people, forcing them to reflect on their own traditions and to think about their deeper meaning. Rather than offering something totally new, Jesus radicalizes the shared traditions. He is the teacher who brings the Torah alive in such a remarkably powerful and direct way that its implications could not be avoided .... He teaches with an authority that is evident to all who hear him (Matt. 7: 29). He is called 'Rabbi' or 'Teacher' .... (Hodgson, 1999, p. 98)

But, of course, Jesus does something that Socrates does not do: he speaks in parables, an event in themselves, insofar as they have no fixed meaning and yet say and mean so much. Theologically, they mirror the incarnation itself in that they are relational, rather than propositional, in character. They are bounded stories, and yet they open up horizons of possibility and vision that is part of the economy of God's freedom. In parables, everyday logic is turned on its head: errant sons are welcomed back with celebration; 99 sheep are abandoned, wastefully, for fear of losing just one; workers are seldom rewarded in proportion to their effort. Parables can be read and reread, but their meaning and interpretation is never exhausted, because as agents of instruction, teaching and learning, they 'live' as stories that continue to shape and mould individuals and communities.

Hodgson concludes his meditation on wisdom in theological education by identifying the 'depth dimension or transformative power' of three basic elements in wisdom. These are: critical thinking, heightened imagination and liberating practice. What is noteworthy about these qualities is his insertion of qualifiers. No-one could really dispute that wisdom consists of thinking, imagination and practice. But the insertion of 'critical', 'heightened' and 'liberating' gives a different edge to his theology of education. To some extent, the proper place of the critical has already been touched upon in this chapter – the necessity of encouraging faithful doubt as a means to growth is a given within education, especially theological. The heightening of imagination, however, depends on the ability and courage of individuals to 'think outside the box' – to take risks with formation in the wider pursuit of transformation. A heightened (and deepened) imagination is, clearly, an appropriate quality to encourage within any discipline, but it is, at the same time, something that confesses that the discipline is incomplete and requires new insight. Liberating practice, in turn, requires the courage to challenge, reject, overthrow, recreate and more besides, and places education once again at the service of freedom and social flourishing; the liberal spirit is connected to liberation.

In order to draw this together more, let me offer a concrete and practical example of wisdom operating within a context of 'collective vocation', namely an all-age parish weekend.[5] The theme of the weekend was studying scripture, and part of the education and formation of the church members (all ages, from 7 to 70 plus) was to consider the question of how to read the Bible. Rather than simply ask the question, several manageable groups (again mixed, all-age) were created and given large sheets of paper, crayons, glue and magazines to make collages or drawings. The exercise was introduced by the facilitor holding up a large plain leather-bound black Bible and inviting the groups to design a cover for it that reflected its contents. They were also told that 'Bible' is a word that only means 'collection of books' and asked to come up with a better title. As the groups worked, small historical stories were offered to feed their imaginations: the first English Bible; how the Bible came to be divided into chapters and verses; amusing mistakes in early printings of the Bible; early Celtic illuminated manuscripts.

The covers that were produced were remarkable, as children and adults had contributed ideas on mostly equal terms. Naturally, the inspiration behind each individual idea was what the group thought the Bible meant to them, or perhaps their idea of the most memorable or significant stories. This, in turn, quite naturally promoted a discussion about why stories or sayings were valued by some but not by others, and vice versa. Even more illuminating was the attempt to 'capture' the Bible in a new title. There were some humorous ones (*Would you Adam and Eve it?*), some dogmatic (*The Truth, the Whole Truth and Nothing but the Truth*), and some that tried to bridge dogma and humour (*God: The Autobiography*).[6]

However, the whole group – almost 100 people in all – eventually settled on a new title: *God – Some Stories By His Friends.* But the agreement was by no means unanimous. Some felt that 'his' was too gender-specific, which led to further (slightly heated) discussion. A few felt that the word 'stories' implied that what the Bible said might not be true or who, at best, fable-like. Others protested that the Bible was full of stories that were not 'true' (such as the parables), if 'truth' meant something that was 'historically verifiable'. Others said that large parts of the Old Testament were fables and shouldn't be read as history. Some people were agitated that an essentially 'fun' and collaborative exercise was now exposing some quite deep divisions in the group about the nature of scripture – a book that, in theory, unites Christians. But the discussion was well managed, and nobody lost their temper.

---

[5] This is an exercise I have used myself on several occasions, but I was first introduced to it by the Reverends Debbie and Michael Peatman, to whom I am grateful.

[6] This latter title was rejected, as participants said biblical writings were *about* and not *by* God.

As I reflect on this event, I realize that I have rarely been part of a meeting where critical thinking, heightened imagination and liberating practice came together so well, and for such a diverse range of people. Naturally, there was, in the end, no agreement about the precise nature of the Bible, but that is what the exercise taught us. You can't know a book by its cover; you can't judge a book by its title. Perhaps there was a hidden wisdom in such an economic title, and (normally) such dull or generic covers. Perhaps what we learnt was this. When we stood outside the Bible, we couldn't agree on what it was. But when we read it together, we were mysteriously united, even as we were transformed. As Auden (1955, p. 46) says:

> Truth in any serious sense
> Like Orthodoxy, is a reticence ...

Education and Vocation

In an important contribution to this debate, Nicholas Wolterstorff argues that the question of vocation not only goes to the heart of theological endeavour, but also raises profound questions in society about the nature and purpose of education. Basing his analysis on North American schools and colleges, Wolterstorff argues that amongst the primary purposes of Christian education are forming persons within a pluralistic society and 'educating for shalom' (Wolterstorff, 2002, pp. 253ff). According to Wolterstorff, this type of vocation involves risk and care, and also requires churches to resist indoctrinating people into faith. For Wolterstorff, addressing his own Evangelical constituency, such an approach to education is utterly deficient:

> It may seem true to you that a college is a place for people to soak up a tradition and not to learn to think, but do not suppose then that what you are proposing is Christian education. It may seem safer to you to advise your students to keep out of contact with opposing religious systems, but do not suppose then that the still-born, culture-abstracted system you present has much at all to do with Christian education. It may seem surer to you to demand of your students that they memorize a whole list of dogmatic propositions ... but never for a moment delude yourself that you are participating in Christian education .... (Wolterstorff, 2002, p. 10)

That risk and care should emerge as themes within the consideration of vocation need not surprise us. Wolterstorff is arguing for pluralism to be taken seriously as a *co-educator*; without risking dogmatic certainties in conversation, trial and critical inquiry there can be no true education. But, of course, the character of this engagement must be shaped around the care of the student and an overall care for the process of engagement. The reason for this is that the deeper purpose of education is revealed, according to Wolterstorff, in the collective aspect of vocation: educating for shalom. And this is achieved through care in the enunciation of the tasks and invitation of education – 'teaching for gratitude' and 'teaching for justice'. Thus:

> Education is ultimately always shaped by a vision of the nature and possibility of human flourishing... the vision of human flourishing that underlies the biblical narrative and proclamation is what biblical writers call shalom. Shalom is harmony and delight in all one's relationships – with God, with other human beings, with culture, with nature, with oneself. The picture... is an essentially relational picture – and then, a multi-relational picture... Christian education is education that strives both to exhibit shalom and equip for shalom.... (Wolterstorff, 2002, p. 262)

Wolterstorff's vision is a particularly 'biblical' one that naturally arises out of his Evangelical and Bible-based hermeneutics. Although useful in a number of respects, many will struggle with his theological strategy – an inductive methodology that legitimizes praxis from a scriptural base for the purposes of establishing a definitive type of 'Christian' education. Much more promising are the essays in the collection from Jones and Paulsell, entitled *The Scope of Our Art* (2002). In this volume, the authors set out to explore the common nature of the vocational task in theological education, but from a wide representation of disciplines. The editors acknowledge that there were 'profound theological differences among us' and that 'our pedagogical practices were diverse, as were our understandings of our tasks as theological teachers' (Jones and Paulsell, 2002, p. vii). Nevertheless, a rich conversation ensues, which deepens and heightens the sense of what vocation might mean.

For example, Clark Gilpin sees the vocation of theological education as a 'vibrant attachment to public thoughts' (ibid., pp. 3ff). For Paul Griffiths it is 'particularly Christian intellectual habits' (ibid., pp. 32ff). Paul Wadell sees the task as enabling his students 'to grow captivated by God' (ibid., pp. 120ff). Susan Simonaitis argues that it is to initiate students into 'the difficult discipline of genuine conversation' (ibid., pp. 99ff). Bonnie Miller-McLemore and Rosemary Skinner Keller press their case for an understanding of vocation that includes the whole of one's life and is therefore linked to values, behaviour and discipleship. But there is a unity in the collection of essays which further supports our contention that theological education needs to be seen as more of a collective vocation:

> ...several common touchstones emerged. We had all been influenced, it seemed, by Simone Weil's work on attention, especially in relation to intellectual work. All of us were intrigued by her claim that academic study can hone our capacity for attention, making us better able to be present to God and to our suffering neighbour. We felt that cultivation of attention in our teaching and our learning, our reading and our writing, our relationships with our colleagues and our administrative work was crucial to the practice of our vocation. Mindfulness, generosity, hospitality, and discipline also emerged as common themes.... (Miller-McLemore and Keller in Jones and Paulsell, 2002, p. ix)

The essays – space does not permit a detailed, individual discussion of each – are remarkable for their identification of the costly nature of teaching. Essayists speak easily of the 'cultivation of wisdom', the need for 'generative lectures' that encourage conversation, discipline that enhances 'compassionate listening', and sharing in the 'constant struggle to understand the world of their students'. There is, however, in the final analysis, no agreement on the nature of vocation for the theological educator, although most of the authors are drawn to an illustration from the early church father (Cappadocian) Gregory Nazianzen (329–390 CE):

> ...[our] vocation is the care of souls...the scope of our art is to provide the soul with wings.... If it abides we are to take it by the hand; if it is in danger, to restore it; if it is ruined...[to redeem it]. (Jones and Paulsell, 2002, p. 202)

In view of these remarks, we can say that vocations are better understood in terms of calling and gift, which we might say, theologically speaking, are extensions of the generosity of God. Yet, as we have already hinted, there can be no avoidance of the political and social implications of even the most spiritualized vocation, and certainly not of those vocations that are related (more generally) to the caring or formation of persons. Arguably, a key task for theology and the churches at the turn of the millennium is to underline the imperative of vocations as an essential fundament in the proper ordering of a just society. This does not necessarily return society to religion or to some kind of spirituality, whether specific, collaborative or general. Yet such a move might at least prevent the ethos and ethic of service from becoming overwhelmed by inimical market forces. The restoration of the vocational holds out some real possibilities for the reconstitution of society not only in terms of gift, offering and collaboration, but also in terms of a thorough and prophetic critique of the prevailing cultural and political powers that shape educational praxis.

Understanding

Understanding theological education as a collective vocation – something shared out within ecclesial communities and between students and teachers – has emerged as a major key to the renewal of theological education in churches, seminaries and theological colleges. The renarration of the nature and tasks of theology, and the argument against its clericalization and professionalization, have led us to a point where we can now begin to make some tentative closing remarks. However, like all conclusions within the realm of practical theology – especially one that is concerned with theological education – the words will have to be tested, honed and implemented with a proper praxis. This is because vocational professions such as teaching are of vital interest to theology. As Jenkins suggests, proper reflection on the nature of service and vocation is part of theology's task and its contribution to public life:

> ...to revive a proper priestliness right across our society, we [need to] persuade one another widely that the time is ripe not only for the rehabilitation of the caring professions but also for a readiness to speak up in the form of a caring *confession*...quality of life is more important than consumption of goods...cher-

ishing people and sustaining the earth is more important than growth... and belonging and finding meaning and enjoyment together is more important than competition.... (Jenkins, 1990, p. 76)

Correspondingly, it is important to recall that the task of practical theology itself is not simply to provide empathy with a well-meaning and articulate theological gloss. It is, rather, more serious and costly: 'constructive statements about God's relation to human experience which leads to strategies of liberating action... [and]... the analysis of experience and culture through the use of critical [theory]' (Graham and Poling, 2000, pp. 163–66). A good practical theology of theological education will, in other words, seek the necessary transformations that might advance liberation and critical self-reflection, helping the churches, individuals and colleges come to terms with the nature and tasks of theology in fresh and relevant ways that might further enable social and human flourishing.

But where exactly does this take us? What does it mean to talk about 'faith in the church' in the same breath as 'the meaning of theological education'? The title chosen for this chapter was deliberately provocative, and I have been arguing throughout that the church, in all its plurality as a culture, place, repository of belief and customs, is the primary location for theological education and formation. It is in working in, through and with the whole church that the whole people of God encounter wisdom and gain under-standing. Although I have been arguing against specific specialization in theological education, I have, of course, recognized that some are called to that vocation. What is at issue, then, is the manner of their engagement with the community and the extent to which educators *listen* and pay proper attention to the important theological disclosures that are present in ecclesial and spiritual qualia. This leads me to make several points about the character of theological education by way of conclusion. Clearly, these points are not exhaustive, but they do resonate with the concerns expressed at the beginning of this chapter, and their adoption opens up new and rich possibilities for understanding theology as a collective vocation.

First, theological education is a dialogue or conversation. In Christian theology, there is no 'abstract' or 'pure' method of theology. It is essentially a responsive, reflective and reliable means of resolving issues in relation to problems and particular contexts. As I have argued from the outset, all theology is, essentially, *practical*: the discipline is birthed in praxis. This means that the discipline not only has to teach; it has to listen. Moreover, the discipline is concerned with educating 'listening persons into [being] active learners' (Melchert, 1998, p. 293).

Second, theological education is a kind of schooling in apprenticeship, and it steers individuals and communities through life; it is not just an abstract philosophy or part-time pursuit. The New Testament bears witness to a variety of apprenticeship models that are concerned with discipleship, some of which are quite radical (for example, Jesus' call to leave families, leave the dead unburied, and so on), and others which are perhaps more obvious (for example, Paul and Timothy). But it is important to grasp that apprenticeship is more dialogical than hierarchical: guidance prevails over obedience. As Melchert states:

> [The apprentice] begins by watching, performing routine tasks, gradually learning to understand...often this cannot be taught, yet must be learned...[some things] cannot be transmitted in a purely verbal manner....there are some things that only 'make sense' when they have been mastered.... (Melchert, 1998, p. 293)

Third, theological education can be playful and teasing: 'it does not command so much as it seeks to persuade' (Murphy, 1990, p. 15). I have already touched upon the parabolic pedagogy of Jesus, which is, of course, as intrinsically playful as it is unsettling. The idea of playfulness is not meant to imply that education is not serious; it clearly is. It is, rather, to discover again that play is one of those means through which we learn more than we can be taught, and that certain types of teasing can unpick new meanings and open different vistas of interpretation. (As we saw earlier, an essentially playful exercise about the nature of scripture exposed serious opinions about how the Bible was to be regarded and read).[7]

Fourth, theological education is concerned with forming persons of integrity (Melchert, 1998, p. 301). This points to some of the self-critical dynamics that we explored earlier. Biblical wisdom literature is peppered with biting satire and exposures of hypocrisy, and consistently points out the gaps (to use modern idiom) between rhetoric and reality, belief and behaviour. This is important for theological education, because integrity is closely linked to the 'integral' or 'whole', and here again we return to the theme of discipleship in relation to theological education, and the nature and purpose of theology. Good theological education, rightly conceived, can explore and address the 'gaps' in churches and Christian lives, putting together those things that have long been held apart (ibid., p. 302).

Fifth and finally, theological education is a type of death and resurrection. Just as Fowler's stages (with which we began) have to fall and die before a new stage can be born and lived, so it is with theological education. To learn in theology, one must constantly let go of cherished truths and dogma, and learn to face the possibility of death and new life together. Too often, ecclesial communities, seminaries and theological colleges, like many other institutions, invent traditions, customs or beliefs that deny death or seek to evade it. Sometimes educators, in order to avoid conflict, will collude with this. At other times, the death of an idea or school of thinking is forced too quickly and eagerly, leaving the student no time to grieve for cherished ideas that they may need to let go of. It is at this point that the vocational nature of the theological educator reaches its peak:

---

[7] See the extended discussion in Melchert (1998, pp. 295–301). Melchert argues that Socrates, Plato and other classical philosophers understood that 'serious play' was a profound catalyst and agent within the pedagogical economy. Furthermore, the wisdom literature of the Bible is full of ironic play and wise teaching that is, on the face of it, simply 'folk humour'.

[It] is both to allow the needed death of the old and then to use one's caring to sustain and support the learner in finding and shaping new truth and thus new life. There are even times when a teacher has to do the hoping for a learner, for experience has taught the teacher that there is a path on the other side of the pain.... (Melchert, 1998, p. 304)

Furthermore, as I noted in the Introduction, the study of congregations is also something that is not taught at theological colleges. This means that the qualia of the church are too often easily dismissed and that 'operant religion' is not treated as seriously as 'formal religion' (Roof, 1985). The ancestry of this absence lies in a profound imperfection in the notion of theological education, and in an extremely poor understanding of theology. James Hopewell once again draws our attention to the agenda:

... an analysis of both local congregational idiom and the way the gospel message confronts and yet is conveyed by that language would be a better starting point for efforts to assist the local church. Rather than assume that the primary task of ministry is to alter the congregation, church leaders should make a prior commitment to understand the nature of the object they propose to improve ... many strategies for operating upon local churches are uninformed about the cultural constitution of the parish; many schemes are themselves exponents of the culture they seek to overcome. (Hopewell, 1987, p. 11)

Thus, the theological enterprise for which we are ultimately arguing emerges as something altogether richer and more empathetic:

To ponder seriously the finite culture of one's own church, given the promise of God's redemptive presence within it, opens up a vast hermeneutical undertaking. The congregation recedes as primarily a structure to be altered and emerges as a structure of social communication within which God's work in some ways already occurs. The hermeneutical task is not merely the mining of biblical revelation in ways meaningful to individuals. It is more basically the tuning of the complex discourse of a congregation so that the gospel sounds within the message of its many voices. (Ibid.)

This means that theological education is about finding God both in the church and in the wider culture of ordinary life, knowing and experiencing faith in its operant, as well as formal, expressions and their capacity to teach, form and transform.

I began Part II by noting that reform of theological education was a live issue for the churches. I have then tried to show how the traditional 'teaching church' (and its theological education) lacks an appropriate philosophy of education to guide the formation of its theological education. This is due to narrowly conceived definitions of theology that take little account of the multiplicity of ways in which people learn about God and acquire their own theology. All too frequently, those who want to offer theological education want to exclude certain types of knowledge and experience from the 'discipline', as though this somehow constituted a proper delimiting and concentration of the subject. So, the 'teaching church' fails to connect with authority because it dismisses authenticity and the integrity of the lives and experiences of individuals. It also tends to concentrate its 'education' for clergy or ministers into one single period (prior to ordination or licensing) and puts few resources into ongoing educative processes that take place throughout ministerial life.[8]

In contrast I have attempted to show that theology is for everyone. I have advanced the argument through a classic type of 'practical theological approach', which takes issues and contexts seriously and allows them to shape and form the theological debate. This has allowed me to suggest that theological education is more about shared and different world-views than it is about linear progression through stages. It is more about discipleship, apprenticeship, mothering, parenting and nurturing than most will want to admit. And, if it is education at all, it should be about the transformation and liberation of individuals rather than the preservation of ideas and institutions. But to get to this point requires letting go, listening deeply and patiently, and becoming a learner yourself.

Conclusion

After all that has been said, curricular questions necessarily come to the surface. What could or should a theological college programme look like? How would such a programme, concentrated in a seminary or theological college, flow out into the life of the church? How does the life of the church flow into the seminary? Following Van de Ven (1998) and Jones in Jones and Paulsell (2002), here are some brief but revolutionary suggestions for curricular development, which are mindful of the need for seminaries to become 'settings for formal enquiry in which people's beliefs are tested, nurtured, criticized and revised' (Jones and Paulsell, 2002, p. 202).

1 First, the teaching of critical–reflective skills should be extended across all disciplines offered at theological college, and encouraged in churches. Such skills should not be confined to pastoral or practical theology.
2 Congregational Studies should be taught as a separate discipline, enabling ministers to read and learn from their congregations. (The possibilities for this are indicated in Part III of this book.)
3 Congregations should be reconceived by 'professional' theologians or trainee ministers as 'communities of practice', in which the theological understanding, knowledge and practice of a given church can help shape theology itself. A community of practice can teach those who come with knowledge, and seek to deposit it. Congregations should also be understood as contexts of 'informal' learning and teaching, where beliefs and understandings are shaped by shared practice, rather than shared dogma.

---

[8] Inevitably, the 'deposit-banking-episodic' approach to education is replicated in parishes and congregations by the ministers themselves, leading to further impoverishment in collaborative learning and a deficiency in the idea of theology being a shared vocation.

4   Educational philosophy should be taught and developed as a distinct area within theological colleges. Given that one of the primary tasks of a minister is to fulfil the office of teaching, it is a scandal that educational theory (teaching and learning) is not addressed explicitly.

5   Correspondingly, challenges to tradition should be squarely faced with research – the continual interrogation of the basis for faith and ministry, both for the individual and the community.

6   Practical theology should be taught in more depth than it is at present. Currently, theological colleges tend to view the area as 'pastoral' or 'reflective' for ministry; it is not seen as sufficiently significant to be able to probe mainstream traditions. But as we have seen, this is not the case at all. Practical theology is, arguably, the *core* professional discipline for clergy.

7   The range and compass of subjects offered at seminaries should be expanded; at present there is little attention to cultural studies or to social sciences. This inevitably makes theological education into a discipline that either ignores the world or attempts to dominate or outnarrate it, without ever really engaging with it. The result is either ignorance or arrogance – neither of which is desirable or necessary.

8   Correspondingly, it should be recognized that any reflection on theological education is, *prima facie*, an inquiry into the nature of the discipline itself. Constant critical reflection can enable and empower the academy, churches and the public sphere to change. Education-as-transformation is a vital vocation.

9   Finally, churches should consider setting up research and development units which help shape the educative agenda for their seminaries and the formative ecclesial and missiological horizons for churches. In other words, research should lead and inform teaching. This is not only an educational strategy; of itself, it constitutes a powerful statement about the life and work of the Holy Spirit in the church and world at large. Put another way, to inspire, theology and theological education should primarily be inspired. This is both its calling and fulfilment.

PART III
THEOLOGICAL CULTURE
AND THE CONCRETE
CHURCH

Chapter 7

Adventure and Atrophy in a Charismatic Movement[1]

Introduction

In Part III of this book we turn to the study of the concrete church and deploy the interpretative framework of James Hopewell (1987). Successive chapters sketch how his work, applied to various ecclesial situations, illuminates the study of the church and practical theology. This chapter explores the romanticism of a Charismatic congregation. The next chapter looks at the tragic world-view of a movement within the Church of England. The closing chapter in this Part identifies a denomination (Anglicanism) as comic–ironic in its outlook. To the best of my knowledge, this is the first time that Hopewell's interpretative framework has been used on something more than congregation, and, although one should be cautious about its applicability to movements and denominations, I suspect that there are valuable insights that gained from such an analysis.

Dating from 1994, the 'Toronto Blessing' is the name for a phenomenon that is associated with the Toronto Airport Christian Fellowship. From its very foundation, the Vineyard Christian Church in Toronto had experienced many of the things that would be typical for Christians within the fundamentalist–revivalist tradition: miracles, healings, an emphasis on deliverance, speaking in tongues, and a sense of the believers being in the vanguard of the Holy Spirit's movement as the new millennium approached. However, what marked out the Toronto Blessing for special consideration were the more unusual phenomena that occurred. A number of followers trace the initial outpouring back to Father's Day, the result being that some prefer to call the movement 'the Father's Blessing' (Chevreau, 1994).[2] There was an unusually high *reportage* of people being 'slain in the Spirit'. A number would laugh uncontrollably, writhing on the floor (the leaders of the movement dubbed this 'carpet time with God'), make animal-like noises, barking, growling or groaning as the 'Spirit fell on them'. Others reported that this particular experience of God was more highly charged than anything that had preceded it (see Hunt, 1995;

---

[1] I am grateful to the American Academy of Religion for the award of a research grant in 2002, which helped me to undertake some of the fieldwork reflected in this study.

[2] Ironically, and according to the late John Wimber, a founder member of the Vineyard Church, the seminal moment in the formation of Vineyard ministry, the parent movement for the Toronto Blessing, is traced to Mom's Day, 1980.

Poloma, 1996; Percy 1996a, 1996b, 1998, pp. 281–89; Richter and Porter, 1995; Smail, Walker and Wright, 1995).

Thus, the 'blessing' became known by the place where it was deemed to be most concentrated. To date, around 2 million visitors or 'pilgrims' have journeyed to Toronto to experience the blessing for themselves. Many of these pilgrims report dramatic miracles or supernatural interventions, substantial changes in their lives, and greater empowerment for Christian ministry. More unusual claims have included tooth cavities being miraculously filled with gold, and 'dustings' of gold on the hair and shoulders of believers, indicating a specific spiritual anointing. Some have even claimed that children born to believers will have supernatural resurrection bodies. A small number of other women of child-bearing age claimed to have had spiritual pseudo-psychetic experiences.

Despite the extraordinary success of the church, John Wimber (1934–97), founding pastor of the Vineyard network, excommunicated the Toronto fellowship for '(alleged) cult-like and manipulative practices'. Some Evangelical critics of the 'Toronto Blessing Movement' cited the influence of the Rhema or 'Health and Wealth' movement, through the Toronto Fellowship's own connections with Benny Hinn and Rodney Howard-Browne, as another reason for Vineyard-led secession (Hilborn, 2001, pp. 4–10). In January 1996 the Toronto Vineyard became independent. But, under the leadership of its pastor, John Arnott, it has flourished and continues to exercise an international ministry in the fundamentalist–revivalist tradition.

The Toronto Airport Christian Fellowship still meets in a converted trade centre on an industrial estate that is less than a mile away from the main city airport. Contextually, it is conveniently located in a matrix of highways that criss-cross downtown Toronto. There are no residential areas remotely near the fellowship, and members or visitors need a car to travel to meetings – but this is not unusual in North American churchgoing. Local hotels that are linked to the airport and conference economy also enjoy a good reciprocal relationship with the fellowship and its 'pilgrims'. The fellowship building is functional, comprising offices and meeting rooms, plus a large sanctuary area for celebrations. It is a spacious, adaptable building. For example, there was once a large area at the back of the church that was segregated into track lanes. This is where worshippers, at the end of a service, could stand waiting for individual ministry to take place. A minister stood in front of the worshipper, and a 'catcher' was positioned behind them. When, or if, a worshipper fell to the ground – 'slain in the Spirit' – they were caught, and the minister moved on to the next worshipper on their track, leaving the previous one on the floor to 'marinade in the Spirit'. Worship or revival meetings can last several hours, but pilgrims can also avail themselves of cafe facilities if they need physical rather than spiritual refreshment. Yet as a cultural creature of its time, the Toronto Blessing, despite its claims to represent a pre-eminent type of pneumatological power, ironically seemed to place *less* emphasis on aggressively reified spiritual power (a particular feature of John Wimber's teaching in the 1980s – for example, 'power evangelism'), and, through its distinctive grammar of worship, put more *accent* on concepts such as the 'softness' and 'gentle touch' of God and the desirability of acquiescence in the believer. The popular worship song 'Eternity' (by Brian Doerksen, 1994, Vineyard/Mercy Publishing), sung many times over by followers and set to a soft melody, perhaps captures this best:

> I will be yours, you will be mine.
> Together in eternity
> Our hearts of love will be entwined.
> Together in eternity,
> Forever in eternity.
> No more tears of pain in our eyes;
> No more fear or shame.
> For we will be with you,
> Yes, we will be with you,
> We will worship,
> We will worship you forever.

It is through this distinctive grammar of assent that the fellowship continues to configure its life. The motto of the fellowship is 'to walk in God's love and give it away', and the life of the congregation emphasizes this in its ministerial distinctiveness. Thus, there are programmes for single parents (for example, *'Just Me and the Kids* – Building Healthy Single Parent Families: a twelve week program for single parents and their kids'), a conference entitled *Imparting the Father's Heart* ('Are you called to minister the Father Heart of God? This course will take you deeper into the Father's love...giving you the tools to give it away...topics include the need to be fathered, hindrances to receiving the Father's love, shame, Father issues, prodigal issues, orphan heart...') and various schools of ministry or programmes that centre on spiritual–therapeutic approaches to brokenness, abuse, neglect and failure.[3] There are also some social and welfare programmes that reach out to the poor and homeless.

More generally, we should also note that the Toronto Blessing was one of the first revivalist movements to be promoted through the Internet, and to a lesser extent on television networks such as CNN. (Indeed, I debated with John Arnott live on television on the BBC 2 *Newsnight* programme in 1996.) Through skilful marketing and public relations, the Toronto Blessing spread its message and testimonies quickly and easily; it rapidly developed into an 'internet-ional' movement. But, with the benefit of hindsight, the net benefit of the 'Blessing' seems to have been individual and atomized, rather than a spur for the world of revivalism. Indeed, the epiphenomena associated with the 'Toronto Blessing' succeeded in dividing many constituents within the world of Charismatic Renewal, with some declaring that the manifestations of spiritual outpouring (for example, laughter, howling and animal noises) were Satanic, whilst others proclaimed them to be a pre-eminent sign that this was the prelude to the greatest revival ever. In retrospect, neither side – promoter or detractor – could claim an interpretative victory (see Hilborn, 2001).

---

[3] All taken from leaflets on display at the Toronto Airport Fellowship.

Perhaps all that now can be said is that the experiences of those attending Toronto Blessing meetings since 1994 seem to have been primarily cathartic; one could almost describe the effect of the Blessing on worshippers as having been something like a cleansing spiritual enema. However, the influence of the Toronto Blessing has steadily waned since the late 1990s, and its position and prominence within global revivalism and the Charismatic marketplace have been quickly forgotten. The movement, after a period of intense etiolation, has been subject to some serious atrophy. There are now comparatively few visitors to the Toronto Fellowship, and the phenomenon is now rarely mentioned in revivalist circles.[4] Scholars such as Festinger (1957) might see this as a simple matter of cognitive dissonance – the process whereby a belief or expectation, having been disconfirmed, is nonetheless adhered to (and perhaps even more strongly). In this scenario, the much anticipated fruits and blessings of revival are usually deemed to have arrived as promised and predicted, but have just not been widely perceived and reified. Margaret Poloma (1996) pays some attention to this perception in her analysis of the Toronto Blessing. However, the majority of churches that were initially supportive of the Toronto Blessing seemed to have moved on quickly, redeveloping their focus as well as their interpretation of the phenomenon. For some, the promised revival is deemed to be 'manifest' in the phenomenal success and growth of Alpha courses (see Hunt, 2000). Only a few Christian fellowships and churches have continued to focus on exotic spiritual epiphenomena, such as miraculous gold fillings occurring in tooth cavities, or dustings of gold on the shoulders and the hair, indicating a special anointing. (Suffice to say and, despite the claims made for these miracles on various websites, the evidence for such miracles remains circumstantial and uncorroborated.) We should also note that a small number of Vineyard churches have become more liturgically-oriented in the wake of the Blessing: spiritual experience has led to an embracing of tradition and order.

Interpreting Toronto: A Methodological Sketch

On my return to the Toronto Airport Christian Fellowship, I wanted to see how it was dealing with the decline in demand for its conferences, and how it was coping in a post-millennial climate in which the rhetoric of a much-anticipated global Charismatic revival had patently receded. The added grist for such a study was that, strictly speaking, for the past 25 years many scholars have only been predicting uniform growth for conservative churches, especially those with a Charismatic flavour (see, for example, Kelley, 1972; Tamney, 2002; Cox, 1994; Miller, 1997 cf. Weber 1946, pp. 295ff). Only a small minority

---

[4] Visitor figures are hard to procure. The Fellowship claimed – with some justice – that up to 2 million had visited between 1994 and 2000. The visitor figures are now harder to calculate, as the Fellowship runs so many commercial conferences that delegates are indistinguishable from pilgrims. My own estimation is that the combined numbers of delegates and pilgrims visiting annually is between 50 000 and 75 000.

of scholars have predicted the very opposite of this in relation to Charismatic Renewal and revivalism, especially in relation to the Toronto Blessing (see Walker, 1998, pp. 313–15; Hunt, Hamilton and Walter, 1997).

In this micro-study, I wanted to explore how participants now understood the movement of which they were still a part – one that had witnessed stunning but ultimately unsustainable growth, followed by 'wilting' – a process that biologists know as etiolation. Put more colloquially in the rhetoric of the 1980s and 1990s that partly constructed the language and vistas of 'power evangelism' and 'power healing' programmes, I wanted to see how adherents have lived through the 'boom and bust' years.

So how did they now interpret the apparent atrophy of revivalism? Of course, pilgrims and members tend not to construct their self-understanding in these terms, and this immediately raises some sensitive questions not only about appropriate methodological approaches within the field, but also about participant observation. Nevertheless, there can be no substitute for being there. As James Hopewell notes:

> ... the fullest and most satisfying way to study the culture of a congregation is to live within its fellowship and learn directly how it interprets its experiences and generates its behaviour ... participant observation ... as the term suggests [involves the analyst] in the activity of the group to be studied [whilst] also maintaining a degree of detachment .... (Hopewell, 1987, p. 86)

As a general guide, three distinctive, but closely related, tactical trajectories have conditioned my reading and reappraisal of the Toronto Blessing some six years after my first visit. The first is drawn broadly from anthropology, the second from ethnography and the third from 'congregational studies'. Each focus their attention upon first-hand accounts of *local* practices and beliefs, rather than solely being concerned with 'official' texts (see, for example, Geertz, 1973, 1983; Dey, 1993; Maykut and Morehouse, 1994; Hammersly and Atkinson, 1995; Atkinson, 1990; Mishler, 1991; Burgess, 1984). In this regard, the disciplines are more 'behaviourist' than 'functionalist'. The distinction is important, for it moves research away from concentrating on the primary claims of 'pure' or 'central' religion (or its analysis) towards the grounded reality of praxis. (For example, it might assess a number of Roman Catholic congregations and their practices, rather than ask the Vatican or theologians what such churches should be doing or believing.) In other words, the focus shifts from 'blueprints' about the way the church or congregation could or should be to that of 'grounded ecclesiology' – discovering how and why Christian communities are put actually together in their localized context (see Healy, 2000). It is through a matrix of conversation, interviews, observation and the savouring of representative vignettes that one can begin to piece together a more coherent picture of what it is like to belong to a group, to be a pilgrim and to believe (see Harrington-Watt, 2002; Bramadat, 2000; Dempsey, 2002).

For the purposes of this study, the work of Clifford Geertz has proved to be most illuminating. Geertz is an anthropologist of religion, and his two principal works are *The Interpretation of Cultures* (1973) and *Local Knowledge* (1983). Both these works argue for research that consists of ethnography and theoretical approaches. In my own research, I have tended to treat religion as a complex cultural system. That is not to say that I, in any way, ignore or reject any idea of revelation, divinity or 'genuine' religious experience. Theologically, I expect such things to be treated seriously, and I expect their reality to have some sort of impact on any empirical study. But I do not think that 'religion' is only the repository for revelation. I regard it as a complex system of meaning: a mixture of description and ascription; of deduction and induction.

For Geertz, a cultural system is a collection of symbols – objects, gestures, words, events and the like – which all have meanings attached to them, exist outside of individuals and yet work inwardly to shape attitudes and guide actions. Referring to Max Weber, Geertz takes the view that man is 'an animal suspended in webs of significance he himself has spun'. Furthermore, to explain cultures, Geertz takes the view that analysts and interpreters have to engage in 'thick descriptions', not thin ones. It is important to understand what people *mean* by a word or gesture, so that we can understand its *significance*. An obvious example is two boys – one with a twitch of the eye and another who winks. A 'thin' description would say they made the same movement. A 'thick' description' unpacks the significance of the wink, what the gesture means and infers, why it is unspoken language and so forth. That said, the study of culture is not just about meanings, as though the currency of behaviour was agreed. People often do things that are countercultural. This means that anthropologists can often do little more than faithfully reconstruct what people did and meant, and then interpret this. Cultural analysis is 'guessing at meanings, assessing the guesses, and drawing explanatory conclusions . . .' (Geertz, 1973, p. 20). Geertz regards his interpretative anthropology as being constituted through 'ethnographic miniatures' – small studies that paint a bigger picture of society, a tribe or culture.

This means that Geertz tends not to be in favour of 'general' theories. He sees anthropology not as 'an experimental science in search of a law, but as an interpretative one in search of a meaning' (ibid., p. 5). Thus, an anthropologist, like a doctor, cannot predict what will happen – say, that a child will develop flu – but an anthropologist can *anticipate* what might happen, based on patterns they have observed, studied and interpreted. At this point, anthropologists have a variety of ideas at their disposal: ritual, structure, identity, world-view, ethos, to name but a few. Thus, Geertz is primarily interested in religion as a cultural system, or the 'cultural dimensions' of religion, because he sees culture as a pattern of meanings or ideas, carried by symbols, by which people pass on knowledge and express their attitudes to knowledge. 'Common sense' can be a system as much as any political ideology. So for Geertz, as we noted earlier, religion is:

> [1] a system of symbols which acts to [2] establish powerful, pervasive, and long-lasting moods and motivations in men by [3] formulating conceptions of a general order of existence and [4] clothing these conceptions with such an aura of factuality that [5] the moods and motivations seem uniquely realistic . . . . (Geertz, 1973, p. 90)

Geertz expands this definition by reminding his readers that religions distinguish between world-views and ethos. A world-view is the way things could be or should be: 'blessed are the poor, for theirs is the kingdom of heaven'. And an ethos is the way things are: 'they gave alms to the poor'. In ritual and belief, ethos and world-view are often fused together; religion expresses both. The moods and motivations created within an ethos reach towards a world-view – the ways things could or should be. Of course, there are limits to what can be done with Geertz's work. Many scholars regard him as a functionalist, but this may be more of a compliment than an insult. Like many anthropologists, he is compressing complex data into a system of agreed symbols and contours – not unlike a cartographer. And, as with cartography, there is no map that is drawn to a 1:1 scale, which records what the observer sees. A good map is a *guide* to a field or an area; the chosen symbols help us to look on unfamiliar terrain with some agreement – churches with spires, a pub, a post office, an incline and a forest of deciduous trees. Insofar as it goes, Geertz offers us a reasonable, accurate and creative way of navigating through complex data and making some judgements about the shape of the subject. And as with maps, each is *specific*, but uses general ideas to help us create an accurate impression.

As a discipline, ethnography (our second tactical trajectory) comes in all shapes and sizes: some is mainly quantitative, whilst other kinds can be mostly qualitative; some depends on formal questionnaires and clearly proscribed methods; other kinds are more like 'participant observation' and accept the partiality of the observer/interpreter as a given. As Wuthnow points out, ethnography is 'a highly diverse set of techniques and practices' (1997, p. 246). It can be closely related to anthropology – the direct observation of social events, and reflections on first-hand accounts, drawn from the field. Equally, however, ethnography can also be a matter of data collection: church records, interviews and other kinds of primary data are brought together to help construct an assemblage of resemblance (Wuthnow, 1997, p. 246). But fundamentally, as Courtney Bender notes, ethnography is also always:

> ...about human relationships: it is built (or broken) through trust and through barter and exchange of various kinds. Although [we] focus on fieldwork relationships, ethnographers carry on simultaneous dialogue and exchange (and human relations) with the scholarly community and other texts as well. These concurrent dialogues make ethnographic research unique amongst investigative journeys.... (Bender, 2003, p. 148)

Bender describes the delicate balance between stepping into 'streams' of events and conversations and the need to stay just outside them. There is an ambiguity in making 'their' talk 'our' talk, in order to bridge the gap between the gaze of the ethnographer and the lives that are being lived. Inevitably, the ethnographer is not simply a passive listener, but is an active agent in conversations, and becomes a reflective partner in dialogue. This requires a degree of self-awareness in the ethnographer; they must not only be attentive to the words and moods they study, but also be conscious of their own vocabulary and emotions in a given situation.

Bender recognizes that her ethnography does not 'reproduce' the voices of others. Those events that are recorded are inevitably shaped by the particularity of the ethnographer – what strikes them will not necessarily be what strikes another. As Foucault famously quipped of his own ethnography, 'I am not a pipe': there is no neutral conduit through which 'pure' information flows from source to receptor (this seems to me to be more of a common-sensical observation than anything particularly postmodern). This means, as Bender notes (quoting James Clifford), that dialogue occurs as ethnographers 'try on' different languages and perspectives:

> Dialogic[al] textual production goes well beyond the more or less artful presentation of 'actual' encounters. It locates cultural interpretations in many sorts of reciprocal contexts, and it obliges writers to find diverse ways of rendering negotiated realities as mini-subjective, power-laden and incongruent. . . . (Clifford, 1986, pp. 14–15)

Put more succinctly, the expression of dialogue in an ethnographer's text will inevitably contain more than the author could intend. Granted, the text will convey what the author wants to say, and the recorded dialogue will 'fit' their interpretative framework. But there will also be, as Bender says, enough 'surplus' to question these interpretations. This admission is important, for it alludes to the limits of explanation, but without implying a necessary equality between speakers and the ethnographer. The ethnographer is therefore free to identify those common 'stories' and 'typical' events that they deem to occur most frequently, or to be of most significance for a community. This, in turn, can allow such communities to be 'read' for 'deep meanings'. But the door is always open for others to listen to the community under investigation in quite different ways, and offer a different interpretation (Bender, 2003, p. 150). However, the keys to good ethnography remain constant: immersion in a community; many hours of patient and deep listening; conversation and rapport; not jumping to premature conclusions; not adopting interpretative matrices too early on in an investigation; faithful (or verbatim) recording of narratives and voices; shaping the material coherently; being attentive to the fact that nothing can be studied without being changed – either the material or the investigator.

As Bender quips, there are, in the end, really only two kinds of (intellectual) books: (1) the stranger who comes to town, and (2) someone who goes on a journey. In ethnography, she notes, one always finds oneself in the second category, but always with some sympathy for the first:

> [T]he ethnographer is always in some sense a pilgrim . . . a seeker . . . we go on trips to undiscovered countries or, armed with notepads and a 'critical eye', we make our own countries strange . . . [but] fieldwork [also] compels us to circle back on ourselves, our ideas, and our worlds, just as it also compels us to keep moving toward answers to our questions about the worlds of those around us. . . . (Bender, 2003, p. 151)

The third methodological trail – appropriately enough – draws upon the burgeoning field of congregational studies (see Ammerman, 1997; M. Williams, 1974; Eiesland, 1998; Dorsey, 1985), but with a special focus on the interpretative framework provided by James Hopewell (Hopewell, 1987; Ammerman *et al.*, 1998, pp. 91–104). In many ways, the discipline is a natural complement to anthropology and ethnography, since practitioners of congregational studies pay particular attention to the local or 'concrete' church rather than to the 'ideal' constructions; such studies stress the value of uncovering 'operant' rather than 'official' religion. In other words, and reflecting what I noted earlier:

> As slight and predictable as the language of a congregation might seem on casual inspection, it actually reflects a complex process of human imagination. Each is a negotiation of metaphors, a field of tales and histories and meanings that identify its life, its world, and God. Word, gesture, and artefact form local language – a system of construable signs that Clifford Geertz, following Weber, calls a 'web of significance'. Even a plain church on a pale day catches one in a deep current of narrative interpretation and representation by which people give sense and order to their lives. Most of this creative stream is unconscious and involuntary, drawing in part upon images lodged long ago in the human struggle for meaning. Thus, a congregation is held together by much more than creeds, governing structures and programs. At a deeper level, it is implicated in the symbols and signals of the world, gathering and surrounding them in the congregation's own idiom. (Hopewell, 1987, p. 11)

Hopewell, rather like certain anthropologists (he was heavily influenced by Geertz) and ethnographers in the field, takes the many and multifaceted *stories* of faith seriously. Rather than simply attending to the credal statements and articles of faith that are said to provide ecclesial coherence, ethnography and congregational studies probe deeper and listen to (and observes) the expressive narratives of belief that make up the practice of a community. It is by attending to the apparently *trivial* – testimonies, sayings, folk wisdom, stories, songs and so forth – that one can begin to understand the truer theological construction of reality under which believers shelter. But what exactly emerges from this 'narrative trawl'? As we shall see, there are many rhetorical shards that speak of heroism, romance, adventure, risk and reward, and, whilst these may lie scattered on the surface of congregational storytelling, their origin comes from deep within the movement. To repeat Wade Clark Roof's observations, the beliefs of churches cannot be construed entirely in terms of their credal statements:

> Theological doctrines are always filtered through people's social and cultural experiences. What emerges in a given situation is 'operant religion' will differ considerably from the 'formal religion' of the historic creeds, and more concern with the former is essential to understanding how belief systems function in people's daily lives. (Roof, 1985, pp. 178–79)

So, in telling the story of the congregation, we unravel its plot:

...church culture is not reduced to a series of propositions that a credal checklist adequately probes. The congregation takes part in the nuance and narrative of full human discourse. It persists as a recognizable storied dwelling within the whole horizon of human interpretation. (Hopewell, 1987, p. 201)

This observation is important, for it would be a mistake to read or judge the Toronto Blessing movement by its formal declarations of belief. (Most adherents are, in any case, unaware of these and would regard them as unimportant.) So, although the Toronto Airport Christian Fellowship does have a Statement of Faith and also adheres to certain formal credal articles, its main purpose is to position itself as a mainstream (Evangelical) ecclesial organization. To focus on these elements as constituting the core identity of the fellowship would be to entirely miss the point, however. It is the combination of divine dramaturgy (healings, miracles and the like) and the distinctive romantic grammar of assent that attracts believers by the thousand and then enriches their lives. Phrases such as 'you will be led into greater intimacy [with God] and personal renewal' are abundantly present in literature and teaching, peppering pamphlets and 'pep talks' alike. Similarly, worship songs such as 'I Can Feel the Touch of Your Presence' and 'Dancing in Daddy's Arms' are manifestly more important for the constituent contouring of belief and practice within the fellowship than any creed. The operant stress is on tactile, almost romantic–somatic encounters with God, which lead to deep cathartic spiritual moments, which then provide liberating and generative possibilities for individual spiritual renewal and further empowerment.

Immersed in the River of Revival: Returning to Toronto

Given the context of atrophy – the pretext for this short study – it might be asked how the stories of faith within the Toronto Airport Christian Fellowship are beginning to change. Given that the much-hyped and predicted global revival has not taken place, what kinds of narratives do 'pilgrims' and members now use to describe their ongoing commitment to a fellowship whose influence and popularity has manifestly waned (cf. Festinger, 1957)? Interestingly, there is both some continuity and development to focus on here, but it is the latter which highlights a theme I had not fully developed in my earlier study. In my original research, based on my 1996 visit, I had especially registered the romantic metaphors and motifs in worship, teaching and testimony that seemed to shape the overall horizon of belief and possibility. There was a superabundance – almost an overwhelming – of appeals to the romantic nature of God and of the believer's desire for intimacy and oneness with God, and of the reciprocal desire of God, Jesus and the Holy Spirit for the believer's heart and soul. Much of this was constituted in a grammar of paternalism and passionate (or quasi-erotic) intimacy (see Percy, 1997, pp. 71–106; Heather, 2002, pp. 28–38).

Yet during my visit of 2002, I was struck by just how little the appetite for this faith-world had abated. There had been some routinization of Charisma in the Weberian sense. There was less spontaneity and more order; there were signs that a Charismatic movement was evolving into a young church. But there were also factors that pointed to a sustained and original vibrancy. 'Pilgrims' and members were still hungry and thirsty for God; and God was, apparently, still hungry and thirsty for them too, for the rhetoric of passionate and romantic intensity remained buoyant. That said, the numbers of attendees were a fraction of what they were, and the rhetoric that anticipated (and to some extent hyped) the possibility of global Charismatic revival had all but disappeared. How then, I wondered, did members and 'pilgrims' understand the failure of God to slake their desire for global revival? Given that 'intimacy with God' had been (and still was) advocated as the path to ultimate individual spiritual empowerment, which would then pave the way for the pre-eminence of Charismatic renewal throughout the world, surely followers of the Toronto Blessing would have a theological narrative that dealt with the growing sense of dissonance?

The answer to these questions lay in paying closer attention to narratives that emphasized a spiritual theme that is closely related to the romantic world-view, but which I had underestimated in my earlier research. I speak, of course, about adventure and the idea that 'pilgrims' and members are caught up in God's own narrative of involvement in the world, which in revivalist and Charismatic world-views is often understood as a form of adventure, of which romance is but only one type. In focusing on narratives of adventure, the language and actuality of atrophy could be located and understood – read not in terms of dissonance but, rather, understood as a vindication of 'the ongoing story of struggle'.

But before reflecting further upon the theme of adventure and its relation to Charismatic atrophy, it is first necessary to describe the present situation of the Toronto Airport Christian Fellowship in a little more detail. Turning up for a regular nightly revival meeting, which begins at 7.30p.m. and normally ends about four hours later, I was greeted at the door by a smartly dressed woman who introduced herself: 'Hello – tonight will be your night for a miracle.' All revival and prayer meetings commence with intense periods of corporate worship. Participants sometimes dance to the music, but most make gestures with their hands or arms, either raising them high (and then keeping them still) and some also move them in a slow sweeping, encompassing or wiping fashion, as though polishing an invisible giant globe.

Some of the gestures seem to be more eccentric than this, at least to an observer. As I stood amongst the worshippers, a woman near me clapped her hands haphazardly around her body, as though swatting a fly, and cried out 'Ho!' or 'Hah!' (loudly) with each clap. A man in front of me raised his hands during the sermon at points where he was in intense agreement with the speaker and cried out words such as 'transformation!' and 'change!'. During praise, some women danced around freely, twirling brightly coloured flags and ribbons. A male member of the ministry team moved along rows of seats and prayed with people by blowing on them forcefully and loudly, making a wind-like sound. As he did so, the supplicant, normally already standing with arms raised, buckled and fell to the ground, where others then gathered around and prayed. As the worship continued, the songs proclaimed that believers are 'dancing on the mountain top with God'; another song announced 'God of the Breakthrough...all things are possible through you'. Still another worship song declared that:

> You are my health
> Your are my hope
> Your are my help,
> So I'm gonna lift You up....

On my return to Toronto, I had expected the distinctively romantic and mildly quasi-erotic accent of the movement that had permeated the worship to have subsided. But, if anything, the romantic genre had become even more explicit and intense than before. The structuring and grammar of worship made overt use of sexual analogies that were drawn from biblical and Christian tradition, but then intensified as they were interpreted. One worship leader explained that 'worship means "to kiss towards" – to come into His tender presence; so let Jesus *respond* to your loving...'. There was a real sense in which worship regularly progressed through three distinct phases: wooing or courting Jesus; 'mystical foreplay', often accompanied by heightened use of musical instruments, but with little singing (that is, delicately stroking or touching the chords of a guitar or keys of a piano – brushing them *so* lightly yet intensely in an erotic and suggestive sequence of notes rather than 'music'); relational consummation, which could include signing in tongues and other activity, sometimes leading to cathartic responses. But is such an interpretation fair, or merely tendentious?

The key is to recognize the way in which the encounter with Jesus is understood in specifically romantic terms. Thus, recent praise compilations (available on CD, tape and in books) offer '*Intimate Bride* – gentle worship for soaking in God's presence', '*Warrior Bride*' (with a picture of a young woman in full bridal regalia holding a large sword) and '*Passionate Bride* – songs of intimacy and passion for soaking in God's presence'. These products are illustrated with pictures of a bride embracing or encountering Jesus, the biblical analogy of 'marriage' to Jesus having been literalized and individualized. Other collections of songs include 'How Big is He?', 'I Can Feel the Touch', 'Take Me' and 'Soaking in Glory (in the River)'.

It seems that this worship continues to appeal more to women than men. At the daily morning meetings ('Wake Up Call for Revival', 10.30–12.30), close to 95 per cent of the attendees were women, with an average age of 57. These meetings are far smaller but no less intense than those I encountered six years ago and attract around 50 people. But the format remains almost identical, with the meeting opening in worship songs that suggest a unique, tactile intimacy with Jesus:

> Lord, Show me your face,
> So I can touch your brow
> Lord, show me your face
> So I can see your smile....

These prayer meetings are led by women, and are mainly for women, and the rhetoric reflects the desires and concerns of the dominant age group (50–60 plus).[5] Prayer is offered for those who suffer from anxiety or sleepless nights. Women are advised to try to create a prayer room in their homes, 'tastefully decorated in colours that help you to *relax*'. Other advice includes to 'keep a "Dream Journal", and share them with your Cell Group leader'. During ministry, the value of 'resting' was frequently stressed; resting with Jesus would combat stress, alleviate anxiety and also bring stillness and strength back into the family home. Sometimes this counsel would extend into vivid analogy: 'reach out your hand – can you sense the fragrance of the Lord here? This is a place of peace, and it feels like *velvet*....' In the fellowship's bookshop and resource centre customers can buy fragrant oils for the house as well as scented candles with names such as 'Rose of Sharon', 'Myrrh', 'Frankincense' and 'Lily of the Valley'.

The morning meetings tend to contain a smattering of teaching drawn from the Bible, but are mostly distinguished by a constant resort to 'folk wisdom', stories and aphorisms that seem to engage the audience. More often than not, the talks are aimed at giving handy and homely hints for living a distinctive Christian lifestyle. Again, this thematic approach to teaching is reflected in the fellowship's resource centre. Adherents can buy books on Christian approaches to parenting, family life, marriage, health and healing, devotion, revival, leadership and ministry. There are also books on men's and women's spirituality, and books for children and teenagers. Books on doctrine or theology would be a rare find. Furthermore, there is no neglect of watery or liquid analogies to remind adherents that they are part of a 'wave' or 'river' of revival. Several letters in the fellowship's magazine, *Spread the Fire*, now include endings such as 'yours in the flow' and 'yours, in the river'. One article headline states bluntly: 'Power Conference Leaves Everyone Saturated.'

Worship in the larger revival meetings also shows no sign of being less intense than it was six years ago, although the numbers of participants are also smaller. But worship continues to be central; one leader proclaims that 'as we bless the Lord, his presence begins to fall'. If I may make an aside here, the study of the *theology* of worship is interesting at the Toronto Fellowship, because it effectively marks out the activity of intimate worship as the primary mediator between God and humanity. Worship becomes the conduit for encounter with God – an agency and catalyst that manifests the 'I–thou' relationship.[6] Performative worship is therefore elevated to a high sacramental status (that is, God is 'reified' *in* this activity, not simply inferred, described, remembered or represented). This observation is also borne out by close attention to the numerous slick aphorisms that pepper presentations. Thus,

---

[5] Although on one morning I attended, there were ten people only, and the time of fellowship consisted of watching a video of an old revival meeting on a wide videoscreen.

[6] Thus, a typical sermon from a visiting speaker argues that God appears *in* glory, and therefore the task of the worshipping community is to *produce* the glory so that God will appear. If the glory

'God is looking for a reason to come to you, not a reason to leave you', and 'God is looking for a reason to bless you, not a reason to punish you' sound fairly reasonable and, to some extent, comforting. But deeper reflection on the phraseology might suggest that these aphorisms create a sense of *distance* between God and the individual (an accidental trope), which only intimate worship can bridge. In other words, the rhetoric implies a doctrine of *conditional* grace, despite appearing to say the very opposite of this.

But some aspects of the fellowship continue to produce surprises. The novelty of a 'spiritual car wash', in which the congregation pass through a 'tunnel' of pastors who 'spray and brush' each individual with the 'anointing power of God' is a typically innovative form of ministry that combines a theology of immediate and reified divine power with a contemporary mechanistic cultural construction of reality. Equally, some worshippers bring their own musical instruments to meetings. One evening when I was present, a woman had brought a giant rams' horn with her, and the speaker, when he saw this, insisted that she blow it hard to announce the presence of the Lord in the 'Holy of Holies'. 'Let the horn proclaim Zion!' he cried, and the people joined in with whoops of delight and loud acclamations of 'Amen!' and 'Praise God' as the horn was blown loud and long.[7] On another evening, one visiting speaker from South Africa, who appeared to be at complete liberty to address the congregation, prophesied at length in rhyming couplets, albeit in a fairly rudimentary way:

> ... thus the Lord *says*,
> I am with you until the end of *days*,
> and though you may have *striven*,
> know that you shall be *forgiven* ....

The slightly 'corny' or 'retro' language of revival that is spoken in meetings is perhaps a surprise, but speakers are probably doing no more than trying to link the present to the past. Inevitably, as the movement wanes, a 'tradition' is being appealed to in order to sustain momentum and provide a historical repository for memories that can recontextualize the dramaturgy. There are often allusive appeals to previous Great Revivals (and their leaders, such as Smith Wigglesworth, George Whitfield amongst others), presumably in an attempt to establish a sense of historic continuity (or rapport?) for 'pilgrims' and members. References enhance the sense of spiritual adventure for believers,

---

is *created* by the congregation, or in the heavenly realm by angels, God can appear, but it is a quality of worship that is deemed to *produce* glory, which is regarded as the necessary context for God's presence to be manifest.

[7] The Toronto Fellowship exhibits an intense interest in Israel as the fulfilment of God's purposes 'as we near the end times'. Many of the talks elide the identity of Israel with the pioneering spirit of the fellowship. In sermons, the Old Testament appears to be more of a resource than the New Testament.

underlining the requisite pioneering and 'tarrying identity'[8] that is so endemic within revivalism.

There is also plenty of audible praying in tongues, which is encouraged and orchestrated from the stage by speakers and worship leaders alike. Worship continues to be punctuated by individuals in the congregation crying out loud sporadically, groaning or moaning loudly, and letting out involuntary yelps of agreement, occasional piercing cries of ecstasy, or offering loud interjectory words of encouragement. Many people in the congregation twitch and shake, with some appearing to have their legs regularly buckle, as though being oppressed by a great weight. Many who are prayed for fall backwards, apparently 'slain in the Spirit'. But the numbered tracks and lanes that used to filter and organize believers for this ministry have now been replaced. More ambiguous thick green lines or bands which are woven into the pattern of the carpet, and which run in several areas of the sanctuary, now demarcate where believers should stand before they fall during times of 'soaking' ministry. Here again, we should note that where there was once one large area for this ministry, there is now a range of much smaller areas scattered around the sanctuary, marked out on the carpet, only a few of which are used in any one evening.

However, the types of people coming forward for healing ministry have altered little in six years: caucasian, middle-class and (late) middle-aged. The list of diseases and ailments cured is also a familiar canonical litany that reflects the needs of the congregation. Thus, there are 'suspected cancers' said to be healed on the spot, with 'depression', 'nightmares', 'back pain', 'angina', 'urinary tract infections', 'cancer of the ovaries and colon' and 'persistent headaches' all dealt with by Jesus, immediately. Naturally, each of these complaints is internal, usually unverifiable and not normally linked to any social cause such as malnutrition or poverty. But to make such an observation is simply to point to the fact that the 'healings' are part of the overall performative experience within the revivalist context. Their efficacy lies not in being 'proved', but in their power to persuade and perform within the divine dramaturgy that unfolds each day within the sanctuary.

So far, these reflections suggest that the life of the Toronto Airport Christian Fellowship remains buoyant and continues to evolve, albeit centred on fewer participants who are concentrating more intensely on some of the core themes that marked out the fellowship for attention and research in the first place. But, given that a process of atrophy is also underway, how does a Charismatic movement such as the Toronto Blessing and its parent fellowship come to understand itself? How does it reconcile its belief in a global revival with a steady decrease in its own popularity? I want to suggest that part of the answer to this question lies in repositioning the romantic genre (that dominates the

---

[8] That is, addressing the primary spiritual tasks through a variety of works, which may include 'spiritual warfare'. Here, we are dealing with a sense of the perpetual journey and struggle to bring about the kingdom of god on Earth, and also to be able to present yourself spotless at heaven's gate on the Last Day.

world-view and worship of the fellowship) and seeing romance as being derivative of a theology of adventure, which in turn can make space for atrophy.

Adventure and Atrophy

According to Hopewell's congregational studies, based on participant observation and thematic analysis and interpretation, Charismatic Christians and revivalists configure their lives and meaning through a primarily romantic genre:

> ...the charismatic narrative is a more frightening and thrilling place...souls are eternally damned in it, yet God does not fail those who trust in him...the world in which the charismatic lives is fundamentally equivocal and dangerous, challenging the believer to seek its blessings amid the peril of evil forces and events. God's steady providence, however, accompanies the self who launches out toward God in an exciting romantic adventure.... (Hopewell, 1987, p. 76)

The romantic world-view generally eschews mundane reality in favour of witnessing supernatural signs. It deliberately ventures into a world of uncertainty; it is the world of the 'perilous journey'. But this search or spiritual quest is rewarded, for, as Hopewell points out, 'the romantic journey ends in the triumph of God's love': 'the hero becomes the home of God's Spirit' (ibid., p. 78). In a romantic world-view (that is, a congregation's perception of how things should or could be), the primary motif is adventure. Individually, the response to weakness is tarrying, and the resolution is empowerment. Corporately, conventionality is overcome by charism, which leads to transformation. Cosmically, perpetuity is usually addressed by signs and wonders, which will then lead to the coming of the Day of the Lord. In the world of adventure, authority is discovered in the evidence of God's immanence, the continuity of God's providence and the recognition of God's blessings. Critically, a romantic world-view understands that spiritual adventure is the context in which the strength of the romantic relationship with God is discovered, tested and refined. The 'heroes' of romantic stories are those who persevere through trials and tribulations, and who remain constant and faithful in the midst of adversity. In this respect, the underlying romantic theology of the Toronto Blessing movement depends, to some extent, on 'reading' Jesus' life as part of God's adventure with humanity. Just as it is an adventure following Jesus, so Jesus himself is often portrayed as the proto-adventurer, and as the 'pioneer of faith'. In talking to individuals at the Toronto Fellowship, and in listening to speakers and their talks and sermons, one is continually struck by the emphasis on *blessing* – those who receive it are those who venture beyond conventionality. Furthermore, the adventure to acquire blessing only becomes possible when one has been pre-empowered and equipped with some kind of anointing, divine charge or what some describe as being filled with 'the liquid love of God'.

In a Christian community that mainly configures its life through the romantic genre, there is a close relationship between *ethos* and *world-view*. The ethos of a place is the palpable experience and tone of a place – the very character of the culture that is encountered. A world-view, in contrast, is a philosophy of life that indicates how the world could or should be. In the romantic genre, ecclesial reality, no matter how imperfect, is normally regarded as a significant foretaste of what is to come; heaven is already partly revealed. The perceived experience of divinity within the worshipping community is regarded as an aperitif; the banquet is to follow. Correspondingly, the sense of adventure that both sources and governs the romantic genre tends to take on elements of dramaturgy and narrativity that stress exploration and pioneering. This might sound like a mundane remark, but it is in fact crucial. Adventurers not only pass over and through boundaries, they also return to the worlds from which they claim, with new stories, fresh revelations and novel perspectives from afar, which change the environment of their homecoming.

Furthermore, an adventure is not, strictly speaking, quite like a vacation, pilgrimage or ordinary journey. An adventure is something that happens *to* someone. People seldom opt to go on adventures; adventures are events, dramas and stories upon which individuals and communities are *taken* – they are event-driven, with no obvious plot. In the course of an adventure, there is no control over the beginning or end of the drama (one can only choose to see it through, or to opt out). Furthermore, because the outcomes of adventures are seldom known, there is no point at which a conclusion can be naturally reached. Necessarily, an adventure engages its subjects; it is packed with risk and reward, uncertainty and vindication, threat and promise. As Georg Simmel suggests, adventure is 'defined by its capacity to have necessity and meaning: [there] we abandon ourselves to the world with fewer defences and reserves than in any other relation'. In other words, the adventurer can be characterized as having 'daring... with which [the adventurer] continually leaves the solidities of life' (Simmel, cited in Levine, 1971, pp. 187–90).

The motif of adventure, then, allows a threefold cyclical sequence of movement for believers: leaving the present life and its conventionality; encountering the new world; returning home, and then transforming the homeland from which one has come with the tales of the new world. But critically, the motif of adventure also begins to offer some clues as to how a Charismatic movement might begin to cope with apparent atrophy.[9] In the world of adventure, the romance (with God or Jesus) may remain constant, or

---

[9] I say 'apparent atrophy', but it is, in reality, undeniable. The sanctuary area had been almost full each night when I visited in 1996. That same area has now been skilfully partitioned such that the size of the area has been reduced by about two-thirds, and this area itself is only two-thirds full each night. The area underneath the mezzanine that was used for ministry is now walled up and used for seminars and offices. A 'chill-out' zone for ministry that was available in 1996 is now fully partitioned off for children's ministry – a giant wooden 'walk-in' 'Noah's Ark'. The overall effect is to create a smaller, more intimate space – but for far fewer people. Evening meetings attract about 300–400 people, and morning meetings only about 50 – sometimes far fewer. This is a significant reduction from 1996.

even steadily intensify, but that does not prevent setbacks. When these occur, they only serve to test the quality of the adventurous romantic relationship and underline its fundamental importance to the believers. So adventure allows for the negotiation of atrophy – it is only a 'blip' or test in the longer, bigger, divine drama. The prevalence of Charismatic authority – 'resting on devotion to...exceptional heroism' (Weber, 1968, p. 24) – provides further support for the romantic world-view.

Similarly, a reappraisal of sermons at the Toronto Airport Christian Fellowship also suggests that the ideal 'model' Christian that is being promoted is the 'Pilgrim-Adventurer'. The highs and lows of Christian living are sustained by a deep, romantic, passionate and intense relationship with Jesus. But it is this foundation that creates the context for coping with apparent atrophy and setbacks. In a world where the horizons of possibility are shaped by the promise of adventure – including rewards – tarrying for revival is a duty and a joy. Correspondingly, the biblical archetypes of heroism that are most frequently appealed to in sermons tend to be Old Testament figures who are reconstructed as pioneers. Characters such as Abraham, Moses, Joshua, Noah, and even Jonah, are represented as proto-Pilgrim-Adventurers who set an example for believers today. This is intriguing, for in my original research on the Toronto Blessing in 1996, I suggested that, strictly speaking, visitors to the Toronto Airport Christian Fellowship were not really 'pilgrims' at all, because the location of the church was immaterial to receiving the Blessing. I now accept that this view needs to be modified. Visitors to Toronto are unquestionably pilgrims, but not in any conventional anthropological sense. For a believer, the pilgrimage is entirely internal – a thrilling adventure that takes place within the individual's rugged and breathtaking interior spiritual landscape, in which adversity and reward combine within the overall ecology of the broader spiritual adventure that constitutes the divine drama for each visitor or member.

To some extent, this observation can be verified when one talks to individuals about how they now understand the term 'harvest'. Six years ago, references to 'harvesting' peppered many talks and sermons. The Toronto Airport Christian Fellowship launched 'Partners in Harvest', an umbrella term for other North American and Canadian churches that wanted to belong to a network that linked revivalism to Evangelism. 'Harvest' was suggestive of produce and growth and had a clear resonance with Gospel imagery and analogy. But the term now seems to have evolved into a cipher for the spiritual fruits within the lives of individuals. The 'harvest' is now less 'out there' – whole 'fields' of potential converts, as it were – and more concerned with the growth, development and the interiority of the individuals' spiritual life. Of course, this means that the phenomenon of atrophy is much more difficult to assess, since 'growth' is still always being claimed, despite appearances to the contrary. In an interview, one member of staff explained to me that the cell meetings that produce the most growth are those for men or women only. When I gently press the question, 'Does that mean numerical growth?', the reply is modest and temperate: 'Oh, you know, growth takes many forms; like it could be spiritual growth, or growth of another kind. It could be Evangelism, yes, I suppose. It depends.'

The cellular structure of the Toronto Airport Christian Fellowship has existed from the outset. The cells comprise small groups of people meeting in specific localities for prayer, worship and fellowship. Cell groups meet in each others' homes on a weekly basis, for perhaps an hour or two. The numbers involved in cell groups are perhaps the best indication of the present size of the Toronto Fellowship; by their own estimation there are 150 groups with perhaps 1000 members. There are cell groups for families, young adults, men, women and couples. The fellowship believes that the most popular cell groups are single-sex. The advocacy of the cell structure is not unusual in a North American church context, but its promotion at the Toronto Fellowship tells us something about its direction and development, namely that it is leaving its 'movement identity' behind and is on the way to becoming a church. Being a committed member of the fellowship is now constituted through belonging to a cell. This also helps the fellowship differentiate between members and attendees; the leadership's estimates are that there are about 2000 regularly coming to meetings, but 'core' membership is around 1000 – a noticeable reduction in numbers from the figures I collected in 1996.

Naturally, the fellowship does not see this picture in terms of atrophy or decline. The language of harvest and the 'Pilgrim-Adventurer' world-view ensures that any notion of fallowness is only read as part of an overall narrative of growth. Thus, one of the noticeable changes from six years ago is the more intense concentration on youth work. There are about 250 children in the youth programme, approximately 100 teenagers and around 50 in the 'young adult' category (20–30). Part of the main sanctuary has been partitioned to create a giant 'walk-in' Noah's Ark, in which some of the youth ministry can take place. For older youths, it is also interesting to note that the Toronto Fellowship now practises 'Christian Bar Mitzvah' with its children, in which the passage from childhood to adulthood is marked with a ceremony of blessing (by pastors and parents), which also includes walking across a makeshift bridge as part of the symbolic ritual. Here again, there is a ritual of pioneering and journeying to complement the movement to childhood to adulthood. The ritual creates a sense of freedom fused with security: a *safe* journey in life – with the Lord.

The new focus on youth and children's work indicates that the adults who have settled in the church are now raising the next generation of revivalists: routinization is settling in, and the fellowship is moving quickly away from a movement identity into an ecclesial one. Six years ago there was little youth work to speak of; now it is essential to ensure the future of the fellowship through organic growth, as it seems not to be occurring in other ways that are numerically significant (that is, through evangelism). The new rituals seem to inculcate the youth into the 'Pilgrim-Adventurer' and pioneering identity that so intensely flavours the Toronto Fellowship. It is here that they learn that the true meaning of being a pioneer – they are both travellers and settlers, doing something wholly new, yet totally familiar.

Conclusion

The apparent atrophy of a Charismatic movement – in this case, the Toronto Blessing – is indeed a complex phenomenon. For adherents within the movement, the decrease in numbers attending the fellowship, and the overall waning influence of the movement as a whole, means little. Thus, a conversation with an administrator at the fellowship reveals that they 'are cutting back on [staff] numbers at the moment, because we don't want to be, like, well you know, top heavy'.[10] But this is not interpreted as being indicative of decline. The Pilgrim-Adventurer travels lightly. There is no real narrative of deterioration in the romantic adventure – only temporary setbacks and the embracing of leanness, so that travel may be swifter and more reflexive. Romantics are incurably positive and optimistic about their future: in the arena of adventure, the faithful pilgrim always prevails. In such a world-view there are times of abundant harvest to look back on and cherish, and there are times to look forward to when the harvest will be plentiful again. Living between the lands of sowing and reaping (to borrow a well-worn phrase from Pentecostalism) only serves to consolidate the identity of the fellowship, and invites the faithful to cease travelling (for the time being), and begin settling. Indeed, such consolidation may turn out to be the Promised Land – the harvest of plenty that was promised.[11]

So, strictly speaking, adherents would regard any apparent routinization as merely temporary, since the culture of revivalism requires believers to be ready, at any point, to become restless pilgrims and adventurers once more. Meanwhile, the fellowship dwells within that unique hinterland of adventure and security; being neither a church nor a movement, but a *fellowship* (settled, yet reflexive), it knows that its time will come again. Adherents have no need of theories of cognitive dissonance to explain themselves (they do not, in any case, really apply here), and nor do they perceive themselves to be in decline. In the mind's eye of the faithful, God 'is doing a new thing' each day, and the temporary lull in revivalist intensity is simply regarded as a period of waiting, during which time the Toronto Airport Christian Fellowship continues to hone and intensify its distinctively passionate grammar of assent and quasi-erotic spirituality.

Further afield, we should note that the Vineyard movement as a whole (the parent church for the Toronto Fellowship) has found it difficult to sustain growth and maintain identity in the wake of the death of their founder and

---

[10] Source: interview, November 2002. Staff numbers are difficult to calculate, as some are paid, some are voluntary and some part-time in both categories. There may be as many as 150 staff spread across all areas of work, including the School of Ministry and international development.

[11] In conversations with other members of Vineyard churches and those who have left the Toronto movement altogether, but remained within Charismatic Renewal, these motifs seem to persist: a new journey is underway – a new adventure with God. There is an irony here. Those who leave the movement do not necessarily regard it as having failed. Rather, they see their identity and purpose as being continually restructured within a romantic world-view, in which all journeys and pilgrimages are ultimately ascribed some worth.

patron, John Wimber, in 1997. Under Wimber's leadership, Vineyard fellowships were bound together by a concept of 'kinship' and an understanding of their leader's charismatic and apostolic authority. This meant that the fellowships enjoyed a degree of homogeneity in their praxis; there was, in effect, a distinct 'Vineyard style' that marked out the fellowships from other types of Charismatic Renewal and contemporary revivalism. Indeed, one of Wimber's legacies to the Association of Vineyard Churches was the proscribing of ten 'vital signs' that provided a 'genetic code' for all Vineyard churches. But, in the space of five years, much of this has changed.

Privately, a number of the Vineyard leadership now acknowledge that three key divisions have emerged within the Vineyard movement. Some churches have attempted to return to the 'original recipe' that first made the reputation of Wimber and his churches, namely a concentration on 'power evangelism' and 'power healing'. A second stream have developed an ethos that is close to that of 'Seeker Churches'.[12] A third stream has seen some pastors adopting a more liturgical and sacramental tone in their fellowships or churches. Some pastors now robe for worship, and the Eucharist has become the central rite for the congregation. There are now women pastors too – something that Wimber would not have permitted. Where there was once homogeneity, there is now considerable diversity in liturgical style and theological substance: the Vineyard movement is losing its coherence, and becoming a broad-based (but small) denomination. At the same time, a degree of routinization is already apparent in those Vineyard churches that are faithful to their past. A survey of some British Vineyard fellowships reveals that worship now follows a set pattern or 'recipe': worship, offertory, weekly announcements, teaching, more worship, ministry, before ending with coffee and doughnuts.[13]

At the same time, many Evangelical churches of various denominational persuasions have adopted aspects of Vineyard praxis – in effect, giving themselves a Vineyard 'make-over' – but have nonetheless remained true to and within their denominations. This has ensured further diversity for revivalism, and also ironically blunts the impact of various Charismatic movements. In effect, mainstream churches feel free to adopt those traits and teachings that they find congenial from within the world of revivalism, but they do not actually transfer their allegiance to that world. In other words, they treat the revivalism as a collation of resources from which they can pick and

---

[12] 'Seeker Churches' exist in various forms throughout North America in a variety of denominational guises, although they are predominantly Evangelical and Charismatic in ethos. Bill Hybels, pastor of Willow Creek Church in South Barrington, Chicago, is widely regarded as their pioneer. Seeker Churches deliberately set out to remove all 'churchy' barriers that might prevent people from attending or joining churches. Thus, at the Willow Creek church itself, there are no robed ministers, no hymn books, no altar, nor obvious Christian symbolism. The church 'services', as such, resemble accessible 'magazine-style' TV chat shows – interviews, features, 'staged' discussions or seminars, and perhaps some drama. The church attracts enquirers and committed members, and aims to cultivate patterns of Christian lifestyle that resonate with contemporary culture.

[13] Source: Bristol Vineyard, UK – weekly notice sheet, October 2001.

choose, and also discard, as they seek to maintain and renew their own traditions. This means that their Jerusalem – the Golden City of Revivalism – is simply *not* being built; the contemporary revivalist movement is becoming a widely dispersed resource, rather than a concentrated settlement of believers that might rival mainline denominations. It is becoming enculturated and syncretic, reflecting its spiritual and ecclesial pragmatism, together with its theological alterity (see Hunt, 1995, pp. 257–72; Jongeneel, 1992; Hunt, Hamilton and Walter, 1997).

The implications of all this for Charismatic Renewal, the future of the Toronto Blessing movement and for Vineyard churches are by no means easy to predict. Clearly, the primary motif of the 'Pilgrim-Adventurer', although peculiarly intense in Toronto, might be said to have emerged as a major interpretative key for Charismatic Renewal more generally within this study.

Hermeneutically, we can now see that the notion of the Pilgrim-Adventurer provides a viable narrative and world-view, through which Charismatic Christians can construct and reconstruct their identity in the midst of change and decline, as much as in growth. Whilst careful limits would have to be placed upon the 'pioneering' identity, it should be clear that the principal contribution made by the Toronto Blessing movement to Charismatic Renewal is not the exotic miracles and the spiritual epiphenomena, so much as the confirmation and consolidation of the identity of Charismatic Christianity as faith for those who seek to venture beyond conventionality. Understood like this, the evolution of the Pilgrim-Adventurer in Charismatic Renewal can be read as a romantic and conservative movement that is morphologically similar to some of the radicalism that broke out of liberal Christianity in the 1960s and 1970s. Both now share a sense of purpose that stresses moving on, breaking existing paradigms and thereby renewing the tradition. But the question marks that hang over such movements remain stubbornly simple. How can the identity of a revolutionary, radical, renewing movement be maintained if it subsequently becomes mainstream? How can a 'movement' ever become 'settled' and thereby consolidate itself? I suspect, at least in this case, that it can't. Charismatic Renewal, like the Toronto Blessing itself, is destined to wander. The faith of the Pilgrim-Adventurer demands movement, not security, which is both its strength and weakness.

In my final 24 hours at the fellowship, I listened intently to a talk given in the morning by a woman who told her small congregation (numbering perhaps 40), that she thought 'Jesus really wanted us all to just rest at the moment'. 'We were battle-weary', she added, 'and Jesus was longing to just let us rest with him, soak in his presence, and be still.' We were, in effect, being offered a cipher for the temporary hibernation of revivalism. In the romantic world-view, a period of rest for the warrior bride or pilgrim adventurer is naturally only a precursor to a new quest, or perhaps even a fresh battle. As the time of ministry began (more 'carpet time', 'soaking' and 'marinading in the Spirit') several women simply stretched out on the floor and relaxed. They were resting with Jesus – being still in the presence of God.

Ultimately, this quiet hibernation of a small but influential branch of revivalism cannot be surprising; this is the reality of its organic but temporary atrophy. As the writer of Ecclesiastes reminds us, there is a time to rest, and a time to wake and rise. And after all the feverish and intense activity of the Toronto Blessing movement at its absolute peak, worshippers were now being quietly encouraged to embrace a period of passivity, punctuated only by the stirrings of our romantic–passionate and personal relationship with Jesus. And as I tried to slip out of the main sanctuary meeting that same night, where the prayer and praise had been as exuberant as ever, lasting for more than four hours, a woman seated on the ground near the doorway beckoned me over. 'You look tired,' she said.

'I am', I replied.

'We're all tired', she added, 'and I feel the Lord is just using me to tell you that what you need to do is go home and rest. I think the Lord is telling me to tell you that. It's a word of encouragement for you. We all need rest – we all need to rest with Jesus. He'll take good care of us.'

I nodded in agreement. Every good adventure story ends with a well-deserved rest for the hero and reader alike. The Pilgrim-Adventurers were now having their respite, for the time being, at least. Perhaps it was still too early to close the story and utter the words 'The End'?

Chapter 8

A Blessed Rage for Order

Before theology and doctrine can ever exist, there must first be stories. They are stories of faith, of course. And before stories, there must be encounters, experiences and reflection. Churches are, moreover, as James Hopewell reminds us, primarily 'storied communities and dwellings'. Ecclesial communities and their members occupy, for the most part, that precognitive hinterland: a place where lives and norms are not so much governed by formal religious rules and dogma, as by a complex tapestry of stories and affinities that bind believers together. This is true religion – being continually bound together by shared narratives, common interests and particular practices, that turns a group of individuals into a 'congregation'.

I make no apology for beginning in this way, as I, too, want to start with a story from 15 years ago. In many ways it is a simple story. At the theological college I attended for my ordination training (1988–90), I was walking down the corridor one day, returning to my study. I ran into a fellow ordinand whom I had seen that morning in chapel. It was now afternoon, but there was something different about him. He usually wore smart jeans or corduroys, well-polished brown brogue shoes, a shirt (sometimes with a tie) and a smart-casual sports or tweed jacket. However, on this particular day I couldn't help noticing that his arm was in a sling, and he was trying to conceal his injury. I asked him if he was all right. He replied that he was fine. So I asked him how he came by the injury. He explained that he had been having a discussion that morning with a close friend, who normally shared his theological views. The discussion was about whether or not righteousness was 'imputed' or 'imparted', but it had developed into a raging argument. So much so, in fact, that the ordinand now standing in front of me had finally smashed his fist into a college noticeboard in disgust at his friend's views. The force of the impact had fractured some bones, and he had had to go to the local hospital for treatment. He didn't seem to be embarrassed by this 'accident'; the injury he sustained, he suggested, showed just how important the issue was. And with that, he left.

I recall the story for several reasons. First, because of the force, passion and aggression that colours the narrative, coupled with the incongruity of this story being spoken softly, deeply and earnestly by a young man who one would not normally have associated with violence. Second, because the display of violence did seem to reveal a hidden rage for ordering the church and policing its theology. Third, because the display of force was immediately justified: this showed 'just how important' the issue was.

I recognize at once that this story is both unusual and atypical in relation to Conservative Evangelicalism. Furthermore, the event took place in 1989, some four years before the formation of Reform, and it is the analysis of this movement within the Church of England that we are primarily concerned with in this chapter. There can be no doubt that, had Reform existed in the late 1980s, my bandaged colleague would have been a member. He was an ardent disciple of the Revd Dick Lucas, then rector of St Helen's Bishopsgate, London, an avid proponent of *Read, Mark, Learn* (Lucas, 1986), a regular mentor to the Christian Union and a staunch opponent of women's ordination (on grounds of headship). But, at the same time, the story, with its overtones of violence and aggression, reflects a commonly held perception about Reform. Even the secular British media have dubbed Reform 'the Taliban of the Church of England'. The story, of course, chimes with such sentiments: it points towards the deep and barely controlled spiritual and theological *rage* that many regard as one of the defining hallmarks of the movement. And, paradoxically, this rage is being expressed by otherwise (normally) ultra-polite and (allegedly) upper-middle-class Christians who mostly hail from the home counties or the prosperous suburbs of larger cities throughout England. In what follows, I want to explore not only the rise of Reform in the Church of England, but also examine some of the reasons why, theologically and sociologically, a movement made up of people who really know how to *behave* (both culturally and in terms of manners) has also developed a decidedly aggressive side to its character, and how this has been done within a church and worldwide Communion (or Commonwealth) of churches that are implicitly bound together by a code of manners (Percy, 2000, pp. 114–25).

After briefly considering the history of Reform – a movement that is now more than ten years old – I will go on to look at some methodological perspectives before turning to some of the key issues that define Reform's agenda. Some further analysis will examine the prospects for denominations (Anglicanism in this case) in a postmodern world, where churches are bound together less and less by a common form of governance and more and more by a shared ethos and moral affinity. The conclusion looks at the implications of the relative strength of Reform within the context of the Anglican communion as a whole. Suffice to say, this chapter is more exploratory in nature, and as much an exercise in testing methodologies within the broad penumbra of modern ecclesiology. It is not intended to be a definitive account or interpretation of Reform: from the outset, I recognize that the movement itself merits far more attention than a single chapter in a book can possibly give it.

The Origin and Anatomy of Reform

One of the surprising aspects of Reform is its size. It currently has approximately 1600 members. The number of churches that would categorically identify with the movement is probably less than 50, and perhaps as few as 30. It is difficult to be precise about this last statistic, as clergy who lead churches may well insist that their congregation is 'fully supportive of Reform', but hard data to back this up simply do not exist.[1] Clergy will often assume that a congregation's support of them and their ministry amounts to their tacit agreement with his or her theological position. In fact, such concord is quite rare, even in the most apparently homogenous congregations. Congregations – even those that may be content to be identified as Conservative Evangelical – are likely to be places of doctrinal divergence rather than credal concurrence. However, statistics that seem to reveal a relatively low level of support for Reform should not be used to underestimate the scale and importance of the movement. It wields considerable national influence and also has a significant international profile through links with the diocese of Sydney (cf. Jensen, 2002), and enjoys other liaisons in North America.

As a movement, Reform was born on 22 February 1993. The text of the original leaflet, stating the aims and purposes of the movement, identifies its fundamental doctrinal core before listing its major concerns:

> ...for some years groups of mainstream Evangelicals have met to discuss issues in the church and nation. These issues include the authority of and sufficiency of Scripture; the uniqueness and finality of Christ; the priority of the local church; the complementarity of men and women...[We are] Christians first, Evangelicals second, and Anglicans third...[we have] committed ourselves to unite for action under the authority of Scripture as God's word...Historic Anglican theology is committed to continuous Reformation of the church. We are committed to the reform of ourselves, our congregations and our world by the gospel...Reform is urgently needed...[because] the gospel is not shaping and changing our church and our society: our society seems to be shaping and changing us. A biblical Christian voice is heard too little in our society. The Church of England seems to have lost confidence in the truth and power of the gospel.... To reverse these trends we are committed to change and growth. Such change will be costly.... We do not believe this change can come from the denominational centre. The local church must take back responsibility for the denomination... (Holloway, 1993)

The agenda outlined is specific and direct. The leaflet identifies a particular kind of stance as being 'orthodox' and implies that the wider denomination has lapsed in its belief, confidence and responsibility. In terms of process, this inevitably leads to a call for financial realignment and establishing the local church as the primary locus of mission and discipleship. This agenda is, in turn, driven by a broad appeal to the ongoing work of the Reformation. In effect, the leaders of Reform are doing nothing less than eliding their own identity and agenda with that of the original Reformers of the sixteenth and seventeenth centuries. Except that, this time, the enemy is not the papacy: it is modernity and liberalism, which is deemed to have betrayed the historic missiological calling of a national church.

---

[1] For example, the Revd Philip Hacking, the former chair of Reform and a former vicar of Christ Church Fulwood, Sheffield, estimates that some 60 members of his congregation joined Reform out of a possible 1200 regular attendees. But he maintains that the vast majority of attendees, whilst not being members of Reform, would be fully supportive of its agenda.

Although the precise birth date of Reform can be easily identified, the date (and process) of its conception is a little more contentious. Worth mentioning are several recent moments in postwar English Evangelical history, each of which may stake a claim to have been influential in the genesis of Reform. First, the decision of the General Synod of the Church of England to ordain women to the priesthood in November 1992 could undoubtedly be seen as the 'final straw' or 'trigger' that galvanized Evangelical leaders into action. As Ian Jones points out, those Conservative Evangelical leaders who opposed women's ordination were wholly unprepared for the measure to be approved and thereafter vowed to be more organized in order to address other key issues that they saw on the horizon (such as women bishops, the ordination of homosexuals and so on – see Jones, 2004).

Second, Reform also owes a partial debt to the (relatively successful) campaigning of the Revd Tony Higton during the 1980s. Higton, the rector of Hawkwell in Essex, launched an influential pressure group called Action for Biblical Witness to Our Nation (ABWON) which petitioned the General Synod, published several tracts and engaged in numerous high-profile public debates, most notably on sexuality and interfaith worship. Higton, himself a member of General Synod, also edited *Sexuality and the Church: The Way Forward* (1987), which was a systematic and robust Conservative Evangelical refutation of homosexuality. Higton was a kind of middle-aged *enfant terrible* within the General Synod, and his terrorizing tactics, use of the media and strident polemical voice won him many admirers. More particularly, Higton demonstrated that the 'liberal centre', which many assumed to be at the heart of the Church of England's governance, could be seriously challenged and called to account by some well-organized campaigning.

Third, the growing presence of Conservative Evangelicals within the Church of England can be traced, in part, to the seminal (Evangelical Congress) Keele Conference of 1967. Dr Martyn Lloyd-Jones had called upon Evangelicals to leave their respective denominations and form a new denomination. But within the Church of England, this move was tenaciously resisted by John Stott and Jim Packer, amongst others, who eventually won the day. But this moment in modern church history set a course for Evangelicals that would lead to other kinds of conflict. Specifically, in deciding to remain within Anglicanism and to work for 'evolution within', Conservative Evangelicals quickly organized themselves into groups and networks that could maintain their identity and promote their causes.

Fourth, and despite the numerical strength of postwar Evangelical Anglicanism, some tensions were beginning to emerge within the movement. On the issue of women's ordination, it was increasingly apparent that many Evangelicals felt that there were no longer any clear biblical reasons that should prevent women being made priests. Evangelical identity was also successively transformed and eroded by Charismatic Renewal, which seemed, at least to its Conservative Evangelical detractors, to pay far too much attention to the realm of feelings and not enough to the Bible. Furthermore, the gradual emergence of a broader and more accommodating mainstream 'Anglican-Evangelical' identity, which grew increasingly popular from the

1970s onwards, put Conservative Evangelicals much more on the defensive, even to the point of making them appear reactionary. This is perhaps best illustrated by the debacle that surrounded the publication of *Churchman* in 1984. The editor at the time, Revd Peter Williams, was dismissed from his post for publishing some articles about the authority and inspiration of scripture, which departed from the normal 'classic' Conservative Evangelical stance. To the non-Evangelical eye, the slight differences between the views of, say, Jim Packer and James Dunn would hardly seem to be significant, but the trustees of *Churchman* saw it differently. The argument led to several committee members breaking away from *Churchman* and a new journal, *Anvil* being launched. *Anvil* subsequently became the voice of those who were more inclined to call themselves Anglican-Evangelicals; *Churchman* retained the loyalty of those who preferred to call themselves Evangelical-Anglicans.[2]

Fifth, a particular kind of elite Conservative Evangelicalism has also been influential in the genesis of Reform. Bodies such as the Church Society, Inter-Varsity Fellowship (IVF), and its successor UCCF (Universities and Colleges Christian Fellowship) have naturally played a significant part in forming future leaders within Evangelicalism. In the latter case, with its distinctive Articles of Faith (a ten-point doctrinal schema), UCCF/IVP have been able to secure a degree of credal homogeneity amongst Christian Union groups that has eluded other denominational affiliations and more radical groups such as the Student Christian Movement. However, what is particularly intriguing about Reform is that some of its leaders had their Christian faith formed within a relatively small cartel of elite public schools, often followed by a university education at Oxford or Cambridge. The backbone of the student work will often have included some exposure to the Iwerne Minster Camps, which offered a very specific kind of programme under the tutelage of Nash and the Fletcher brothers.[3] (These camps would include 'lady helpers', but not women speakers.) Sociologically, these camps and meetings appeared to be promoting what some scholars now refer to as 'muscular Christianity' – particular kinds of male bonding centred on exercise and spiritual study (Money, 1997; Magdalinski and Chandler, 2001). Thus, a typical Iwerne Minster midrash of instruction (which I have often overheard), and aimed at students, runs like this (paraphrased):

> Living the Christian life can be likened to three cats walking on a wall, one named Facts, one named Faith and the other named Feelings. Now they have to walk on the wall in the right order, or they will all fall off. Facts must always lead, and then

---

[2] But Reform takes the view that whilst 'Anglican-Evangelicals' have developed 'caring, intelligent and thorough local parochial ministry', they have always been unable to challenge the dominant 'liberal-Catholic leadership' of the church.

[3] However, Reform leaders are at pains to point out that many of its council members lack this 'pedigree'. The previous chair, Philip Hacking, suggests that Reform is more of a grassroots movement. Similarly, the support enjoyed by the Jensen brothers within the diocese of Sydney is to be found more amongst the lower-middle classes and skilled blue-collar workers than amongst Sydney's elite social circles. See Jensen (2002) and Judd and Cable (1987).

followed by Faith, with Feelings coming last. If Feelings ever leads, Facts and Faith both fall off the wall....

Sixth, over the last 25 years a number of other pressure groups have grown up that have directly contributed to the genesis of Reform. Several could be named, but one of the groups most closely allied to Reform has been the Proclamation Trust, founded by the Revd Dick Lucas, formerly rector of St Helen's Bishopsgate. The Proclamation Trust has enjoyed a wide ministry in the Church of England and is primarily devoted to promoting a particular kind of expository preaching and the promulgation of courses that teach 'Christian basics' (for example, *Read, Mark, Learn*). It should be noted, however, that Reform, in common with other Conservative Evangelicals, regard the Alpha course (a product of a more Charismatic–Evangelical mindset, and originating from Holy Trinity Brompton) as too liberal and quite unsound. (Indeed, prominent Conservative Evangelicals such as Philip Jensen, archbishop of Sydney, have consistently attacked the Alpha course.)

Seventh, and finally, some leaders within Reform appeal directly to the early heroes of the Reformation (such as Wycliffe) or to seventeenth-century Anglican thinkers who were themselves heavily influenced by Cromwellian Puritanism. In this regard, some Reform leaders are inclined to oppose the 'liberal-catholic drift [which] is destroying the Church of England' (Holloway, 1993, p. 3). The claim to be Reformist is therefore to be treated with the utmost seriousness within Anglicanism. Reform leaders are not simply arguing for a particular kind of moral coherence as the basis for ecclesial communion, they are also advocating a specious form of Protestantism that will exclude the excesses of Charismatic Renewal and the aesthetics of Anglo-Catholicism. In other words, Reform is promoting a kind of clear, plain, morally certain and pedagogically cerebral Christianity. Conversion is achieved through intellectual persuasion; discipleship is maintained through embodying the convictions of the mind in disciplined living. There is little scope for ambiguity or difference, for the Bible is held to be clear on all matters of importance. It is a case of 'Trust and Obey' – there is no other way.

To conclude this section, we turn to the Reform Covenant itself. Besides identifying its fundamental life through the usual credal formulae, it is important to understand the association as a movement of *resistance*. Throughout Reform's documents, the themes of correction, confrontation, reformation and reassertion are prominent:

> ...[We affirm]...the divine *order* of male headship, which makes the headship of women as priests-in-charge, incumbents, dignitaries and bishops *inappropriate*...the *rightness* of sexual intercourse in heterosexual marriage, and the *wrongness* of such activity both outside it and in *all* its homosexual forms...the *urgent* need for decentralisation at national, diocesan and deanery level, and the need to *radically reform* the present shape of episcopacy and *pastoral discipline*.... (Holloway, 1993, p. 1, emphasis added)

Properly speaking, we might say that Reform exists because of concerns with money, sex and power. As an organization, it is more focused than the Church

Society, an older and more traditional body for Conservative Evangelicals. In particular, Reform seeks to campaign on a specific range of issues, each of which is underpinned by a concern to reaffirm the authority of scripture and the priority of the local church as the primary locus for mission and evangelism. Were it not for the anxieties of Conservative Evangelicals on these matters, Reform would probably not exist. This is an issue to which we shall return, but, before doing so, we need to explore the ethnography of the movement in more detail.

Reform: An Ethnographic Sketch

The primary material for this study has been gathered within the context of a broad ethnographic framework. This has principally been achieved in four ways: through interviews with key leaders in Reform, and also with individuals on its periphery;[4] through searching through Reform's records and statements (accessible on its own website); by reflecting on stories, encounters and vignettes gathered over the last decade; and by collecting over 50 newspaper articles and commentaries drawn from a wide variety of sources. The written pieces collected came from secular national newspapers, church newspapers, and articles in church journals, which were all published in 2003 at the height of the Jeffrey John, Gene Robinson and New Westminster debates.

Granted, I have not conducted formal quantitative fieldwork in my research of Reform, at least in a form that might be understood by Bender, Clifford and others and was sketched in the previous chapter, (although the interviews I conducted have been a very important feature in constructing this study). Instead, I have chosen to write from the vantage-point of someone who, as an Anglican priest and theologian, is constantly caught up in the narrative streams and cross-currents that the movement creates. I have known a number of Reform's members throughout my ordained life. Indeed, Reform is now a recognizable feature of the landscape of English Anglicanism: it has become a necessary part of the ecclesiological 'cultural furniture'. Encountering Reform is unavoidable, and I have long been puzzled by the sombre effervescence of the movement, and have aspired to study its characteristics and interiority. But what would qualify me, as a more distant observer than a decidedly engaged fieldworker, to claim any knowledge of the movement at all?

First, although it is true that Reform came into being in 1993, the seeds for the movement were germinating in the soil of Conservative Evangelicalism long before that. As someone who was raised in a 'normal low Anglican Church', I lived through, first-hand, a number of the emergent tensions between Charismatic Renewal and Conservative Evangelicalism, as they were expressed in a local congregation. They fascinated me at the time, and continue

---

[4] Specifically with a former chair of Reform, a member of the Council, a leading moderate Conservative Evangelical, and a clergyperson from the Diocese of Sydney (who is not an Evangelical, and provided comment as an 'outsider').

to do so. The conflict between spiritualities that celebrated the sensate and those that embodied the cerebral, the arguments over worship, sermons, order and gifts of the Spirit: these are but a few examples. There is now, of course, some interesting literature that explores the phenomenon of the 'post-Evangelical' (see P. Ward, 1997; Tomlinson, 1995).

Second, my own exposure to the wider Anglican–Evangelical culture has been continuous. For the most part, this has been as a direct result of studying and researching Charismatic Renewal for the past 15 years, and therefore being unable to avoid the Conservative Evangelical forces that have typically opposed it. In the course of such research, I have often encountered texts and individuals who were happy to espouse a proto-Reform agenda after they had finished critiquing contemporary revivalism. This was especially true of my ordination training (1988–90) where followers of the Revd Dick Lucas, although small in number, made their presence felt and disclosed their theological schema publicly, and in fairly unambiguous terms.

Third, in my own research and writing, I have always been careful to distinguish between Conservative Evangelicalism and fundamentalism. I have been critical of James Barr for lumping the two together, even though it can sometimes *feel* that there are morphological similarities (Percy and Jones, 2002; cf. Bebbington, 1989). In my view, avoiding the 'fundamentalist' label is important. Using such a label for movements such as Reform is often no more than a lazy attempt to demonize and dismiss the movement. In fact, Reform is far too complex and specific to be included as a world within the fundamentalist universe. I mention this only to make clear that much of my information about Reform and Conservative Evangelicalism has been gleaned from the *underside* of my primary research on Charismatic Renewal, revivalism and fundamentalism (see Percy, 1996a; Percy and Jones, 2002; Harris, 1998). On the one hand, I have encountered Conservative Evangelical movements and exponents through their tussles with Charismatic Renewal, which might even include their opposition to Alpha courses. On the other hand, in my study of fundamentalism, I have inevitably had to study certain aspects of Conservative Evangelicalism, partly in order to clarify, at least in my own mind, that it is not really a form of fundamentalism.

Fourth, as a curate, university chaplain and post-ordination training tutor, I have encountered ordained and lay members of Reform at several levels. During training as a curate, clergy colleagues who were members of Reform would habitually boycott deanery and diocesan events that did not fit with their priorities. Reform curates would normally absent themselves from any kind of additional training programmes, as they were deemed to be 'unsound'. As a university chaplain in Cambridge, I would routinely discover that students were being urged to stay away from college chapel by 'Reform-type' clergy. As a post-ordination tutor, I would later listen patiently as a young Reform curate explained to me and other curates how and why they barred people from Holy Communion, and effectively excommunicated individuals for such 'offences' as divorce and remarriage.

Fifth, and to return to Bender's earlier observation, I find myself constantly caught up in the streams of events and conversations that characterize

Conservative Evangelicals and the Reform movement. Over several years, I have collected a substantial litany of vignettes that have slowly demanded systematization and interpretation – like collecting the individual pieces of a jigsaw over a long period of time. For example, I recall meeting Revd Tony Higton at NEAC in 1988 and discussing with him his principled stance to not stand and applaud the archbishop of Canterbury's address, as other delegates did. On another occasion, I puzzled over a small number of fellow ordinands who, when they did not entirely agree with the content of a sermon, would pointedly leave chapel before receiving communion, usually slamming the heavy oak door as they left. As G.K. Chesterton once famously quipped, 'a gentleman is never unintentionally rude'. If that is true, it left me, as an observer, with an uncomfortable paradox – namely that these normally well-mannered young men, mostly from upper-middle-class backgrounds, educated in elite public schools and often with an Oxbridge pedigree, *meant* to demonstrate rudeness. But over something as trivial as a sermon that they found troubling? It would seem so.

Finally, in the process of this research, and more typically within the ethnographic framework, I have conducted interviews with key individuals and engaged in correspondence with others, both formal and informal. I cannot claim that this endeavour is comprehensive; it has been limited by lack of resources and time. Whether or not what follows is reasonable and representative is for others to judge, but I hold that it is. At the same time, I readily acknowledge that I am not *reproducing* the voice of Reform in this exercise; instead, I am inviting the reader to see a relatively new Christian movement in a particular way. What follows is a critical contemplation of a Christian tradition that is proud of its zeal and tenacity, and is unashamed of its politics; my invitation is to ponder the ways in which the world of Reform is put together, both culturally, sociologically, ecclesiologically and theologically.

Briefly, my approach is primarily ethnographic insofar as I attempt to provide an in-depth account of a movement. The study also takes the cultural aspect of religion seriously and tries to make some serious sense of its complexity. Furthermore, as an ethnographic study, it also aims to describe the texture of the movement. As such, the study tries to avoid theoretical generalizations as far as possible in favour of concentrating on details. To paraphrase Durkheim's comment on religion, a study of this kind accepts that any representation it offers is necessarily metaphorical and symbolic but, in being like this, it is not inevitably unfaithful (cf. Wuthnow, 1997, p. 247). An ethnographic sketch is, in other words, just that: a sketch. Like any map or drawing, it can never reproduce reality; it can only represent it as accurately and artistically as possible.

An Interpretative Horizon

Within the field of Congregational Studies, James Hopewell (1987) provides a promising perspective from which to gain some understanding of Reform. Hopewell contends that individual congregations and, more broadly, networks of churches are united less by credal formulae and more by world-views, which in turn are configured through the kinds of narratives that 'construct' specific households of faith:

> ... world views reflect and give a focus to group experience, providing a map within which words and actions make sense. The setting of a congregation is the order by which its gossip, sermons, strategies and fights – the household idiom gain their reasonableness. What is expressed in *daily intercourse* about the nature of the world is idiomatic, responsive to a particular pattern of language, expressing a particular setting for narrative. Tales in a local church tend to travel in packs: one good story evokes another, one member's account of an illness, for example, is usually reciprocated in kind. In comradeship and commiseration members top each other's stories, building up the world setting that they together inhabit. (Hopewell, 1987, p. 85, emphasis added)

Although Hopewell's primary interest is in local congregations, his work offers considerable illumination in exploring and analysing Reform's world-view. Hopewell, following Northrop Frye (1957), argues that churches are essentially 'storied communities' and that these stories can be understood as corresponding to the four basic literary genres, namely irony, comedy, romance and tragedy. This means, in effect, that the principal stories configuring a church or cluster of churches will usually turn out to be primarily oriented towards one of these major genres. However, Hopewell is careful to point out that individuals, movements and congregations must be properly situated within this 'quadripolar analysis' and are therefore unlikely to be, say, entirely ironic or romantic in their world-view – there will be mixtures and variables.

The literary genre that most closely corresponds to the world-view espoused by members of Reform (and more generally to that of Conservative Evangelicalism) is the 'tragic' – what Hopewell calls the 'Canonic negotiation'. According to Hopewell, the Canonic negotiation is:

> [r]eliance upon an authoritative interpretation of a world pattern, often considered [to be] God's revealed world or will, by which one identifies one's essential life. The integrity of the pattern requires that followers reject any gnosis (i.e., knowledge) of union with the pattern but instead subordinate their selfhood to it. Characteristics of the Canonic orientation are similar to Frye's tragic genre .... (Hopewell, 1987, p. 69)

Developing this observation, Hopewell exports and converts the basic literary theory into some explicitly theological and ecclesiological conceptualizations. When comparing Hopewell's basic framework to the Reform Covenant, we can see how illuminating the reading can become. For example, Hopewell claims that the primary narrative motif of the Canonic negotiation is sacrifice and that its movement is 'union toward subordination' (ibid., p. 70). The Reform Covenant seems to reflect this: 'we who subscribe to this Covenant *bind* ourselves together in fellowship to *uphold, defend* and *spread* the gospel of Jesus Christ according to the doctrine of the Church of England ... ' (emphasis added).

Personally, socially and cosmically, there are specific theological resolutions to certain scenarios. In a personal situation of hubris, the response is generally surrender and the resolution is justification. In a social context a situation of vice is met with the response of righteousness and the resolution is judgement. Cosmically, principalities and powers are engaged with passion and the resolution is the arrival of the kingdom. Similarly, Hopewell identifies the cognitive features of this world-view. Authority is posited in God's revealed Word and will; the focus of integrity is scripture; valued behaviour is obedience. Conceptually and typically, God is Father, Jesus the saviour, and evil (or the enemy) is a personal devil. The Bible is the word of God; a minister a messenger of God; the Eucharist a memorial; the church a covenant; and the Gospel salvation.

In the Reform Covenant, the Articles of Faith seem to reflect the Canonic world-view sketched by Hopewell:

> ... specifically we lay emphasis on the universality of sin, the present justification of sinners by grace through faith in Christ alone, and their supernatural regeneration and new life through the Holy Spirit... the calling of the church and all Christian people to a life of holiness and prayer according to the Scriptures... the significance of personal present repentance and faith as determining eternal destiny... the infallibility and supreme authority of 'God's Word written' and its clarity and sufficiency for the resolving of disputes about Christian faith and life.... (Hopewell, 1987, pp. 60ff)

Hopewell, in his explication of the Canonic world-view, suggests that:

> ... in this negotiation, the controlling canon provides integrity... for Canonic Protestants the inviolable canon is God's word, the Holy Scripture. The Bible in their Canonic eyes is completely reliable and authoritative. (Hopewell, 1987, p.79)

In other types of negotiation, the self or reason might be deemed to be the arbiter in the midst of life's complexities. But in the Canonic negotiation, God's revealed Word and will is already predetermined in the canon of scripture. As Northrop Frye notes, 'whether the context is Greek, Christian or undefined, tragedy seems to lead to an epiphany of law, of that which is and must be' (Frye, 1957, p. 79). But what does an 'epiphany of law' mean here, exactly? Hopewell answers this question by describing the Canonic outlook in more detail:

> One is not free and good. One is lost and sinful, and one's story develops the costly consequences of one's depraved nature. If the self remains disobedient, refusing to recognise the sovereignty of God, then life continues to deteriorate and ends in hell. If, however, one repents and accepts the lordship of Christ, one takes on a different yoke, of suffering love and obedience. (Hopewell, 1987, p. 80)

In other words, an apotheosis of the self is an anathema to the Canonic world-view. Everything – the self, church and world – must submit to the predetermined will of God that is clearly and unambiguously revealed.

Correspondingly, this personal spiritual programme, when mapped on to a movement and brought into a church or denomination as an agent of transformation, is inevitably and radically insistent on its agenda:

> The moral fibre of the nation is decaying; families, schools, cities and [the media] are close to disaster. Only by a massive mission can this nation be saved. Churches must become obedient, 'Bible-centred, Bible-believing, Bible teaching churches'.... (Hopewell, 1987, p. 80)

Hopewell's observation can be compared with that of a mainstream exponent of Conservative Evangelicalism. The 'fit' is precise:

> It is the tragedy of much modern theology, and of whatever church life is influenced by such theology, that it has chosen to follow its culture rather than the word of God. It has accepted the negative verdict on the Bible of movements such as the Enlightenment, and has tried to substitute other revelations or other versions of revelation. These must be doomed to failure.... (Jensen, 2002, p. 274)

Although I think that Hopewell is entirely correct to emphasize these aspects of the Canonic negotiation, I am less convinced that the full features of Frye's definition of tragedy necessarily apply to Conservative Evangelicals or to movements such as Reform. In Hopewell's use of Frye, it is suggested that the Canonic negotiation anticipates failure, death and tragedy; in effect, rewards and 'ultimate happiness is deferred to an afterlife'. But whilst the Canonic Christian life is undoubtedly characterized by submission and obedience, these should be properly understood as disciplines or virtues of empowerment for this life. In other words, the sombre, sober and serious ways in which Canonic Christians approach the church and shape their own spirituality is intended to achieve some measure of triumph in the midst of tragedy. In other words, Canonic Christians believe that they operate within a tragic world and also in tragic consequences for that world. However, these consequences can normally be avoided by resolute obedience and faithfulness. If tragedy continues to afflict a believer who is faithful to this calling, the rewards (usually deferred until the afterlife) will necessarily outweigh the consequences.

The Canonic world-view, then, is a particularly tight and resilient type of Christian belief. It sees the affliction of the self or the persecution of a movement as confirmation of its value and righteousness. It sees the triumph of the self or of a movement as God's vindication of principled Christian living. Ultimately, individuals and movements shaped by the Canonic negotiation are quite *prepared* to be defeated – unlike Hopewell, I do not accept that the Canonic negotiation *expects* defeat. In my view, the Canonic negotiation could more properly be said to anticipate grinding out a gritty, disciplined and ultimately righteous victory, in which falsehood and compromise were comprehensively defeated and shown to be less than the full Gospel. Put another way, Canonic conservative Christians are not to be compared to a latter-day St Sebastian, tied to a stake of persecution and stoically awaiting the onslaught of the many arrows of modernity and liberalism to pierce their skin, as they surely await the bliss of heaven. Rather, they are more like St George (or at least he of the popular iconography and myth), spearing the dragon of error and heresy and rescuing that fair damsel (that is, the church) from the suggestive and seductive whisperings of that great tempter, liberalism. In the fight for righteousness and truth, injury and perhaps even death may be anticipated, but the risks are nothing when compared to the eternal rewards on offer. The journey ahead may be perilous, but the valiant knights of canonic Christianity are bidden to the fight, to go forth and crusade.

In one way, Hopewell could be said to have already understood my reservation about the actual extent of his narrative theory. In his discussion of tragic tales he acknowledges that 'the self in tragedy, as in romance, is heroic'. However, tragic heroes in the Canonic genre are vindicated and saved rather than cured or freed. Only by identifying with God's revealed Word or will can salvation be obtained. So the heroes (or leaders) within the Canonic genre are not necessarily those who embody exemplary suffering. They will, instead, be those who devote themselves to a disciplined and selfless life in which sacrifice and obedience are paramount. As Linda Bamber puts it, the Canonic world is one:

> ... that is separate from us who inhabit it; it will not yield to our desires and fantasies...this means that tragedy, recognition – *anagnorisis*, the banishing of ignorance – is a major goal.... (Bamber, 1982, p. 22)

Here we have an account, developed from the Hopewellian reflections on tragedy, that partially explains why Reform concentrates so heavily on teaching, preaching and instruction to constitute its essential life and identity. It is important to note here that, from my discussions with members of Reform about the priorities of Jesus in his earthly ministry, it seems that the majority of individuals within the movement propagate the view that Jesus was primarily a teacher. Of course, although the most common title for Jesus used in the Gospels is indeed 'Rabbi' – teacher – most people I have talked to within Reform go further than this and suggest that the primary mode of Christ's teaching was preaching. This is, in itself, contestable. Moreover, even if it were true, little, if any, account is taken of the ambiguity of parabolic interaction, the multifaceted ways in which parables can be taken and interpreted, what actually constitutes teaching and learning (one suspects a very un-Freirian 'banking model' rather than anything shrewd or revolutionary), nor the other ways in which Jesus 'taught', such as through specific actions, practices or behaviour.

From the perspectives gleaned so far, the Reform world-view can be properly summarized as follows. The world is a sinful place, from which the individual must be saved. The church, in order to fulfil its missiological task as an agent of salvation, must be opposed to the world and its vices as well as to any form of accommodation of worldly standards. The tragic or Canonic outlook expects that serious, sober and disciplined discipleship to be a primary means of ensuring that the tragic nature of the world does not have tragic consequences for those caught within its snares. This is ultimately, then, an advocation of a form of separatism, which of course can lead to something akin to sectarianism. However, within the Canonic world-view, the purpose of separatism is centred on prophetic condemnation, individual purgation and a sharing in salvation; there is no separatism for the sake of it. In other words, the Canonic world-view is a means by which participants – either individuals or movements – can imagine the reordering and cleansing of the church itself. It is a form of systematic postmodern Puritanism; saving the church from itself and the world, and thereby rescuing souls from the inevitable and tragic consequences of disobedience and unbelief. The Canonic world-view is a gnosis of certitude; the faith rests on 'received facts' that are sufficient and clear. Those who think otherwise are leading the church astray and destined for annihilation either in this life or the next.

Money, Sex and Power

One consequence of the tragic outlook is that it inevitably tends to treat the church as an acultural entity. Because the Gospel is absolute, it must also be expressed, embodied and reified in ways that ultimately transcend culture, and perhaps even subjugate it. I do not propose to take issue with that particular missiological presupposition in this chapter. Suffice to say, such issues have been dealt with perfectly well by a number of theologians over the years, as well as by scholars within Evangelicalism, and also by some notable novelists (one only has to recall Barbara Kingsolver's recent *The Poisonwood Bible* or Herman Melville's *Omoo* and *Tipee*.) My observation is, rather, intended to question the wisdom of a world-view that does not pay proper attention to enculturation. It should perhaps be obvious that, even within a strictly biblical framework of understanding, no-one speaks or learns their Christianity *without* a distinctly local accent. The story of the outpouring of the Holy Spirit at Pentecost is a reminder – as though one were ever needed – that Christianity has always spoken in the many-and-tilthed tongues of its adherents. There is no type of Christianity that does not bear the trace of its 'accent of origin'. Even Alpha courses, despite their global appeal, feel and sound like they grew up in Knightsbridge. Roman Catholicism (that great oxymoron), retains its 'Roman' accent (a concentrated, imperial and centralized power), despite its 'Catholic' (global) claim.

These preliminary observations aside, the focus of this short section is concerned with three key themes that appear to preoccupy the public agenda of Reform: money, sex (or gender) and power. The concerns over these issues are, I want to suggest, not at the *heart* of the Reform. Rather, they are better understood as symptomatic of the deeper disquiet that accompanies the tragic world-view. It is far too easy, in my view, to narrate Reform as an ultra-Protestant schismatic body that simply wants its own way on certain issues and will go to almost any lengths to secure their purity, identity and autonomy. Witness, for example, how one commentator expresses a widely shared perception of Reform:

In effect, this is exactly the strategy pursued with such success by Reform and Forward in Faith within the Church of England. Behave as if the schism were an accomplished fact, withhold your money, treat your bishop with the distant ecumenical courtesy normally due to a neighbouring Imam, control your own appointments, and tell your congregations that everyone else is a doomed heretic or dupe of doomed heretics .... (Brown, 2003, p. 16)

In contrast, I have found that, in my interviews with Reform members and leaders, there are more measured views to be harvested. For many, if not most, the central concerns are the authority of the Bible and the priority of local mission: clashes over money, sex/gender and power are simply identified as prominent obstacles that can impede the effectiveness of the local church and undermine the authority of scripture. But the obstacles themselves do not constitute a 'cause'. Nor do ministers of Reform see themselves as 'congregationalist', turning their backs on the obligations and opportunities of parochial ministry. On the contrary, such ministers seem to be deeply engaged in parish or 'local-contextual' ministry and seek to draw in significant numbers of people that reflect the culture in which their native ministry operates. Increasingly, a number of churches in the Reform penumbra see 'church planting' in other parishes as an extension of that missiological strategy. Having perceived – correctly, to some extent – that a parish church will not appeal to all its parishioners, they do not seek to undermine the parochial framework, but instead see their activity as complementing a 'system' that no longer works as comprehensively and deeply as it once did. In that respect, they are merely demonstrating a nascent prowess: to develop an effective missiology within a consumerist, postmodern and post-institutional world. For Reform members, the demands of the Gospel and the call to repentance must supersede any 'man-made' regulations about the ordering and governance of the church. So any rigid appeal relating to 'parish boundaries' that impedes a wider mission and ministry will simply be interpreted as yet another obstacle to be overcome, for the sake of the Gospel.

Strictly speaking, the issues of money, sex/gender and power belong together in any assessment of Reform. Analysts tend to treat them as separate foci of concern, whereas in reality these issues form an interrelated nexus of problems to which Reform addresses itself in a particularly systematic manner. Moreover, as we have noted before, the issues are merely deemed to be the presenting 'symptoms' that riddle a sick body (the church). The deeper malaise is, from the perspective of the tragic world-view, disobedience to God, and a failure to honour the authority of scripture. Thus, David Holloway writes:

> ... [we] met in London to discuss, think and pray about financial issues in the Church of England. [We] were discussing the right way forward for 'net-givers' in responding to the ever-larger financial demands for central church funds – 'the quota'. Huge sums of money are now subsidizing work that Evangelicals often believe is frustrating the gospel.... The context is increasing theological liberalism in the church at large; and growing bureaucratic centralism especially at the Diocesan but also at the General Synod levels. As a response some mainstream larger Evangelical churches that are 'net-givers' are already capping their quotas.... The

goal of this action is not merely responsible stewardship, financial competence and long-term viability but mission. The needs of the nation are seen as more important than the comfort of the church. The conversion of England in our nation's desperate spiritual and moral condition is a priority.... (Holloway, 1993, p. 1)

In this narration, it is the wider church that is being written-up as 'deviant'. Withholding income from central funds is therefore 'responsible' and a foundation for reconstructing a more faithful form of mission that is less centred on the 'comfort' of the church and more focused on evangelism and the moral renewal of the nation. It therefore follows that Reform members see themselves as acting correctively, prophetically and creatively rather than obstructively. Thus, Holloway notes that 'many mainline Evangelical churches are no longer willing to pay for a combination of ineffectiveness and doubt at the centre' (Holloway, n.d., p. 2).

Reform's concern with sex and gender are, perhaps surprisingly, a little more difficult to access. On the matter of gender, Reform continues to assert 'the divine order of male headship' as an important article of faith. But, privately, many leaders within the movement acknowledged that there are considerable differences of opinion and varieties of practice within Conservative Evangelicalism. Some openly admitted that the issue of women priests was now 'water under the bridge'. Thus, although some Reform churches are 'Resolution A' parishes, and would therefore not welcome a female incumbent, there was little sign of real opposition to the ministry of women priests in general. Some had no real difficulty with women preaching and celebrating the Eucharist. Some went further and indicated that women bishops would not necessarily be a divisive or decisive issue for them, nor perhaps even a crisis. In that respect, Reform seems to have already anticipated that a campaign against women bishops is likely to divide Evangelicals more than it unites them.

However, the same cannot be said for sex outside marriage, and in particular, homosexual practice. Again, it is important to report that, in my interviews with Reform leaders and in conversations with other Conservative Evangelicals, all were concerned to emphasize that they were not 'obsessed' with the issue; that they were not homophobic; and that they were not seeking to make the issue into a litmus test of orthodoxy or unity. Such claims seem to be reasonable when one considers that there are far fewer publications from Reform on sex and gender when compared to the volume that address money and power. Whilst the nomination of Jeffrey John and Gene Robinson as bishops of Reading and New Hampshire respectively has pushed the 'gay issue' to the fore, Reform seems to have put relatively few resources into addressing homosexuality. The reason for this, I suspect, is that Reform needs relatively few 'formal' religious statements on the matter, given that coherent opposition is widespread within the culture of 'operant' Evangelicalism. For example, R.T. France's recent *A Slippery Slope?* (2000), a rather slight publication in many ways, seems to be characterized more by reassertion than by argument.

In some of my interviews with Conservative Evangelicals and Reform members, I pressed the question of what it would take to establish a conversation on the 'gay issue'. With more or less uniformity, interviewees could not foresee a conversation with 'practising' gay Christians taking place at all, since they regarded homosexuality itself as sinful. Dialogue with bodies such as the Lesbian and Gay Christian Movement (LGCM) was also seen as fairly pointless as, in the words of one commentator, 'both sides seem to regard the other as intransigent, shrill fundamentalists'. But for Reform members, the foundation for any dialogue on the issue would have to respect the authority of scripture on such matters. Correspondingly, the kind of agenda laid out by Jakobsen and Pellegrini (2003) in their recent book on sexual regulation, and arguing for freedom and tolerance, is the very antithesis of a Reform-type position which would assert that such freedom and tolerance amounts to a rebellion against, and a rejection of, God's sovereignty (cf. Jensen, 2002, pp. 266ff; Higton, 1987).

But the issue of sexuality is not quite as closed as it might first seem. In one interview with a Reform member, I mused on the fact that what the dialogue needed was another Michael Vasey – an 'out' gay priest who would not let go of his mainstream Evangelical identity, but who published one of the few good hermeneutical books on the issue in recent years, *Strangers and Friends* (1997). During one interview, a Reform leader spoke regretfully about the Revd Roy Clements, a Baptist minister who had been a close mentor to, and supporter of, both Reform and the Proclamation Trust and had been a senior figure in the Evangelical Alliance. But Roy left his pastorate in Cambridge when, after 20 years of marriage, he became 'reconciled' to his homosexual nature and went to live with a male partner. He now works independently as a minister and has some involvement with LGCM. The Reform leader said that he still could 'not understand this', and that their parting was a cause of deep grief to him, but he could no longer see how they could dialogue anymore. This was a genuine 'tragic' story, and narrated by the Reform member in classically tragic terms: a stalwart of the Gospel who had lost his way. Or put in more Bunyanesque terms, the Vasey–Clements stories are akin to *Pilgrim's Regress*.

Finally in this section, we turn to power. As an issue, it is closely related to money. As we have already suggested, it is a mistake to conceive of Reform as schismatic or 'congregationalist'. Members and leaders are not against parish ministry and pro-eclectic. Neither are they necessarily intent on working against the dioceses in which they minister. They are, rather, radically attempting to reposition the local church as the primary locus of mission and evangelism within a community. In Reform's understanding of the church, the local is the catholic. Correspondingly, excessive centralization is seen as a threat to ministry, by being a drain on resources. Reform, contrary to what its critics say, does not want to withhold money. Instead, it wants to exercise some degree of choice in how it is spent and, in particular, to see that it is spent effectively. In that regard, Reform's position on money and power can be interpreted, in Hopewellian terms, as 'mechanistic' with its focus on effectiveness, evangelism and results (Hopewell, 1987, pp. 22–24). That said, there is also a sense in which the argument for the local church to define itself and self-govern has a long tradition within mission history. Evangelical missionaries such as Henry Venn, Henry Wright and James Johnson were at the forefront of Victorian missiology, arguing for the independent 'native church' as a controlling objective (cf. P. Williams, 1990). So it really cannot be very surprising that such ideas, once nourished, have now spread from their colonial seedbeds and returned to their churches of origin. Moreover, Anglicanism itself can be properly said to have promoted a 'self-governing, self-supporting and self-extending' ecclesiology (Sachs, 1993, pp. 241–44).

But the focus on power also has another side to it: the efficacy and righteousness of its bearers. Reform's call for 'godly leadership' is a cipher and a trope. It is an attack on liberal Catholics in positions of authority, who betray the heritage of the church and abuse its resources: 'we believe this liberal-Catholic drift is destroying the church' (Holloway, 1993, p. 3). In this light, the unprecedented campaign against Jeffrey John should be understood as a focused attempt to draw attention to what Reform perceives as being a wider malaise, in which the appointment of Rowan Williams is also implicated. In talking to Reform members, they are unhappy with the appointment of the archbishop generally, and not simply because of his views on sexuality. It should also be said that some Reform members were not entirely happy with George Carey's tenure as archbishop either, as they felt that he made too many accommodations to Charismatic Renewal and to 'unsound' initiatives such as Alpha courses. Put more sharply, anything that takes away from the primacy of propositional faith – the revelation of God, expressed clearly and unambiguously through scripture, and most especially the Gospels – is seen to be, at best, a form of heterodoxy (cf. Jensen, 2002, pp. 257–69) and therefore dangerous.

Reading Reform Differently

One of the advantages of studying a movement like Reform is that it is relatively easy to position within the wider Evangelical culture and, by so doing, one can gain a preliminary understanding of its controlling fundaments; the basic ethos can also be quickly grasped. However, the deeper socio-theological task will always depend on disciplines such as ethnography, and in more nuanced reflections based on the primary material that is gathered. That said, the aim of this section is to locate Reform within Evangelicalism, and then to situate it within the broader penumbra of Anglicanism.

Graham Kings' recent study of contemporary Anglican Evangelicalism maps the shape of the movement by using the metaphor of watercourses (Kings, 2003, pp. 167–84). He equates Conservative Evangelicalism with canals; moderate or open Evangelicalism is identified with broad rivers; Charismatic Evangelicalism is said to resemble rapids or waterfalls. This slightly innocent and playful set of analogies is more penetrating than it first appears. It allows Kings to sketch the strengths and weaknesses of each and, in so doing, reflect something of their truer nature:

> ...canals also have very positive aspects to them...they are the only watercourse where there can be movement uphill; they are steady and calm.... (Kings, 2003, p. 169)

Of course, canals cut through all manner of materials to maintain their course; they do not negotiate or compromise with what stands in their way, as rivers might. Another advantage of Kings' analogy is that the watercourse suggests fluidity and movement. In the case of Charismatic Evangelicals, it may be fast and frothy, and this can be usefully contrasted within the constrained, controlled and majestic movement of canals. But whether canal, river or waterfall, the clear implication of the analogy is that each movement is bound to history and therefore also to development. Kings, in summing up his analogical 'map', reminds his (Evangelical) audience that there is a commonality about Evangelicalism, just like the water of the watercourses: 'Evangelical is not a party word' (ibid., p.184).

Viewed from a slightly different perspective, David Tracy (1975) identifies five basic models of contemporary theology for engaging with modernity. They are: orthodox, liberal, neo-orthodox, radical and revisionist. Space does not permit a discussion of each of these in their own right, but Tracy's concern is to identify how the models attempt to negotiate with the complexity of the modern world. The closest 'model' to Conservative Evangelicalism that Tracy identifies is orthodox:

> In an orthodox theological model, the claims of modernity are not understood to have any inner-theological relevance.... Orthodox theologians do not seem impressed with the counter-claims of modern scientific, historical, or philosophical scholarship.... (Tracy, 1975, p. 24)

Certainly there are traces of the Conservative Evangelical approach in Tracy's other models (especially the neo-orthodox), but the orthodox is a particularly good fit for the same reasons that Kings equates the movement with canals. Tracy sees strengths in the sophisticated and single-minded approach; he understands that canals are complex to construct. But, like Kings, Tracy also sees weaknesses in the orthodox model:

> ...[the] major weakness...lies in [the] inability to make intrinsic (i.e., inner-theological) uses of other scholarly disciplines...[and the] theological inability to come to terms with the cognitive, ethical, and existential counter-claims of modernity. The weakness is directly dependent upon the presence of a relatively narrow self-referent (the explicit believer) and of an object-referent of parallel narrowness (an understanding of the beliefs and values of his own church tradition).... (Tracy, 1975, p. 25)

The outcome of this model is, in Tracy's words, a clear and 'blessed rage for order'. Writing over a decade before Hopewell, Tracy identifies the link between anger (a fury at the chaos and confusion modernity and contemporary culture allegedly wreaks upon the church and theology) and the desire to develop stability and regulation to combat this. Of course, the genius of Tracy's contribution to mapping the shape of modern theology is to see that *each* of the models is responsive and is also an attempt to reorder the tasks of theology and the nature of the church in the face of sustained challenge. The rage for order, then, is a particular feature of more conservative models of theology that tend to resist rather than make peace with, or embrace, the forces of secularity, modernity and cultural change.

At this point in our discussion, confirmation of this emergent thesis comes from a surprising source. William Pickering's study of Anglo-Catholicism (1989) suggests that the heirs of the Tractarian movement were able to form a distinctive ecclesial culture that was able to cope with ambiguity and differences by appealing to aesthetics and the sublime. But perhaps more than this, there was some real sense in which Anglo-Catholicism actually revelled in ambiguity (for example, its stance on sexuality, its position on Rome, and so on), precisely because the unity of the movement was primarily sacramental. Through metaphor, liturgical practice, cultural bonds and appeals to the sublime, a degree of diversity came to be expected, which went hand-in-hand with hospitality towards ambiguity (Pickering, 1989, pp. 184ff).

Pickering's perceptive historical and sociological analysis identifies ambiguity as a key issue for Anglo-Catholicism:

> ...all religions contain ambiguities. Such ambiguities arise initially out of the very nature of religion itself in trying to bridge two orders of reality – that of this world and the world beyond, a transcendental world. All religions have had to come face to face with such ambiguities or ambiguities dependent on their premises. They have either to accept them fairly and squarely and perhaps say they are irresolvable, or else to attempt to deal with them in such a way as to satisfy [man's] intellect but never completely gratify it. If ambiguity is resolved, religion disappears.... (Pickering, 1989, p. 141)

The key feature of Anglo-Catholicism is that it does not resolve its inherent ambiguities at all; it defers resolution constantly and refers all deep questioning and contested issues to art, aesthetics, the sublime, mystery and the continually open texture of the sacraments. Arguably, this is why the Church of England's decision to ordain women to the priesthood presented such a deep crisis to Anglo-Catholics. A resolution had finally been reached; it was now impossible for some to rejoice in the characteristic 'unsolvedness' of Anglo-Catholic ecclesiology and identity, which had hitherto been its genius. The simple 'fact' of women priests could no longer be ignored. The sacramental understanding of the church is, generally, an adequate way of keeping a broad range of views together, since plurality of belief is always deemed to be 'under' a higher mystery. But when faced with deep divisions and hotly contested views, a sacramental understanding of the church often tends to lack the ability to create conditions under which conflicts can be successfully negotiated.

The discussion of Pickering's thesis is important here, for it helps us to understand why Reform opposes 'liberal Catholics'. As we can now see, the problem is not simply with liberalism; it also lies with the relative comfort that Anglo-Catholics have with ambiguity. Rather than valuing ambiguity, Conservative Evangelicals resist it vigorously and wish to express their Christianity through emphasizing virtues and practices associated with clarity. In contrast with the Anglo-Catholic absorption with the sensate, ethereal and mysterious, Conservative Evangelicals wish to base their faith on a kind of scriptural rationalism. Thus, the Anglo-Catholic attachment to sacramentality, the sublime and mystery is seen by Conservative Evangelicals as heterodox: it elevates the relational and aesthetic above the propositional. It runs the risk of placing experience above revelation; of the church above the Gospel.

Correspondingly, to Conservative Evangelicals, liberal Catholics are an even more despised breed than Anglo-Catholics. Conservative Evangelicals feel that at least they could join hands with Anglo-Catholics on a 'traditionalist' platform, provided that the construction and constitution of that tradition is not scrutinized too closely. But liberal Catholics tend to be regarded as being beyond the pale, for they are deemed to have abandoned such traditionalism and embraced the many and varied forms of modernism and liberalism. To a Conservative Evangelical, that looks like nothing more than performative (but watered down) liturgy, coupled to a post-Enlightenment and modernist theology. Of course, I am aware that these remarks are, to some extent, a characterization. But they serve a purpose, namely to reveal some of the deeper, nascent reasons why the proposed appointment of Jeffrey John evoked such reaction amongst Reform members. It wasn't simply his sexuality that some found problematic; it was everything he stood for.[5]

This last remark leads us, finally in this section, to return to the question of authority. In many ways, an understanding of the sources and purposes of authority has been shown to be the key to understanding Reform. As I have noted earlier, the movement is not primarily preoccupied with money, sex and power. These issues are simply symptomatic and indicate the deeper and most contested issue: the authority of the Bible. Paula Nesbitt, in her reflections on the 1998 Lambeth Conference, shows how the Anglican communion has been unable to avoid being gradually split: caught between increasing cultural diversity, on the one hand, and the need to provide coherence and identity, on the other. She notes how successive Lambeth Conferences have moved sequentially from being grounded on traditional authority (that is, the establishment of churches and provinces during the colonial era), to rational authority (which presupposes negotiation through representative constituencies for dominance over meeting outcomes) to negotiated authority (which, however, normally lacks the power to stem the momentum of change). She notes that these kinds of authority, when pursued through the four 'instruments' of unity[6] in the Anglican Communion, are usually capable of resolving deep disputes. However, although they enable complex interaction

---

[5] Of course Canon Dr Jeffrey John was one of the key founders of Affirming Catholicism, a movement begun ten years ago to accommodate those Anglo-Catholics who supported the ordination of women and a more progressive faith. Rowan Williams was also one of the architects of the movement, and Reform's opposition to both should be understood as hostility towards the agenda of progressive liberal Catholic thinking.

[6] The four instruments of unity are the archbishop of Canterbury, the Lambeth Conference, the Anglican Consultative Council and the Meetings of the Primates. In turn, these 'instruments' generally consider how issues fall within the 'Anglican Quadrilateral': Scripture, Tradition, Reason and Culture.

and conversation, they do not lead to clear and firm resolutions. Correspondingly, Nesbitt argues that, within the Anglican Communion, a new, fourth authoritative form has emerged, which has in some senses been present from the very beginning and is now tied up with the identity of scripture. She writes of this authority:

> [It] could be used to countervail the relativism of cross-cultural alliances without affecting their strategic utility: symbolic authority. The symbol, as a locus of authority, has a tangible and timeless nature. Where the symbol is an authoritative part of the institutional milieu, either traditional or rational authority must acknowledge its legitimacy . . . scripture is an authoritative symbol . . . . (Nesbitt, 2001, p. 257)

Nesbitt points out, as I noted earlier, that the symbolic authority of sacraments may create shared bonds and enhance communal cohesion, but are normally unable to regulate or negotiate conflict. However, in contrast:

> Scripture, when canonized as complete or absolute, becomes symbolic of a particular era or set of teachings and beliefs. However, unlike sacraments, the use of scripture as symbolic authority can be constructed and constituted according to selecting those aspects or passages that address an issue at hand. Furthermore, scripture as symbolic authority can be objectified or absolutized, which transcends cultural boundaries in a way that other forms of authority can less easily do. The appeal of scriptural literalism provides an objectification of authority that is independent of the influence or control of dominant perspectives, social locations, and circumstances. As symbolic authority, it can be leveraged against cultural dominance as well as provide common ground for cross-cultural alliances . . . . (Ibid.)

In other words, with scripture raised almost to the level of apotheosis, a cross-cultural foundation for authority exists that can challenge the dominance of rational authority, which is normally associated with highly educated elite groups from the West or First World. Scripture, given symbolic authority, becomes an important tool in the hands of Southern (non-elite) Christians who are seeking to counter-legitimate more conservative perspectives. Of course, this strategy not only plays directly into the hands of groups like Reform: it can in fact be resourced by them. As Nesbitt notes, 'scriptural literalism as symbolic authority represents the easiest and most accessible form of counter-legitimation across educational or cross-cultural divides' (ibid., p. 258). And as Lambeth Conferences, like the Anglican communion itself, have become increasingly diverse in their cultural expression, symbolic authority has risen to the fore. This means that, at present, the only contender for being a focus of symbolic authority is the Bible, since cross-cultural negotiation only leads to sterile relativism – and as long as this situation continues, the dominance of Reform within the Church of England looks set to continue. We should note that the only other alternative to the Bible as symbolic authority – the Communion itself – has so far failed to attain this status, mainly because the very enabling of that possibility would require a looser, more elastic view of truth-claims and a necessary tolerance towards competing convictions.

Typically, those who press for the Anglican Communion as a natural focus for symbolic authority tend to be liberal Catholic, and, as we have already noted, the lack of clarity that this tradition embodies is largely unacceptable to Conservative Evangelicals.

Conclusion

In a Communion that is now in a state of considerable flux, caution should be exercised in drawing firm conclusions from such a short study as this. What I have attempted to show here is that the rise of Reform in the Church of England belongs to a wider set of cultural, ecclesiological and theological trends in global Anglicanism from which Reform currently benefits. These trends include a move towards emphasizing the power and autonomy of the local church and a renewed interest in scriptural literalism as a focus for symbolic authority (cf. Ndungane in Douglas and Pui-Lan, 2001, pp. 233–46). There is also a sense, in a primarily English context, in which we are witnessing the resurgence of the cultural differences between Roundheads and Cavaliers – between the architects of a Puritan regime and a later Caroline settlement. Furthermore, the inherent 'tragic world-view' of Conservative Evangelicals seems to provide individuals and churches with a certain kind of steely resolve which makes accommodation unlikely, if not an anathema.

Having sketched the origins of Reform and attempted to suggest some of the reasons why its rise within the Church of England has been so influential, we are now in a position to hazard some guesses about the future of the movement within the church and the wider Communion. Such suggestions are, of course, contingent, but four preliminary points can be made by way of conclusion.

First, and following Nesbitt (2001), we can say that in a post-denominational age (arguably a natural development arising from postmodernity and postcolonialism), the churches that can survive as denominations will be those with a shared affinity of feeling and a shared moral consensus. This closely matches Harvey Cox's (1994) postulation that denominational labels will matter less and less in the twenty-first century and that the battle lines between liberalism and traditionalism will be redrawn. Those churches that celebrate the sensate, embodied and experiential will increasingly network together, just as those that emphasize the propositional and credal will attempt to work together. (For an alternative and theologically richer vision for the Communion, see Sagovsky, 2000.)

Second, we should note that Anglicanism, ever since the first Lambeth Conference (which was called to head off schism and therefore arguably marks the beginning of the end for the coherent 'globalization' of the Church of England), has struggled to maintain its unity amidst diversity. Indeed, Seabury's consecration as a bishop for North America by the Scottish episcopal bishops in 1784, goes hand-in-hand with the first significant blow to British imperial interests, the American War of Independence, and ably demonstrates that the Church of England could not restrain its own spread from Canterbury. It could not challenge the idea that Anglicanism was 'self-supporting, self-governing and self-extending' (Sachs, 1993, pp. 241–44). Subsidiarity and individuation in each newly established province was then virtually inevitable. In one sense, the Anglican Communion is continually destined to play 'catch up' with an expansion and diversity that it consistently sows but cannot control (see Sachs, 1993; Douglas and Pui-Lan, 2001; Rowell, 1992).

Third, and again following Nesbitt, we note that, in the first phase of denominationalism, institutional relations can be governed through obedience, and, if necessary, punishment. However, in the second phase, interpersonal contracts emerge between congregations, regions and individuals. Here 'ecclesial citizenship' is born, and law and order develop into an agreed, rather than imposed, rule. In the third phase (postmodernity), more complex social contracts emerge between parties, which require a deeper articulation of a shared ethos and an agreement about the nature of a shared moral community. Correspondingly, any arguments about women or, more especially, 'gay issues' are far more likely to cause schism than unity in liturgy or order, since some will see this as a betrayal of the ethos. We should therefore expect arguments on key issues to increase in volume and severity. Indeed, so far, they have only been contained by an assertion of rational, traditional or negotiated authority. However, with the focus of authority posited in the Communion quickly giving way to the symbolic authority of the Bible, we should expect denominational fortunes to closely match hermeneutical coherence or fragmentation (cf. Ndungane in Douglas and Pui-Lan, 2001, pp. 233–46).

Fourth, Reform's championing of the primacy of the local congregation can be read as pro-reticulate, but as anti-denominational. It is, arguably, a postmodern movement with a premodern agenda. Reform, as an organization, seeks to renarrate denominations as shared moral communities with an explicitly harmonized ethos. This is in sharp contrast to the normative narration of Anglicanism as a civilized community of disagreement (cf. Rowell, 1992; Percy, 2000), a matrix of competing convictions and a church where its identity is ambiguous and unresolved. Here, Reform's major contribution to the future of Anglicanism is to offer clarity against ambiguity: decision instead of 'fudge', and precision and transparency in place of uncertainty and haziness. Ultimately, then, Reform represents a blessed rage for (Godly, biblical) order. It is not anger for anger's sake. It is a righteous anger, the very mirror of the fear-inspiring God that features so strongly in their core doctrine, namely that of penal substitution. The anger is directed and purposeful: it is for a new order in the Church of England, and more broadly for the nation.

Finally, the overall achievement of Reform in its first decade should not be underestimated. The movement, in concert with other initiatives and developments in the Anglican communion, has established Conservative Evangelicalism as a major force within the church. The efforts of Sydney diocese, as well as the contribution of conservative and southern bishops, have posed a serious challenge to the historic and hegemonic governance of liberal-catholic theology and its Western bishops. Moreover, it has helped to fundamentally alter the sense of balance within the Anglican churches, by making the symbolic authority of the Bible both higher and mightier than that of the Communion itself. Reform has, like its sixteenth century precursors who pioneered the original Reformations across Europe, done no more than light the proverbial match. It still remains to be seen whether the new fire will catch and hold, but, for supporters of Reform, the signs look promising. The church looks set to be caught ablaze in new fires of passion and purgation. Such flames will test the Church of England and the Anglican Communion to its natural limits.

Chapter 9

Comic Turns

Introduction

A candidate for one of the most teasing opening lines in modern English literature must be from Rose Macaulay's *The Towers of Trezibond*:

> 'Take my camel, dear', said my Aunt Dot, as she climbed down from this animal on her return from High Mass.... (Macaulay, 1956, p. 3)

The Towers of Trezibond is an absurd, comic and beautiful tale, which offers the inimitable Aunt Dot, her niece Laurie and Father Chantry-Pigg, and their expedition to Turkey to explore the scope for converting the Turks – not just to any old Christianity, but to Anglicanism. By establishing a High Anglican mission, the trio hope to bring salvation and civilization to the country. Aunt Dot is particularly keen on the emancipation of Turkish women – through a wider use of the bathing hat.

Despite Macaulay's comic novel, there is, ironically, a well-established Anglican presence in Turkey. But the scope of this chapter is not to take issue with parodies of Anglicanism. It is, rather, to use the work of James Hopewell once more to examine the comic and ironic identity of mainstream Anglicanism, and thereby identify those hidden aspects of its appeal that have turned a single English denomination into a worldwide presence. Globally, there are around 77 million Anglicans. They are spread over 36 self-governing churches, comprising 500 dioceses, 30 000 parishes with around 65 000 congregations, located in a total of 165 countries. Whilst not ranking amongst the largest groupings of Christians, the Anglican Church is, after the Roman Catholic Church, arguably one of the most widespread and influential denominations in the world. (Anglicanism is by no means confined to the Commonwealth, which has 53 countries – less than a third of the total in which Anglicanism is to be found.)

The study of Anglicanism (or Anglican Studies, which would be slightly different) can be undertaken in several ways. As a faith that is both widespread and concentrated, it can be scrutinized from a variety of different intellectual disciplines. Naturally, its theology can be assessed theologically. Anglicanism has a rich, distinctive and historic theological tradition, being rooted in both Catholicism and Protestantism. These theological roots condition Anglican liturgy, ecclesiology and missiology. At the same time, Anglican identity is a contested concept, and, although it has distinct instruments of unity (for example, the archbishop of Canterbury, the Anglican Consultative Council, the Lambeth Conference, and the Meetings of the Primates), its authority is broadly dispersed (see Sykes, 1995; Avis, 2000; Sykes and Booty, 1988; Sachs, 1993). More recently Caddick and McDonald (2002) have suggested that Anglicanism is the answer to modernity. Pemberton and others (1998) have also written lucid trenchant defences of the Anglican Communion. Equally, its corporate life can be opened up to the full range of disciplines within the penumbra of social sciences. Culturally and theologically, Anglicanism tends to be a mediating and accommodating ecclesiology, rather than imposing and authoritative. Globally, each province has its own distinct history, flavour, sense of purpose and mission, yet still within the broad framework of a worldwide 'family' or Communion of churches (see Thomas, 1987). As we noted in the previous chapter, each branch or province of the Anglican family is 'self-supporting, self-extending and self-governing' (Sachs, 1993).

Yet the 'Anglican Communion' also evokes what Benedict Anderson describes as an 'imagined community' (1983, pp. 15–16). Most of its members have never met one another, and never will. Yet members will readily acknowledge a deep, horizontal comradeship of belonging. The Communion is bound together by an ethos, codes, memories and aspirations that allow it to cohere in the minds of its members, but without that coherence necessarily being practised at either a deep or extensive level. In this regard, we can regard the Anglican Communion as a kind of filial network of understanding, again like a family (see Thomas, 1987, pp. 18–143), in which certain types of belief and certain modes of behaviour are cherished. As Pascal Boyer notes:

> One thing modern humans did and still do vastly more than any other species is exchange information of all kinds and qualities, not just about what is the case but also what should be or could be; not just about their emotions and knowledge but also about their plans, memories and conjectures. The proper milieu in which humans live is that of information, especially information provided by other[s]. It is their ecological niche. (Boyer, 2002, p. 374)

There can be no question that Anglicanism and its ecological niche contains elements of coherence and a notion of a shared life and identity, bound together through a common sense of purpose, history and teleology. But what exactly are those 'things' that are particular to Anglican identity? Authors such as Sykes, Avis, Booty and Wright would be able to nominate particular theological priorities. From a sociological perspective, we can point to Pickering's work that identifies ambiguity and aesthetics as being culturally significant (Pickering, 1989), or to my own suggestion that Anglicanism is a 'sacralised system of manners' as being somehow vital to its understanding (Percy, 2000, pp. 114–25). Analogically, Boyer suggests that:

> If we consider the whole domain of information [within an organization] over time we have a gigantic 'soup' of representations and messages. The messages are constantly changing because the contexts change…. However, we also find that there are lumps in this soup of messages, that is, bits of information that seem to appear in rather similar form at different times and in different places. They are not strictly identical but we find a small number of templates that seem to organise them. Religious concepts and behaviours are like that…. (Boyer, 2002, p. 374)

In this chapter I want to suggest that the 'soup' of the Anglican Communion contains such lumps. As with the previous chapters that work with James Hopewell's interpretative methodology, I am less interested in the obvious theological priorities of the Communion, and more concerned here with the nascent cultural distinctives that shape and flavour it. In exploring and analysing these, I will seek to demonstrate that much of Anglicanism is an inherently ironic and comic type of faith which, when understood culturally, can in turn illuminate some of the current theological debates that preoccupy the church. Again, as Boyer notes:

> Religion is cultural. People get it from other people, as they get food preferences, musical tastes, politeness and dress sense. We often tend to think that if something is cultural then it is hugely variable. But it then turns out that food preferences and other such cultural things are not so variable after all. Food preferences revolve around certain recurrent flavours, musical tastes within strict constraints, and so do politeness codes and standards of elegance.... (Boyer, 2002, p. 54)

The next section will therefore look at Hopewell's 'cultural reading' of the church in order to identify and explicate these 'lumps', 'tastes' and 'preferences'. From that vantage-point, it will then be possible to explore the Anglican Communion as a cultural system (albeit strained and multi-flavoured), before moving into a brief excursion on Continuing Anglican Churches, which I hold to represent a form of non-ironic alternative comedy. A final section returns to the idea of Anglican culture, and evaluates its coherence.

Anglicanism as Irony and Comedy

Hopewell is well aware that it is only recently that 'participant observation' has gained any credibility in academic studies of culture and that this has been driven by anthropologists and ethnographers, who have urged scholars to immerse themselves in the very field of their inquiry. However, participant observers who have studied congregations in any depth are still comparatively rare. Most studies tend to be, in Hopewell's words, 'travelogues', giving accounts of churches and congregations that are based on anecdotes and texts. In contrast, Hopewell, who in turn acknowledges his debt to the work of Melvin Williams and Samuel Heilman (Hopewell, 1987, p. 89), argue for the studies of congregations to be undertaken through the 'observing participant' – congregations themselves learning to function 'as if' they were themselves outsiders. It is through such strategies that congregations and scholars can become attuned to the myriad manners and codes that participants often take for granted. Thus, Hopewell suggests that 'sounding the depths' of a congregation must be a deeper task that pays attention to such things as:

> jokes, stories, lore... parish conversations that follow administrative meetings... sermons, classroom presentation... use of space... line of authority... use of time... conscious and unconscious symbols... conflict.... (Hopewell, 1987, p. 89)

But how could paying attention to such trivia and ephemera reveal something about the fundamental nature and identity of a church or something as complex as the Anglican Communion? To illustrate this simply, consider the following three jokes about Anglicanism:

1 **Question**: How many Anglicans does it take to change a lightbulb?
   Answer: Five – one to put in the new one and four to admire the old one.

2 One day, the archbishop of Canterbury is sitting alone on the beach, trying to enjoy a holiday and a retreat. It has been another hard year. He gazes out towards the horizon where the sun is still rising and sighs. Presently, his eye catches something gleaming in the sand. He brushes away the grains and pulls out a brass canister. Seeing an inscription, he spits on it and polishes it, but before he can read it, the canister explodes in a haze of blue smoke. The archbishop rubs his eyes and is surprised to find, standing before him, a large genie. 'Your Grace', says the genie, 'I will grant you one wish – whatever you want: just name it.'
   The archbishop reaches inside his cassock pocket, and pulls out a map of the Middle East. With a crayon, he draws a large red circle around the whole area. 'I'd like you to bring peace to this region', he says.
   The genie does not reply. He sits on the sand and looks at the rising sun. He says nothing for ten minutes. Then, turning again to the archbishop, he says: 'I have never said this to anyone before, but what you ask is beyond me. It is too difficult. But if you have another wish, I will grant that.'
   The archbishop pauses, and then reaches inside for another map. This is a map of the world, with 165 countries coloured in. 'This is the Anglican Communion', he explains, 'and all I ask is that you help all the many different parts to get on a little better.'
   The genie sits back down on the sand again and looks towards the sun. Again, for ten minutes, he says nothing. Then he stands up, and turns to the archbishop. 'Your Grace', he says, 'do you think I could have another look at that first map?'

3 One day, the queues of people to get into heaven are so long and thick that the angels guarding the Pearly Gates begin to panic. They fly off to see Jesus and ask for advice. Jesus suggests that potential entrants are graded. He will ask a question of everyone seeking entry and, depending on how they answer, they will either be placed in the slow track or granted immediate entry. The question Jesus proposes to use is the same question he once put to the disciples: 'Who do you say that I am?'
   The first person Jesus encounters at the gates is a Methodist minister. Jesus asks her, 'Who do you say that I am?'
   The minister hesitates and then answers 'Well, at Conference last year . . . '.
   But Jesus interrupts her immediately. 'I am sorry', he says, 'but I asked you for your opinion, and not for your denominational line. Would you mind going to the back of the queue? Thank you.'
   The next person to step forward is a Roman Catholic monk. Jesus poses

the same question, to which the monk replies, 'Well, our pope says...'.

But Jesus again interrupts and points out that he wanted the monk's opinion, not the pope's.

Third, a Baptist minister approaches. His response to Jesus' question is emphatic: 'The Bible says...'.

But Jesus again interrupts and reminds the minister that he wanted his opinion, not his knowledge. Finally, an Anglican priest approaches. Jesus regards the minister somewhat quizzically, but puts the question to him nonetheless. The Anglican replies categorically: 'You are the Christ – the Son of the living God.'

Jesus is slightly taken aback by such an ardent response from an Episcopalian, and is about to let the Anglican priest in, when he adds, 'but then again, on the other hand...'.

These jokes reveal several things about the nature of Anglicanism. First, they are jokes told by Anglicans, suggesting that they possess a capacity for gentle self-mocking comic irony. Second, the lightbulb joke makes a serious point: admiration of the past is an important feature of Anglican life – but it can get of out hand. Third, the joke about the archbishop and the genie recognizes the acute difficulties in maintaining Anglican polity. Fourth, the joke about the Anglican priest at the Pearly Gates celebrates the inherent ambivalence of Anglicanism – the way in which it glories in seeing situations from different points of view and holds a variety of viewpoints together, even though such convictions may compete with another and cause a degree of tension. Fifth, the jokes reveal a real fondness for the way Anglicanism is, including its flaws. Indeed, the flaws are being intrinsically linked to its virtues, which the jokes highlight, albeit ironically.

The careful noting of this apparently incidental material is important for any ethnography of a church, let alone an entire Communion. Paul Willis, in his *The Ethnographic Imagination* (2000) suggests that many conventional types of ethnography overlook the sensate and felt aspects of bodies, societies or situations under scrutiny. He argues that careful attention paid to artefacts, poetry, sayings, humour and sensations can provide important registers of the mood and shape of a given subject. Therefore trying to capture the visual, sensate and experienced aspects of a community can provide important indicators that conventional fieldwork might normally miss. In this respect, Willis is doing no more than building on Raymond Williams' (1976, 1986) earlier work on cultures, arguing that they are often constituted through 'structures of feeling'. Indeed, we might go further here and suggest that the Anglican Communion itself is a 'structure of feeling'; its senses its kinship, ties and shape, but hardly ever sees these fully reified.

Thus, and to return to the Anglican jokes, the mere fact that Anglicans appear to be able to tolerate (or even celebrate?) a certain amount of gentle self-mocking comic irony reveals something about the nature of the movement itself. In the previous chapter we looked in some detail at the problem of moral coherence within a post-denominational framework. Nevertheless, it still appears to be meaningful to speak of Anglicanism as a 'community of moral discourse', despite the stresses and strains associated with particular issues (Hopewell, 1987, p. 144). But what exactly is a community of moral discourse? Hopewell suggests that it is a gathering of people that are explicitly intent on surveying and critically assessing their personal, social and moral convictions *together*, because there is already some prior nascent consensus about the loyalty that binds them together as a group. Such ties need not be explicit. Indeed, we might say that any attempt to make them so can be problematic. Part of the genius of Anglicanism arguably lies in its fundamental 'unsolvedness'. Its major problems of moral coherence only emerge when it attempts to *clarify* itself, instead of allowing competing convictions to continue to gestate within a broadly sacramental understanding of the church.

To press the discussion a little further, it is noteworthy that anthropologists such as Geertz distinguish between the ethos of a community and its world-view. The world-view is the 'ideal' shape of the world (to come?) that guides the life of community. In contrast, the ethos refers to those values and codes that the group currently maintains. The two are, of course, related and, as Hopewell points out, the bonds that link ethos and world-view are not only creeds and formal religious statements, but also whole value systems and narrative streams that may seldom be understood or explicitly revealed. In my own participant observation of Anglicanism (indeed, as an observing participant, since I am an ordained Anglican priest), I have been continually struck by the capacity of the wider Communion for what I have already described as gentle self-mocking comic irony. Could it be, in Hopewell's and Geertz's terminology, that this characteristic actually links the ethos and world-view in Anglicanism? In other words, is the cultural ecclesiology of Anglicanism mild, temperate, given to measured humour, but also anticipative of the ultimacy of a sacramental resolution to all serious forms of dispute and the threat of schism or incoherence? In order to investigate this further, it is necessary to explain Hopewell's understanding of comedy and irony in ecclesiological narrative streams and then test this 'reading' of Anglicanism against current debates.

Anglicanism: Comic and Ironic

In David Hare's *Racing Demon* (1990), an ironic and comic play about Anglican clergy in London during the 1980s, a central feature of the plot is the division between those who think 'things will work out alright', and those for whom the church has reached breaking point. The latter position is represented by a fictitious bishop of London, who consistently narrates a 'tragic' understanding of the church and the world – a more 'catholic' version of the type discussed in the previous chapter. In Hare's play the divisions between the characters are, on the surface, theological. But Hare is able to exploit the deeper partitions that separate the characters, and these are more typically concerned with world-views and expectations. Although the play ends, to a degree, in a mire of tragedy, its overall character is ironic-comic. According to Hopewell, true comedies begin with a world in which there is misunderstanding, crisis and calamity, but end:

...in unions, pacts, embraces and marriages – that symbolize the ultimately trustworthy working of the world. Created in misinformation and convoluted by error, a comedy is resolved by the disclosure of a deeper knowledge about the harmonious way things really are.... (Hopewell, 1987, p. 58)

Hopewell sees the comic genre as one that pivots on integration. Personally, a situation of ignorance is responded to with enlightenment, with the resolution being peace. Socially, discord is met with wisdom and leads to harmony. Cosmically, illusion is addressed by process and resolved through union. The key cognitive feature of the comic world-view is wisdom, and, because of this, the minister is most commonly a 'guide', the Eucharist a 'sacrament', the church a 'pilgrimage' and the Gospel 'consciousness' (Hopewell, 1987, pp. 70–71). As with our previous studies in Chapters 4 and 5, Hopewell's descriptions must, to some extent, be understood as characterizations. But they are a reasonable 'fit' for much of the 'inner life' of Anglicanism. For example, when Canon Jeffrey John was forced to withdraw from his nomination as bishop of Reading in the diocese of Oxford in the summer of 2003, his parting shot was to write to the local paper in Reading and state that 'love, in the end, will win'. This was his response to the chaos of potential schism and disharmony: to reassert that there was bound to be a truly 'comic' ending to a tragic farce.

For many people reading Hopewell, the denominational thinking that would most closely correspond to the comic genre (or 'gnostic negotiation', as Hopewell prefers to call it) is Quakerism. This is not an unreasonable assumption, based on Hopewell's own understanding of the world-view that he articulates. Quakerism, perhaps of all the mainstream Protestantism denominations, is the one most comfortable with universalism, interreligious dialogue and religious pluralism. Quakers have been at the forefront of placing greater emphasis on the spirituality of the individual rather than on corporate credal formulae; as a religious movement it tends to eschew articles of faith in favour of a deep commitment to 'comic' inclusiveness. However, the genre also closely resonates with the kind of idealized and slightly mystical sacramentalism that characterizes much of Anglicanism's own absorption with its (imagined) Communion. Put another way, doctrinal differences or moral incoherence will ultimately 'melt away', since the Communion is gathered around one table, sharing in one common baptism, and will be unable to resist exchanging the kiss of peace. Differences over gender, sexuality and other matters will be seen in their true light – as secondary issues that do not interfere with the primacy of the sacramental nature of the Communion.

In this regard, as Hopewell correctly points out, the comic genre is 'utterly dependable': bafflement and confusion are ultimately overcome by wisdom and love; harmony replaces discord. This is, of course, a positive and optimistic ecclesiology, which assumes a kind of 'inner energy' within the ethos that drives it, teleologically, towards its world-view. Ultimately, all in the end is harvest. Not even death can stand in the way of a mystical unity, for which, at worst, a broken Communion points us towards.

The positivism of the comic genre is, of course, only one half of the equation that shapes Anglicans' self-understanding of the Communion. The other half is more contingent and is habitually posited in irony:

> Miracles do not happen; patterns lose their design; life is unjust, not justified by transcendent forces. Trapped in an ironic world, one shrugs one's shoulders about reports of divine ultimacies and intimacies. Instead of expecting such supernatural outcomes, one embraces ones brothers and sisters in camaraderie.... (Hopewell, 1987, p. 61)

Hopewell, in developing the ironic genre, tends to put a more reductionist gloss on the world-view than many would normally be prepared to own. The genre is characteristically 'liberal' in its orientation, with a strong sympathy for organic and contextual ecclesiological models. But this does not, in my view, necessarily mean that those who inhabit the ironic world-view are likely to dismiss the realm of the supernatural, which Hopewell often assumes will be the case. That said, Hopewell's characterization of ironic ecclesiology contains many features that will resonate with Anglicans. The key motif is testing; variation leads (ultimately) to conformity. At a personal level, a situation of bondage is met with honesty and resolved through love. Socially, oppression is met by justice and resolved through the establishment of community. The focus of valued behaviour is realism and integrity. Theologically, Jesus is a 'teacher', the minister an 'enabler', the church a 'fellowship' and the Gospel 'freedom' (ibid., pp. 70–71).

In discussing this outlook, Hopewell recognizes that ironic ecclesiologies and world-views are in fact best characterized as 'cosmopolitan religion'. Living with differences is a sign of integrity. Thus, and following Wade Clark Roof, Hopewell notes that those who are most attracted to 'ironic' religion may want to avoid organized religion altogether, but tend nonetheless to be faithful church members who affirm:

> (a) the centrality of ethical principles in their meaning systems; (b) a parsimony of beliefs, few attributions of numinosity; (c) breadth of perspective; (d) piety defined as a personal search for meaning; and (e) licence to doubt. (Hopewell, 1987, p. 82)

Perhaps inevitably, this draws those with primarily ironic world-views towards a theological terrain that is packed with deep ambiguity and paradox. Within Anglicanism this tradition is perhaps best exemplified by writers such as David Jenkins, John Habgood and the early work of Richard Holloway. In working with congregations and groups where the ironic world-view dominates, one can observe how paradox is not only testing, but also persuasive and nourishing. Thus, phrases that can speak of the incarnation in angular ways (for example, Launcelot Andrewes' 'the Speechless Word', or Rowan Williams' more recent notion of the 'spastic Christ-child') will invariably absorb individuals and groups in hours of patient spiritual musings. In the ironic world-view, anomaly and paradox are givens.

Given these remarks, it is perhaps reasonable to suggest that the core proponents of the Anglican Communion are, in Hopewellian terms, comic-ironic in orientation. Or, to return to Boyer, these are just two of the 'lumps' in the soup that is Anglicanism. They anticipate a form of sacramental unity that will ultimately bear its own fruit. But they are sagacious enough to know that the path to unity is littered with pitfalls and potholes that require the mind of an empiricist rather than an idealist. Again, in Hopewellian terms, the 'model' of the church that emerges from this world-view is a combination of perspectives. On the one hand, it comprises *organicist* views: 'developing towards a final integrated reality which is unapparent in its present state' (ibid., p. 200). On the other, it is both *mechanist* and *formist*, recognizing that the church is a collectivity of structures that can be regulated and adjusted. Moreover, the church is *contextualist*, shaped by the very cultural forces that it seeks to shape. For Hopewell, the analogy of the church (or Communion in this case) as a house allows an analyst to see that

> ...as a house within the world, 'house' emphasizes its participation in the frame of all language. Human imagination as a whole provides the particular idiomatic and narrative construction of a congregation; its members communicate by a code derived from the totality of forms and stories by which societies cohere. In such a picture...church culture is not reduced to a series of propositions that a credal checklist adequately probes. Rather, the congregation takes part in the nuance of and narrative of full human discourse. It persists as a recognizable storied dwelling within the whole horizon of human interpretation. (Hopewell, 1987, p. 201)

The features of this 'household of faith' in relation to its problems of ordering and identity are indeed complex, and space only permits a few brief paragraphs by way of summary. So let us begin with some questions. Can Anglicanism survive the deep and divisive arguments that seem to have rocked it for more than a quarter of a century? Women priests, women bishops, liturgical reform and gay bishops have all threatened splits and schism. So what is it that holds the church together in the midst of such public disagreement? And assuming there are some virtues, instruments or habits that provide the necessary social and ecclesial glue (or lumps in soup), can such things be appealed to again in the midst of the current divisions centred on sexuality? In addition to the comments already made on irony and comedy, three further observations come to mind.

First, Anglicanism has a rich, distinctive and historic theological tradition, being rooted in both Catholicism and Protestantism. These theological roots condition its liturgy, ecclesiology and missiology. At the same time, Anglican identity is a contested concept. Classically, it is the quintessential *via media*. The genius of Anglicanism is that it has *not* resolved its identity. It is broad yet particular, synodical, yet episcopal, Protestant, but also Catholic. One might say that all the main crises in Anglican identity stem from one party or another trying to resolve its innate ambiguity.

Second, the complexity of Anglicanism is mirrored within its structures. For example it has at least four distinct instruments of unity: the archbishop of

Canterbury, the Anglican Consultative Council, the Lambeth Conference, and the regular Meetings of the Primates. But this means that authority within the Communion is broadly and peculiarly dispersed. Culturally and theologically, Anglicanism tends to be a mediating and accommodating, rather than an imposing and authoritative, ecclesiology. The archbishop of Canterbury wields no kind of putative papal power. Globally, each Anglican province has its own distinct history, flavour, sense of purpose and mission, yet still within the broad framework of a worldwide 'family' of churches.

Third, Anglicanism has tended to conduct its theological debates through a trilateral of scripture, tradition and reason – and one might add, through well-mannered and patient exchange. Indeed, the elevation of manners within Anglicanism is a significant feature of its polity. It has therefore managed, for the most part, to retain its poise within a trilateral framework which has created space for differences to emerge, but without losing sight of mutual recognition and fostering relatively peaceful coexistence. Over the past century, with the emergence of postcolonial and modern societies, the trilateral has increasingly been understood as a quadrilateral that has had to take account of context and culture. For example, the concession to 'culture' might allow some conservative Anglicans to make allowances for polygamous practices in African churches – or at least turn a blind eye. Similarly, many American Anglicans think that the concession to culture should be similarly extended theologically, and to thinking differently about gay and lesbian people.

Theoretically, this (soup) recipe ought to be good enough to guarantee continuity of identity and existence for Anglicanism. But somehow, at least at the moment, it seems strangely inadequate. Is it the case, to paraphrase Yeats, that 'things fall apart; the centre cannot hold . . . the ceremony of innocence is drowned. The best lack all conviction, [and] the worst are full of passionate intensity'? To be sure, there are many reasons why the Anglican Communion (or federation?) faces so many problems at present. But one of the main ones must surely be that Anglicanism has forgotten that it was, first and foremost, a complex and well-mannered community in which differences and ambiguities remained unresolved. Indeed, these were part of its very foundations.

Yet despite, and because of, this, Anglicanism flourished. It prospered as a church because it was possible to belong to a broad community of belief in which some liberty of conscience and practice was respected, but with enough morphological similarity to foster homogeneity. It was, in short, a community of civilized disagreement. And far from hampering itself as a body, its example invited the world to take note. It embodied plurality: you can belong to one another without always seeing eye-to-eye, and you can witness like this too, because God is bigger than 'my' church.

So, and from my own Anglican perspective, the arguments that currently disturb the soul of Anglican polity somehow need to become calmer. Only when the intense heat of the argument begins to cool can Anglicanism recover its poise and start talking and listening rather than shouting. At its best, Anglicanism is, arguably, like the English weather: an essentially temperate affair. It is often cloudy, but with some sunny intervals, and the occasional outburst of rain. It is seldom born well from a climate of extremes. Given these remarks, we now turn to the notion of the Anglican Communion as a 'house' or 'estate'.

Excursion: Continuing Anglican Churches as Alternative Comedy

In describing Anglican identity, I have argued elsewhere that the Anglican Communion can analogically be visualized as a vast mansion, replete with Evangelical and Catholic wings (Percy, 2000, pp. 114–25). It remains a large stately home, albeit one in which the vast rooms are now being sealed off and converted into self-contained flats. Everyone still has the same official address and shares the imposing exterior and frontage, but different internal relations within the 'storied dwelling' mean that the union is not as it once was. Not only does this analogy fit the current state of Anglicanism, but it also allows us to briefly consider the intriguing phenomenon of Continuing Anglican Churches, whose numbers have multiplied over the last 30 years. A Continuing Anglican Church is, strictly speaking, one that still continues to use the Anglican 'family name', practise various kinds of Anglican liturgy and claim Anglican identity, but has nevertheless formally removed itself from communion with Canterbury.

Mention of 'family names' raises an important issue about ecclesial identity: it remains the case that very few denominations choose their own names. 'Anglicanism' is a term that was popularized by James VI of Scotland and contains a degree of mocking irony. Similarly, 'Anabaptists' had their family name bestowed upon them by their detractors; equally, 'Methodist' can also be read as a dubious compliment. Yet these names have been adopted and redeemed by their respective denominational families. Even the curious double-barrelled (and oxymoronic?) 'Roman Catholic' is, in some sense, an externally imposed nomenclature. 'Catholic' should mean universal and comprehensive, but 'Roman' implies imperialist centralization and hegemonic domination. No less of an oxymoron is the triple nomenclature 'House Church Movement'. Again, participants in the movement have not chosen this name for themselves; it is 'given' by the wider Christian family. But the name somehow captures the ambiguity and potentiality of the movement.

Returning to pursuing the 'family' and 'household' analogy, the phenomenological problem can be outlined as follows. Continuing Anglican Churches are often very similar in style, operation, theology and 'culture' to those they have separated from, which might raise questions about their distinctiveness. Therefore, for Anglicans who remain in the mansion, understanding Continuing Anglican Churches and conducting a dialogue with them is unlikely to be part of any normal, neat, linear process of negotiation or reception. Granted, many of the issues that created the conditions for separatism have become secondary over time, which suggests that, in some cases, Anglicans may be dealing with formalized estrangement rather than trying to undo a messy divorce or, to continue the analogy, deal with groups that have moved out of the mansion but are still living on the family estate. Negotiating on understanding demands evidence-based research as there is no obvious meta-ecclesiological or 'high theological ground' that can settle issues of difference or determine relations. The very existence of Continuing Anglican Churches suggests some rather more 'fuzzy borders' for Anglican identity.

Continuing Anglican Churches that still use the Anglican 'family name' are usually doing so for 'operant' rather than 'formal' religious reasons. This means that some understanding of the reasons for cession – case-by-case – is needed if the field is to be approached with any degree of care and sensitivity. Given that the nature of Continuing Anglican Churches is a contested issue and subject to some degree of flux, any debate about Continuing Anglican Churches is ultimately about the nature of Anglicanism per se. Thus, the 'subject' of Continuing Churches should therefore not be regarded as extraneous to mainstream Anglican identity.

There are about approximately 50 different types of Continuing Anglican Churches in the USA and Canada, with a combined membership of around 82 000. The larger 'denominations' within the 'family' include the Anglican Province of Christ the King (founded in 1978), with a membership of around 15 000 and the Reformed Episcopal Church (founded in 1873) with 12 000 members. Continuing Anglican Churches in the USA/Canada can claim a total of 966 parishes or missions, 105 dioceses, 159 bishops and 1133 priests.[1] Outside the USA and Canada, Continuing Anglican Churches exist in South Africa, India, Britain and throughout the Commonwealth. Numbers are more difficult to estimate here, but it is probable that, globally, the combined membership of Continuing Anglican Churches is at least 100 000. Of these, the vast majority can be found in North America, which also boasts the greatest span of variety in terms of 'denominations'.

The causes of secession – that is, no longer being in communion with Canterbury – can be reasonably traced to two areas of dispute: reactions to liturgical reform, either because of modernization or concern about 'Anglo-Catholic' or 'Protestant' tendencies being promoted or eroded; concerns about perceived theological and ecclesiological liberalism (for example, the ordina-tion of women to the priesthood and so on). It is rare to find a Continuing Anglican Church that does not owe its *raison d'être* to one or both of these contested arenas. Thus, many Continuing Anglican Churches typically uphold the *Book of Common Prayer* and its North American variants, and do not ordain women. An exception is the International Anglican Communion (founded in 2002), which does ordain women but adheres strictly to 'traditional' worship. However, broadly speaking, Continuing Anglican Churches are evenly divided between those that seek to uphold a more obviously Protestant version of Anglicanism (a number of whom can trace their foundation to the nineteenth century) and those of a more Anglo-Catholic persuasion that have reacted to perceived 'liberal' trends within the Episcopal Church of the USA (or ECUSA) and therefore have more recent foundations. The multiplication of *types* of Continuing Anglican Churches is

---

[1] An interesting statistic in its own right, since the ratio of stipendiary priests to bishops in the Church of England is around 100:1. In Continuing Anglican Churches it is 10:1.

the result of: internal schism, leading to separation and the formation of a new 'denomination'; and 'local' theological and ecclesiological responses (for example, the Missionary Diocese of Texas).

An ethnographic sampling of statements of faith from Continuing Anglican Churches can reveal much about their self-understanding and identity:

> ...Anglicans found it no longer possible to continue being Anglican in the 'official' Anglican Church...so they decided to continue Anglicanism outside 'official' Anglican parameters....

> We simply consider ourselves to be ordinary, conventional Anglicans who have neither added anything non-Anglican or subtracted anything....

> [We were] created to preserve, to uphold, and to transmit unimpaired, the whole catholic and apostolic Christian faith and religion as received and set forth by the Church of England in the Book of Common Prayer and the Thirty-Nine Articles of religion....

> The Independent Anglican Church of Canada is not in communion with, nor part of, the 'Continuing Anglican Movement', nor with any other 'independent Anglicans'.

> [We were created] in defense of the Catholic faith....

> We enjoy intercommunion with Forward in Faith, England....

> We do what the apostles did; we don't add or take away from what the apostles did; the 1928 BCP comes closest to what the apostles did... (Interview)

> We were formed to assure the continuity of our 'low church' liturgical life....

> [We were created because of] the lack of preaching of the Bible's strong salvation message in ECUSA....

> We were created to ensure the continuation of historic Anglican Christianity in America...[preserve] traditional Episcopal liturgy and polity...intercommunion with FIF...[use] BCP 1928, American Missal, English Missal, etc...indifferent to 39 Articles....

Hearing some of the Continuing Anglican Churches speak with their own voice enables us to see that it is 'traditionalism' that tends to unite the churches across liturgical, theological and ecclesiological spectra. Moreover, these churches do not see themselves as 'schismatic', but as 'continuing', which places them outside most conventional categories and definitions in the sociology of religion, or even within ecclesiology itself.

That said, there is an immediate problem with the term 'Continuing Anglican Churches', since it lacks any agreed value amongst users or analysts. It may be fair to describe such churches as 'neo-conservative' or 'neo-traditionalist', but this does not quite capture their diversity. For example, some of the Continuing Anglican Churches are strongly flavoured by their appeal to the idea of 'returning' – either to the Roman Catholic Church, or to a 'purer' form of Evangelical faith. So far from preserving Anglican identity, certain Continuing Anglican Churches see themselves as restorationists, and therefore as progressive.

In Hopewellian terms, it is therefore possible to conceive of Continuing Anglican Churches as a form of 'alternative comedy'. However, this comedy is unlike mainstream Anglicanism, since it lacks its irony (which in turn gives 'licence to doubt'). The union Continuing Anglican Churches seek is almost wholly beyond their means, and yet many individuals and groups persist in the belief that 'we did not leave the Anglican Communion – it left us'. In this respect, a tragic world-view is being espoused, similar to that identified in the previous chapter. This notion of each specific Continuing Anglican Church being an essentialist 'faithful remnant' is vital for the maintenance of ecclesial identity, for it leaves open the possibility of a full comic reunion, in which the discord of separatism is ultimately overcome when the errant majority turn from their ways and rejoin those who, having been ostracized, are recognized as being true and faithful. Peace, wisdom and will ultimately reunite the loose threads and filial ties.

Further Reflections

If Continuing Anglican Churches remain related to the wider Anglican Communion by virtue of the link established through non-ironic alternative comedy, there are further issues that can be explored through Hopewellian analysis and interpretation. For example, there may be several reasons to be hesitant in adopting the term 'Continuing Anglican Churches'. First, within the 'imagined Communion' of Anglicanism, it is commonplace to suppose that there is clarity about its ordering and definition. This is, ironically, a mechanistic ideology that finds itself located within a more organic under-standing of the church. For example, is it not the case that the Methodist Church and smaller bodies, such as the Countess of Huntingdon's Connexion, technically qualify as progressive (rather than neo-conservative) Continuing Anglican Churches? Second, where does the call for a Third Province fit in with the definition of a Continuing Anglican Church? Come to that, what is one to make of the small number of churches that have moved themselves into a more semi-detached relationship with their bishop and diocese, such as St Helen's Bishopsgate in London? In both cases, there is a desire to retain the Anglican label, but not to be in communion with Canterbury – at least for the time being. Third, certain churches have actively encouraged 'church planting', sometimes collaboratively with the bishop/diocese, but this has not always been the case. Again, there seems to be some toleration for the idea that there can be an Anglican 'missionary' church within an existing parish.

Allied to these concerns, there are also some intriguing micro-capital issues to be considered. In both North America and Britain, the ownership of the church property can have a significant bearing on the nature and extent of schism or the formation of a Continuing Church. Recent cases in the dioceses of Philadelphia (USA) and Worcester (UK) come to mind. In both situations, a priest declared himself to be no longer in communion with his bishop. In North America, because the congregation owned the church property and plant, and the bishop's powers of sequestration were therefore limited, a settlement was possible. In contrast, Charles Raven, the priest-in-charge of a potentially schismatic congregation in Kidderminster would have needed to renew his licence (and therefore reaffirm his canonical obedience) to remain in post – and the congregation did not own 'its' church buildings.

Having said this, surely the challenge of St Helen's Bishopsgate to the diocese of London, and to communion with Canterbury, should be looked at afresh? It should be obvious that, even with the economic and authority structures of the Church of England, it may be possible to operate like a Continuing Anglican Church yet remain within the fold of Anglicanism. As we began to see in the previous chapter, under the umbrella of Reform, or other comparable organizations, St Helen's Bishopsgate can operate an autonomous ministry that actively opposes the Church of England and declares itself to be out of communion with the archbishop of Canterbury. In other words, a continuing schism/church *within* a Communion is a viable option for some congregations, just as much as a schism/church *without* a Communion.

It should now be clear why a Hopewellian approach to this knotty problem is a reasonable way of exploring and assessing Continuing Anglican Churches. First, the evidence-based research relating to those churches that are happy to identify themselves as Continuing Anglican Churches suggests that the definition and category of the term is ambiguous. Second, by allowing individual Continuing Anglican Churches to speak with their own voice, we can see that, in terms of aspiration, they are more than mere sects. They are neo-conservative in character, but also 'comically restorationist' in tone and, in some respects, radical and inventive as much as they may be counted as traditionalist. Third, we can also see that beyond the penumbra of 'obvious' Continuing Anglican Churches, there are a host of situations (that is, schisms remaining *within* churches) that closely relate to the phenomenon we are exploring and assessing. In short, the study of Continuing Anglican Churches does not easily lend itself to 'pure' meta-theological assessment or to the making of 'blueprint' ecclesiological judgements. The very subject requires a combination of grounded research, interdisciplinarity and theological reflection.

So how are we to make some sense of this complex ecclesial landscape – the very *terroir*[2] of Anglicanism, where habits, customs, rubrics, liturgy, ethos and world-view can clearly survive (and flourish?) outside the 'official' Communion? James Gordon Melton's work talks of 'family types' in relation to ecclesiological categorization. A useful analogy, it permits us to recognize a morphological resemblance between churches, even where divorce or estrangement has taken place. Thus, in claiming a nomenclature – in this case,

---

[2] A Gallic word for which there is no obvious English counterpart, *terroir* refers to a combination of ethos and context. Used by sommeliers, it encompasses soil, climate, geography, tradition and human input.

'Anglican' – we can see that the label continues to be invested with appeal, signifies roots and continues to construct identity. So building on the family and mansion analogies, three points can now be made.

First, the nineteenth and twentieth centuries have seen a number of congregations abandoning their respective Evangelical or Catholic wings altogether. Some have continued to use the Anglican nomenclature, and, indeed, to replicate as much of the ecclesial *terroir* of the mansion as possible. Thus, the *Book of Common Prayer* is retained, the 39 Articles remain fundamental, and so forth. But, in every other way, the congregation has become separatist.

Second, there are congregations who wish to remain within the original mansion, family or household, but now desire to seal off the wing from contact with the centre. Separate entrances to the wing are created (for example, 'Flying Bishops',[3] alternative Episcopal oversight and so on). Continued occupancy is an uneasy truce between the centre and wing, and questions of capital, ownership and financial responsibility have yet to be tested. But the seeds of developing Continuing Anglican Churches *within* the Communion (mansion) are already present.

Third, the analogies allow us to think not only of the Anglican family and mansion, but also of the broader and more extensive 'estate' of Anglicanism, which might include the Church of South India, and perhaps even Methodism. In other words, in this third option, there is some recognition that the very boundaries of Anglicanism are not as precise as one might perhaps hope. Now this is not meant to be a (cheap) ecumenical remark, which fails to take seriously the differences between denominations. Rather, it is intended to acknowledge some part of the generative power of culture (that is, national identity, history and so on) which has some hand in shaping denominations and their interrelation. Moreover, it suggests that wherever we locate ecclesial differences – and this may be in doctrine – there are other, subtle causes of fracture and fissure that might have to be faced. This may be personality (a key factor in certain Continuing Churches that divide, then form two or three 'denominations' as the result of a single split), class (I use an elitist analogy intentionally to underline this point, to remind Anglicans of one possible contributory factor in Methodism), and gender (which may be repositioned as authority or order).

In summary, and despite the ambiguities I have highlighted, we can say that Continuing Anglican Churches are those that have consciously chosen to leave the Anglican Communion and have elected to identify their life as being separate from that of the See of Canterbury. They have taken a decision to leave, even if they deploy a reverse comic narrative: 'they left us – but we expect all true believers to eventually join us'. Those churches that continue within the

---

[3] 'Flying Bishops' – or, to give them their proper title, 'Provincial Episcopal Visitors' – are bishops set aside by the church to minister to those congregations that cannot accept the priestly ministry of women. They are formally recognized by the Church of England, and a number of Anglican provinces have now constructed informal arrangements for such congregations.

Anglican Communion, and yet wish to be hermetically separated within the tradition, can be identified as *potential* Continuing Anglican Churches, but are otherwise pursuing that honoured course within mainstream Protestant ecclesiology that is normally termed 'loyal dissent'. Inevitably, where ecclesial unity in North America is primarily achieved through *confessional* harmony and agreement, the number of Continuing Anglican Churches rises in direct proportion to the number of ecclesial spats.

In the Church of England, however, ecclesial unity is primarily maintained through *structural* and *organizational* apparatus. What makes the study of the Anglican Communion so fascinating in the light of Hopewell's work is the extent to which individual provinces throughout the world reflect this dualistic heritage. Furthermore, if individual churches in the Church of England can opt out of structural and organizational obligations and apparatus (and it appears that some are already attempting this), then it is possible to envisage the emergence of an even larger number and range of Continuing Anglican Churches that will eventually become an adjunct of the Church of England.

Given these remarks, we now turn to a brief consideration of a parallel (and unavoidable) subject that necessarily accompanies an exploration and assessment of Continuing Anglican Churches, namely the nature of Communion. Thus far, we have spoken of the Anglican Communion as though it were obvious and coherent or, at least in comic terms, as a body with a 'plot that shares a common desire for a happy and reconciled ending'. However, I wish to suggest that this is not quite the case and that an important factor in addressing Anglicanism and its offshoots lies in beginning with a more realistic understanding of the nature and reality of the Anglican Communion.

The Cultural Nature of Anglican Communion

'Communion' in relation to the worldwide Anglican Church is primarily a postcolonial construction of reality. That is, the present sense of 'Communion', whatever meaning is attached to it, is unquestionably a descendant of a more imperialist ecclesiology. The gradual colonization of territory in the seventeenth to nineteenth centuries often meant that it was the Church of England that was 'established' in British dominions. The emergence of the American Episcopal Church after the Revolution of 1776 was the first indication that Anglicanism could retain its shape without reference to political establishment or monarchical power. It is no accident that the first Episcopal bishop in the USA, Bishop Samuel Seabury, received his consecration through Scottish Episcopalians, who were likewise not established, although they remained loyal to the British Crown.

Ownership of the colonial past and postcolonial present is an important step in understanding the evolution of the Anglican Communion. Inevitably, in meta-ecclesiological constructions of reality, it is tempting to assume that the very idea of 'communion' was somehow the starting point for worldwide Anglicanism. True, it may be possible, using Hooker and other Anglican theologians, to construct such an argument. But rather like orthodox doctrine, it is important to understand that such a thing normally emerges at the *end* of a series of complex negotiations and compromises, often taking account of several different understandings along the way. Orthodox doctrine does not arrive created, *ex nihilo*, as it were. It does not *commence* debates that then become more convoluted and complex as time goes on. Christian orthodoxy is the focused, end point of several types of debate, not the origin of arguments in which a pre-existent 'pure' ideology is sullied in the process of reception. Similarly, the proper way to understand the Anglican Communion is to see it as the default matrix for provincial relationality, following the collapse of the British Empire and its mutation into the British Commonwealth. Dependents became partners; colonies became member states; where there was once patronage, equivocal relationships begin to emerge.

It is important to appreciate this, since there can be a lazy assumption, sometimes made by Anglicans, that 'our' or 'the' Communion only differs from the Roman Catholic Church in terms of size and scope, whereas in reality the sources and notions of the Communion are quite different. The 'Communion' to which Anglicans belong has fuzzy edges. It embraces churches that are not Anglican (for example, those in the Porvoo Agreement), the Church of South India which is krypto-Anglican, and, at various levels, recognizes and affirms the ministry and authority of a wide variety of other churches. Allied to the 'fuzzy edges', the lines of authority are not as clear as those enjoyed by other denominations. In some provinces it is possible to be doctrinally deviant or innovative (depending on your point of view), but removal from office (say, as a priest) is only possible when canon law has been breached. Anglican ecclesiology, in both its principal monarchical and non-monarchical expressions (that is, English and American Anglicanism) protects the liberty of individual conscience to a remarkable degree. The tradition of 'loyal dissent' is tolerated and can sometimes be honoured.

This leads us to state that the idea of an Anglican Communion is not primarily about a 'static' state of being. 'Communion' is a noun, to be sure. But, in Anglicanism, the term should mainly be understood as a verb; in other words, 'in communion with' someone or something. The stress is on the 'in' and the 'with'; 'communion' is the action. It is not a description of an ideal, static state of being; rather, it describes a quality of relationship. Understood like this, we can see that there is a tension in Anglican self-understanding in relation to identity. To borrow once again a distinction from Clifford Geertz, there is a difference between *ethos* and *world-view*. An ethos is the way things are – the actual ecclesial *terroir*. A world-view, on the other hand, is what the churches could or should be. When considering the Anglican Communion, we are immediately caught between the tension of ethos and world-view, of verb and noun. To talk of the Anglican Communion is, in reality, to talk of the activity of being in communion *in* or *with*; the Communion is yet to come.

The reason that this reflection is important for the study of Anglican churches is simple enough. If the Anglican Communion is, in reality, a kind of 'serious fiction', an imagined ironic or comic community replete with 'fuzzy' edges, porous boundaries and the like, then how is it held together? Structurally, we have already pointed to the four instruments of unity, namely the archbishop of Canterbury, the Anglican Consultative Council, the Meeting of Primates and the Lambeth Conference. But this does not suggest to us a 'Communion' in the sense that Roman Catholics might mean the term. Thus, coherence and control is not there in the same way for Anglicans as it is for Roman Catholics. For 'Communion' in Anglicanism, therefore, read 'federation'.

The use of the word 'federation' is not meant to imply that the idea of Communion has no currency for Anglicans. Clearly, it does. But federations can take many forms, and, in the case of Anglicanism, I want to suggest that the liturgical, doctrinal and ecclesial unity makes for far more than a morphological similarity across provinces. At the same time, the reality of self-determination in individual provinces and dioceses cannot be overlooked (consider Sydney and New Westminster for example). The acid test for a Communion is whether or not it would expel churches or provinces it held to be deviant. But excommunication is an uncommon phenomenon and language for Anglicans, and all the signs are that the ecclesiology is characterized by a preference for looser ties to maintain a degree of unity, rather than stricter criteria for remaining within the Communion. Put more definitively, Anglicans seem to prefer being 'in communion' with a variety of ecclesiological and theological positions than having a secure sense of belonging 'within *the* Communion' with its clear implication that there are certain lines that, when crossed, automatically render individual congregations, dioceses or provinces to be in breach of order and ecclesial polity.

Here we might ask whether this is any different from (or worse than) the Orthodox Church. Orthodoxy has similarly complex issues to negotiate. In the USA, for example, there is a range of different Orthodox traditions – Russian, Romanian, Greek, Serbian, to name but a few. But these congregations may be divided between those that still look to Europe for their priests and bishops and those that have developed along more North American lines. Thus, a recently appointed Romanian Metropolitan for North America only has authority over those congregations that continue to relate to Bucharest. His authority does not extend to Romanian Orthodox churches, which are self-governing within the USA and Canada, although relationships between the two tend to be reasonably (but not always) cordial.

The fact that the Orthodox Churches (the plural is important) can tolerate diversity and a certain degree of competition may be something that Anglicanism can learn from. After all, in speaking of an Anglican Communion, or even a federation, it must be acknowledged that one is really describing a range of Anglican Churches, with at least as much diversity as that found in Orthodoxy. Moreover, the lack of clear, central power in Orthodoxy suggests that Anglicanism may not have as much to fear as it supposes from those churches that keep the Anglican 'title', whilst at the same time trying to keep their distance. As with so many things in ecclesiology, the issue revolves around power and ownership. And it must be clear that there are many more 'Anglicans' than those who are actually in communion with Canterbury.

This last point leads us to make a number of supplementary points that relate to this discussion. First, Anglicans must be wary of being tainted by (the fiction of) perfectionism. It is important to remember and respect the cultural forces that have both generated and shaped its polity. The activity of God – even when it can be said to be *actus purus* – is inevitably mediated through agencies that are less than perfect. Notions of 'perfected' ecclesiology are a danger to both the 'parent' denomination and to the rebelling 'child'.

Second, there is usually some scope for pastoral and ecclesial pragmatism in reception. A number of cathedrals now admit ministers from other denominations as ecumenical canons. Whilst the Anglican Church may be a very long way off from recognizing the ministry of Continuing Anglican Churches in such a way (and it must be repeated that such invitations, may, in any case, be scorned), there are nonetheless conventional modes for establishing rapport that are somewhere between the local and the diocesan.

Third, there has always been space for 'loyal dissent' within the Church of England and the wider Anglican Church. Hooker's *Laws*, the covert attacks on Anglicanism's Puritan strain and the desire for compliancy coupled to diversity all point to a church whose identity has been contested in every generation since the Reformation. Yet it is important to recognize that those traditions that press, probe and question the identity and boundaries of Anglicanism have often nourished and enriched the church at the same time. Sometimes the art of practical ecclesiology is in retaining rebellion, not in silencing it.

Fourth, there is a fundamental ecclesial reality about being 'divorced', yet 'still related'. As an analogy, it provides an important 'fit' for Anglican–Roman Catholic relations, and relations between the branches of the Orthodox Church. The recognition of this aspect in modern ecclesiology raises some teasing questions about dialogue, continuing relations and their restoration and mediation between once hostile parties.

Fifth, Anglican 'independentism' seems to be increasingly difficult to police and control. Some recognition that Anglicanism is more of a federation than a Communion may help the Anglican Church to live a little easier with its own reality and identity. Instead of feeling (almost all the time) that it is a weak Communion, it may begin to appreciate that it is, in fact, a strong federation.

Sixth, we should note that the language of 'Communion' creeps into ecumenical dialogue and thinking where it is very probably unwarranted. For example, it is common practice to refer to the 'Porvoo Communion'. Indeed, this is how those churches within are described in successive *The Church of England Yearbooks*. However, the reality of Porvoo is that it is an understanding of federalism and a mutual recognition of ministries at which a significant level of intercommunion takes place. In other words, and to repeat, a Communion is not *a* static, easily identifiable body. There is no 'a', because communion is a state of relations and being (that is, *with* or *in*). There can be *some* communion between churches or individuals, but churches that talk of being *the* or *a* Communion are expressing a world-view (that is, what could or should be); they are seldom describing their ethos (the ways things are). Thus, the 'Anglican Communion of Churches' or the 'Communion of Anglican Churches' is a far better nomenclature than 'The Anglican Communion'. Indeed, the gradual metamorphosis of Anglicanism into denominationalism seems to be almost inevitable (Swatos, 1979).

Comic Endings: What is the Future for the Anglican Communion?

The late and lamented theologian, Robert Carroll, once described the Anglican way of doing theology as 'the Dodo's incorporative principle – a means by which everyone wins'. Anglicans, in trying to sort out doctrinal differences amongst themselves, were always arguing about the precise weight that should be given to scripture, tradition, reason and culture. The ground rules for such debates always guaranteed inclusion for participants and most reasonable points of view – even those one might passionately oppose. All sides in any debate could always claim a moral victory, since final decisions were seldom reached. It is precisely this kind of ecclesiology that has made Anglicanism – rather like a dodo – such a rare bird for several centuries. But is the rarity and novelty of Anglicanism about to slide into self-inflicted extinction?

Certainly, the archbishop of Canterbury has an unenviable task in trying to hold together some hotly held competing convictions. Liberals were calling on him to support the choice of an openly gay bishop, partly to confirm the identity of the church as being relevant and inclusive. Conservatives wanted him to offer unequivocal condemnation, claiming that a gay bishop was a departure from all scriptural and ecclesial norms. It is a no-win situation for the archbishop of Canterbury. Leading the Church of England, it is often said, is like trying to herd cats. Precocious and unbiddable creatures, they roam where they please. The job of leading the Anglican Communion is, therefore, many times more difficult. The Episcopal Church in America will go one way; Anglicans in Sydney and Nigeria will go another.

It seems unlikely, given what we have already said about Anglicanism as a denomination that expresses the comic genre that there is hope for a harmonious future in which discord is ultimately banished. But comedy needs to be rooted in reality, and, in Hopewellian terms, this is where an ecclesial synergy between irony and comedy can come into its own. The comedy can imagine a future together; irony can face the despair of separatism. In this respect, four points about the future of the Anglican Communion need to be made here.

First, it must be accepted that the worldwide Anglican Communion is really a construction of the British Empire that has evolved into a more equitable Commonwealth or federation in the postcolonial era. The Anglican Church is undoubtedly global, but it may now be too diverse to be centrally or collegially governed in a manner that guarantees unequivocal unity.

Second, 'overlapping' or 'extended' episcopal oversight must be possible in a church that has always valued a degree of pluralism. In a 'glocal' world, geographical boundaries mean less and less; congregations and churches are increasingly related by their shared affinities and agreed moral coherence. So models of episcopacy that lean on Constantine or Cyprian are less attractive today, especially in a church that is deeply infused with a democratic spirit, infected by consumerism and choice and has, in any case, always respected dissent and wallowed in differences.

Third, Anglicanism is not, and never has been, one vast 'catholic' continent. It has always been a kind of archipelago – a connection of provincial islands that shares doctrinal, liturgical and cultural aspects. The real power of the archbishop of Canterbury and the Church of England has been waning since the American Anglicans got their own bishop (from Scotland) in the eighteenth century. But Anglicans should remember that such 'schisms' have (so far) never proved fatal.

Fourth, Anglican leaders may like to reflect on the virtues of Anglican elasticity and malleability. It is a very adaptive type of church and it ought to be able to cope with quietly dropping the chimera of 'Communion' and realizing that its identity lies in being more like a 'family' of churches. The 'Anglican family name' could, in future, be used rather like the Baptist family name. The basic essence would be shared and would continue, but the prefix ('American', 'Southern', 'Reformed', 'Strict and Particular' and so forth) would indicate the flavouring.

Whatever Anglicans decide to do, it is now clear that the worldwide Anglican Church already has too many different styles of expression and different emphases of belief to enable it to be governed centrally or collegially. But a degree of separation doesn't necessarily mean schism, let alone divorce. Indeed, a slight loosening of the ties could help the Anglican churches. Those family members that want the space 'to be themselves' should perhaps be allowed to individuate. Since 77 million members in 38 provinces all living under one roof might be a bit too stifling for the twenty-first century, it might be worthwhile exploring the possibility of developing a 'neighbourhood' or 'family' of 'semi-detached' Anglican churches instead of one single monolithic Communion. Arguably, now more than ever, Anglicans should try to be mature and realistic about the real state of the Anglican Church: instead of trying to patch things up through fear of the unknown, we should try to face the future with faith. Specifically, can Anglicans agree to live apart, but still be friends and neighbours – at least for the sake of its children? Such an ironic–comic turn should not be beyond the grasp of an Anglican Communion that combines humour, realism and hope in equal measure.

Concluding and Unscientific Postscript: Quadripolar Anglicanism

Ultimately, Anglicanism is a faith that is formed by worship, prayer, the scriptures and an ecclesial practice that is, at once, local and catholic. It is a religiously suffused and compassionate interwovenness of faith, order, sociality and difference. It is also an extraordinarily optimistic expression of Christianity that anticipates its world-view through its ethos. Faithfully conceived, Anglicanism is a multidimensional quadripolar ecclesial system that engages its adherents in faith through a rich matrix of particularities. For example, the four instruments of unity (the Meeting of the Primates, the Anglican Consultative Council, the archbishop of Canterbury and the Lambeth Conference) link with the Lambeth quadrilateral (that is, scripture, tradition, reason and the historic episcopate).

Through using Hopewell's insights as an analytical and interpretative agent to read the Anglican Communion, we can add a third dimension to this equation. Hopewell's four genres or world-views – ironic, comic, tragic and romantic – permit the Communion to be positioned within the wider global ecclesial milieu. Specifically, this chapter has explored Anglicanism as an ironic–comic world-view. In Chapter 8 we saw how a Conservative Evangelical form of Anglicanism can be understood as 'tragic'. And in Chapter 7 I explored the romantic culture of contemporary revivalism. This allows me to suggest that Anglicanism, faithfully conceived, is also an expression of the full Hopewellian quadripolar ecclesial system, in which the ample range and depth of world-views are allowed representation within a system of trust and hope. Indeed, using Hopewell, we can suggest that the inherent 'tensions' between the romantic, comic, tragic and ironic corners of Anglican world-views are better off when they face one another in tension (but with respect), rather than being apart in self-imposed ghettoes of certainty.

A Communion, then, is a complex body immersed in the complexity of the world, in which all seek to participate in God's purposes for a wide range of reasons. The world-views of the Hopewellian quadrilateral suggests four more corners that necessarily exert some moral force on the shaping of the ethos. How the world could or should be, to an extent, suggests how the world already is. Anglicanism is, then, a kind of practical idea that embodies how people might be together. It is not an abstract idea, and nor is it general. It is, rather, a form of knowledge that is optimistic about the future itself, precisely because it is founded on the conviction that Anglicanism is a form of faith that holds, possesses and shapes people within the dynamic life of God, but in ways that liberate rather than constrain. Part of its genius is its (ironic) attachment to paradox, especially located in ecclesiology (that is, *via media* – Catholic and Protestant) and theologically (for example, the doctrine of the incarnation – humanity and divinity).

We can also say that what singles out Anglicanism for particular attention, as a denomination, is its sheer optimism. This, as I have suggested, is primarily a 'comic' outlook, but one that is rooted in a notion of being bound up in God's future, and a particular view of reconciled humanity and sociality, rather than specific self-belief. But within Hopewellian quadripolar Anglicanism, the optimism is tempered by other particular expressions of Anglican life. For example, those of a 'tragic' hue would see sin as an inextricable (outgrown) part of human nature. But in the broader Anglican compass, the comic and ironic world still prevails strongly, at least in the northern hemisphere and developed world. Thus, 'sin' is essentially regarded as an *infection* of human nature (not as intrinsic to it) and could ultimately be banished. However, the moral optimism of Anglicanism is not habitually constituted through the moral certainty that might be anticipated in other ecclesial traditions.

Alternatively, to locate these remarks within Anglican spirituality, one could consider the synthesis of sources that Anglicans habitually draw upon to constitute and shape their inner life. The pastoral optimism of George Herbert comes to mind. Equally, the spiritual writings of Donne, Stillingfleet, Andrewes and Waterland would also serve as examples, to pick just one rich seam of Anglican expression. But even outside the main corpus of specifically Anglican writing, Julian of Norwich's theological mysticism would represent a typically optimistic outlook that shapes many types of Anglican spirituality. 'All shall be well; and all manner of things shall be well' is an example of 'classic comedy' set within the normative Anglican cultural nexus.

Thus, the hope vested in the future by most Anglicans means that the trust placed in the present, is, perhaps, a little more conditional. The English fondness for inchoate Pelagianism, which is hardly a precise or explicit form of faith-practice, is at the same time a remarkably resilient form of modern Christian discipleship. Ultimately, it is a form of Christian faith that values deep, penetrating conversations, and is also prayerful in the midst of diverse local communities. Globally, Anglicanism is at once romantic, tragic and ironic – differently shaped in each local, regional and ecclesial context. Granted, we now know, using Hopewell, that whichever 'story' of God individuals participate in, it will most likely shape their ecclesiology and missiology. But the three-dimensional quadripolar system that is Anglicanism seems to be especially capable of holding individuals and communities in debates of considerable import and tension. United through mystical and sacramental union, Anglicanism is therefore a model of engaged polity for a complex sociality. It is a credal faith, where beliefs can be affirmed, but also doubted. But it is not a confessional church in which membership is conditional upon precise agreement with articles and statements. Despite the moral and ecclesial internal difficulties that global Anglicanism encounters, it is a faith that foresees its future optimistically. Its strength lies in its apparent weakness; its unity in its diversity; its coherence in its difference; its shape in its diffusiveness; its hope in a degree of faithful doubt; its energy in passionate coolness. It embodies 'feint conviction'; it practises 'truthful duplicity'; it is Protestant and Catholic. Like a classic Shakespearian comedy, the Anglican Communion seems to be mired within dissipation and disunity; but it ultimately anticipates resolution, reconciliation and a truer deepening of relationships. It is comic and ironic:

> We came into the world like brother and brother;
> And now let's go hand in hand, not one before the other.
> (*Comedy of Errors*, V, i)

> All yet seems well; and if it end so meet,
> The bitter part, more welcome is the sweet ....
> (*All's Well That Ends Well*, V, iii)

Conclusion

Authentic Engagement

Part of the burden of this book has been to explore the two main faces of theological and ecclesiological engagement with contemporary culture. The first kind is constituted through an interlocking and combative encounter. Niebuhr would identify this as the 'Christ against culture' perspective, and we have explored, at the more sophisticated end of the spectrum, Radical Orthodoxy as just one example of a theology that attempts to engage with (but then overcome) culture. A second kind, normally identified as more liberal, and in Niebuhrian terms as the Christ for culture, sees the Christianity–culture debates as an interrelated binding covenant or commitment. The work of Lieven Boeve (explored in Chapter 3) was used to exemplify this position. Mediating between these two positions (extreme characterizations, granted) was David Martin's work, which along with Mudge, Healy and others, was held to be a form of sociologically informed ecclesiology that was best placed to engage with culture in a theologically discerning manner.

Within these positions, there are of course differences of emphasis. For example, there are at least two varieties of conservative engagement that vie for pre-eminence. One the one hand, a traditionalist position might make its appeal on the basis of how things used to be (or at least deemed to be). In such thinking, it is normally imagined that the culture of modernity has gone too far and that Christianity's interests would be best served by returning to a form of Christendom. Still within the conservative spectrum, another view may accept the reality of secular and modern culture, but seek to engage with it in ways that are tenacious and critical. Both positions here would be anti-liberal to some degree, but would seek to pursue the Christianity–culture debate in rather different ways. However, there is an in-built paradox with these positions. Whilst holding fast, on the one hand, to the immutability of the Christian tradition, these theological strategies also assume a degree of reflexivity in application, hermeneutics and identity. Similarly, the more 'liberal' positions that attempt to negotiate the nexus of the Christianity–culture debate show little sign of being truly anti-foundationalist. The paradox of the different types of theological and ecclesiological engagement with culture is that more unties than divides them. Each position appears to accept the need for reflexivity and foundationalism. Each, in addressing, engaging or critiquing culture, inevitably inculcates some aspect of that same culture. Furthermore, each ecclesiological or theological position that we have discussed can also, to some extent, also be understood culturally.

It is partly for this reason that the concentration of this book has rested with a focus on the concrete church. As André Dumas notes in his commentary on Bonhoeffer:

> The Church starts from what actually happens when Jesus Christ takes form as
> community. But the event of Jesus Christ is also the advent of a communal being and
> not simply an individual existential encounter. Revelation does not only come *to* the
> community; it takes place *within* the community. (Dumas, 1971, p. 108)

Christianity is, of course, bound to paradox; indeed, the faith revels in it. Its major doctrines (for example, the incarnation) are attempts to hold or fuse together seemingly contradictory positions, understandings or statements. Correspondingly, in its theological engagement with culture, there is something of an incarnational and sacramental paradigm which is itself rooted in the revelation of God, who is revealed both through the ordinary and the extraordinary, the natural and the supernatural, and in agents whose 'nature' (whether ordinary or transformed), are necessarily contestable. The paradoxical natures of the two main forms of theological engagement with culture are an expression of the unresolved and unsettled nature of Christianity. Thus, the church is the body of Christ in one sense, but the hope of the coming of the kingdom of God, and of the return of Christ, suggests that the church habitually lives between the tension of the present, and of the ultimacy of God's future.

When facing the paradoxes of engagement, which naturally arise from the paradoxes of the Christian tradition, I have sought to show that paying attention to the concrete church, stories and contemporary culture can result in a deeper form of theological reflection. The chapters in this book have sought to show a rich theoretical practical theology that can combine the two faces of engagement and, in so doing, restore some sense of public theology as a critical–affirming discourse that is engaged with/to contemporary culture and can also illuminate the potential for a sociologically informed ecclesiology. Indeed, the focus on culture seems to demand this, as religious expressions and institutions within contemporary society appear to be mutating at a rate that requires a significantly higher level of practical and theoretical engagement from theologians and ecclesiologists. It is partly for this reason that the sequencing of the parts and chapters in this book has been so important. Part I explored the Christianity and culture debate through various problems and theological strategies. Part II sought to narrate a vision for theology and theological education that might be more hospitable to this debate. Part III introduced the idea undertaking ecclesiology through a series of concrete studies that, each in their turn, took sociology, ethnography, anthropology and cultural studies seriously. 'Reading' religion as 'culture' can bring some advantages to theology, not least of which is 'seeing ourselves as others see us': it can help prevent (an all too common) ecclesiological self-deception.

However, I have also tried to be careful *not* to privilege social sciences or cultural studies over and against theology. The argument in this book is for fusion and dialogue, not domination. It is borne out of the recognition, ceded by Berger many years ago, that even if we begin our study of the church from an entirely human perspective, we soon run into what he calls 'signals of transcendence'. As Macquarrie points out, this is not an alien world, but simply a deeper dimension of the one we are already immersed in; it is merely a journey from the 'natural' to the 'supernatural' (Macquarrie, 1997, p. 161). Sacramental material is ordinary material – bread, wine, oil, water (or even marriage). But in the hands of another, and in a different context, these same ordinary agents become 'doors to the sacred'. They are utterly ordinary elements and yet infused with mystery – the 'outward and visible sign of an inward grace' (Macquarrie, 1997 p. 5: cf. Martos, 1981).

That said, there is no escaping the other kinds of paradoxes we have sought to explore. Witness the gap between the ideal and real church, between the concrete church and the church triumphant, and between formal and operant religion. Increasingly, the Christianity–culture 'problem' lies in the gaps, and this can lead to a problem of authenticity and credibility for a church that is founded on being ultimate and truthful, yet is also temporal and human. As we explored in Chapter 1, such insights seem to be confirmed at grassroots level when studying almost any denomination, including Roman Catholicism. For example, an American Roman Catholic priest in an interview with *The New Yorker* magazine states that:

> People today are looking for *authenticity*, not just some kind of Catholicism where you go in on Sunday and punch your card, performing your obligation... they are looking for a framework for their lives, inspiration to go on, to be decent... to be good citizens and good people. (*The New Yorker*, 2 September 2002, p. 54)

At the same time, I have also sought to give due recognition to the fact that practices shape beliefs, and religious beliefs also shape practice. In any theology of culture, the infusion of religion within culture (and vice versa) must be given its proper due. As Tanner notes:

> ... religious beliefs are a form of culture, inextricably implicated in the material practices of daily social living on the part of those who hold them... in the concrete circumstances in which beliefs are lived... actions, attitudes, and interests are likely to be as much infiltrated and informed by the beliefs one holds as beliefs are to be influenced by actions, attitudes and interests.... (Tanner, 1992, p. 9)

But lest this sounds too arid, it is worth recalling the attention given to narrativity in Part III. As we saw here, doctrines can be 'dramatic scripts' which Christians perform and by which they are performed. Doctrines 'provide a scripted code for the motions of a Christian's life in much the same way that broader cultural codes and linguistic patterns structure the self' (Volf and Bass, 2002, p. 75). In other words, doctrines practise us; practices are not just things that Christians do in the light of doctrine: 'practices are what we become as we are set in motion in the space of doctrine' (ibid.). In this sense, we are once again close to Lindbeck's theory of theology – its performative dimension as something that is 'cultural–linguistic': it (that is, doctrine, belief and so on) 'gains power and meaning insofar as it is embodied in the total gestalt of community life and action' (Lindbeck, 1984, p. 36). But there is an irony here both for the theologian and for the church. For in gaining an understanding of how the world beliefs and practice begin to cohere, one immediately sees that they, in fact, do not. As Tanner says:

Christian practices do not in fact require (1) much explicit understanding of beliefs that inform and explain their performance, (2) agreement upon such matters among the participants, (3) strict delimitation of codes for action, (4) systematic consistency among beliefs or actions, or (5) attention to their significance that isolates them from a whole host of non-Christian commitments. More often than not, Christian practices are instead quite open-ended in the sense of being undefined in their exact ideational dimensions and in the sense of being always in the process of re-formation in response to new circumstances.... (Tanner, in Volf and Bass, 2002, p. 229).

So, in the light of our theological study of culture, what are Christian practices and beliefs? I take them to be 'resonances of God's engagement with the world' (Volf and Bass, 2002, p. 260). And, in this respect, we might then want to argue that theology should always be in the service of practice and belief – something to do with 'real life', the 'concrete church' and the context of 'operant' or 'vernacular' religion. It is here that the practical theologian will find individuals and communities 'working out their own salvation' (Phil. 2: 12).

It now seems appropriate to turn back to practical theology and its task. Yust reminds us that the cultivation of practical wisdom (*phronesis*) remains one of the primary tasks for the seminary and the church: 'not knowing our tradition leaves us confused; not passing it on creatively and critically transformed identifies us with the past and leaves us closed off to the present' (Yust, 2002, p. 239). So, making sense of religious life is something which practical theology can really use to help inform the church about its identity and life. Similarly, Browning calls the church and theology to account when he writes that:

Theology can be practical if we bring practical concerns to it from the beginning. The theologian does not stand before God, Scripture and the historic witness of the church like an empty slate or Lockean tabula rasa ready to be determined, filled up, and then plugged into a concrete practical situation. A more accurate description goes like this. We come to the theological task with questions shaped by the secular and religious practices in which we are implicated – sometimes uncomfortably. These practices are meaningful or theory-laden. (Browning, 1991, p. 2)

Thus, theologians have to learn that they cannot rely on theological blueprints to determine how congregations could or should be in contemporary culture. In this respect, practical theology needs to work with fields such as Congregational Studies in helping the church to become exegetes of the text of the congregation. And, as Yust reminds us, this requires engagement with 'several social science disciplines...[so that they can] describe congregational life in its thickness' (Yust, 2002, p. 241). The epiphany seems to lead towards what Clark Williamson describes as a 'conversational theology':

The purpose of [conversational] theology is to enter into conversation with such questions [about what we ought to do and why], to interpret the Christian faith in relation to the context in which we live, and to interpret that context in the light of the Christian faith, so that we can...have a conversation...about what God gives and calls us to be and do in this time and place.... Theology is...a practical wisdom...we are not finished with any theological point until we can talk about the difference it makes to how we see things and to what we intend to do.... (Williamson, 1999, pp. 2–8)

Quite so. And this leads us to agree with Roberts, who argues that theology itself, and most especially practical theology, is 'a practical process of discerning God's will...a community activity requiring conversation and interaction' (Roberts, 2002, p. 184). Moreover, this process is tried, tested, evaluated and put to use through the praxis of the church. Here, and in prayerful communion with the Creator and Redeemer, practical theology becomes a transforming activity for both the church and the world.

Bibliography

Abrecht, P. (1961), *The Churches and Rapid Social Change*, London: SCM Press.

Althaus-Reid, M. (2003), *The Queer God*, London: Routledge.

Alves, C. (1972), *The Christian in Education*, London: SCM.

Ammerman, N. (1997), *Congregation and Community*, New Brunswick, NJ: Rutgers University Press.

Ammerman, N., Carroll, J., Dudley, C. and McKinney, W. (1998), *Studying Congregations*, Nashville, TN: Abingdon Press.

Anderson, B. (1983), *Imagined Communities: Reflections on the Origin and Spread of Nationalism*, London: Verso.

Archbishops' Council of the Church of England (2001), *Mind the Gap: Integrated Continuing Ministerial Education for the Church's Ministers*, London: Church House Publishing.

Astley, J. (2002), *Ordinary Theology*, Aldershot: Ashgate.

Astley, J., Francis, L.J. and Crowder, C. (eds) (1996), *Theological Perspectives on Christian Formation: A Reader on Theology and Christian Education*, Leominster: Gracewing.

Atkinson, P. (1990), *The Ethnographic Imagination: Textual Constructions of Reality*, London: Routledge.

Atoun, R. (2001), *Understanding Fundamentalism*, Lanham, MD: AltaMira Press.

Auden, W.H. (1955), *Shield of Achilles*, London: Faber.

Augustine, St (1961), *Confessions*, trans. R. Pine Coffin, Harmondsworth: Penguin.

Austin, J.L. (1962), *How to do Things with Words*, Oxford: Oxford University Press.

Avis, P. (2000), *The Anglican Understanding of the Christian Church*, London: SPCK.

Bamber, L. (1982), *Comic Women, Tragic Men*, Stanford, CA: Stanford University Press.

Barnett, R. (1990), *The Idea of Higher Education*, Buckingham: The Society for Research and Higher Education/ Open University Press.

Barnett, R. (1994), *The Limits of Competence*, Oxford: Oxford University Press.

Bauman, Z. (2000), *Liquid Modernity*, Cambridge: Polity Press.

Beaudoin, T. (2003), *Consuming Faith*, London: Sheed & Ward.

Bebbington, D. (1989), *Evangelicalism in Modern Britain: A History from the 1730s to the 1980s*, London: Unwin Hyman.

Becker, P. and Eiesland, N. (eds) (1997), *Contemporary American Religion: An Ethnographic Reader*, Lanham, MD: AltaMira Press.

Belenky, M. *et al.* (1986), *Women's Ways of Knowing*, New York: Basic Books.

Bell, C. (1996), 'Modernism and Postmodernism in the Study of Religion', *Religious Studies Review*, July pp. 197–90.

Bellah, R.N. and Hammond, P.E. (1980), *Varieties of Civil Religion*, San Franscisco: Harper & Row.

Bender, C. (2003), *Heaven's Kitchen: Living Religion at God's Love We Deliver*, Chicago: Chicago University Press.

Berger, P. (1980), *The Heretical Imperative*, New York: Harper.

Berger, P. and Luckman, T. (1971), *The Social Construction of Reality: A Treatise in the Sociology of Knowledge*, London: Penguin.

Bernstein, J. (1978), 'Christian Affection and the Catechumenate', *Worship*, **52**, pp. 194–210.

Boeve, L. (2003), *Interrupting Tradition: An Essay on Christian Faith in a Postmodern Context*, Louvain: Peeters Press.

Bourdieu, P. (1990), *In Other Words: Essays Towards a Reflexive Sociology*, trans. M. Adamson, Cambridge: Polity Press.

Boyer, P. (2002), *Religion Explained: The Human Instincts that Fashion Gods, Spirits, and Ancestors*, London: Vintage.

Bramadat, P. (2000), *The Church on the World's Turf*, New York: Oxford University Press.

Brierley, P. (1992), *Act on the Facts*, London: Marc Europe.

Brookfield, S. (1995), *Becoming a Critically Reflective Teacher*, San Francisco: Jossey-Bass.

Brown, A. (2003), 'Press Review', *Church Times*, 5 September.

Brown, C. (2000), *The Death of Christian Britain: Understanding Secularisation 1800–2000*, London: Routledge.

Brown, D. (1999), *Tradition and Imagination*, Oxford: Oxford University Press.

Brown, D. (2000), *Discipline and Imagination: Christian Tradition and Truth*, Oxford: Oxford University Press.

Brown, D., Deraney, S.G. and Tanner, K. (2001), *Converging on Culture: Theologions in Dialogue with Cultural Analysis and Criticism*, Oxford: Oxford University Press.

Browning, D. (1991), *A Fundamental Practical Theology: Descriptive and Strategic Proposals*, Minneapolis, MN: Fortress Press.

Bruce, S. (1996), *Religion in Modern Britain*, Oxford: Oxford University Press.

Buckley, F. (2000), *The Church in Dialogue: Culture and Traditions*, New York: University of America Press.

Burgess, R. (1984), *In the Field: An introduction to Field Research*, London: Routledge.

Bynum, C.W. (1982), *Jesus as Mother: Studies in the Spirituality of the High Middle Ages*, Benkeley: University of California Press.

Caddick, C. and Dormor, D. (eds) (2003), *Anglicanism: The Answer to Modernity*, London: Continuum.

Casanova, J. (1994), *Public Religions in the Modern World*, Chicago and London: University of Chicago Press.

Chevreau, G. (1994), *Catch the Fire*, London: HarperCollins.

Chittister, J. (1983), *Women, Ministry and the Church*, New York: Paulist Press.

Chopp, R. (1995), *Saving Work – Feminist Practices of Theological Education*, Louisville, KY: Westminster John Knox Press.

Clark, D. (1982), *Between Pulpit and Pew*, Cambridge: Cambridge University Press.

Clifford, J. (1986), 'Introduction: Partial Truths', in J. Clifford and G. Marcus (eds), *Writing Culture: The Poetics and Politics of Ethnography*, Berkeley, University of California Press.

Collins, S. (2000), 'Spirituality and Youth', in M. Percy [ed] *Calling Time: Religion and Change at the Turn of the Millennium*, Sheffield: Sheffield Academic Press.

Cox, H. (1994), *Fire From Heaven: Pentecostalism, Spirituality and the Re-Shaping of Religion in the 21st Century*, New York: Addison-Wesley.

Cronin, M. (2000), *Advertising and Consumer Citizenship: Gender, Images and Human Rights*, London: Routledge.

Cunningham, H. (1980), *Leisure in the Industrial Revolution*, Beckenham: Croom Helm.

Davie, G. (1994), *Religion in Britain since 1945: Believing without Belonging*, Oxford: Blackwell.

Davie, G. (2000), *Religion in Modern Europe: A Memory Mutates*, Oxford: Oxford University Press.

Davie, G. (2002), *Europe: The Exceptional Case: The Parameters of Faith in the Modern World*, London: DLT.

Davies, D. (2002), *Anthropology and Theology*, Oxford: Berg.

Davis, C. (1980), *Theology and Practical Society*, Cambridge: Cambridge University Press.

Davis, K. (1990), *Emancipation Still Comin': Explorations in Caribbean Emancipatory Theology*, New York: Orbis Books.

D'Costa, G. (ed.) (1996), *Resurrection Reconsidered*, Oxford: Oneworld.

Dean, W. (2002), *The American Spiritual Culture*, London: Continuum.

Dempsey, C. (2002), 'The Religioning of Anthropology: New Directions of the Ethnographer-Pilgrim', *Religion and Culture*, 1(2), pp. 134–52.

Dewey, J. (1966), *Democracy and Education: An Introduction to the Philosophy of Education*, New York: Free Press.

Dey, I. (1993), *Qualitative Data Analysis; A User-Friendly Guide for Social Scientists*, London: Routledge.

Docherty, D. (2000), 'Reservoir Gods' in A. Walker and M. Percy (eds), *Restoring the Image*, Sheffield: Sheffield Academic Press.

Doll, P. (1989), 'Imperial Anglicanism in North America, 1745–1795', Oxford D.Phil. thesis.

Donovan, V. (1982), *Christianity Rediscovered: An Epistle from the Masai*, London: SCM.

Dorsey, G. (1995), *Congregation: The Journey Back to Church*, New York: Viking.

Douglas, I. and Pui-Lan, K. (eds) (2001), *Beyond Colonial Anglicanism: The Anglican Communion in the Twenty-First Century*, New York: Church Publishing Inc.

Dulles, A. (1974), *Models of the Church*, New York: Doubleday. Reprinted 1987.

Dumas, A. (1971), *Dietrich Bonhoeffer: Theologian of Reality*, New York: Macmillan.

Dykstra, C. and Parks, S. (1986), *Faith development and Fowler*, Birmingham, AL: Religious Education Press.

Eagleton, T. (2000), *The Idea of Culture*, Oxford: Blackwell.

Eiesland, N. (1998), *A Particular Place*, New Brunswick, NJ: Rutgers University Press.

Eisner, E. (1979), *The Educational Imagination: On the Design and Education of School Programs*, New York: Macmillan.

Eisner, E. (1985), 'Aesthetic Modes of Knowing', in E. Eisner (ed.), *Learning and Teaching the Ways of Knowing*, Chicago: Chicago University Press.

Evans D. (1979), *Struggle and Fulfillment*, London: Collins.

Everding, E., Huffaker, L., Snelling, C. and Wilcox, M. (1998), *Perspectives of Faith and Christian Nurture*, Harrisburg, PA: Trinity Press International.

Farley, E. (1982), *Ecclesial Reflection: An Anatomy of Theological Method*, Philadelphia, PA: Fortress Press.

Farley, E. (1985), 'Can Church Education be Theological Education?', *Theology Today*, **42**(2), pp. 159–71.

Farley, E. (1987), 'Interpreting Situations: An Inquiry into the Nature of Practical Theology', in L. Mudge and J. Poling (eds), *Formation and Reflection: The Promise of Practical Theology*, Philadelphia, PA: Fortress Press.

Farley, E. (1988), *The Fragility of Knowledge: Theological Education in the Church and the University*, Philadelphia, PA: Fortress Press.

Farley, E. (2003), *Practising Gospel*, Louisville KY: WJK Press.

Ferris, R. (1990), *Renewal in Theological Education: Strategies for Change*, Wheaton, IL: Billy Graham Center.

Festinger, L. (1957), *A Theory of Cognitive Dissonance*, Stanford, CA: Stanford University Press.

Fiorenza, F. Schussler (1988), 'Thinking Theologically about Theological Education', *Theological Education*, **24**(2), pp. 98–119.

Flanagan, K. (1996), *The Enchantment of Sociology: A Study of Culture and Theology*, London: Macmillan.

Flory, R.W. and Miller, D.E. (eds) (2000), *GenX Religion*, New York: Routledge.

Forrester, D. (2000), *Truthful Action: Explorations in Practical Theology*, Edinburgh: T&T Clark.

Forbes, M. and Mahan, J. (eds) (2000), *Religion and Popular Culture in America*, Berkeley, University of California Press.

Foster, L. and Hertzog, P. (eds) (1994), *Defending Diversity: Contemporary Philosophical Perspectives on Pluralism and Multiculturalism*, Amherst, MA: University of Massachusetts Press.

Fowler, J. (1981), *Stages of Faith: the Psychology of Human Development and the Quest for Meaning*, San Francisco: Harper & Row.

Fowler, J. (1984), *Becoming Adult, Becoming Christian: Adult Development and Christian Faith*, San Francisco: Harper & Row.

France, D. (2000), *A Slippery Slope?*, Nottingham: Grove.

Francis, L. and Kay, W. (1995), *Teenage Religion and Values*, Leominster: Gracewing.

Freire, P. (1972), *Pedagogy of the Oppressed*, Harmondsworth: Penguin.

Freire, P. (1973), *Education for Critical Consciousness*, New York: Seabury Press.

Frye, N. (1957), *The Anatomy of Criticism*, Princeton, NJ: Princeton University Press.

Fuellenbach, J. (2002), *Church: Community for the Kingdom*, New York: Orbis Books.

Fuller, R. (2001), *Spiritual, But Not Religious: Understanding Unchurched America*, Oxford: Oxford University Press.

Geertz, C. (1973), *The Interpretation of Cultures*, New York: Basic Books.

Geertz, C. (1983), *Local Knowledge*, New York: Basic Books.

Giddens, A. (1991), *Modernity and Self-Identity: Self and Society in the Late Modern Age*, Cambridge: Polity Press.

Giggie, G. and Winston, D. (eds) (2002), *Faith in the Market: Religion and the Rise of Urban Commercial Culture*, New Brunswick, NJ: Rutgers University Press.

Gittins, A. (2002), *Ministry at the Margins: Strategy and Spirituality for Mission*, New York: Orbis Books.

Goldscheider, F. and Goldscheider, C. (1993), *Leaving Home Before Marriage: Ethnicity, Familism and General Relationships*, Madison, WI: University of Wisconsin Press.

Goodchild, P. (2002), *Capitalism and Religion*, London: Routledge.

Graham, E. (1996), *Transforming Practice*, London: Mowbray.

Graham, E. (2002), *Representations of the Post/Human: Monsters, Aliens, and Others in Popular Culture*, Manchester: Manchester University Press.

Graham, E. and Poling, J. (2000), 'Some Expressive Dimensions of a Liberation Practical Theology', *International Journal of Practical Theology*, **4**, pp. 163–83.

Greeley, A. (1998), *God in Popular Culture*, Chicago: Thomas More Press.

Grenz, S. and Olsen, R. (1992), *20th Century Theology: God and the World in a Transitional Age*, Carlisle: Paternoster.

Grey, M. (1989), *Redeeming the Dream: Feminism, Redemption, and the Christian Tradition*, London: SPCK.

Grigg, R. (1990), *Theology as a Way of Thinking*, Atlanta, GA: Scholars Press.

Grimes, R.L. (1990), *Ritual Criticism: Case Studies on its Practice, Essays on its Theory*, Columbia, SC: University of South Carolina Press.

Grimes, R.L. (ed.) (2003), *Disaster Ritual*, Louvain: Peeters Publishing.

Groome, T. (1980), *Christian Religious Education: Sharing our Story and Vision*, San Francisco: Harper & Row.

Guenther, M. (1992), *Holy Listening: The Art of Spiritual Direction*, London: DLT.

Hacking, P. (ed.) (1993), 'What is Reform?', at www.reform.org.uk.

Hall, J. and Neitz, M. (1993), *Culture: Sociological Perspectives*, Englewood Cliffs, NJ: Prentice Hall.

Hall, J., Neitz, M.J. and Battani, M. (2003), *Sociology on Culture*, New York: Routledge.

Hammersley, M. and Atkinson, P. (1995), *Ethnography; Principles in Practice* (2nd edn), London: Routledge.

Hardy, D. (1996), *God's Ways with the World*, Edinburgh: T & T Clark.

Hare, D. (1990), *Racing Demon*, London: Faber.

Harland, T. (1997), *Stories about Small-Group Teaching: A Problem Based Approach. Vol. 1: Lecturers' Reflections*, Sheffield: University of Sheffield Press.

Harrington Watt, D. (2002), *Bible-Carrying Christians*, New York: Oxford University Press.

Harris, H. (1998), *Fundamentalism and Evangelicals*, Oxford: Clarendon Press.

Hauerwas, S. (1996), 'The Gesture of a Truthful Story', in J. Astley and L. Francis (eds), *Christian Theology and Religious Education: Connections and Contradictions*, London: SPCK.

Hazle, D. (2003), 'Practical Theology Today and the Implications for Mission', *International Review of Mission*, **XCII**(366), July, pp. 345–66.

Healy, N. (2000), *Church, World and Christian Life: Practical–Prophetic Ecclesiology*, Cambridge: Cambridge University Press.

Heather, N. (2002), 'Modern Believing and Postmodern Reading', *Modern Believing*, **43**(1), January, pp. 28–38.

Hebblethwaite, M. (1984), *Motherhood and God*, London: Geoffrey Chapman.

Hervieu-Leger, D. (2000), *Religion as a Chain of Memory*, Cambridge: Polity Press.

Highmore, B. (ed.) (2002), *The Everyday Life Reader*, London: Routledge.

Highmore, B. (2002). *Everyday Life and Cultural Theory*, London: Routledge.

Higton, T. (ed) (1987), *Sexuality and the Church: The Way Forward*, Hockley: ABWON.

Hilborn, D. (ed.) (2001), *Toronto in Perspective*, Carlisle: Paternoster.

Hodgson, P. (1999), *God's Wisdom: Toward a Theology of Education*, Louisville, KY: Westminster John Knox Press.

Hodgson, P. and King, R. (1982), *Christian Theology: An Introduction to its Tradition and Tasks*, Philadelphia, PA: Fortress Press.

Holloway, D. (1993), 'The Background to, and the Need for, Reform' at www.reform.org.uk

Holloway, D. (n.d.), 'Finance, Centralism and the Quota' at www.reform.org.uk.

hooks, b. (1994), *Outlaw Culture: Resisting Representations*, London: Routledge.

Hoover, S. (2000), 'The Cross at Willow Creek' in M. Forbes and J. Hahan (eds), *Religion and Popular Culture in America*, Berkeley: University of California Press.

Hopewell, J. (1987), *Congregation: Stories and Structure*, Philadelphia: Fortress Press.

Horkheimer, M. and Adorno, T. (1972), *Dialectic of Enlightenment*, London: Allen Lane.

Hull, J. (1985), *What Prevents Christian Adults from Learning?*, London: SCM.

Hunt, S. (1995), 'The Toronto Blessing – A Rumour of Angels?', *Journal of Contemporary Religion*, **10**(3), pp. 257–72.

Hunt, S. (2000), *Anyone for Alpha?*, London: Darton, Longman and Todd.

Hunt, S. (2003), *The Alpha Initiative: Evangelism in a Post-Christian Age*, Aldershot: Ashgate.

Hunt, S., Hamilton, M. and Walter, T. (1997), *Charismatic Christianity: Sociological Perspectives*, London: Macmillan.

Huston Smith, J. (1990), 'Postmodernism's Impact on the Study of Religion', *Journal of the American Academy of Religion*, Winter, p. 661.

Hyman, G. (2001), *The Predicament of Postmodern Theology: Radical Orthodoxy or Nihilist Textualism?*, Louisville, KY: Westminster John Knox.

Jakobsen, J. and Pellegrini, A. (eds) (2003), *Love the Sin: Sexual Regulation and the Limits of Tolerance*, New York: New York University Press.

Jamieson, A. (2002), *A Churchless Faith: Faith Journeys Beyond the Churches*, London: SPCK.

Jenkins, D. (ed.) (1990), *The Market and Health Care*, Edinburgh: Edinburgh University Press.

Jensen, P. (2002), *The Revelation of God: Contours of Christian Theology*, Downers Grove, IL, IVP.

Jewett, R. (1988), *The American Monomyth*, Garden City, NY: Anchor/Doubleday.

Jonegeneel, J. (ed.) (1992), *Pentecost, Mission and Ecumenism: Essays on Intercultural Theology*, Frankfurt: Peter Lang.

Jones, I. (2004), *The Ordination of Women: Ten Years On*, London: CHP/LTI.

Jones, L.G. and Paulsell, S. (2002), *The Scope of Our Art: The Vocation of the Theological Teacher*, Grand Rapids, MI: Eerdmans.

Judd, S. and Cable, A. (eds) (1987), *Sydney Anglicans*, Sydney: Anglican Information Office.

Kamitsuka, D. (2002), *Theology and Contemporary Culture*, Cambridge: Cambridge University: Press.

Kelley, D. (1972), *Why Conservative Churches are Growing*, New York: HarperCollins. Reprinted 1986.

Killen, P. and de Beer, J. (1994), *The Art of Theological Reflection*, New York: Crossroad.

Kinast, R. (1996), *Let Ministry Teach: A Guide to Theological Reflection*, Collegeville, MN: Liturgical Press.

Kinast, R. (2000), *What are they Saying About theological Reflection?*, New York: Paulist Press.

King, U. (2002), *Spirituality and Postmodernism*, Oxford: Farmington Institute for Christian Studies.

Kings, G. (2003), 'Canal, River and Rapids: Contemporary Evangelicalism in the Church of England', *Anvil*, **20**(3), pp. 167–84.

Lakeland, P. (1997), *Postmodernity*, Minneapolis, Fortress Press, 1997.

Lakeland, P. (2003), *The Liberation of the Laity: In Search of an Accountable Church*, New York: Continuum.

Levine, D. (ed.) (1971), *Georg Simmel: Selected Writings on Individual and Social Forms*, Chicago: Chicago University Press.

Lindbeck, G. (1984), *The Nature of Doctrine: Religion and Theology in a Post-Liberal Age*, Philadelphia: Westminster.

Lindbeck, G. (2002), *The Church in a Post-Liberal Age*, London: SCM.

Lippy, C. (1994), *Being Religious American Style*, Westport, CT: Greenwood Press.

Lodge, D. (2002), *Thinks*, London: Penguin.

Long, R. (1978), *Theology in a New Key*, Philadelphia: Westminster Press.

Lovin, R. (1995), *Reinhold Niebuhr and Christian Realism*, Cambridge: Cambridge University Press.

Lucas, R. (1986), *Read, Mark, Learn*, London, Proclamation Trust.

Lyon, D. (2000), *Jesus in Disneyland: Religion in Post-modern Times*, Cambridge: Polity Press.

Lyotard, J.F. (1984), *The Postmodern Condition: A Report on Knowledge*, Manchester: Manchester University Press.

Macaulay, R. (1956), *The Towers of Trezibond*, London: Collins.

McCann, D. and Strain, C. (1985), *Polity and Praxis*, Chicago: Winston Press.

McCleod, H. and Ustorf, W. (2003), *The Decline of Christendom in Western Europe: 1750–2000*, Cambridge: Cambridge University Press.

McDannell, C. (1995), *Material Christianity: Religion and Culture in America*, New Haven, CT: Yale University Press.

McFague, S. (1975), *Speaking in Parables: A Study in Metaphor and Theology*, London: SCM.

Macquarrie, J. (1997), *A Guide to the Sacraments*, London: SCM.

Magdalinski, T. and Chandler, T. (eds) (2001), *With God on Their Side: Sport in the Service of Religion*, London: Routledge.

Markham, I. (2003), *A Theology of Engagement*, Oxford: Blackwell.

Markham, I. and Abu-Rabi', I. (2002), *11 September: Religious Perspectives on the Causes and Consequences*, Oxford: Oneworld.

Marling, K. (2000), *Merry Christmas!*, Cambridge, MA: Harvard University Press.

Martin, D. (1967), *A Sociology of English Religion*, London: SCM.

Martin, D. (1969), *The Religions and the Secular*, London: RKP.

Martin, D. (1978), *A General Theory of Secularization*, Oxford: Blackwell.

Martin, D. (1980), *The Breaking of the Image*, Oxford: Blackwell.

Martin, D. (1988), 'Some Sociological Perspectives' in G. Ecclestone (ed.), *The Parish Church*, London: Mowbray.

Martin, D. (1989), *Divinity in a Grain of Bread*, London: Lutterworths.

Martin, D. (1996), *Reflections on Sociology and Theology*, Oxford: Oxford University Press.

Martin, D. (2002), *Christian Language and Its Mutations*, Aldershot: Ashgate.

Martos, J. (1981), *Doors to the Sacred: A Historical Introduction to the Sacraments in the Christian Church*, London: SCM.

Maykut, P. and Morehouse, R. (1994), *Beginning Qualitative Research: A Philosophic and Practical Guide*, New York: The Falmer Press.

Mazur, E. and McCarthy, K. (eds) (2001), *God in the Details: American Religion in Popular Culture*, New York, Routledge.

Melchert, C. (1998), *Wise Teaching: Biblical Wisdom and Educational Ministry*, Harrisburg, PA: Trinity Press International.

Merton, T. (1979), *Love and Living*, ed. N. Stone and P. Hart, London: Sheldon Press.

Middleton, R. and Walsh, B. (1995), *Truth is Stranger Than It Used To Be: Biblical Faith in a Postmodern Age*, London: SPCK.

Milbank, J. (1990), *Theology and Social Theory: Beyond Secular Reason*, Oxford: Blackwell.

Milbank, J. (1991), *Religion and Social Theory: Beyond Secular Reason*, Oxford: Blackwell.

Milbank, J. (1997), *The Word made Strange: Theology, Language, Culture*, Oxford: Blackwell.

Milbank, J., Ward, G. and Pickstock, C. (1999), *Radical Orthodoxy: A New Theology*, London: Routledge.

Miller, D. (1993), *Unwrapping Christmas*, Oxford: Oxford University Press.

Miller, D. (ed.) (1995), *Acknowledging Consumption*, London: Routledge.

Miller, D. (1997), *Re-inventing American Protestantism*, Berkeley, University of California Press.

Miller, D. (1998), *A Theory of Shopping*, Cambridge: Polity.

Miller-McLemore, B. (1994), *Also a Mother: Work and Family as Theological Dilemma*, Nashville, TN: Abingdon Press.

Mishler, E. (1991), *Research Interviewing: Context and Narrative*, Cambridge, MA: Harvard University Press.

Moltmann-Wendel, E. (1982), *The Women Around Jesus*, New York: Crossroad Publishing Co.

Money, T. (1997), *Manly and Muscular Diversions: Public Schools and Nineteenth Century Sporting Revival*, London: Duckworth.

Moore, L. (1994), *Selling God: American Religion in the Marketplace of Culture*, Oxford: Oxford University Press.

Moore, M.E. (1991), *Teaching from the Heart: Theology and Educational Method*, Minneapolis: Fortress Press.

Morgan, D. (1997), *Visual Piety*, Berkeley: University of California Press.

Morgan, D. and Promey, S. (eds) (2001), *The Visual Culture of American Religions*, Berkeley: University of California Press.

Morisy, A. (1997), *Beyond the Good Samaritan: Community Ministry and Mission*, London: Mowbray.

Mudge, L. (2001), *Rethinking the Beloved Community: Ecclesiology, Hermeneutics and Social Theory*, Lanham MD: University Press of America.

Murphy, R. (1990), *The Tree of Life: An Exploration of the Biblical Wisdom Literature*, New York: Doubleday.

Murphy, N. (1996), *Beyond Liberalism and Fundamentalism: How Modern and Postmodern Philosophy Set the Theological Agenda*, Valley Forge, PA: Trinity Press International.

Nesbitt, P. (2001), *Religion and Social Policy*, Lanham, MD: AltaMira Press.

Niebuhr, H.R. (1951), *Christ and Culture*, New York: Harper & Row.

Nieman, J. (2002), 'Attending Locally: Theologies in Congregations', *International Journal of Practical Theology* 6(2), Fall, pp. 198–225.

Nieman, J. and Rogers, T. (2001), *Preaching to Every Pew: Cross-cultural Strategies*, Minneapolis, MN: Fortress Press.

Nissenbaum, S. (1996), *The Battle for Christmas*, New York: Vintage.

Norman, E. (2002), *Secularisation*, London: Continuum.

Nouwen, H. (1975), *Reaching Out: The Three Movements of Spiritual Life*, London: Collins.

Orchard, H. (2000), *Hospital Chaplaincy: Modern, Dependable?*, Sheffield: Sheffield Academic Press.

Pattyn, B. (ed.) (2000), *Media Ethics: Opening Social Dialogue*, Leuven: Peeters.

Pemberton, C. (ed.) (1998), *The Anglican Communion*, New York: Church House Publishing.

Percy, M. (1996a), *Words, Wonders and Power: Understanding Contemporary Christian Fundamentalism and Revivalism*, London: SPCK.

Percy, M. (1996b), *The Toronto Blessing*, Issue 53–54, Oxford: Latimer Studies.

Percy, M. (1997), 'Sweet Rapture: Subliminal Eroticism in Contemporary Charismatic Worship', *Journal of Theology and Sexuality*, 6, March, pp. 71–106.

Percy, M. (1998), 'The Morphology of Pilgrimage in the Toronto Blessing', *Religion*, 28(3), pp. 281–89.

Percy, M. (2000), 'Reluctant Communion', in I. Markham and J. Jobling (eds), *Theological Liberalism*, London: SPCK.

Percy, M. (2001), *The Salt of the Earth: Religious Resilience in Secular Age*, Sheffield: Sheffield Academic Press.

Percy, M. (2003), 'Reconsidering Gifts', in P. Avis (ed.), *Responding to The Gift of Authority*, London: Church House Publishing.

Percy, M. and Jones, I. (2002), *Fundamentalism, Church and Society*, London: SPCK.

Percy, M. and Walker, A. (2001), *Restoring the Image: Essays in Honour of David Martin*, Sheffield: Sheffield Academic Press.

Peterson, E. (1992), *Under the Unpredictable Plant*, Grand Rapids, MI: Eerdmans.

Phillips, T. and Ockholm, D. (1996), *The Nature of Confession: Evangelicals and Postliberals in Conversation*, Downers Grove, IL: Inter-Varsity Press.

Pickering, W. (1989), *Anglo-Catholicism: A Study in Ambiguity*, London: Routledge.

Pinsky, M. (2001), *The Gospel According to the Simpsons*, Louisville, KY: Westminster John Knox Press.

Poling, J. (ed.) (1997), *Towards Viable Theological Education: Ecumenical Imperative, Catalyst of Renewal*, Geneva: World Council of Churches.

Poling, J. and Miller, D. (1985), *Foundations for a Practical Theology of Ministry*, Nashville, TN: Abingdon Press.

Poloma, M. (1996), *A Preliminary Sociological Assessment of the Toronto Blessing*, Bradford-upon-Avon: Terra Nova.

Post, P., Grimes, R., Nugteren, A., Pettersson, P. and Zondag, H. (2003), *Disaster Ritual*, Leuven: Peeters.

Putnam, R. (2000), *Bowling Alone: The Collapse and Revival of American Community*, New York: Simon & Schuster.

Reed, B. (1978), *The Dynamics of Religion: Process and Movement in Christian Churches*, London: Darton, Longman & Todd.

'The Reform Covenant' (1993), published at www.reform.org.uk.

Rengger, N. (1995), *Political Theory, Modernity and Postmodernity*, Oxford: Blackwell.

Richard, L. (1988), *Is There a Christian Ethic?*, New York: Paulist Press.

Richter, P. and Porter, S. (eds) (1995), *The Toronto Blessing – Or Is it?*, London: DLT.

Roberts, D. (2002), 'What Does Theology Have to Do with Ministry?', *Encounter*, **63**, Spring, pp. 24–38.

Roberts, R. (2002), *Religion, Theology and the Human Sciences*, Cambridge: Cambridge University Press.

Roebben, B. and Warren, M. (eds) (2001), *Religious Education as Practical Theology*, Leuven: Peeters.

Roll, S. (1995), *Toward the Origins of Christmas*, Kampen, The Netherlands: Kok Pharos.

Roof, W.C. (1985), *Community and Commitment: Religious Plausibility in a Liberal Protestant Church*, Philadelphia: Fortress Press.

Rothman, J. (2000), *Stepping out into the Field: A Field Work Manual for Social Work Students*, Boston, MA: Allyn & Bacon.

Rowell, G. (ed.) (1992), *The English Religious Tradition and the Genius of Anglicanism*, Wantage, Oxford: Ikon Books.

Ruddick, S. (1983), 'Maternal Thinking', in J. Trebilcot (ed.), *Mothering: Essays in Feminist Theory*, Savage, MD: Rowman & Littlefield, pp. 213–30.

Rycenga, J. (2000), 'Dropping in for the Holidays: Christmas as Consumerist Ritual', in E. Mazur (ed.), *God in the Details*, New York: Routledge.

Sachs, W. (1993), *The Transformation of Anglicanism: From State Church to Global Communion*, Cambridge: Cambridge University Press.

Sagovsky, N. (2000), *Ecumenism, Christian Origins and the Practice of Communion*, Cambridge: Cambridge University Press.

Schreiter, R. (1985), *Constructing Local Theologies*, Maryknoll: Orbis.

Seymour, J. and Miller, D. (eds) (1972), *Contemporary Approaches to Christian Education*, Nashville, TN: Abingdon Press.

Sibley, D. (1995), *Geographies of Exclusion: Society and Difference in the West*, London: Routledge.

Smail, T., Walker, A. and Wright, N. (1995), *Charismatic Renewal*, London: SPCK.

Streng, F., Lloyd, C. and Allen, J. (1973), *Ways of Being Religious*, Englewood Cliffs, NJ: Prentice Hall.

Strinati, D. (1995), *An Introduction to Theories of Popular Culture*, New York: Routledge.

Swatos, W. (1979), *Into Denominationalism: The Anglican Metamorphosis*, Storrs, CT: University of Connecticut/Society of the Scientific Study of Religion.

Sykes, S. (1995), *Unashamed Anglicanism*, London: DLT.

Sykes, S. and Booty, J. (1988), *The Study of Anglicanism*, London: SCM Press.

Tamney, J. (2002), *The Resilience of Conservative Religion*, Cambridge: Cambridge University Press.

Tanner, K. (1992), *The Politics of God: Christian Theologies and Social Justice*, Minneapolis, MN: Fortress Press.

Tanner, K. (1997), *Theories of Culture: A New Agenda for Theology*, Minneapolis, MN: Fortress Press.

Tanner, K., Davaney, S. and Brown, D. (2001), *Convergence on Culture: Theologians in Dialogue with Cultural Analysis and Criticism*, New York: Oxford University Press.

Taylor, D. (1996), *The Healing Power of Stories*, New York: Doubleday.

Taylor, J. (1972), *The Go-Between God: The Holy Spirit and the Christian Mission*, London: SCM.

Thomas, P. (1987), 'A Family Affair: The Pattern of Constitutional Authority in the Anglican Communion' in S. Sykes, (ed.) *Authority in the Anglican Communion*, Toronto: Anglican Book Centre.

Thomas, T. (2001), 'Becoming a Mother', *Religious Education*, **96**(1).

Tomlinson, D. (1995), *The Post-Evangelical*, London: SPCK.

Toulmin, S. (1990), *Cosmopolis: The Hidden Agenda of Modernity*, New York: Free Press.

Towler, R. (1984), *The Need for Certainty*, London: Routledge.

Tracy, D. (1975), *Blessed Rage for Order*, New York: Seabury.

Tracy, D. (1981), 'Defending the Public Character of Theology', in J. Wall (ed.), *Theologians in Transition*, New York: Crossroad.

Tracy, D. (1983), *The Analogical Imagination*, London: SCM Press.

Van Buren, P. (1969), 'On Doing Theology', in *Talk of God*, London: Macmillan.

Van der Ven, J. (1998), *Education for Reflective Ministry*, Leuven: Peeters.

Vasey, M. (1997), *Strangers and Friends*, London: Hodders.

Veblen, T. (1953), *The Theory of the Leisure Class*, New York: Mentor Books.

Visser, M. (2001), *The Geometry of Love*, Harmondsworth, Penguin.

Visser't Hooft, A. (2000), *Teachers and the Teaching Authorities*, Geneva: WCC Publications.

Volf, M. and Bass, D. (eds) (2002), *Practicing Theology: Beliefs and Practices in Christian Life*, Grand Rapids, MI: Eerdmans.

von Balthaser, H-U. (1982), *The Glory of the Lord: A Theological Aesthetics*, Edinburgh: T & T Clark.

Vrame, A.C. (1999), *The Educating Icon: Teaching Wisdom and Holiness in the Orthodox Way*, Brookline, MA: Holy Cross Orthodox Press.

Walker, A. (1998), *Restoring the Kingdom*, Guilford: Eagle.

Ward, G. (1995), *Barth, Derrida and the Language of Theology*, Cambridge: Cambridge University Press.

Ward, G. (2000), *Cities of God*, London: Routledge.

Ward, G. (2003), *True Religion*, Oxford: Blackwell.

Ward K. (2002), *God: A Guide for the Perplexed*, Oxford: Oneworld.

Ward, P. (1997), *Growing Up Evangelical*, London: SPCK.

Ward, P. (2002), *Liquid Church*, Peabody, MA: Hendrickson.

Warren, M. (1997), *Seeing Through the Media*, Harrisburg PA: Trinity Press International.

Weber, M. (1946), 'The Social Psychology of the World Religions', in H. Gerth and C. Wright Mills (eds), *From Max Weber*, New York: Oxford University Press.

Weber, M. (1968), *Economy and Society*, ed. Guenther Roth and Claus Wittich, Vol. 1, New York: Bedminster Press. First published in German in 1925.

Whitehead, J. and Whitehead, E. (1995), *Method in Ministry: Theological Reflection on Christian Ministry*, Franklin, WI: Sheed & Ward.

Williams, M. (1974), *Community in a Black Pentecostal Church*, Pittsburgh: University of Pittsburgh Press.

Williams, P. (1990), *The Ideal of a Self-Governing Church: A Study in Victorian Missionary Strategy*, Leiden: E.J. Brill.

Williams, P. (1999), *Perspectives on American Religion and Culture*, Oxford: Blackwell.

Williams, R. (1976), *Keywords*, London: Fontana.

Williams, R. (1986), *Culture*, London: Fontana.

Williams, R. (1989), *The Making of Orthodoxy: Essays in Honour of Henry Chadwick*, Cambridge: Cambridge University Press.

Williams, R. (2000), *On Christian Theology*, Oxford: Blackwell.

Williams, A. and Davidson, J. (1996), 'Catholic Conceptions of Faith: A Generational Analysis', *Sociology of Religion*, **57**(3), pp. 273–89.

Williamson, C. (1999), *Way of Blessing, Way of Life: A Christian Theology*, St. Louis, MS: Chalice Press.

Willis, P. (2000), *The Ethnographic Imagination*, Cambridge: Polity.

Winquist, C. (1978), *Homecoming: Interpretation, Transformation and Individuation*, American Academy of Religion Studies in Religion, no. 1. 18, Atlanta: Scholars Press.

Winterson, J. (2002), *Oranges Are Not the Only Fruit*, London: Vintage.

Witzel, G. and Witzel, K. (2002), *The Sparkling Story of Coca-Cola*, Stillwater, MN: Voyageur Press.

Wollerstorff, N. (2002), *Educating for Life: Reflections on Christian Teaching and Learning*, Grand Rapids, MI: Eeerdmans.

Woodward, J. and Pattison, S. (2000), *The Blackwell Reader in Pastoral and Practical Theology*, Oxford: Blackwell.

Wright, A. (2002), *Why Bother with Theology?*, London, Darton, Longman and Todd.

Wuthnow, R. (1997), 'The Cultural Turn', in P. Becker and N. Eiesland (eds), *Contemporary American Religion: An Ethnographic Reader*, Lanham, MD: AltaMira Press.

Yust, K. (2002), 'Teaching Seminarians to be Practical Theologians', *Encounter*, **63**, p. 237.

Index

Printed in Great Britain
by Amazon

38920845R00150